CREATIV
HOMEOWN

MOST-POPULAR
2-STORY
HOME PLANS

VP/Publisher: Brian H. Toolan
VP/Editorial Director: Timothy O. Bakke
Production Manager: Kimberly H. Vivas

Home Plans Publishing Consultant: James D. McNair III
Home Plans Editor: Kenneth D. Stuts
Home Plans Designer Liason: Timothy Mulligan

Design and Layout: Arrowhead Direct (David Kroha, Cindy DiPierdomenico, Judith Kroha)

Cover Design: David Geer

Manufactured in the United States

Current Printing (last digit)
10 9

Most-Popular 2-Story Home Plans
Library of Congress Control Number: 2003112523
ISBN-10: 1-58011-185-8
ISBN-13: 978-1-58011-185-0

CREATIVE HOMEOWNER®
A Division of Federal Marketing Corp.
24 Park Way
Upper Saddle River, NJ 07458
www.creativehomeowner.com

Note: The homes as shown in the photographs and renderings in this book may differ from the actual blueprints. When studying the house of your choice, please check the floor plans carefully.

PHOTO CREDITS

Front cover: *top* plan 121081, page 175; *bottom row left to right* plan 161022, page 113; plan 161018, page 112; plan 161022, page113; plan 161033, page 184

Back cover: *top* plan 161018, page 112; *center* plan 121017, page 212; *bottom row all* plan 161035, page 170

page 4: courtesy of Trus Joist MacMillan

page 5: Paul M. Schumm/CH

page 6: *top* Freeze Frame Studio/CH; *bottom* courtesy of Trus Joist MacMillan

page 7: Kim, Jin Hong Photo Studio

page 68: courtesy of Merillat Industries

page 69: courtesy of Kraftmaid Cabinetry, Inc.

pages 70–71: *left* courtesy of Kraftmaid Cabinetry, Inc.; *center* courtesy of Jenn-Air; *right* courtesy of Wood-Mode Cabinetry

page 72: *top* courtesy of Kohler; *bottom right* courtesy of Ann Sacks Tile; *bottom left* courtesy of Wilsonart International

page 73: *top row* courtesy of Kraftmaid Cabinetry, Inc.; *bottom* courtesy of Armstrong Floors

page 132: courtesy of Mannington Floors

page 133: courtesy of Congoleum

page 134: *top* courtesy of Congoleum; *bottom* courtesy of Mannington Floors

page 135: courtesy of Dal-Tile

page 136: *left* courtesy of Mannington Floors; *right* courtesy of Congoleum

page 137: *left* courtesy of Mannington Floors; *right* courtesy of Dal-Tile

pages 188–189: *both* George Ross/CH

page 190: Christine Elasigue/CH

page 191: *top* George Ross/CH; *bottom all* Christine Elasigue/CH

page 192: *left* George Ross/CH; *right top to bottom* Christine Elasigue/CH

pages 193–195: *all* Christine Elasigue/CH

pages 267–268: *all* courtesy of Sylvania

page 269: courtesy of Kraftmaid Cabinetry, Inc.

page 270: *all* courtesy of Sylvania

pages 310–313: *all* illustrations by Steve Buchanan

Contents

Getting Started

Maybe you can't wait to bang the first nail. Or you may be just as happy leaving town until the windows are cleaned. The extent of your involvement with the construction phase is up to you. Your time, interests, and abilities can help you decide how to get the project from lines on paper to reality. But building a house requires more than putting pieces together. Whoever is in charge of the process must competently manage people as well as supplies, materials, and construction. He or she will have to

- Make a project schedule to plan the orderly progress of the work. This can be a bar chart that shows the time period of activity by each trade.
- Establish a budget for each category of work, such as foundation, framing, and finish carpentry.
- Arrange for a source of construction financing.
- Get a building permit and post it conspicuously at the construction site.
- Line up supply sources and order materials.
- Find subcontractors and negotiate their contracts.
- Coordinate the work so that it progresses smoothly with the fewest conflicts.
- Notify inspectors at the appropriate milestones.
- Make payments to suppliers and subcontractors.

You as the Builder

You'll have to take care of every logistical detail yourself if you decide to act as your own builder or general contractor. But along with the responsibilities of managing the project, you gain the flexibility to do as much of your own work as you want and subcontract out the rest. Before taking this path, however, be sure you have the time and capabilities. Do you also have the

time and ability to schedule the work, hire and coordinate subs, order materials, and keep ahead of the accounting required to manage the project successfully? If you do, you stand to save the amount that a general contractor would charge to take on these responsibilities, normally 15 to 30 percent of the construction cost. If you take this responsibility on but mismanage the project, the potential savings will erode and may even cost you more than if you had hired a builder in the first place. A subcontractor might charge extra for hav-

Acting as the builder, above, requires the ability to hire and manage subcontractors.

Building a home, opposite, includes the need to schedule building inspections at the appropriate milestones.

ing to return to the site to complete work that was originally scheduled for an earlier date. Or perhaps because you didn't order the windows at the beginning, you now have to pay for a recent cost increase. (If you had hired a builder in the first place he or she would absorb the increase.)

Hiring a Builder to Handle Construction

A builder or general contractor will manage every aspect of the construction process. Your role after signing the construction contract will be to make regular progress payments and ensure that the work for which you are paying has been completed. You will also consult with the builder and agree to any changes that may have to be made along the way.

Leads for finding builders might come from friends or neighbors who have had contractors build, remodel, or add to their homes. Real-estate agents and bankers may have some names handy but are more likely familiar with the builder's ability to complete projects on time and budget than the quality of the work itself.

The next step is to narrow your list of candidates to three or four who you think can do a quality job and work harmoniously with you. Phone each builder to see whether he or she is interested in being considered for your project. If so, invite the builder to an interview at your home. The meeting will serve two purposes. You'll be able to ask the candidate about his or her experience, and you'll be able to see whether or not your personalities are compatible. Go over the plans with the builder to make certain that he or she understands the scope of the project. Ask if they have constructed similar houses. Get references, and check the builder's standing with the Better Business Bureau. Develop a short list of builders, say three, and ask them to submit bids for the project.

Contracts

Lump-Sum Contracts

A lump-sum, or fixed-fee, contract lets you know from the beginning just what the project will cost, barring any changes made because of your requests or unforeseen conditions. This form works well for projects that promise few surprises and are well defined from the outset by a complete set of contract documents. You can enter into a fixed-price contract by negotiating with a single builder on your short list or by obtaining bids from three or four builders. If you go the latter route, give each bidder a set of documents and allow at least two weeks for them to submit their bids. When you get the bids, decide who you want and call the others to thank them for their efforts. You don't have to accept the lowest bid, but it probably makes sense to do so since you have already honed the list to builders you trust. Inform this builder of your intentions to finalize a contract.

Cost-Plus-Fee Contracts

Under a cost-plus-fee contract, you agree to pay the builder for the costs of labor and materials, as verified by receipts, plus a fee that represents the builder's overhead and profit. This arrangement is sometimes referred to as "time and materials." The fee can range between 15 and 30 percent of the incurred costs. Because you ultimately pick up the tab—whatever the costs—the contractor is never at risk, as he is with a lump-sum contract. You won't know the final total cost of a cost-plus-fee contract until the project is built and paid for. If you can live with that uncertainty, there are offsetting advantages. First, this form allows you to accommodate unknown conditions much more easily than does a lump-sum contract. And rather than being tied down by the project documents, you will be free to make changes at any point along the way. This can be a trap, though. Watching the project take shape will spark the desire to add something or do something differently. Each change costs more, and the accumulation can easily exceed your budget. Because of the uncertainty of the final tab and the built-in advantage to the contractor, you should think twice before entering into this form of contract.

Contract Content

The conditions of your agreement should be spelled out thoroughly in writing and signed by both parties, whatever contractual arrangement you make with your builder. Your contract should include provisions for the following:

- The names and addresses of the owner and builder.
- A description of the work to be included ("As described in the plans and specifications dated . . .").
- The date that the work will be completed if time is of the essence.
- The contract price for lump-sum contracts and the builder's allowed profit and overhead costs for changes.
- The builder's fee for cost-plus-fee contracts and the method of accounting and requesting payment.
- The criteria for progress payments (monthly, by project milestones) and the conditions of final payment.
- A list of each drawing and specification section that is to be included as part of the contract.
- Requirements for guarantees. (One year is the standard period for which contractors guarantee the entire project, but you may require specific guarantees on

When submitting bids, all of the builders should base their estimates on the same specifications. Once the work begins, communicate with your builder to keep the work proceeding smoothly.

Inspect your newly built home, if possible, before the builder closes it up and finishes it.

certain parts of the project, such as a 20-year guarantee on the roofing.)
- Provisions for insurance.
- A description of how changes in the work orders will be handled.

The builder may have a standard contract that you can tailor to the specifics of your project. These contain complete specific conditions with blanks that you can fill in to fit your project and a set of "general conditions" that cover a host of issues from insurance to termination provisions. It's always a good idea to have an attorney review the draft of your completed contract before signing it.

Working with Your Builder
The construction phase officially begins when you have a signed copy of the contract and copies of any insurance required from the builder. It's not unheard of for a builder to request an initial payment of 10 to 20 percent of the total cost to cover mobilization costs, those costs associated with obtaining permits and getting set up to begin the actual construction. If you agree to this, keep a careful eye on the progress of the work to ensure that the total paid out at any one time doesn't get too far out of sync with the actual work completed.

What about changes? From here on, it's up to you and your builder to proceed in good faith and to keep the channels of communication open. Even so, changes of one sort or another beset every project, and they usually add to its cost.

Light at the End of the Tunnel.
The builder's request for a final inspection marks the end of the construction phase—almost. At the final inspection meeting, you and the builder will inspect the work, noting any defects or incomplete items on a "punch list." When the builder tidies up the punch list items, you should reinspect. Sometimes, builders go on to another job and take forever to clean up the last few details, so only after all items on the list have been completed satisfactorily should you release the final payment, which often accounts for the builder's profit.

Some Final Words

Having a positive attitude is important when undertaking a project as large as building a home. A positive attitude can help you ride out the rigors and stress of the construction process.

Stay Flexible. Expect problems, because they certainly will occur. Weather can upset the schedule you have established for subcontractors. A supplier may get behind on deliveries, which also affects the schedule. An unexpected pipe may surprise you during excavation. Just as certain, every problem that comes along has a solution if you are open to it.

Be Patient. The extra days it may take to resolve a construction problem will be forgotten once the project is completed.

Express Yourself. If what you see isn't exactly what you thought you were getting, don't be afraid to look into changing it. Or you may spot an unforeseen opportunity for an improvement. Changes usually cost more money, though, so don't make frivolous decisions.

Finally, watching your home go up is exciting, so stay upbeat. Get away from your project from time to time. Dine out. Take time to relax. A positive attitude will make for smoother relations with your builder. An optimistic outlook will yield better-quality work if you are doing your own construction. And though the project might seem endless while it is under way, keep in mind that all the planning and construction will fade to a faint memory at some time in the future, and you will be getting a lifetime of pleasure from a home that is just right for you.

Plan #321042

Dimensions: 71' W x 54'7" D
Levels: 2
Square Footage: 3,368
Main Level Sq. Ft.: 2,150
Upper Level Sq. Ft.: 1,218
Bedrooms: 4
Bathrooms: 3 full, 2 half
Foundation: Basement
Materials List Available: Yes
Price Category: G

If your family loves contemporary interiors and spacious rooms, this could be their dream home.

Features:

• Great Room: A cathedral ceiling with wooden beams adds height and interest to this sunken room. Skylights add to the ambiance, and the masonry fireplace is beautiful in any season.

• Dining Room: Entertain in this lovely room, or use it for quiet family dinners.

• Kitchen: This thoughtfully designed kitchen will thrill any cook, thanks to the ample work and storage space it features.

• Breakfast Room: Octagon-shaped, this room features a domed ceiling with prominent beams, large windows, and a door to the rear patio.

• Master Suite: Located in a separate wing for privacy, this suite is filled with amenities such as the dressing area adjacent to the bedroom and a luxurious bathroom with adequate space for two.

Images provided by designer/architect.

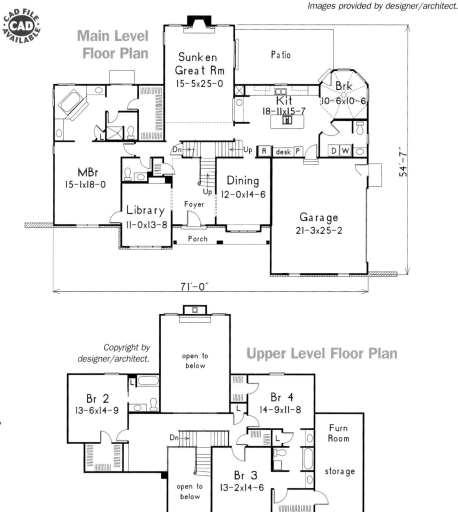

Plan #321048

Dimensions: 77'6" W x 30' D

Levels: 2

Square Footage: 3,216

Main Level Sq. Ft.: 1,834

Upper Level Sq. Ft.: 1,382

Bedrooms: 4

Bathrooms: 4½

Foundation: Basement

Materials List Available: Yes

Price Category: G

You'll love the columns and well-proportioned dormers that grace the exterior of this home, which is as spacious as it is comfortable.

Features:

- Family Room: This large room, featuring a graceful bay window and a wet bar, is sure to be the heart of your home. On chilly evenings, the whole family will gather around the fireplace.

- Dining Room: Whether you're serving a family dinner or hosting a formal dinner party, everyone will feel at home in this lovely room.

- Kitchen: The family cooks will appreciate the thought that went into designing this kitchen, which includes ample work and storage space. A breakfast room adjoins the kitchen.

- Hearth Room: This room also adjoins the kitchen, creating a large area for informal entertaining.

- Bedrooms: Each bedroom is really a suite, because it includes a private, full bath.

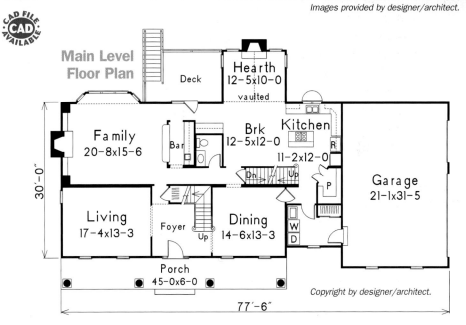

Main Level Floor Plan

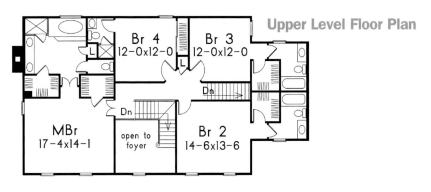

Upper Level Floor Plan

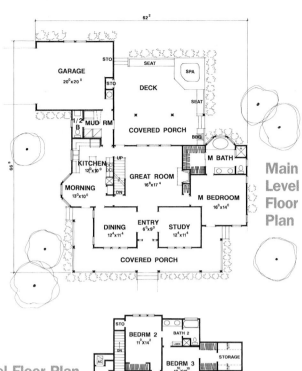

Main Level Floor Plan

Images provided by designer/architect.

GARAGE 20⁰x20⁰

STO

SEAT

SPA

DECK

STO

SEAT

1/2 B | MUD RM

COVERED PORCH

BBQ

KITCHEN 12⁴x10⁰

UP

DN

GREAT ROOM 16⁸x17⁴

M BATH

MORNING 13⁸x10⁰

M BEDROOM 16⁸x14⁰

DINING 12⁴x11⁴

ENTRY 6⁶x9⁰

STUDY 12⁴x11⁴

COVERED PORCH

Upper Level Floor Plan

Copyright by designer/architect.

STO

BEDRM 2 11⁸x14²

BATH 2

LINEN

DN

AC

BEDRM 3 10⁰X16⁰

STORAGE

STO

PLAYROOM 16⁰x9⁴

Plan #331002

Dimensions: 62'2" W x 66'8" D
Levels: 2
Square Footage: 2,299
Main Level Sq. Ft.: 1,517
Upper Level Sq. Ft.: 782
Bedrooms: 3
Bathrooms: 2½
Foundation: Basement, crawl space, or slab
Materials List Available: No
Price Category: E

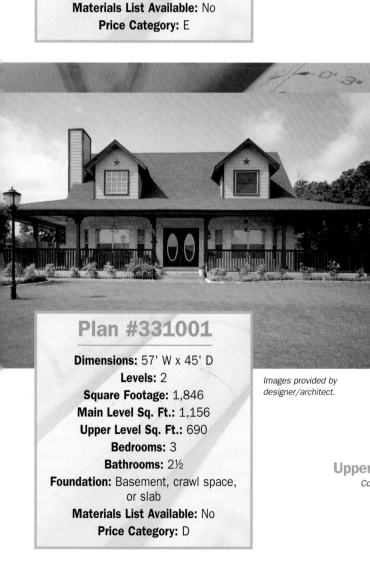

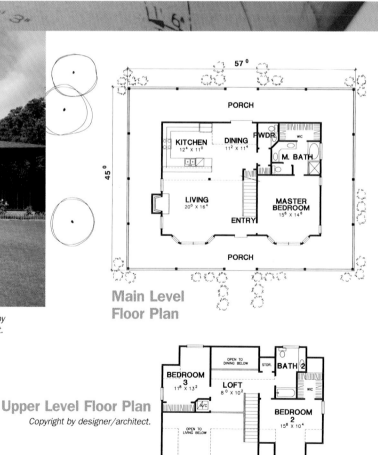

Main Level Floor Plan

Images provided by designer/architect.

57⁰

45⁰

PORCH

KITCHEN 12⁴ X 11⁰

DINING 11² X 11⁴

PWDR.

WIC

M. BATH

LIVING 20⁰ X 16⁴

MASTER BEDROOM 15⁶ X 14⁸

ENTRY

PORCH

Upper Level Floor Plan

Copyright by designer/architect.

BEDROOM 3 11⁸ X 13²

OPEN TO DINING BELOW

STOR.

BATH 2

LOFT 8⁰ X 10²

WIC

A/C

BEDROOM 2 15⁸ X 10⁴

OPEN TO LIVING BELOW

Plan #331001

Dimensions: 57' W x 45' D
Levels: 2
Square Footage: 1,846
Main Level Sq. Ft.: 1,156
Upper Level Sq. Ft.: 690
Bedrooms: 3
Bathrooms: 2½
Foundation: Basement, crawl space, or slab
Materials List Available: No
Price Category: D

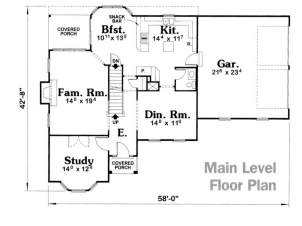

Main Level Floor Plan

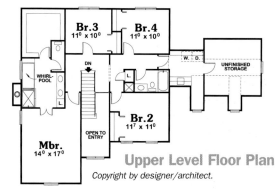

Upper Level Floor Plan

Copyright by designer/architect.

Plan #121097

Dimensions: 58' W x 42'8" D

Levels: 2

Square Footage: 2,417

Main Level Sq. Ft.: 1,162

Upper Level Sq. Ft.: 1,255

Bedrooms: 4

Bathrooms: 2½

Foundation: Basement

Materials List Available: Yes

Price Category: E

Images provided by designer/architect.

This home, as shown in the photograph, may differ from the actual blueprints.

For more detailed information, please check the floor plans carefully.

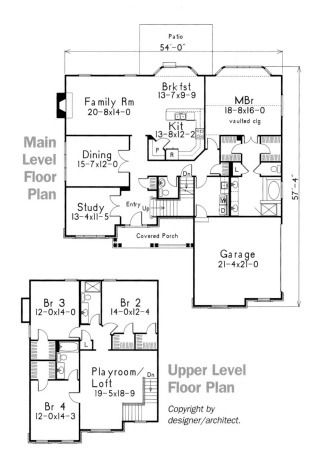

Main Level Floor Plan

Upper Level Floor Plan

Copyright by designer/architect.

Plan #321062

Dimensions: 54' W x 57'4" D

Levels: 2

Square Footage: 3,138

Main Level Sq. Ft.: 1,958

Upper Level Sq. Ft.: 1,180

Bedrooms: 4

Bathrooms: 3½

Foundation: Basement

Materials List Available: Yes

Price Category: G

Images provided by designer/architect.

This home, as shown in the photograph, may differ from the actual blueprints.

For more detailed information, please check the floor plans carefully.

Plan #121091

Dimensions: 56' W x 50' D
Levels: 2
Square Footage: 2,689
Main Level Sq. Ft.: 1,415
Upper Level Sq. Ft.: 1,274
Bedrooms: 4
Bathrooms: 2½
Foundation: Basement
Materials List Available: Yes
Price Category: F

This home, as shown in the photograph, may differ from the actual blueprints. For more detailed information, please check the floor plans carefully.

Photo provided by designer/architect

You'll love the unusual details that make this home as elegant as it is comfortable.

Features:

- Entry: This two-story entry is filled with natural light that streams in through the sidelights and transom window.

- Den: To the right of the entry, French doors open to this room, with its 11-ft. high, spider-beamed ceiling. A triple-wide,

transom-topped window brightens this room during the daytime.

- Family Room: A fireplace and built-in entertainment center add comfort to this room, and the cased opening to the kitchen area makes it convenient.

- Kitchen: With an adjoining breakfast area, this kitchen is another natural gathering spot.

Main Level Floor Plan

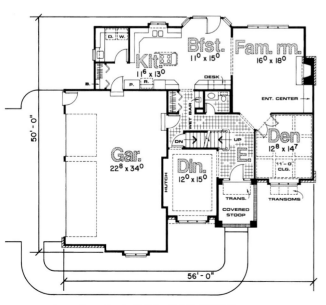

Upper Level Floor Plan

Copyright by designer/architect.

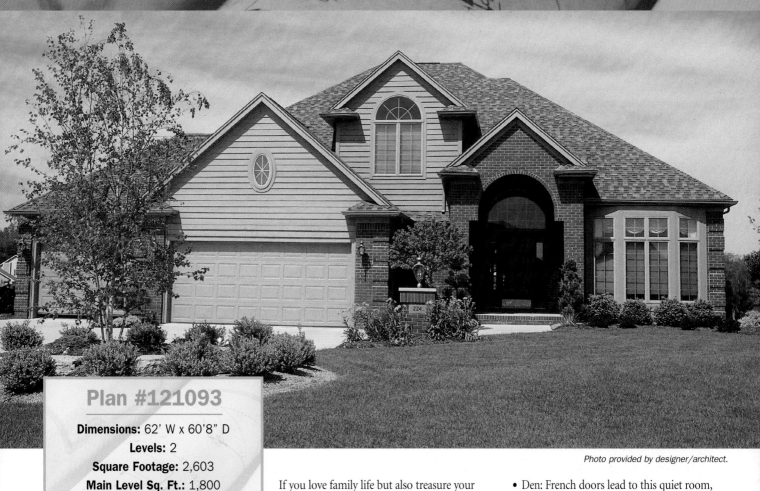

Plan #121093

Dimensions: 62' W x 60'8" D
Levels: 2
Square Footage: 2,603
Main Level Sq. Ft.: 1,800
Upper Level Sq. Ft.: 803
Bedrooms: 4
Bathrooms: 3½
Foundation: Basement
Materials List Available: Yes
Price Category: F

Photo provided by designer/architect.

If you love family life but also treasure your privacy, you'll appreciate the layout of this home.

Features:

- Entry: This two-story, open area features plant shelves to display a group of lovely specimens.

- Dining Room: Open to the entry, this room features 12-ft. ceilings and corner hutches.

- Den: French doors lead to this quiet room, with its bowed window and spider-beamed ceiling.

- Gathering Room: A three-sided fireplace, shared with both the kitchen and the breakfast area, is the highlight of this room.

- Master Suite: Secluded for privacy, this suite also has a private covered deck where you can sit and recharge at any time of day. A walk-in closet is practical, and a whirlpool tub is pure comfort.

CAD FILE AVAILABLE

Main Level Floor Plan

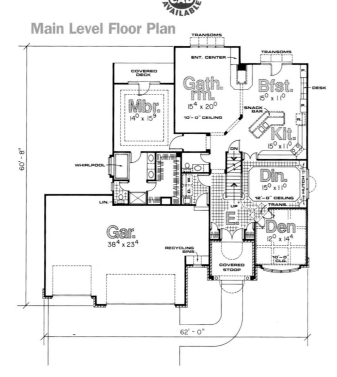

Upper Level Floor Plan

Copyright by designer/architect.

**Main Level
Floor Plan**

**Upper Level
Floor Plan**

*Illustration provided by
designer/architect.*

Copyright by designer/architect.

Plan #151100

Dimensions: 69'6" W x 31' D

Levels: 2

Square Footage: 2,268

Main Level Sq. Ft.: 1,168

Upper Level Sq. Ft.: 1,000

Bedrooms: 3

Bathrooms: 2½

Foundation: Crawl space, slab,
basement, or walk-out

CompleteCost List Available: Yes

Price Category: E

**Upper Level
Floor Plan**

**Main Level
Floor Plan**

*Illustration provided by
designer/architect.*

*Copyright by
designer/architect.*

Plan #151118

Dimensions: 54'2" W x 73'6" D

Levels: 2

Square Footage: 2,784

Main Level Sq. Ft.: 1,895

Upper Level Sq. Ft.: 889

Bedrooms: 4

Bathrooms: 2½

Foundation: Crawl space, slab,
or basement

CompleteCost List Available: Yes

Price Category: F

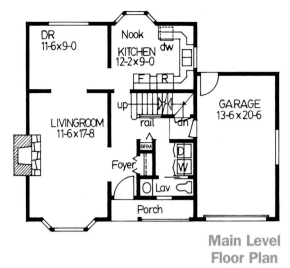

**Main Level
Floor Plan**

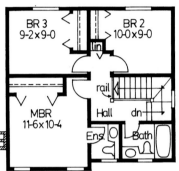

**Upper Level
Floor Plan**

*Copyright by
designer/architect.*

*Illustration provided by
designer/architect.*

Plan #281007

Dimensions: 37' W x 31' D

Levels: 2

Square Footage: 1,206

Main Level Sq. Ft.: 670

Upper Level Sq. Ft.: 536

Bedrooms: 3

Bathrooms: 1 full, 2 half

Foundation: Full basement

Materials List Available: Yes

Price Category: B

Main Level Floor Plan

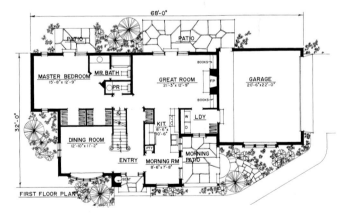

Copyright by designer/architect.

*Illustrations provided by
designer/architect.*

Upper Level Floor Plan

Plan #291011

Dimensions: 68'6" W x 33' D

Levels: 2

Square Footage: 1,898

Main Level Sq. Ft.: 1,182

Upper Level Sq. Ft.: 716

Bedrooms: 4

Bathrooms: 2½

Foundation: Basement

Materials List Available: No

Price Category: D

Plan #121078

Dimensions: 50' W x 48' D
Levels: 2
Square Footage: 2,248
Main Level Sq. Ft.: 1,568
Upper Level Sq. Ft.: 680
Bedrooms: 4
Bathrooms: 2½
Foundation: Slab
Materials List Available: Yes
Price Category: E

This home, as shown in the photograph, may differ from the actual blueprints. For more detailed information, please check the floor plans carefully.

Photo provided by designer/arc

This design is wonderful for any family but has features that make it ideal for one with teens.

Features:

- Family Room: A vaulted ceiling gives a touch of elegance here and a corner fireplace makes it comfortable, especially when the weather's cool.

- Living Room: Both this room and the dining room have a formal feeling, but don't let that stop you from making them a family gathering spot.

- Kitchen: A built-in desk, butler's pantry, and a walk-in pantry make this kitchen easy to organize. The breakfast nook shares an angled eating bar with the family room.

- Master Suite: A walk-in closet and corner tub and shower make this suite feel luxurious.

Main Level Floor Plan

Copyright by designer/architect.

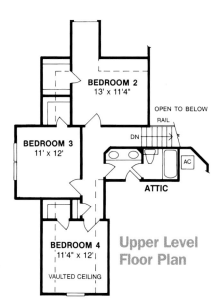

Upper Level Floor Plan

Plan #121079

Dimensions: 50' W x 60' D

Levels: 2

Square Footage: 2,688

Main Level Sq. Ft.: 1,650

Upper Level Sq. Ft.: 1,038

Bedrooms: 4

Bathrooms: 3½

Foundation: Slab

Materials List Available: Yes

Price Category: F

This home, as shown in the photograph, may differ from the actual blueprints. For more detailed information, please check the floor plans carefully.

Photo provided by designer/architect.

You'll love this open design if you're looking for a home that gives a spacious feeling while also providing private areas.

Features:

- Entry: The cased openings and corner columns here give an attractive view into the dining room.

- Living Room: Another cased opening defines the entry to this living room but lets traffic flow into it.

- Kitchen: This well-designed kitchen is built around a center island that gives you extra work space. A snack bar makes an easy, open transition between the sunny dining nook and the kitchen.

- Master Suite: An 11-ft. ceiling sets the tone for this private space. With a walk-in closet and adjoining full bath, it will delight you.

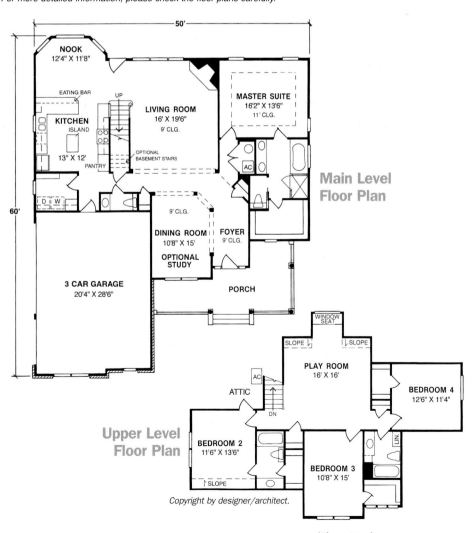

Main Level Floor Plan

Upper Level Floor Plan

Copyright by designer/architect.

Main Level Floor Plan

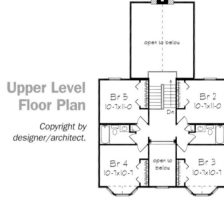

Upper Level Floor Plan

Copyright by designer/architect.

Plan #321054

Dimensions: 70'6" W x 55'6" D
Levels: 2
Square Footage: 2,828
Main Level Sq. Ft.: 2,006
Upper Level Sq. Ft.: 822
Bedrooms: 5
Bathrooms: 3½
Foundation: Basement
Materials List Available: Yes
Price Category: F

Images provided by designer/architect.

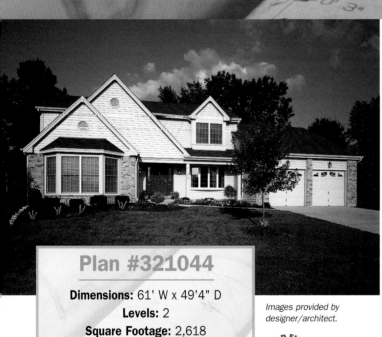

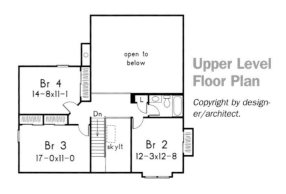

Main Level Floor Plan

Upper Level Floor Plan

Copyright by designer/architect.

Plan #321044

Dimensions: 61' W x 49'4" D
Levels: 2
Square Footage: 2,618
Main Level Sq. Ft.: 1,804
Upper Level Sq. Ft.: 814
Bedrooms: 4
Bathrooms: 2½
Foundation: Basement
Materials List Available: Yes
Price Category: F

Images provided by designer/architect.

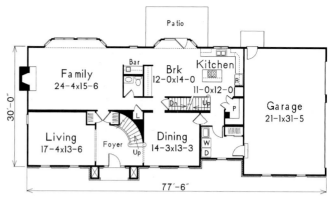

Main Level Floor Plan

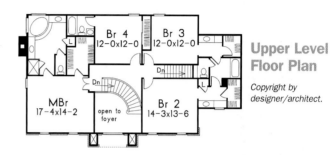

Upper Level Floor Plan

Copyright by designer/architect.

Plan #321049

Dimensions: 77'6" W x 30' D
Levels: 2
Square Footage: 3,144
Main Level Sq. Ft.: 1,724
Upper Level Sq. Ft.: 1,420
Bedrooms: 4
Bathrooms: 4½
Foundation: Basement
Materials List Available: Yes
Price Category: G

Images provided by designer/architect.

CAD FILE AVAILABLE

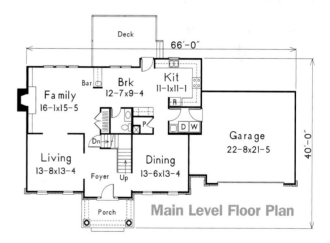

Main Level Floor Plan

Upper Level Floor Plan

Copyright by designer/architect.

Plan #321046

Dimensions: 66' W x 40' D
Levels: 2
Square Footage: 2,411
Main Level Sq. Ft.: 1,293
Upper Level Sq. Ft.: 1,118
Bedrooms: 4
Bathrooms: 2½
Foundation: Basement
Materials List Available: Yes
Price Category: E

Images provided by designer/architect.

CAD FILE AVAILABLE

This home, as shown in the photograph, may differ from the actual blueprints.

For more detailed information, please check the floor plans carefully.

Plan #341015

Dimensions: 57' W x 36'4" D

Levels: 2

Square Footage: 2,418

Main Level Sq. Ft.: 1,083

Upper Level Sq. Ft.: 1,335

Bedrooms: 4

Bathrooms: 2½

Foundation: Crawl space; slab or basement for fee

Materials List Available: Yes

Price Category: E

You'll be charmed by the surprising amenities in this comfortable home, with its old-fashioned country farmhouse appearance.

Features:

- **Front Porch:** Put out a couple of rockers and a swing, hang baskets of fragrant flowering plants, and watch the world go by from this cozy porch.

- **Living Room:** Use this room for entertaining or as a place for quiet talks and reading in the evening.

- **Family Room:** Everyone will gather in this room, with its handsome fireplace and French doors leading to the yard.

- **Kitchen:** This well-planned room features corner dual sinks, a large pantry, lots of work space, and a breakfast bar where everyone will perch.

- **Master Suite:** Retreat to this luxurious suite at the end of the day. You'll love the large walk-in closet here, as well as the bath, with its deluxe tub, dual vanities, and walk-in shower.

Images provided by designer/architect.

Main Level Floor Plan

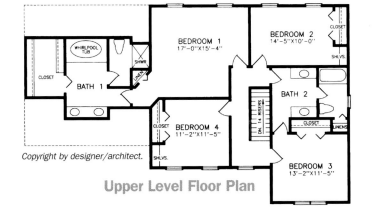

Copyright by designer/architect.

Upper Level Floor Plan

Plan #341014

Dimensions: 57'9" W x 40' D

Levels: 2

Square Footage: 2,128

Main Level Sq. Ft.: 1,064

Upper Level Sq. Ft.: 1,064

Bedrooms: 3

Bathrooms: 2½

Foundation: Crawl space; slab or basement for fee

Materials List Available: Yes

Price Category: E

Images provided by designer/architect.

You'll love the serene appearance of this traditionally styled home, with its romantic front porch and practical backyard deck.

Features:

- Foyer: Look onto this two-story foyer from the sunlit upper floor balcony.

- Dining Room: A tray ceiling sets the formal tone for this lovely room.

- Living Room: A fireplace, built-in cabinets or shelves, and generous windows make this room as practical as it is welcoming.

- Kitchen: A pantry and a work island make this an ideal kitchen for all the cooks in the family.

- Master Suite: A walk-in closet and private bath with double vanities, garden tub, and separate shower make this suite a pleasure.

- Bonus Room: Use this room however you wish — as a study, media room, or play space.

Main Level Floor Plan

Upper Level Floor Plan

Copyright by designer/architect.

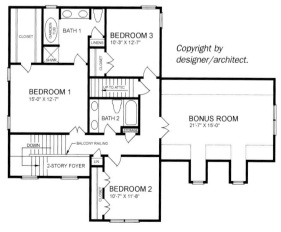

Plan #121080

Dimensions: 56' W x 49' D

Levels: 2

Square Footage: 2,384

Main Level Sq. Ft.: 1,616

Upper Level Sq. Ft.: 768

Bedrooms: 4

Bathrooms: 2½

Foundation: Slab

Materials List Available: Yes

Price Category: E

This home, as shown in the photograph, may differ from the actual blueprints. For more detailed information, please check the floor plans carefully.

Photo provided by designer/arch.

This design is ideal if you want a generously sized home now and room to expand later.

Features:

- Living Room: Your eyes will be drawn towards the ceiling as soon as you enter this lovely room. The ceiling is vaulted, giving a sense of grandeur, and a graceful balcony from the second floor adds extra interest to this room.

- Kitchen: Designed with lots of counter space to make your work convenient, this kitchen also shares an eating bar with the breakfast nook.

- Breakfast Nook: Eat here or go out to the adjoining private porch where you can enjoy your meal in the morning sunshine.

- Master Suite: The bayed area in the bedroom makes a picturesque sitting area. French doors in the bedroom open to a private bath that's fitted with a whirlpool tub, separate shower, two vanities, and a walk-in closet.

Main Level Floor Plan

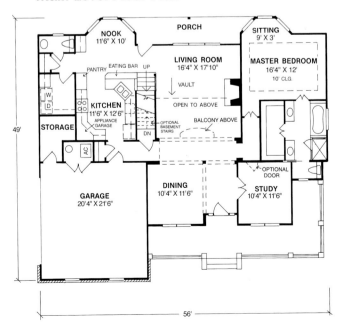

Upper Level Floor Plan

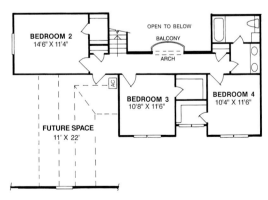

Copyright by designer/architect.

Plan #121090

Dimensions: 60' W x 58' D
Levels: 2
Square Footage: 2,645
Main Level Sq. Ft.: 1,972
Upper Level Sq. Ft.: 673
Bedrooms: 4
Bathrooms: 2½
Foundation: Basement
Materials List Available: Yes
Price Category: F

Photo provided by designer/architect.

You'll be amazed at the amenities that have been designed into this lovely home.

Features:

- Den: French doors just off the entry lead to this lovely room, with its bowed window and spider-beamed ceiling.

- Great Room: A trio of graceful arched windows highlights the volume ceiling in this room. You might want to curl up to read next to the see-through fireplace into the hearth room.

- Kitchen: Enjoy the good design in this room.

- Hearth Room: The shared fireplace with the great room makes this a cozy spot in cool weather.

- Master Suite: French doors lead to this well-lit area, with its roomy walk-in closet, sunlit whirlpool tub, separate shower, and two vanities.

Main Level Floor Plan

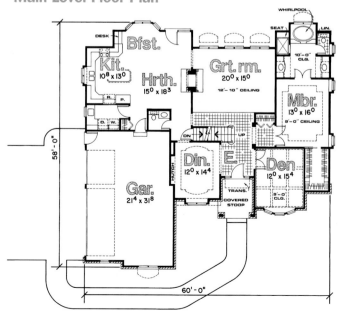

Upper Level Floor Plan

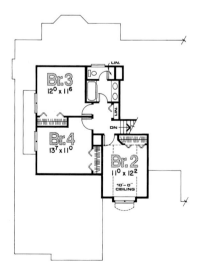

Copyright by designer/architect.

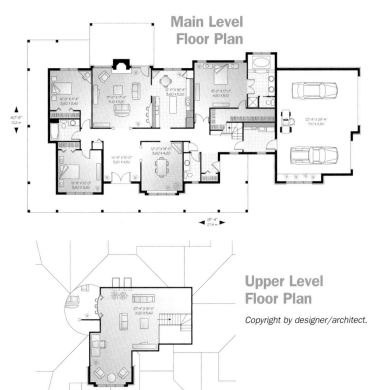

**Main Level
Floor Plan**

*Images provided by
designer/architect.*

**Upper Level
Floor Plan**

Copyright by designer/architect.

Plan #181064

Dimensions: 91'4" W x 40'8" D

Levels: 2

Square Footage: 2,802

Main Level Sq. Ft.: 2,219

Upper Level Sq. Ft.: 583

Bedrooms: 4

Bathrooms: 2½

Foundation: Crawl space

Materials List Available: Yes

Price Category: F

**Main Level
Floor Plan**

*Images provided by
designer/architect.*

**Upper Level
Floor Plan**

*Copyright by
designer/architect.*

Plan #381019

Dimensions: 62' W x 49'6" D

Levels: 2

Square Footage: 2,535

Main Level Sq. Ft.: 1,740

Upper Level Sq. Ft.: 795

Bedrooms: 3

Bathrooms: 2½

Foundation: Crawl space

Materials List Available: Yes

Price Category: E

Main Level Floor Plan

Upper Level Floor Plan

Illustration provided by designer/architect.

CAD FILE AVAILABLE

Copyright by designer/architect.

Plan #181137

Dimensions: 68' W x 34' D

Levels: 2

Square Footage: 2,353

Main Level Sq. Ft.: 1,281

Upper Level Sq. Ft.: 1,072

Bedrooms: 3

Bathrooms: 2½

Foundation: Full basement

Materials List Available: Yes

Price Category: E

Plan #251014

Dimensions: 53'8" W x 61' D

Levels: 2

Square Footage: 2,210

Main Level Sq. Ft.: 1,670

Upper Level Sq. Ft.: 540

Bedrooms: 3

Bathrooms: 2½

Foundation: Crawl space, basement

Materials List Available: Yes

Price Category: E

Illustration provided by designer/architect.

Main Level Floor Plan

Upper Level Floor Plan

Copyright by designer/architect.

Images provided by designer/architect.

Plan #341008

Dimensions: 55'6" W x 61'7" D

Levels: 2

Square Footage: 2,508

Main Level Sq. Ft.: 1,500

Upper Level Sq. Ft.: 1,008

Bedrooms: 4

Bathrooms: 4½

Foundation: Crawl space; slab or basement for fee

Materials List Available: Yes

Price Category: E

This traditional-looking home is filled with contemporary amenities that the family will love.

Features:

- Family Room: Enjoy the fireplace in cool weather, and walk through the French doors to the screened porch when it's warm.

- Dining Room: Two tall windows give extra stature to this formal room, which is ideal for entertaining.

- Kitchen: A pantry and ample work area make this room a cook's dream come true.

- Breakfast Room: You'll use this convenient room all through the day, not just at breakfast.

- Bonus Room: Use the extra room and full bath over the garage as an office, media room, or play space for the children.

- Bedroom Suites: Suites on both the main and upper floors feature a private bath filled with amenities that make you feel pampered.

CAD FILE AVAILABLE

Main Level Floor Plan

Upper Level Floor Plan

Copyright by designer/architect.

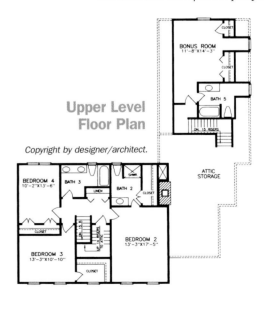

Plan #341002

Dimensions: 62' W x 37'6" D
Levels: 2
Square Footage: 2,528
Main Level Sq. Ft.: 1,193
Upper Level Sq. Ft.: 1,335
Bedrooms: 4
Bathrooms: 2½
Foundation: Crawl space; slab or basement for fee
Materials List Available: Yes
Price Category: E

You'll love the amenities and versatility found in this comfortable family home.

Features:

- **Front Porch:** Enjoy the view from this porch, which opens into the elegant entryway of the home.

- **Ceilings:** The 9-foot ceilings add dimension to this home's already spacious rooms.

- **Dining Room:** This formal room features a large bayed area, which is a treat to decorate.

- **Family Room:** This room is large enough for a crowd and cozy enough for the family.

- **Kitchen:** Planned for convenience, this kitchen features an elevated bar and good storage area.

- **Deck:** Use this space as an outdoor dining room, a grilling porch, or a sunning area.

- **Master Suite:** Enjoy the walk-in closet and bath with double vanity, shower, and garden tub.

Images provided by designer/architect.

CAD FILE AVAILABLE

Main Level Floor Plan

Upper Level Floor Plan

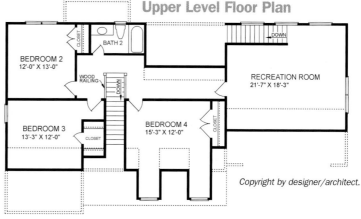

Copyright by designer/architect.

Plan #121064

Dimensions: 44' W x 40' D
Levels: 2
Square Footage: 1,846
Main Level Sq. Ft.: 919
Upper Level Sq. Ft.: 927
Bedrooms: 4
Bathrooms: 2½
Foundation: Basement
Materials List Available: Yes
Price Category: D

Photo provided by designer/architect.

You'll love the features and design in this compact but amenity-filled home.

Features:

• **Entry:** A balcony overlooks this two-story entry, where a plant shelf tops the coat closet.

• **Great Room:** A trio of tall windows points up the large dimensions of this room, which is sure to be the hub of your home. Arrange the furniture to create a cozy space around the fireplace, or leave it open to the room.

• **Kitchen:** You'll love to work in this well-designed kitchen area.

• **Master Suite:** On the second floor, this master suite features a tiered ceiling and two walk-in closets. In the bath, you'll find a double vanity, whirlpool tub, and separate shower.

Main Level Floor Plan

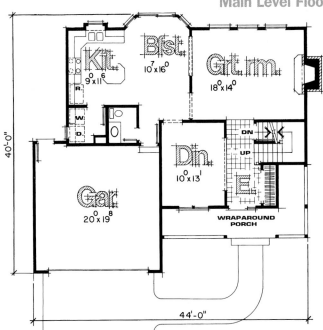

Upper Level Floor Plan

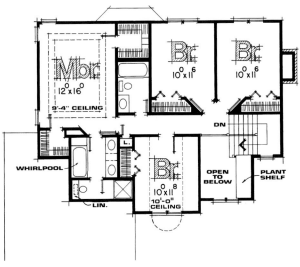

Copyright by designer/architect.

Plan #121066

Dimensions: 46' W x 41'5" D
Levels: 2
Square Footage: 2,078
Main Level Sq. Ft.: 1,113
Upper Level Sq. Ft.: 965
Bedrooms: 4
Bathrooms: 2½
Foundation: Basement
Materials List Available: Yes
Price Category: D

Photo provided by designer/architect.

This lovely home has an unusual dignity, perhaps because its rooms are so well-proportioned and thoughtfully laid out.

Features:

• Gathering Room: This room is sunken, giving it an unusually cozy, comfortable feeling. Its abundance of windows let natural light stream in during the day, and the fireplace warms it when the weather's chilly.

• Dining Room: This dining room links to the parlor beyond through a cased opening.

• Parlor: A tall, angled ceiling highlights a large, arched window that's the focal point of this room.

• Breakfast Area: A wooden rail visually links this bayed breakfast area to the family room.

• Master Suite: A roomy walk-in closet adds a practical touch to this luxurious suite. The bath features a skylight, whirlpool tub, and separate shower.

Main Level Floor Plan

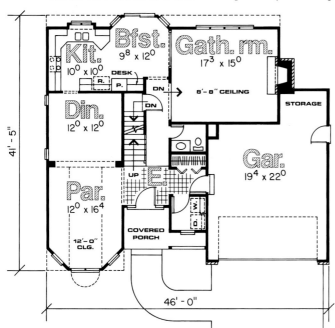

Upper Level Floor Plan

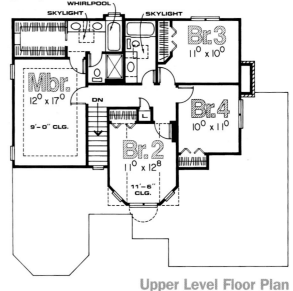

Copyright by designer/architect.

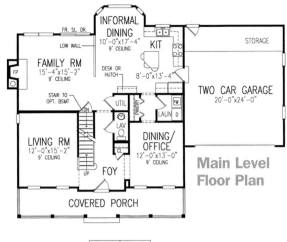

**Main Level
Floor Plan**

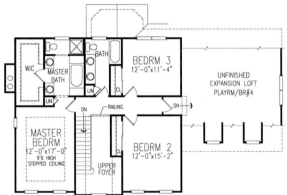

**Upper Level
Floor Plan**

Copyright by designer/architect

Plan #131022

Dimensions: 54'8" W x 43' D
Levels: 2
Square Footage: 2,092
Main Level Sq. Ft.: 1,152
Upper Level Sq. Ft.: 940
Bedrooms: 3
Bathrooms: 2½
Foundation: Basement, crawl space, or slab
Materials List Available: Yes
Price Category: E

Images provided by designer/architect.

This home, as shown in the photograph, may differ from the actual blueprints.

For more detailed information, please check the floor plans carefully.

Main Level Floor Plan

Upper Level Floor Plan

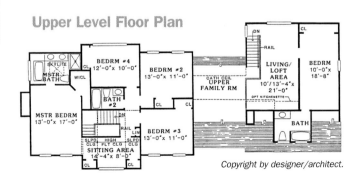

Copyright by designer/architect.

Plan #131023

Dimensions: 78'8" W x 36'2" D
Levels: 2
Square Footage: 2,460
Main Level Sq. Ft.: 1,377
Upper Level Sq. Ft.: 1,083
Bedrooms: 4
Bathrooms: 3½
Foundation: Basement, crawl space, or slab
Materials List Available: Yes
Price Category: F

Images provided by designer/architect.

Plan #271093

Dimensions: 74' W x 52' D
Levels: 2
Square Footage: 2,813
Main Level Sq. Ft.: 1,828
Upper Level Sq. Ft.: 985
Bedrooms: 3
Bathrooms: 3
Foundation: Full basement
Materials List Available: No
Price Category: F

Images provided by designer/architect.

Main Level Floor Plan

Upper Level Floor Plan

Copyright by designer/architect.

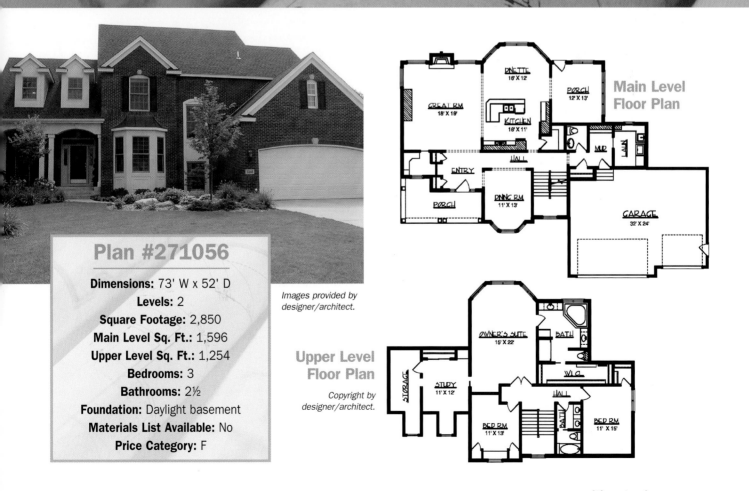

Plan #271056

Dimensions: 73' W x 52' D
Levels: 2
Square Footage: 2,850
Main Level Sq. Ft.: 1,596
Upper Level Sq. Ft.: 1,254
Bedrooms: 3
Bathrooms: 2½
Foundation: Daylight basement
Materials List Available: No
Price Category: F

Images provided by designer/architect.

Main Level Floor Plan

Upper Level Floor Plan

Copyright by designer/architect.

Plan #211070

Dimensions: 46' W x 68' D

Levels: 2

Square Footage: 1,700

Main Level Sq. Ft.: 1,160

Upper Level Sq. Ft.: 540

Bedrooms: 3

Bathrooms: 2½

Foundation: Crawl space, optional slab, or basement

Materials List Available: Yes

Price Category: C

Photo provided by designer/architect.

Features:

- Living Room: With 9-ft. ceilings throughout the living room, dining room, and kitchen merge to maximize usable space and create a spacious, airy feeling in this home. You'll find a fireplace here and three pairs of French doors.

- Dining Room: Walk through this room to the rear covered porch beyond that connects the house to the garage.

- Kitchen: Designed for convenience, this kitchen features a wet bar that is centrally located so that it can easily serve both the living and dining rooms.

- Master Suite: A sloped ceiling with a skylight and French doors leading to the front porch make this area luxurious. The bath includes a raised marble tub, dual-sink vanity, and walk-in closet.

CAD FILE AVAILABLE

You'll be charmed by the three roof dormers and the full-width covered porch on this traditional home.

Main Level Floor Plan

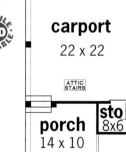

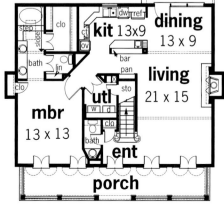

Upper Level Floor Plan

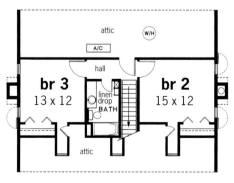

Copyright by designer/architect.

Plan #121094

Dimensions: 40'8" W x 46' D

Levels: 2

Square Footage: 1,768

Main Level Sq. Ft.: 905

Upper Level Sq. Ft.: 863

Bedrooms: 3

Bathrooms: 2½

Foundation: Basement

Materials List Available: Yes

Price Category: C

Photo provided by designer/architect.

You'll love this design if you're looking for a home to complement a site with a lovely rear view.

Features:

- **Great Room:** A trio of lovely windows looks out to the rear of this home. The French doors in this room open to the breakfast area for everyone's convenience.

- **Kitchen:** Designed to suit a gourmet cook, this kitchen includes a roomy pantry and an island with a snack bar.

- **Breakfast Area:** The boxed window here is perfect for houseplants or a collection of culinary herbs. A door leads to the rear porch, where you'll love to dine in good weather.

- **Master Suite:** On the upper level, the bedroom features a cathedral ceiling, two walk-in closets, and a window seat. The bath also has a cathedral ceiling and includes dual lavatories, a large dressing area, and a sunlit whirlpool tub.

Main Level Floor Plan

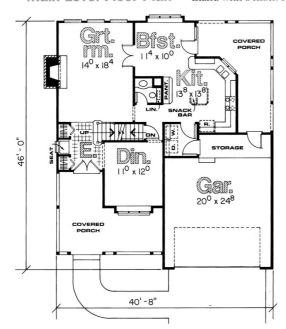

Upper Level Floor Plan

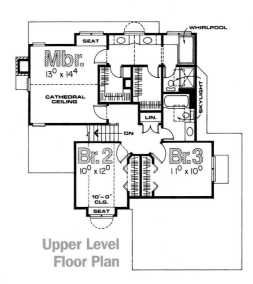

Copyright by designer/architect.

Plan #131028

Dimensions: 69'2" W x 50'2" D
Levels: 2
Square Footage: 2,696
Main Level Sq. Ft.: 1,960
Upper Level Sq. Ft.: 736
Bedrooms: 4
Bathrooms: 3½
Foundation: Crawl space, slab, or basement
Materials List Available: Yes
Price Category: G

Imagine owning a home with Victorian styling and a dramatic, contemporary interior design.

Features:

- Foyer: Enter from the curved covered porch into this foyer with its 17-ft. ceiling.

- Great Room: A vaulted ceiling sets the tone for this large room, where friends and family are sure to congregate.

- Dining Room: A 14-ft. ceiling here accentuates the rounded shape of this room.

- Kitchen: From the angled corner sink to the angled island with a snack bar, this room has character. A pantry adds convenience.

- Master Suite: A 13-ft. tray ceiling exudes elegance, and the bath features a spa tub and designer shower.

- Upper Level: The balcony hall leads to a turreted recreation room, two bedrooms, and a full bath.

Main Level Floor Plan

Upper Level Floor Plan

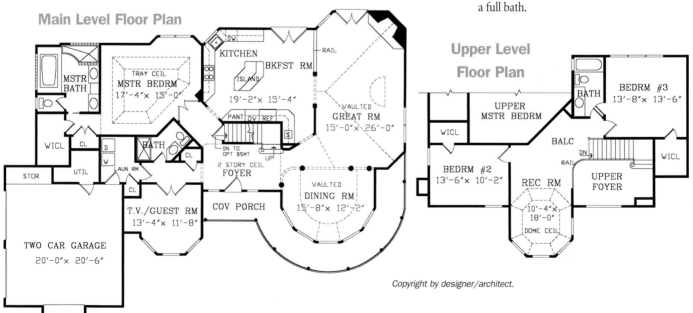

Rear View

Entry

Dining Room

Kitchen View to Great Room

Great Room

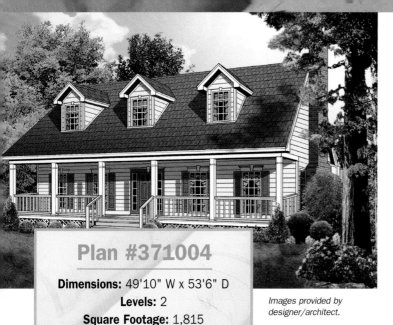

Plan #371004

Dimensions: 49'10" W x 53'6" D

Levels: 2

Square Footage: 1,815

Main Level Sq. Ft.: 1,245

Upper Level Sq. Ft.: 570

Bedrooms: 3

Bathrooms: 2

Foundation: Slab
(crawl space option for fee)

Materials List Available: No

Price Category: D

Images provided by designer/architect.

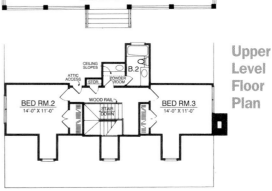

Main Level Floor Plan

Upper Level Floor Plan

Copyright by designer/architect.

Plan #391033

Dimensions: 48' W x 48' D

Levels: 2

Square Footage: 2,007

Main Level Sq. Ft.: 1,345

Upper Level Sq. Ft.: 662

Bedrooms: 3

Bathrooms: 2½

Foundation: Basement,
crawl space, slab

Materials List Available: Yes

Price Category: D

Images provided by designer/architect.

This home, as shown in the photograph, may differ from the actual blueprints. For more detailed information, please check the floor plans carefully.

Main Level Floor Plan

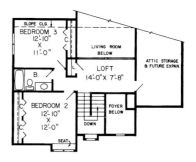

Upper Level Floor Plan

Copyright by designer/architect.

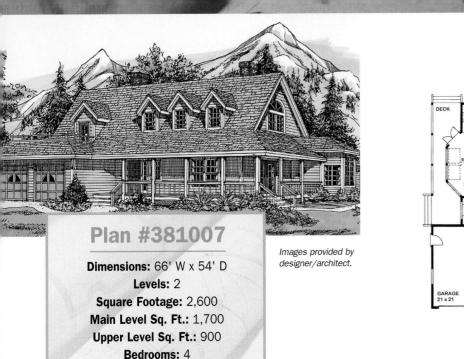

Main Level Floor Plan

Plan #381007

Dimensions: 66' W x 54' D

Levels: 2

Square Footage: 2,600

Main Level Sq. Ft.: 1,700

Upper Level Sq. Ft.: 900

Bedrooms: 4

Bathrooms: 2½

Foundation: Crawl space

Materials List Available: Yes

Price Category: F

Images provided by designer/architect.

Upper Level Floor Plan

Copyright by designer/architect.

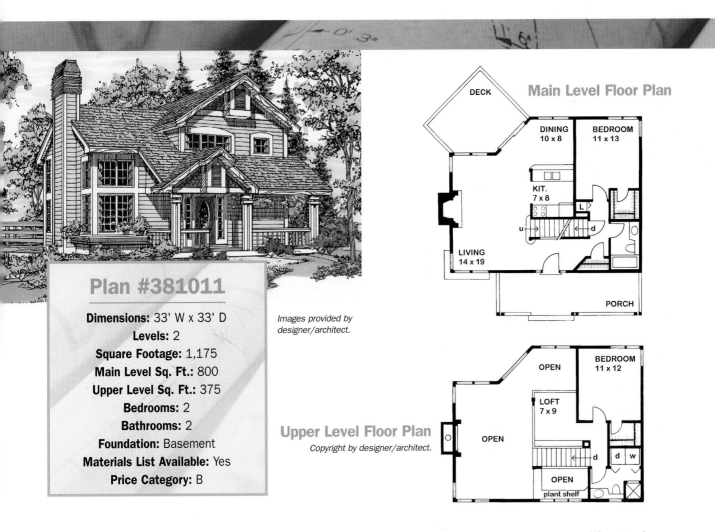

Plan #381011

Dimensions: 33' W x 33' D

Levels: 2

Square Footage: 1,175

Main Level Sq. Ft.: 800

Upper Level Sq. Ft.: 375

Bedrooms: 2

Bathrooms: 2

Foundation: Basement

Materials List Available: Yes

Price Category: B

Images provided by designer/architect.

Main Level Floor Plan

Upper Level Floor Plan

Copyright by designer/architect.

Plan #121027

Dimensions: 46' W x 48' D

Levels: 2

Square Footage: 1,660

Main Level Sq. Ft.: 1,265

Upper Level Sq. Ft.: 395

Bedrooms: 3

Bathrooms: 2½

Foundation: Basement

Materials List Available: Yes

Price Category: C

This elegant home is designed for architectural interest and gracious living.

Features:

• Ceiling Height: 8 ft. unless otherwise noted.

• Great Room: Family and guests will be drawn to this inviting, sun-filled room with its 13-ft. ceiling and raised-hearth fireplace.

• Formal Dining Room: An angled ceiling lends architectural interest to this elegant room. Alternately, this room can be used as a parlor.

• Master Suite: Corner windows are designed to ease furnature placement. The master bedroom is served by a private bath. The sunlit whirlpool bath invites you to take time to luxuriate and rejuvenate. There's a double vanity, separate shower, and a walk-in closet.

• Garage: This two bay garage offers plenty of space for storage in addition to parking.

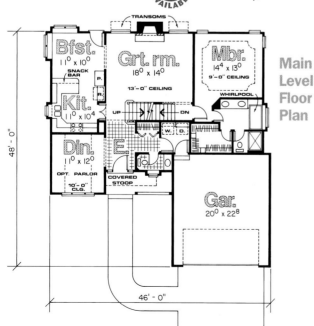

Main Level Floor Plan

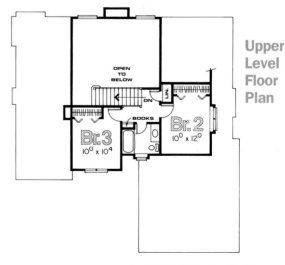

Upper Level Floor Plan

Plan #121032

Dimensions: 54' W x 45'4" D
Levels: 2
Square Footage: 2,339
Main Level Sq. Ft.: 1,665
Upper Level Sq. Ft.: 674
Bedrooms: 4
Bathrooms: 2½
Foundation: Basement
Materials List Available: Yes
Price Category: E

This home is designed for gracious living and is distinguished by many architectural details.

Features:

- Ceiling Height: 8 ft. unless otherwise noted.

- Foyer: This is truly a grand foyer with a dramatic ceiling that soars to 18 ft.

- Great Room: The foyer's 18-ft. ceiling extends into the great room where an open staircase adds architectural windows. Warm yourself by the fireplace that is framed by windows.

- Kitchen: An island is the centerpiece of this handsome and efficient kitchen that features a breakfast area for informal family meals. The room also includes a handy desk.

- Private Wing: The master suite and study are in a private wing of the house.

- Room to Expand: In addition to the three bedrooms, the second level has an unfinished storage space that can become another bedroom or office.

Main Level Floor Plan

Upper Level Floor Plan

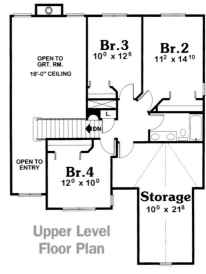

**Main Level
Floor Plan**

*Images provided by
designer/architect.*

**Upper Level
Floor Plan**

*Copyright by design-
er/architect.*

Plan #271067

Dimensions: 72'2" W x 46'5" D
Levels: 2
Square Footage: 3,015
Main Level Sq. Ft.: 1,367
Upper Level Sq. Ft.: 1,648
Bedrooms: 3
Bathrooms: 2½
Foundation: Basement or crawl space
Materials List Available: No
Price Category: G

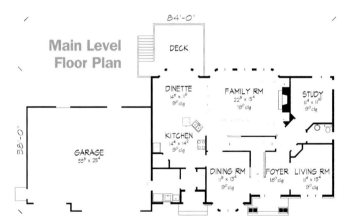

**Main Level
Floor Plan**

*Images provided by design-
er/architect.*

**Upper Level
Floor Plan**

*Copyright by design-
er/architect.*

Plan #271071

Dimensions: 84' W x 38' D
Levels: 2
Square Footage: 3,194
Main Level Sq. Ft.: 1,709
Upper Level Sq. Ft.: 1,485
Bedrooms: 4
Bathrooms: 2½
Foundation: Basement or crawl space
Materials List Available: No
Price Category: G

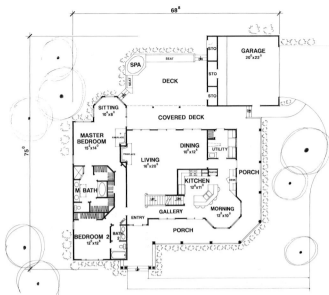

Main Level Floor Plan

Plan #331003

Dimensions: 68'8" W x 75' D

Levels: 2

Square Footage: 2,661

Main Level Sq. Ft.: 2,000

Upper Level Sq. Ft.: 660

Bedrooms: 4

Bathrooms: 3

Foundation: Basement, crawl space, or slab

Materials List Available: No

Price Category: F

Upper Level Floor Plan

Main Level Floor Plan

Plan #331004

Dimensions: 81' W x 49'10" D

Levels: 2

Square Footage: 3,125

Main Level Sq. Ft.: 2,147

Upper Level Sq. Ft.: 978

Bedrooms: 4

Bathrooms: 3½

Foundation: Basement, crawl space, or slab

Materials List Available: No

Price Category: G

Upper Level Floor Plan

GREAT ROOM
18'-0" X 15'-6"
(VAULTED)

CL.
LIN
SHOWER
F/P
UTIL
D
W
F
1/2 BATH
CL.
MASTER BATH
DOUBLE GARAGE
20'-0" X 21'-0"
38'-6"
UP
REF
PANT
ISLAND
KIT
S
D.W.
MASTER SUITE
13'-0" X 16'-0"
(VAULTED)
FOYER
DINING
10'-0" X 12'-4"
PORCH
EATING BAR
BRK.
12'-0" X 11'-0"

Main Level Floor Plan

Images provided by designer/architect.

GREAT ROOM BELOW
FLUE
BALCONY
FUTURE PLAYROOM
20'-5" X 12'-0"
DN
W.I.O.
BEDR'M-3
10'-0" X 12'-4"
BATH
LIN
CL.
BEDR'M-2
12'-0" X 12'-0"

Upper Level Floor Plan

Copyright by designer/architect.

Plan #241009

Dimensions: 62'9" W x 38'6" D

Levels: 2

Square Footage: 1,974

Main Level Sq. Ft.: 1,480

Upper Level Sq. Ft.: 1,154

Bedrooms: 3

Bathrooms: 2½

Foundation: Slab

Materials List Available: No

Price Category: G

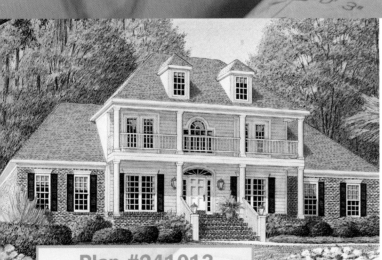

Main Level Floor Plan

BRK
11'-0" X 13'-6"
SUNROOM
20'-7" X 12'-4"
UTIL
D
W
F
F/P
REAR ENTRY
1/2 BATH
GLASS SHOWER
F/P
MASTER BATH
CL.
GREAT ROOM
19'-1" X 16'-1"
LIN
EATING BAR
KIT.
STOR
UP
46'-0"
REF
OVEN MICRO
S
D.W.
U/S
MASTER SUITE
15'-1" X 16'-0"
HALL
CL.
LANDING
DINING
10'-8" X 13'-0"
DOUBLE GARAGE
20'-1" X 21'-0"
STUDY
7'-8" X 9'-1"
DROP CEILING
UP
FOYER
PORCH
68'-0"

Images provided by designer/architect.

BEDROOM 2
11'-2" X 16'-6"
BEDROOM 3
12'-9" X 12'-0"
BATH-3
CL.
LANDING
DN
PLAYROOM
14'-0" X 15'-1"
SEAT
BALCONY
CL.
CL.
BATH 2
CL.
LIN
SHOWER
SEAT
DN
LANDING
FOYER BELOW
BEDROOM 4
11'-0" X 11'-3"
LANDING
BALCONY

Upper Level Floor Plan

Copyright by designer/architect.

Plan #241013

Dimensions: 68' W x 46' D

Levels: 2

Square Footage: 3,072

Main Level Sq. Ft.: 1,918

Upper Level Sq. Ft.: 1,115

Bedrooms: 4

Bathrooms: 3½

Foundation: Slab, crawl space, or walk-out

Materials List Available: No

Price Category: G

Plan #261004

Dimensions: 82' W x 48'8" D
Levels: 2
Square Footage: 2,707
Main Level Sq. Ft.: 1,484
Upper Level Sq. Ft.: 1,223
Bedrooms: 3
Bathrooms: 2½
Foundation: Basement
Materials List Available: No
Price Category: F

Inside the classic Victorian exterior is a spacious home filled with contemporary amenities that the whole family is sure to love.

Features:

- **Porch:** This wraparound porch provides space for entertaining or sitting out to enjoy the evening.
- **Foyer:** Two stories high, the foyer opens to the formal dining room and front parlor.
- **Family Room:** French doors open from the parlor into this room, with its cozy fireplace.
- **Sunroom:** A cathedral ceiling adds drama to this versatile room.
- **Kitchen:** A pantry and a work island make this well-planned kitchen even more convenient.
- **Master Suite:** A tray ceiling and French doors to the bath give the bedroom elegance, while the sumptuous bath features a deluxe tub, walk-in shower, and split vanities.

Images provided by designer/architect.

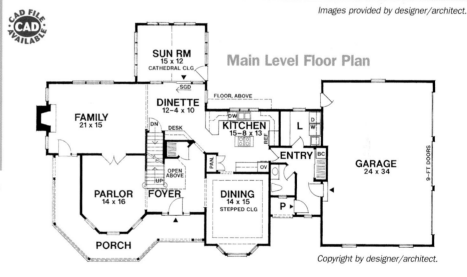

Main Level Floor Plan

Copyright by designer/architect.

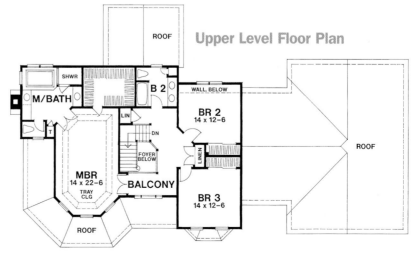

Upper Level Floor Plan

Plan #391018

Dimensions: 93' W x 54' D
Levels: 2
Square Footage: 3,747
Main Level Sq. Ft.: 1,978
Upper Level Sq. Ft.: 1,768
Bedrooms: 4
Bathrooms: 3½
Foundation: Basement
Materials List Available: Yes
Price Category: H

This home, as shown in the photograph, may differ from the actual blueprints. For more detailed information, please check the floor plans carefully.

Images provided by designer/architect.

While the façade of this house suggests the level of detail within, it gives no hint of the home's uniquely designed rooms.

Features:

• Kitchen: This L-shape kitchen, with its large, angled island, provides plenty of workspace and storage.

• Built-ins: Shelving, bookcases, and a built-in desk add extra usefulness throughout the home.

• Porch: This three-season porch is an ideal place to relax and enjoy the outdoors when the weather doesn't permit use of either of the two decks.

• Garage: This garage holds up to three vehicles, though the third bay can be used to storage or shop space.

• Fireplaces: The master suite, great room, and kitchen/breakfast area are all warmed by fireplaces.

Main Level Floor Plan

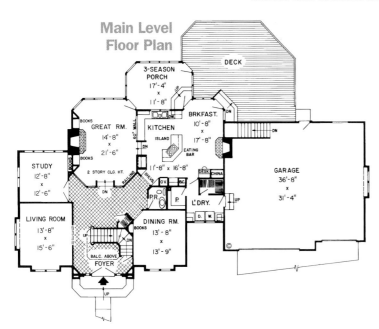

Upper Level Floor Plan

Copyright by designer/architect.

Plan #121088

Dimensions: 56'8" W x 48' D
Levels: 2
Square Footage: 2,340
Main Level Sq. Ft.: 1,701
Upper Level Sq. Ft.: 639
Bedrooms: 4
Bathrooms: 2½
Foundation: Basement
Materials List Available: Yes
Price Category: E

Photo provided by designer/architect.

You'll love this cheerful home, with its many large windows that let in natural light and cozy spaces that encourage family gatherings.

Features:

• Entry: Use the built-in curio cabinet here to display your best collector's pieces.

• Den: French doors from the entry lead to this room, with its built-in bookcase and triple-wide, transom-topped window.

• Great Room: The 14-ft. ceiling in this room accentuates the floor-to-ceiling windows that frame the raised-hearth fireplace.

• Kitchen: Both the layout and the work space make this room a delight for any cook.

• Master Suite: The bedroom has a tray ceiling for built-in elegance. A skylight helps to light the master bath, and an oval whirlpool tub, separate shower, and double vanity provide a luxurious touch.

Main Level Floor Plan

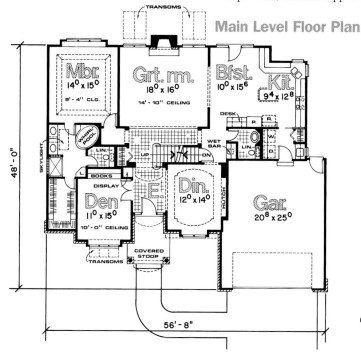

Upper Level Floor Plan

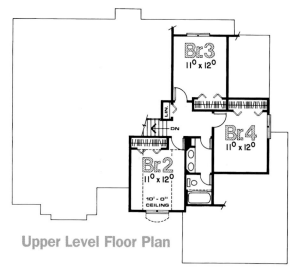

Copyright by designer/architect.

Plan #131078

Dimensions: 72'8" W x 47' D
Levels: 2
Square Footage: 3,278
Main Level Sq. Ft.: 2,146
Upper Level Sq. Ft.: 1,132
Bedrooms: 3
Bathrooms: 3
Foundation: Crawl space, slab, or basement
Material List Available: Yes
Price Category: H

This attractive home is a delight when viewed from the outside and features a great floor plan inside.

Images provided by designer/architect.

Features:

• Great Room: This spacious room, with a vaulted ceiling and skylights, is the place to curl up by the fireplace on a cold winter night. Sliding glass doors lead out to the backyard.

• Kitchen: A center island adds convenience to this well-planned kitchen. The bayed breakfast area adds extra room for a table.

• Master Suite: The 10-ft.-high stepped ceiling sets the tone for this secluded area, which features a large walk-in closet. The master bath boasts a whirlpool tub and dual vanities.

• Bonus Room: Located above the garage, this space can be finished as a fourth bedroom or home office.

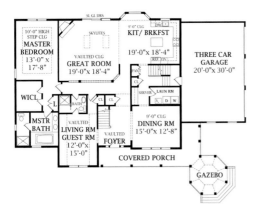

Main Level Floor Plan

Upper Level Floor Plan

Copyright by designer/architect.

Plan #261005

Dimensions: 64' W x 31' D
Levels: 2
Square Footage: 2,419
Main Level Sq. Ft.: 1,228
Upper Level Sq. Ft.: 1,191
Bedrooms: 4
Bathrooms: 2½
Foundation: Basement
Materials List Available: No
Price Category: E

You'll love the spacious rooms and convenient lay-out of this lovely Colonial-style home.

Features:

- Ceilings: Ceilings are 9 ft. tall or higher, adding to the airy feeling inside this home.

- Foyer: This two-story foyer gives a warm welcome.

- Family Room: Everyone will gather in this well-positioned room, with its handsome fireplace and generous dimensions.

- Living Room: Both this room and the dining room are ideal for formal entertaining.

- Kitchen: A cook's dream, this kitchen has ample counter space, a large island, and a pantry.

- Master Suite: Enjoy the luxury of the walk-in closet, dual vanities, whirlpool tub, and shower here.

- Additional Bedrooms: Extensive closet space makes it easy to live in each of the bedrooms.

Images provided by designer/architect.

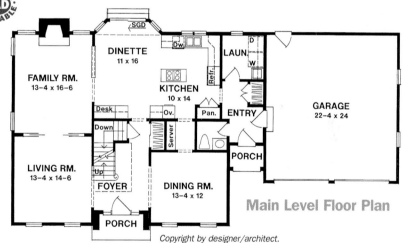

Main Level Floor Plan

Copyright by designer/architect.

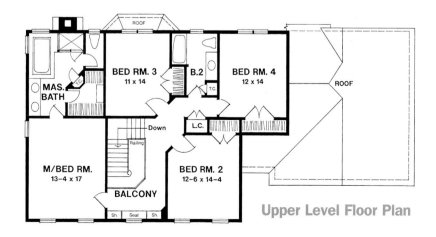

Upper Level Floor Plan

Main Level Floor Plan

Upper Level Floor Plan

Copyright by designer/architect.

Plan #151087

Dimensions: 55'4" W x 53'10" D
Levels: 2
Square Footage: 2,942
Main Level Sq. Ft.: 1,547
Upper Level Sq. Ft.: 1,395
Bedrooms: 5
Bathrooms: 4
Foundation: Crawl space, slab
Materials List Available: No
Price Category: D

Images provided by designer/architect.

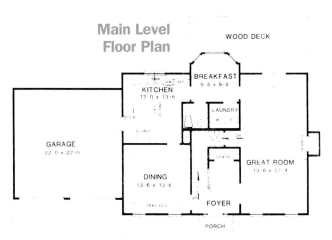

Main Level Floor Plan

Copyright by designer/architect.

Plan #301006

Dimensions: 60' W x 32' D
Levels: 2
Square Footage: 2,162
Main Level Sq. Ft.: 1,098
Upper Level Sq. Ft.: 1,064
Bedrooms: 3
Bathrooms: 2½
Foundation: Crawl space, slab, or basement
Materials List Available: Yes
Price Category: D

Images provided by designer/architect.

Optional Third Level   **Upper Level Floor Plan**

Plan #251010

Dimensions: 53' W x 52' D
Levels: 2
Square Footage: 1,854
Main Level Sq. Ft.: 1,317
Upper Level Sq. Ft.: 537
Bedrooms: 3
Bathrooms: 2½
Foundation: Basement
Materials List Available: Yes
Price Category: D

Illustration provided by designer/architect.

CAD FILE AVAILABLE

Main Level Floor Plan

Upper Level Floor Plan

Copyright by designer/architect.

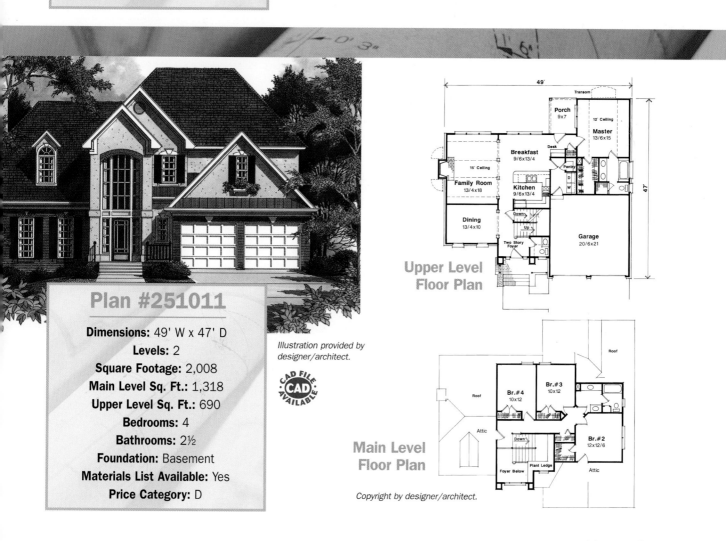

Plan #251011

Dimensions: 49' W x 47' D
Levels: 2
Square Footage: 2,008
Main Level Sq. Ft.: 1,318
Upper Level Sq. Ft.: 690
Bedrooms: 4
Bathrooms: 2½
Foundation: Basement
Materials List Available: Yes
Price Category: D

Illustration provided by designer/architect.

CAD FILE AVAILABLE

Upper Level Floor Plan

Main Level Floor Plan

Copyright by designer/architect.

Images provided by designer/architect.

Plan #291009

Dimensions: 74'8" W x 41'4" D

Levels: 2

Square Footage: 1,655

Main Level Sq. Ft.: 1,277

Upper Level Sq. Ft.: 378

Bedrooms: 3

Bathrooms: 2

Foundation: Basement

Materials List Available: No

Price Category: C

If your family loves a northern European look, they'll appreciate the curved eaves and arched window that give this lovely home its character.

Features:

- **Entryway:** The front door welcomes both friends and family into a lovely open design on the first floor of this home.

- **Living Room:** The enormous arched window floods this room with natural light in the daytime. At night, draw drapes across it to create a warm, intimate feeling.

- **Dining Room:** Windows are the highlight of this room, too, but here, the angled bay window area opens to the rear deck.

- **Kitchen:** The family cook will be delighted with this well-planned kitchen, which is a snap to organize.

- **Master Suite:** Located on the first floor, this suite includes a private bath for total convenience.

Main Level Floor Plan

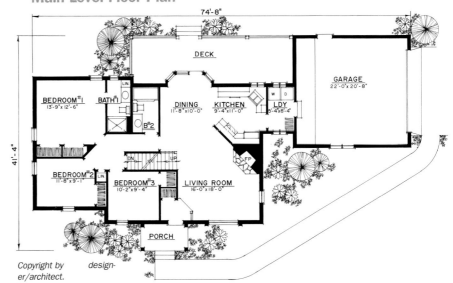

Copyright by designer/architect.

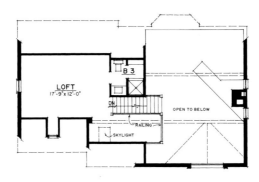

Upper Level Floor Plan

Plan #141010

Dimensions: 43'4" W x 37' D
Levels: 2
Square Footage: 1,765
Main Level Sq. Ft.: 1,210
Upper Level Sq. Ft.: 555
Bedrooms: 3
Bathrooms: 3
Foundation: Basement
Materials List Available: No
Price Category: C

A Palladian window in a stone gable adds a new twist to a classical cottage design.

Features:

- Ceiling Height: 8 ft. unless otherwise noted.

- Living Area: Dormers open into this handsome living area, which is designed to accommodate gatherings of any size.

- Master Suite: This beautiful master bedroom opens off the foyer. It features a modified cathedral ceiling that makes the front Palladian window a focal point inside as well as out. The master bath offers a dramatic cathedral ceiling over the tub and vanity.

- Balcony: U-shaped stairs lead to this elegant balcony, which overlooks the foyer while providing access to two additional bedrooms.

- Garage: This garage is tucked under the house to improve the appearance from the street. It offers two bays for plenty of parking and storage space.

Main Level Floor Plan

Upper Level Floor Plan

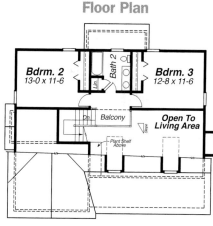

Basement Floor Plan

SMARTtip

Stone Tables

Marble- and stone-topped tables with plants are perfect for use in light-filled rooms. Warmed by the sun during the day, the tabletops catch leaf droppings and can stand up to the splatters of watering cans and plant sprayers.

Plan #121075

Dimensions: 57'4" W x 30' D

Levels: 2

Square Footage: 2,345

Main Level Sq. Ft.: 1,000

Upper Level Sq. Ft.: 1,345

Bedrooms: 4

Bathrooms: 3½

Foundation: Basement

Materials List Available: Yes

Price Category: E

Photo provided by designer/architect.

Imagine owning a home with a Colonial-styled exterior and a practical, amenity-filled interior with both formal and informal areas.

Features:

- Family Room: This room will be the heart of your home. A bay window lets you create a special nook for reading or quiet conversation, and a fireplace begs for a circle of comfortable chairs or soft cushions around it.

- Living Room: Connected to the family room by a set of French doors, you can use this room for formal entertaining or informal family fun.

- Kitchen: This kitchen has been designed for efficient work patterns. However, the snack bar that links it to the breakfast area beyond also invites company while the cook is working.

- Master Suite: Located on the second level, this suite features an entertainment center, a separate sitting area, built-in dressers, two walk-in closets, and a whirlpool tub.

Main Level Floor Plan

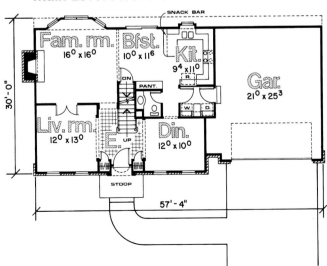

Upper Level Floor Plan

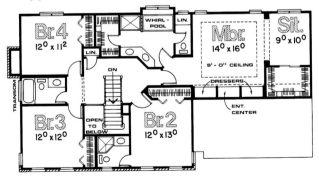

Copyright by designer/architect.

Plan #161019

Dimensions: 54'6" D x 41'10" W

Levels: 2

Square Footage: 2,428

Main Level Sq. Ft.: 1,309

Upper Level Sq. Ft.: 1,119

Bedrooms: 4

Bathrooms: 2½

Foundation: Basement

Materials List Available: No

Price Category: E

Elegant and designed for comfortable family living, this home is full of amenities.

Features:

- Foyer: The elegant staircase and arched opening to the living room are visible from this foyer, and a balcony on the upper level lets you look into it.

- Family Room: Let the family relax and play here so that you can save the formal living room for entertaining and quiet activities.

- Kitchen: The central location of this kitchen makes it the heart of this home. It's visually open to the family room and breakfast area and naturally lit by a bank of rear windows.

- Master Suite: Relax in this quiet area, or enjoy the luxury of the master bath, with its whirlpool tub, separate shower, and dual vanities.

- Upper Level: 3 bedrooms and a bath with a skylight and double-bowl vanity make this area comfortable for guests or family.

This home, as shown in the photograh, may differ from the actual blueprints. For more detailed information, please check the floor plans carefully.

Images provided by designer/architect.

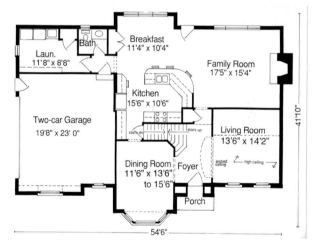

Main Level Floor Plan

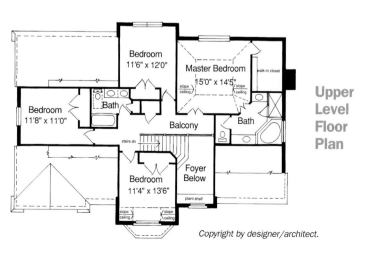

Upper Level Floor Plan

Copyright by designer/architect.

Plan #111008

Dimensions: 43' W x 69' D

Levels: 2

Square Footage: 2,011

Main Level Sq. Ft.: 1,331

Upper Level Sq. Ft.: 680

Bedrooms: 3

Bathrooms: 2½

Foundation: Slab or basement

Materials List Available: No

Price Category: E

Photo provided by designer/architect.

Main Level Floor Plan

Upper Level Floor Plan

Copyright by designer/architect.

Plan #111023

Dimensions: 46'11" W x 73'5" D

Levels: 2

Square Footage: 2,356

Main Level Sq. Ft.: 1,516

Upper Level Sq. Ft.: 840

Bedrooms: 4

Bathrooms: 2½

Foundation: Slab

Materials List Available: No

Price Category: F

Photo provided by designer/architect.

Main Level Floor Plan

Upper Level Floor Plan

Copyright by designer/architect.

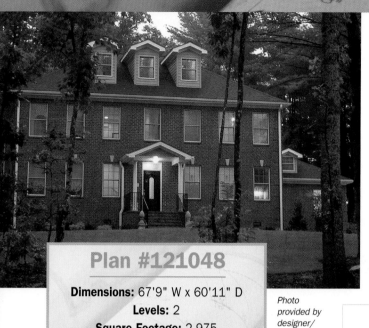

Main Level Floor Plan

Photo provided by designer/architect.

Upper Level Floor Plan

Copyright by designer/architect.

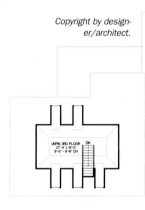

Bonus Area

Plan #121048

Dimensions: 67'9" W x 60'11" D
Levels: 2
Square Footage: 2,975
Main Level Sq. Ft.: 1,548
Upper Level Sq. Ft.: 1,427
Bedrooms: 4
Bathrooms: 3½
Foundation: Slab
Materials List Available: Yes
Price Category: F

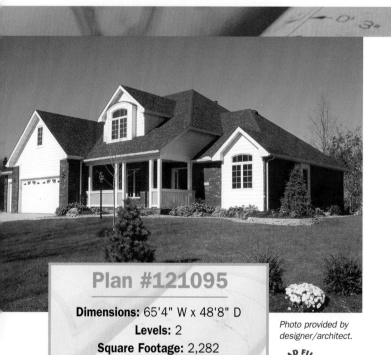

Main Level Floor Plan

Photo provided by designer/architect.

Plan #121095

Dimensions: 65'4" W x 48'8" D
Levels: 2
Square Footage: 2,282
Main Level Sq. Ft.: 1,597
Upper Level Sq. Ft.: 685
Bedrooms: 4
Bathrooms: 2½
Foundation: Basement
Materials List Available: Yes
Price Category: E

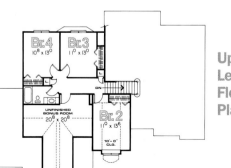

Upper Level Floor Plan

Copyright by designer/architect.

Plan #121068

Dimensions: 54' W x 49'10" D

Levels: 2

Square Footage: 2,391

Main Level Sq. Ft.: 1,697

Upper Level Sq. Ft.: 694

Bedrooms: 4

Bathrooms: 2½

Foundation: Basement

Materials List Available: Yes

Price Category: E

This home, as shown in the photograph, may differ from the actual blueprints. For more detailed information, please check the floor plans carefully.

Photo provided by designer/arch

This home allows you a great deal of latitude in the way you choose to finish it, so you can truly make it "your own."

Features:

• Living Room: Located just off the entryway, this living room is easy to convert to a stylish den. Add French doors for privacy, and relish the style that the 12-ft. angled ceiling and picturesque arched window provide.

• Great Room: The highlight of this room is the two-sided fireplace that easily adds as much design interest as warmth to this area. The three transom-topped windows here fill the room with light.

• Kitchen: A center island, walk-in pantry, and built-in desk combine to create this wonderful kitchen, and the attached gazebo breakfast area adds the finishing touch.

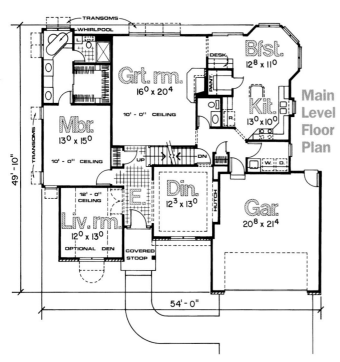

Main Level Floor Plan

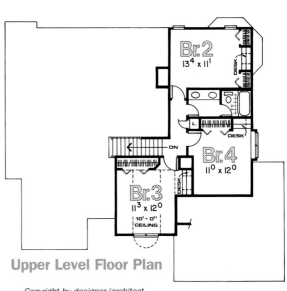

Upper Level Floor Plan

Copyright by designer/architect.

Plan #121071

Dimensions: 72'8" W x 51'4" D
Levels: 2
Square Footage: 2,957
Main Level Sq. Ft.: 2,063
Upper Level Sq. Ft.: 894
Bedrooms: 4
Bathrooms: 4½
Foundation: Basement
Materials List Available: Yes
Price Category: F

You'll appreciate the mix of open public areas and private quarters that the layout of this home guarantees.

Features:

- **Entry:** From this entry, the formal living and dining rooms, as well as the great room, are all visible.

- **Great Room:** A soaring cathedral ceiling sets an elegant tone for this room, and the fireplace that's flanked with lovely transom-topped windows adds to it.

- **Den:** French doors from the great room lead to this den, where you'll find a generous bay window, a wet bar, and a decorative ceiling.

- **Master Suite:** On the main floor to give it needed privacy, this master suite will make you feel at home the first time you walk into it. The private bath has an angled ceiling and a whirlpool tub.

Main Level Floor Plan

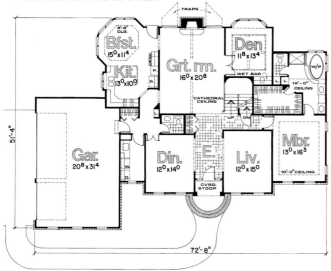

Upper Level Floor Plan

Main Level Floor Plan

Illustration provided by designer/architect.

CAD FILE AVAILABLE

Plan #251012

Dimensions: 57'9" W x 62'10" D

Levels: 2

Square Footage: 2,009

Main Level Sq. Ft.: 1,520

Upper Level Sq. Ft.: 489

Bedrooms: 3

Bathrooms: 2½

Foundation: Basement

Materials List Available: Yes

Price Category: D

Upper Level Floor Plan

Copyright by designer/architect.

Illustration provided by designer/architect.

CAD FILE AVAILABLE

Plan #251013

Dimensions: 58' W x 44' D

Levels: 2

Square Footage: 2,073

Main Level Sq. Ft.: 1,441

Upper Level Sq. Ft.: 632

Bedrooms: 4

Bathrooms: 2½

Foundation: Basement

Materials List Available: Yes

Price Category: D

Main Level Floor Plan

Upper Level Floor Plan

Copyright by designer/architect.

Main Level Floor Plan

68'-0"

32'-0"

MASTER BEDROOM
15'-8" x 12'-9"

MR. BATH

PR.

PATIO

PATIO

GREAT ROOM
21'-3" x 12'-9"

FP

BOOKS

BOOKS

GARAGE
20'-6" x 22'-0"

DINING ROOM
12'-10" x 11'-2"

KIT.
8'-6" x
10'-6"

W D

LDY

ENTRY

MORNING RM
6'-6" x 7'-8"

MORNING
PATIO

CLOSET

FIRST FLOOR PLAN

Plan #291010

Dimensions: 68'6" W x 33' D
Levels: 2
Square Footage: 1,776
Main Level Sq. Ft.: 1,182
Upper Level Sq. Ft.: 594
Bedrooms: 3
Bathrooms: 2½
Foundation: Basement
Materials List Available: No
Price Category: C

Upper Level Floor Plan

BATH #2

OPEN TO VAULTED CEILING

BEDROOM #2
13'-4" x 14'-4"

RAILING

BEDROOM #3
11'-0" x 14'-11"

35'-0"

PORCH

FAMILY ROOM
18'-0" x 19'-6"

MORNING ROOM
8'-0" x 11'-6"

KITCHEN
10'-0" x 11'-6"

DINING ROOM
13'-9" x 14'-4"

VAULTED CEILING

FAMILY ENTRY

FP

DN

DN

PANTRY

LAUNDRY
W D

LAV.

UP

ENTRY FOYER

LIVING ROOM
13'-9" x 18'-6"

44'-0"

TWO-CAR GARAGE
23'-4" x 23'-2"

PORCH

Main Level Floor Plan

58'-0"

Plan #291012

Dimensions: 68'6" W x 33' D
Levels: 2
Square Footage: 1,898
Main Level Sq. Ft.: 1,182
Upper Level Sq. Ft.: 716
Bedrooms: 4
Bathrooms: 2½
Foundation: Basement
Materials List Available: No
Price Category: D

Upper Level Floor Plan

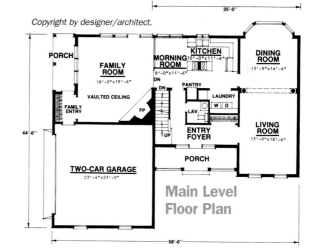

BEDROOM
13'-0" x 8'-10"

WIC

BEDROOM
12'-8" x 11'-0"

DN

LIN

BATH

UPPER HALL

MASTER BATH

BEDROOM
12'-0" x 11'-0"

WIC

MASTER BEDROOM
13'-9" x 14'-2"

32'-0"

35'-0"

Plan #121084

Dimensions: 40' W x 42' D
Levels: 2
Square Footage: 1,728
Main Level Sq. Ft.: 845
Upper Level Sq. Ft.: 883
Bedrooms: 4
Bathrooms: 2½
Foundation: Basement
Materials List Available: Yes
Price Category: C

Photo provided by designer/architect.

If you're looking for a home where the whole family will be comfortable, you'll love this design.

Features:

- Great Room: The heart of the home, this great room has a fireplace with a raised hearth, a sloped ceiling, and transom-topped windows.

- Dining Room: A cased opening lets you flow from the great room into this formal dining room. A built-in display hutch is the highlight here.

- Kitchen: What could be nicer than this wraparound kitchen with peninsula snack bar? The sunny, attached breakfast area has a pantry and built-in desk.

- Master Suite: A double vanity, whirlpool tub, shower, and walk-in closet exude luxury in this upper-floor master suite.

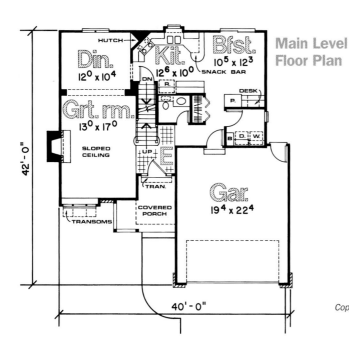

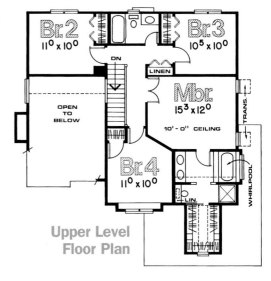

Copyright by designer/architect.

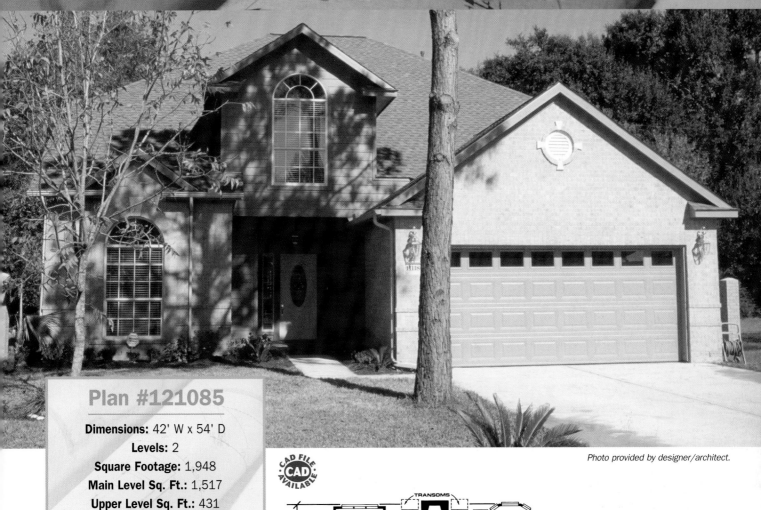

Plan #121085

Dimensions: 42' W x 54' D
Levels: 2
Square Footage: 1,948
Main Level Sq. Ft.: 1,517
Upper Level Sq. Ft.: 431
Bedrooms: 4
Bathrooms: 3
Foundation: Basement
Materials List Available: Yes
Price Category: D

You'll love the spacious feeling in this home, with its generous rooms and excellent design.

Features:

- **Great Room:** This room is lofty and open, thanks in part to the transom-topped windows that flank the fireplace. However, you can furnish to create a cozy nook for reading or a private spot to watch TV or enjoy some quiet music.

- **Kitchen:** Wrapping counters add an unusual touch to this kitchen, and a pantry gives extra storage area. A snack bar links the kitchen with a separate breakfast area.

- **Master Suite:** A tiered ceiling adds elegance to this area, and a walk-in closet adds practicality. The private bath features a sunlit whirlpool tub, separate shower, and double vanity.

Photo provided by designer/architect.

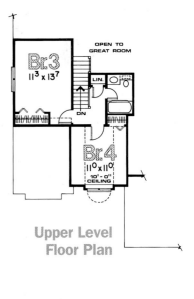

**Main Level
Floor Plan**

**Upper Level
Floor Plan**

Copyright by designer/architect.

- **Upper-Level Bedrooms:** The upper-level placement is just right for these bedrooms, which share an amenity-filled full bathroom.

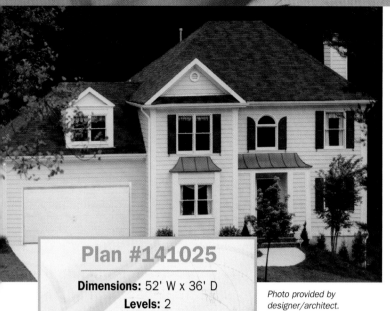

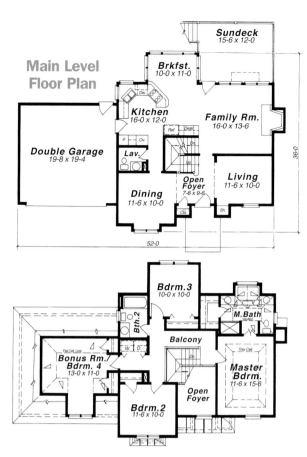

Main Level Floor Plan

Sundeck
15-6 x 12-0

Brkfst.
10-0 x 11-0

Kitchen
16-0 x 12-0

Family Rm.
16-0 x 13-6

Double Garage
19-8 x 19-4

Lav.

Living
11-6 x 10-0

Dining
11-6 x 10-0

Open Foyer
7-6 x 9-6

36-0

52-0

Photo provided by designer/architect.

Plan #141025

Dimensions: 52' W x 36' D

Levels: 2

Square Footage: 1,721

Main Level Sq. Ft.: 902

Upper Level Sq. Ft.: 819

Bedrooms: 4

Bathrooms: 2½

Foundation: Basement

Materials List Available: Yes

Price Category: C

Upper Level Floor Plan

Bdrm.3
10-0 x 10-0

Bth.2

M.Bath

Balcony

Bonus Rm./
Bdrm. 4
13-0 x 11-0

Master
Bdrm.
11-6 x 15-6

Open
Foyer

Bdrm.2
11-6 x 10-0

Copyright by designer/architect.

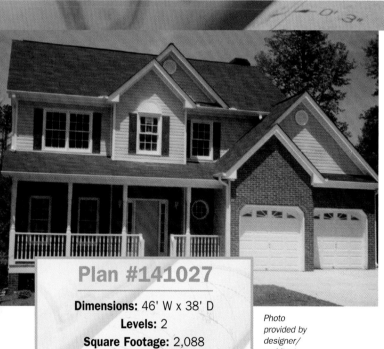

Main Level Floor Plan

Sundeck
21-0 x 12-0

Kitchen
12-6 x 13-4

Brkfst.
12-10 x 13-8

Living Area
20-0 x 13-4

Dining
13-0 x 14-8

Open
Foyer

Double Garage
19-8 x 21-4

Porch

38-4

46-0

Photo provided by designer/ architect.

Plan #141027

Dimensions: 46' W x 38' D

Levels: 2

Square Footage: 2,088

Main Level Sq. Ft.: 1,048

Upper Level Sq. Ft.: 1,040

Bedrooms: 3

Bathrooms: 2½

Foundation: Basement

Materials List Available: Yes

Price Category: D

Upper Level Floor Plan

M.Bath

Bdrm.3
13-0 x 10-10

Master
Bdrm.
13-0 x 18-6

Open
To
Foyer

Bdrm.2
13-0 x 10-0

Copyright by designer/architect.

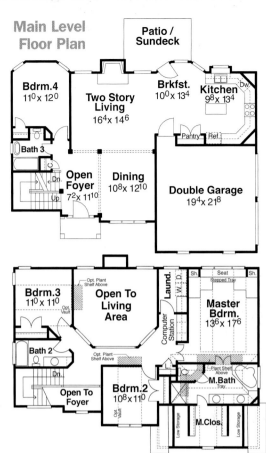

Patio / Sundeck

Bdrm.4
11⁰ x 12⁰

Two Story Living
16⁴ x 14⁶

Brkfst.
10⁰ x 13⁴

Kitchen
9⁸ x 13⁴

Bath 3

Open Foyer
7²x 11¹⁰

Dining
10⁸ x 12¹⁰

Pantry | Ref.

Double Garage
19⁴ x 21⁸

Dn. | Up

Plan #141028

Dimensions: 48' W x 36'4" D

Levels: 2

Square Footage: 2,215

Main Level Sq. Ft.: 1,075

Upper Level Sq. Ft.: 1,140

Bedrooms: 4

Bathrooms: 3

Foundation: Basement

Materials List Available: Yes

Price Category: E

Photo provided by designer/architect.

Bdrm.3
11⁰ x 11⁰

Opt. Plant Shelf Above

Open To Living Area

Laund. | W. D.

Sh. | Seat Stepped Tray | Sh.

Master Bdrm.
13⁶ x 17⁶

Opt. Vault

Computer Station

Bath 2

Opt. Plant Shelf Above

Plant Shelf Above

M. Bath
Tray.

Upper Level Floor Plan

Copyright by designer/architect.

Dn.

Open To Foyer

Bdrm.2
10⁸ x 11⁰

Opt. Vault

Low Storage | M.Clos. | Low Storage

8-0

Sundeck
12-0 x 11-0

Lnd. | W. D.

Lav.

Brkfst.
10-4 x 11-0

Opt. Plant Shelf

Living Area
16-10 x 15-6

Master Bdrm.
13-6 x 15-6

Command Center

Kit.
12-4 x 9-4

Pant.

M. Bath

Dining
10-6 x 12-6

Open Foyer

Up

Stor.

42-0

Main Level Floor Plan

Double Garage
21-4 x 20-8

Plant Shelf

55-0

Plan #141029

Dimensions: 55' W x 42' D

Levels: 2

Square Footage: 2,289

Main Level Sq. Ft.: 1,382

Upper Level Sq. Ft.: 907

Bedrooms: 4

Bathrooms: 2½

Foundation: Basement

Materials List Available: Yes

Price Category: E

Photo provided by designer/architect.

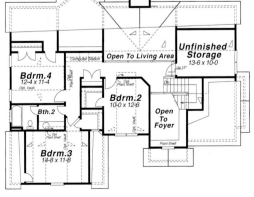

Computer Station

Open To Living Area

Unfinished Storage
13-6 x 10-0

Bdrm.4
12-4 x 11-4

Opt. Plant Shelf

Opt. Vault

Upper Level Floor Plan

Copyright by designer/architect.

Bdrm.2
10-0 x 12-6

Open To Foyer

Bth.2

Opt. Vault

Plant Shelf

Bdrm.3
14-8 x 11-8

Upper Level Floor Plan

br 3
13⁸ x 12

br 4
12 x 12⁴

open to foyer

porch 33 x 10

eating
14 x 10

util
8 x 10

sto
6 x 8

kit

den
19 x 20

mbr
14 x 16

Main Level Floor Plan

garage
22 x 22

dining
12 x 14

foy
9x10

br 2
12 x 14

porch 4 x 21

ledge

Copyright by designer/architect.

Plan #201103

Dimensions: 57'10" W x 56'10" D
Levels: 2
Square Footage: 2,490
Main Level Sq. Ft.: 1,911
Upper Level Sq. Ft.: 579
Bedrooms: 4
Bathrooms: 3
Foundation: Crawl space, slab
Materials List Available: Yes
Price Category: E

Illustration provided by designer/ architect.

Plan #181080

Dimensions: 44'8" W x 36' D
Levels: 2
Square Footage: 2,042
Main Level Sq. Ft.: 934
Upper Level Sq. Ft.: 1,108
Bedrooms: 3
Bathrooms: 2½
Foundation: Full basement
Materials List Available: Yes
Price Category: E

Illustration provided by designer/architect.

CAD FILE AVAILABLE

36'-0"
10,8 m

44'-8"
13,4 m

14'-0" X 8'-4"
4,20 X 2,80

18'-8" X 11'-8"
5,60 X 3,50

12'-4" X 22'-8"
3,70 X 6,80

19'-8" X 22'-0"
5,90 X 6,60

Main Level Floor Plan

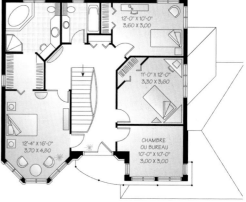

Upper Level Floor Plan

12'-0" X 10'-0"
3,60 X 3,00

11'-0" X 12'-0"
3,30 X 3,60

12'-4" X 16'-0"
3,70 X 4,80

CHAMBRE OU BUREAU
10'-0" X 10'-0"
3,00 X 3,00

Copyright by designer/architect.

Main Level Floor Plan

Upper Level Floor Plan

Plan #101017

Dimensions: 57' W x 51' D

Levels: 2

Square Footage: 2,253

Main Level Sq. Ft.: 1,719

Upper Level Sq. Ft.: 247

Bedrooms: 4

Bathrooms: 2½

Foundation: Basement

Materials List Available: No

Price Category: E

CAD FILE CAD AVAILABLE

Upper Level Floor Plan

Main Level Floor Plan

Plan #181102

Dimensions: 58' W x 58'4" D

Levels: 2

Square Footage: 2,265

Main Level Sq. Ft.: 1,371

Upper Level Sq. Ft.: 894

Bedrooms: 4

Bathrooms: 3½

Foundation: Full basement

Materials List Available: Yes

Price Category: E

CAD FILE CAD AVAILABLE

Plan #131026

Dimensions: 55'10" W x 41' D
Levels: 2
Square Footage: 2,796
Main Level Sq. Ft.: 1,481
Upper level Sq. Ft.: 1,315
Bedrooms: 4
Bathrooms: 2½
Foundation: Basement, crawl space, or slab
Materials List Available: Yes
Price Category: G

Images provided by designer/architect.

Handsome half rounds add to curb appeal.

Features:

• Ceiling Height: 8 ft.

• Library: This room features a 10-ft. ceiling with a bright bay window.

• Family Room: A 10-ft. ceiling adds to the spacious feeling of this room, while the fireplace gives it an intimate feeling. Sliding glass doors at the rear of the room open to the backyard.

• Dining Room: This formal room adjoins the great room, allowing guests and family to flow between the rooms, and it opens to the backyard through sliding glass doors.

• Breakfast Room: Turrets add a Victorian feeling to this room, which is just off the kitchen and overlooks the front porch.

• Master Suite: Privacy is assured in this suite, which is separated from the main part of the house. A separate bath and large walk-in closet add convenience to its beauty.

Master Bathroom

Family Room

Rear Elevation

Upper Level Floor Plan

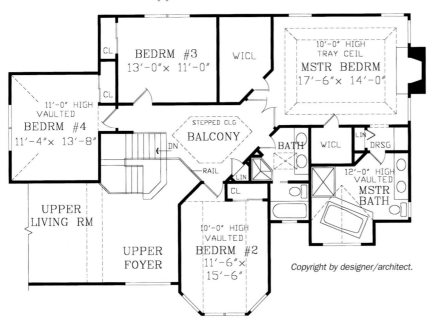

BEDRM #3
13'-0" × 11'-0"

CL

CL

WICL

10'-0" HIGH
TRAY CEIL
MSTR BEDRM
17'-6" × 14'-0"

11'-0" HIGH
VAULTED
BEDRM #4
11'-4" × 13'-8"

STEPPED CLG
BALCONY

DN

RAIL

LIN

BATH

WICL

LIN

DRSG

12'-0" HIGH
VAULTED
MSTR
BATH

CL

UPPER
LIVING RM

UPPER
FOYER

10'-0" HIGH
VAULTED
BEDRM #2
11'-6" ×
15'-6"

Copyright by designer/architect.

Main Level Floor Plan

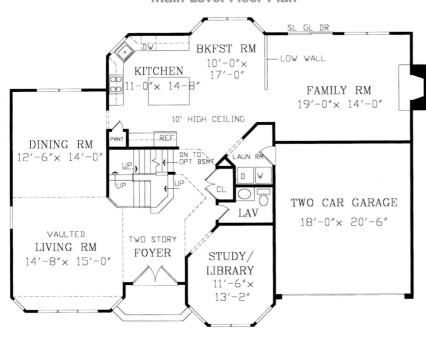

DW

BKFST RM
10'-0" ×
17'-0"

SL GL DR

LOW WALL

KITCHEN
11'-0" × 14'-8"

10' HIGH CEILING

FAMILY RM
19'-0" × 14'-0"

DINING RM
12'-6" × 14'-0"

PANT

REF

UP

DN TO
OPT BSMT

LAUN RM

D   W

UP

UP

CL

LAV

TWO CAR GARAGE
18'-0" × 20'-6"

VAULTED
LIVING RM
14'-8" × 15'-0"

TWO STORY
FOYER

STUDY/
LIBRARY
11'-6" ×
13'-2"

Creating a Stylish Kitchen

Style meets state of the art in the kitchen. If you need inspiration when the time comes to make decorating decisions about your new kitchen, think about some of today's popular decorating styles: country, contemporary, cottage, French country, Shaker, and Arts and Crafts. Which one says the most about you and your lifestyle? You might try starting with the cabinets, which will have the most impact on how your kitchen will look because they will be the largest element in the space. The key is to build a room around a theme while incorporating your personality into it. A favorite color is one way to do this; another way is a repeated pattern or theme.

For inspiration, visit showrooms and read magazines. Is there someone you know who has a kitchen that you've particularly admired? Was it a painted finish on the cabinetry? The color or pattern of the wallpaper or window treatment? A handsome wood floor? A pretty collection displayed in a hutch or on a wall? How did the room make you feel? Cheerful? Relaxed? Animated? Nostalgic? This is the kind of thinking that will help you to zero in on a design that will have staying power.

In addition, look for clues in the details you are planning for the rest your house. What is the intended architectural style?

Will there be elaborate trimwork, or will the walls, doors, and windows be streamlined and spare? Even if the rest of the house will be plain, you can introduce a period flavor in the kitchen with reproduction cabinets and fixtures, window treatments, wallpaper, and accessories.

Do you like antiques or modern art? Are you a collector or someone who prefers pared-down space? You can build on these

Today's traditional styles, below, are updated with fresh finishes and details.

Moldings and raised-panel doors, opposite, dress up any style of cabinetry.

preferences or depart from them entirely. If your kitchen will be open to other areas, such as the family room, link the two spaces with color or related materials.

Whatever you do, your approach to decorating the new kitchen should be deliberate. Let it evolve over time; don't rush your choices. Live with paint, tile, and wallpaper samples for a while.

You might start with some of the ideas that are discussed here. They are just suggestions, however. Let your own preferences be your ultimate guide. If you're not sure about something, don't do it right away or just keep your decorating simple until you're ready to add the details.

Traditional Style

Today's traditional style incorporates elements of English and American eighteenth- and early nineteenth-century design. Marked by symmetry and balance and enhanced by the look of fine-crafted details, it is dignified, rich, and formal.

Choose wood cabinetry finished with a cherry or mahogany stain or painted white, with details such as fluted panels, bull's-eye corner blocks, and dentil and crown molding. For the door style, a raised cathedral panel (top slightly arched) is typical. On the countertop, use marble or a laminate faux version, and install tiles on the back-

splash. Polished brass hardware and fittings add a refined touch.

Colors to consider include classic Wedgwood blue or deep rich tones. Windows and French doors with true divided lights or double-hung units with pop-in muntins have great traditional-style appeal. Dress them with formal curtain panels or swags. Botanical-inspired patterns, formal stripes, or tapestry fabrics are perfect for window treatments or for chair cushions and table linens.

Furnish the kitchen with an antique or reproduction hutch, where you can display formal china, and a table and chairs in traditional Windsor or Queen Anne style.

Contemporary Style

What's referred to as "contemporary" style evokes images of clean architectural lines; an absence of decoration and color; and materials such as stainless steel, chrome, glass, and stone. Indeed, its roots are at the turn of the last century, when architects and designers flatly rejected the exaggerated artificial embellishments of the Victorians by turning to natural products and pared-down forms. Various modern movements, evolving over the course of the industrialized twentieth century, gradually incorporated new man-made materials into their streamlined forms. Hence the high-tech look popularized in the 1970s and 1980s.

Today, contemporary style is taking a softer turn, even in the kitchen, a place where hard edges, cool reflective surfaces, and cutting-edge technology abound. It's not unusual to see updated versions of tra-

Color finishes on cabinets, below, can be combined with artful wall treatments.

Furniture-like pieces, right, make a kitchen less utilitarian looking.

Reproduction light fixtures, opposite, capture a mood or period style.

ditional fixtures and fittings or new uses for natural materials in a contemporary kitchen, especially as improved finishes make these products more durable and easier to maintain.

Although a contemporary room is often monochromatic or neutral, don't be afraid to use color or to mix several materials. Combinations of wood and various metals—stainless steel, chrome, copper, brass, and pewter on surfaces like cabinet doors, countertops, and floors—make strong statements, as do stone and glass.

Country Style

Country cabinets are typically made of wood with framed or raised-panel doors. Beadboard cabinets are a typical American country choice. Or leave the doors off, allowing colorful dishes and canned and boxed goods to create a fun display. For the countertop, install butcher block or hand-painted or silk-screened tiles. Another option is a colorful or patterned countertop fabricated from inlaid solid-surfacing material. A working fireplace will

definitely add charm to your country kitchen, but a simple potted herb garden on the windowsill will, too.

Wood floors are a natural choice in this setting. For a custom touch, add a stenciled backsplash or wall border. Or try a faux finish like sponging, ragging, or combing. These techniques are fun and easy, and they add texture to your walls.

Install double-hung windows. (Standard casement windows look too contemporary in this setting.) Finish them with full trim, and dress them with simple curtains.

The Cottage Look

This vintage look, inspired by quaint English-country style, is appealing in the kitchen because it's cozy, casual, and warm. Framed wood cabinets with an unfitted or unmatched appearance provide a good starting point for building on this theme, especially in a finish such as a honey maple paired with a color stain that looks properly distressed but not shabby. Muntin-glass doors, plate or pot racks, and open shelves should be part of the cabinetry's design. Milk- or clear-glass knobs and pulls complement cottage cabinets. But you could also mix a couple of different styles for mismatched chic.

Beadboard on the walls or ceiling always looks at home in this style kitchen, as does brick. Use brick as a backsplash or as a surround at the cooker. An English import, the AGA cooker, is a great way to bring the old-time European look of a cast-iron stove into the room while providing all the modern-day conveniences. Install an exposed-apron (farmhouse-style) sink with a reproduction chrome-and-porcelain faucet set to add more charm. On the floor, use wide wood planks or stone with a colorful hand-painted floorcloth on top. Bring more color into the room with blue-green surfaces accented in varying shades of rose and cream.

A double-hung window lends a traditional note, but if you can make the style work with the exterior of your house, a Gothic-inspired architectural design would tie it all together. Accent with lighting fixtures that resemble old-fashioned Victorian gas lamps.

For furniture, include a good-size farmhouse table in your plan, as well as a Welsh dresser and plate rack for displaying a pretty collection of transferware.

French Country Style

To create the rustic charm of a French-country farmhouse, whitewash the walls or apply a subtle glaze finish in an earth tone, such as rose ocher or sienna. Install wood ceiling beams with an aged or distressed look. Use limestone tile or clay pavers, which also have a warm, earthy appeal, on the floor. For the appearance of a hearth, design a cooking alcove to house the range or cooktop. Accent it with colorful tiles or brick. Create a focal point at the cooking area with a handsome copper range hood. Hang a rack for copper pots and pans. Pair an exposed apron sink with a high-arc spout.

Use unfitted cabinetry, open shelves, or a baker's rack for storage. Decorate with provincial mini-prints in mustard yellow, clay red, and deep blue. Dress windows with lace café curtains, and stencil a pretty fleur de lis border around the trim.

Add details such as flavored oils and vinegars displayed in pretty glass bottles, fresh herbs growing from racks in sunny windows, and blue and white tiles.

An exposed-apron sink, left, comes in many finishes and colors.

A stone look, below left, can be reproduced in solid-surfacing material.

A high-arc faucet, below, captures nostalgic styles and practicality.

Cabinet Door Style Choices

Shaker Style

The Shakers' plain, practical designs featured dovetailed joints and hand-planed tops, plain panels on doors, and legs tapered almost to a pencil point. The finishes on original Shaker cabinets were always dyes and oils, never varnishes, to enhance the wood.

Accent woodwork in colors inspired by natural dyes—terra cotta, yellow ochre, olive green, green-blue, and denim. Ceramic tile installed in a quiltlike pattern on the countertop or backsplash or as a mural above the cooktop can add more color accents and a reasonable amount of decoration, unless you're a purist at heart. The fixtures could be white, bisque, or black, with plain fittings in a brushed chrome or pewter finish. Trim kits, available from appliance and cabinet manufacturers, can camouflage modern-day appliances that the Shakers eschewed.

A traditional double-hung window, with or without muntins, fits in fine with the Shaker theme. Install plain wood shutters and panel-style curtains with simple cotton tab tops.

Shaker-inspired furniture is widely available today. Tall ladder-back chairs with tape-woven seats look at home around a simple trestle table. A pegged chair rail is a Shaker classic. Installed high on the wall, it can be a display for a collection of hand-woven baskets, dried flowers, tapered candles, or even small wooden chairs.

Many period looks include wood floors, which can be impractical in a kitchen. A laminate look-alike is a good substitute.

Arts & Crafts Style

Styles that are related to or part of the Arts and Crafts movement include Mission, Craftsman, and Prairie, the signature style of the architect Frank Lloyd Wright. Start with plain oak cabinets with a handcrafted appearance. Several manufacturers make reproduction wood cabinets, metal hardware, and period wallpaper and lighting fixtures today.

Decorate with colors that reflect natural hues, such as brown, green, blue, and orange. Accessorize with organically shaped pottery in these colors, too. Pull it all together by incorporating Native American textiles, such as a rug, into this room. Design a custom-tiled backsplash with matte or "art pottery" glazed tiles.

Plain windows should be curtained very simply—if at all—in an Arts and Crafts-style room, using natural fabrics such as linen or muslin with an embroidered border. Typical motifs include ginkgo leaves and poppy seeds. Instead of traditional treatments, use stained-glass or art-glass windows. To complete the look, furnish the kitchen in period style with a Mission table and chairs and a hutch, if there is room for one.

Plan #391009

Dimensions: 73'4" W x 60'4" D

Levels: 2

Square Footage: 3,440

Main Level Sq. Ft.: 2,486

Upper Level Sq. Ft.: 954

Bedrooms: 4

Bathrooms: 3½

Foundation: Basement,
crawl space, slab

Materials List Available: Yes

Price Category: G

This home, as shown in the photograph, may differ from the actual blueprints. For more detailed information, please check the floor plans carefully.   *Images provided by designer/architect.*

This house is like the proverbial genie granting every wish, even down to a special place for storing wine.

Features:

• Master Suite: The master bedroom, alone, is a dream come true with a private outdoor court and hot tub, and a trailing interior hallway that slips into a library with fireplace, built-in shelving and French doors that open to a dramatic two-story foyer.

• Living Room: This centrally located living room curves to a bar, the kitchen, or the sun porch, which is shared with the dining room.

• Kitchen: This kitchen features a cooking island and out-of-the-way laundry room. Most spectacular, though, is the kitchen's morning room with an elegant window to the porch front.

• Upstairs: The staircase overlooks the open foyer and living room. Bedroom #2, charmed by a dormer front window, shares a full bath with bedroom #3, and bedroom #4 gets a private bath.

Main Level Floor Plan

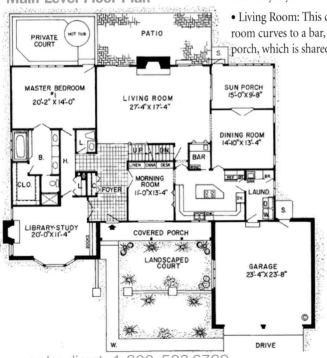

Upper Level Floor Plan

Copyright by designer/architect.

Plan #161038

Dimensions: 58'6" W x 49' D
Levels: 2
Square Footage: 2,209
Main Level Sq. Ft.: 1,542
Upper Level Sq. Ft.: 667
Bedrooms: 3
Bathrooms: 2½
Foundation: Basement
Materials List Available: No
Price Category: E

Brick trim, sidelights, and a transom window at the entry are a few of the many features that convey the elegance and style of this exciting home.

Images provided by designer/architect.

Features:

• Great Room: This great room is truly the centerpiece of this elegant home. The ceiling at the rear wall is 14 ft. and slopes forward to a second floor study loft that overlooks the magnificent fireplace and entertainment alcove. The high ceiling continues through the foyer, showcasing a deluxe staircase.

• Kitchen: This modern kitchen is designed for efficient work patterns and serves both the formal dining room and breakfast area.

• Master Suite: The highlight of this master suite is a wonderful whirlpool tub. Also

included are two matching vanities and a large walk-in closet.

• Bonus Room: A bonus room above the garage completes this exciting home.

Rear Elevation

Main Level Floor Plan

Copyright by designer/architect.

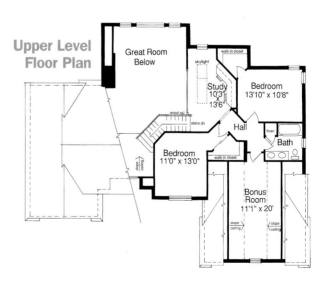

Upper Level Floor Plan

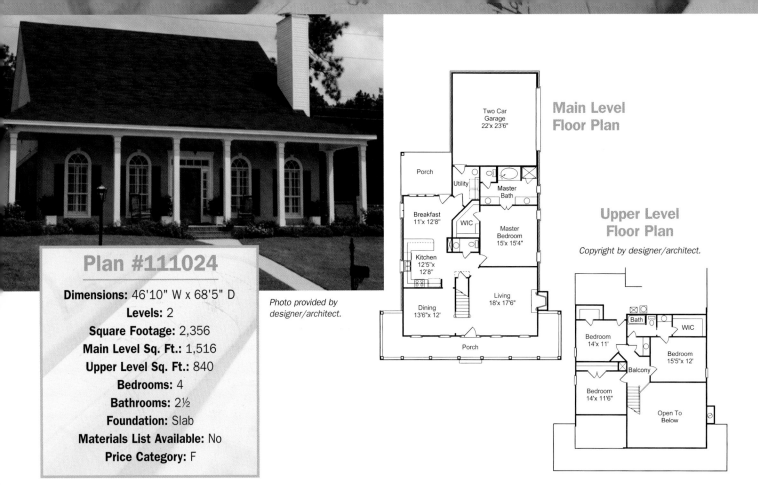

Plan #111024

Dimensions: 46'10" W x 68'5" D
Levels: 2
Square Footage: 2,356
Main Level Sq. Ft.: 1,516
Upper Level Sq. Ft.: 840
Bedrooms: 4
Bathrooms: 2½
Foundation: Slab
Materials List Available: No
Price Category: F

Photo provided by designer/architect.

Main Level Floor Plan

Two Car Garage 22'x 23'6"

Porch

Utility

Master Bath

Breakfast 11'x 12'8"

WIC

Master Bedroom 15'x 15'4"

Kitchen 12'5"x 12'8"

Living 18'x 17'6"

Dining 13'6"x 12'

Porch

Upper Level Floor Plan

Copyright by designer/architect.

Bath

WIC

Bedroom 14'x 11'

Bedroom 15'5"x 12'

Balcony

Bedroom 14'x 11'6"

Open To Below

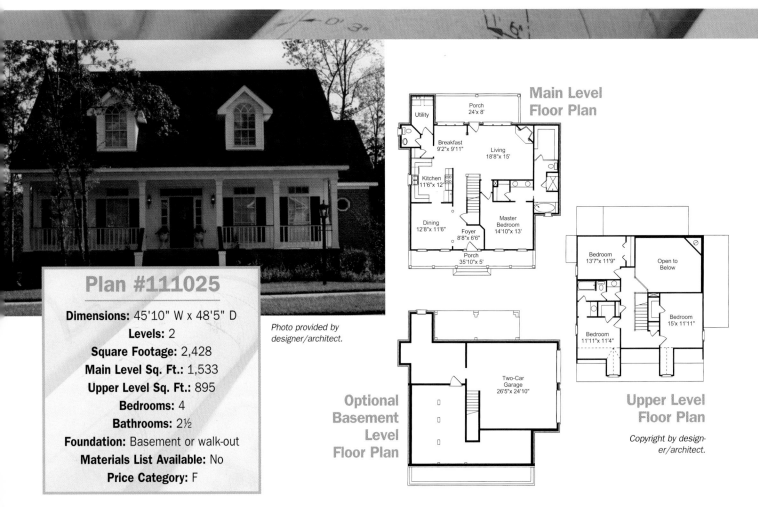

Plan #111025

Dimensions: 45'10" W x 48'5" D
Levels: 2
Square Footage: 2,428
Main Level Sq. Ft.: 1,533
Upper Level Sq. Ft.: 895
Bedrooms: 4
Bathrooms: 2½
Foundation: Basement or walk-out
Materials List Available: No
Price Category: F

Photo provided by designer/architect.

Main Level Floor Plan

Utility

Porch 24'x 8'

Breakfast 9'2"x 9'11"

Living 18'8"x 15'

Kitchen 11'6"x 12'

Dining 12'8"x 11'6"

Foyer 8'8"x 6'6"

Master Bedroom 14'10"x 13'

Porch 35'10"x 5'

Optional Basement Level Floor Plan

Two-Car Garage 26'5"x 24'10"

Upper Level Floor Plan

Copyright by designer/architect.

Bedroom 13'7"x 11'9"

Open to Below

Bedroom 15'x 11'11"

Bedroom 11'11"x 11'4"

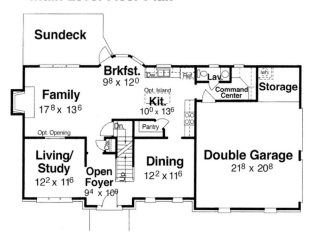

Sundeck

Brkfst.
9^8 x 12^0

Family
17^8 x 13^6

Lav.

Command Center

Storage

Kit.
10^0 x 13^6

Opt. Island

Dw.

Ref.

Wh

Opt. Opening

Dn.

Pantry

Living/Study
12^2 x 11^6

Open Foyer
9^4 x 10^0

Dining
12^2 x 11^6

Double Garage
21^8 x 20^8

Up

Photo provided by designer/architect.

Plan #141031

Dimensions: 58'4" W x 30' D
Levels: 2
Square Footage: 2,367
Main Level Sq. Ft.: 1,025
Upper Level Sq. Ft.: 1,342
Bedrooms: 4
Bathrooms: 2½
Foundation: Basement
Materials List Available: No
Price Category: E

Upper Level Floor Plan

Copyright by designer/architect.

Bdrm.2
12^2 x 12^4

Bth.2

Ln.

Lnd.

W.D.

Sh.

Storage

Computer Station

Sh.

Master Bdrm.
18^{10} x 13^2

Dn.

Balcony

Opt. Opening

Bdrm.3
12^2 x 12^4

Open Foyer

Bdrm.4/Study
12^2 x 11^6

Opt. Opening To Sitting

Tray Ceil.

M.Bath

Opt. Opening

Opt. Sink

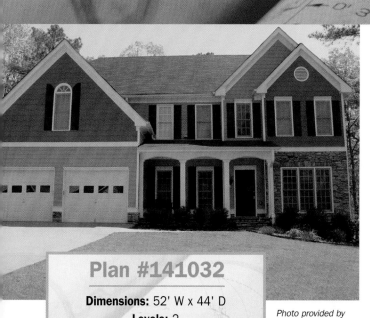

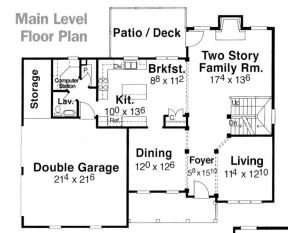

Patio / Deck

Two Story Family Rm.
17^4 x 13^6

Storage

Computer Station

Lav.

P

Dw.

Brkfst.
8^8 x 11^2

Kit.
10^0 x 13^6

Ref.

C.

Up

Dn.

Double Garage
21^4 x 21^6

Dining
12^0 x 12^6

Foyer
5^8 x 15^{10}

Living
11^4 x 12^{10}

Plan #141032

Dimensions: 52' W x 44' D
Levels: 2
Square Footage: 2,476
Main Level Sq. Ft.: 1,160
Upper Level Sq. Ft.: 1,316
Bedrooms: 4
Bathrooms: 2½
Foundation: Basement
Materials List Available: Yes
Price Category: E

Photo provided by designer/architect.

Upper Level Floor Plan

Copyright by designer/architect.

M.Bath
Tray Ceil.

Bdrm.2
11^0 x 11^6
Opt. Vault W/ Plant Shelf

Bth.2

Two Story Family Rm.

Balcony

Dn.

Master Bdrm.
15^4 x 14^6

Opt. Vault W/ Plant Shelf

Bdrm.3
11^8 x 10^6

W.D.

Laund.

Open To Foyer

Opt. Vault W/ Plant Shelf

Bdrm.4
11^4 x 11^0

Tray Ceil.

Opt. Closet

Sitting
10^0 x 7^0

Plan #121086

Dimensions: 55'4" W x 37'8" D

Levels: 2

Square Footage: 1,998

Main Level Sq. Ft.: 1,093

Upper Level Sq. Ft.: 905

Bedrooms: 3

Bathrooms: 2½

Foundation: Basement

Materials List Available: Yes

Price Category: D

You'll love the open design of this comfortable home if sunny, bright rooms make you happy.

Features:

- Entry: Walk into this two-story entry, and you're sure to admire the open staircase and balcony from the upper level.

- Dining Room: To the left of the entry, you'll see this dining room, with its special ceiling detail and built-in display cabinet.

- Living Room: Located immediately to the right, this living room features a charming bay window.

- Family Room: French doors from the living room open into this sunny space, where a handsome fireplace takes center stage.

- Kitchen: Combined with the breakfast area, this kitchen features an island cooktop, a large pantry, and a built-in desk.

CAD FILE AVAILABLE

Main Level Floor Plan

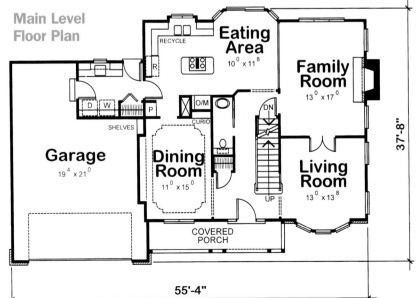

Upper Level Floor Plan

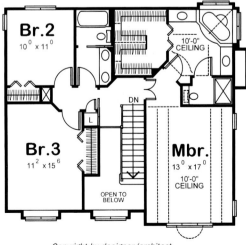

Copyright by designer/architect.

Plan #121087

Dimensions: 50' W x 40' D

Levels: 2

Square Footage: 2,103

Main Level Sq. Ft.: 1,082

Upper Level Sq. Ft.: 1,021

Bedrooms: 4

Bathrooms: 2½

Foundation: Basement

Materials List Available: Yes

Price Category: D

You'll love the comfort and the unusual design details you'll find in this home.

Features:

- **Entry:** A T-shaped staircase frames this two-story entry, giving both visual interest and convenience.

- **Family Room:** Bookcases frame the lovely fireplace here, so you won't be amiss by decorating to create a special reading nook.

- **Breakfast Area:** Pass through the cased

opening between the family room and this breakfast area for convenience.

- **Kitchen:** Combined with the breakfast area, this kitchen features an island, pantry, and desk.

- **Master Suite:** On the upper floor, this suite has a walk-in closet and a bath with sunlit whirlpool tub, separate shower, and double vanity. A window seat makes the bedroom especially cozy, no matter what the outside weather.

Main Level Floor Plan

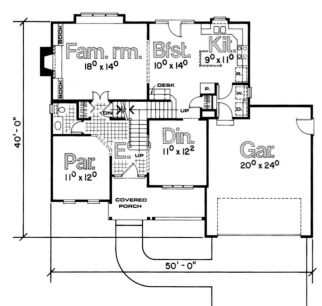

Upper Level Floor Plan

Main Level Floor Plan

Patio 38' x 10'

Vaulted Master Suite 14' x 13'2"

Vaulted Great Room 14'8" x 18'

Vaulted Nook 10' x 10'10"

Kitchen 12'4" x 11'6"

Up

Entry

Den/Dining 12' x 11'4"

Utility

Covered Porch

Garage 21' x 21'6"

Images provided by designer/architect.

CAD FILE AVAILABLE

Plan #361009

Dimensions: 48' W x 53' D
Levels: 2
Square Footage: 1,775
Main Level Sq. Ft.: 1,280
Upper Level Sq. Ft.: 495
Bedrooms: 3
Bathrooms: 2½
Foundation: Crawl space
Materials List Available: No
Price Category: C

Upper Level Floor Plan

Open to Great Room Below

Dn

Bedroom 11' x 10'2"

Bedroom 11' x 13'2"

Copyright by designer/architect.

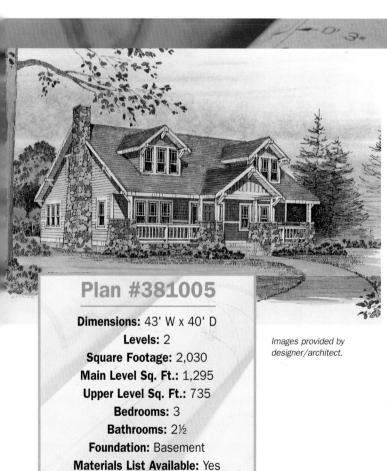

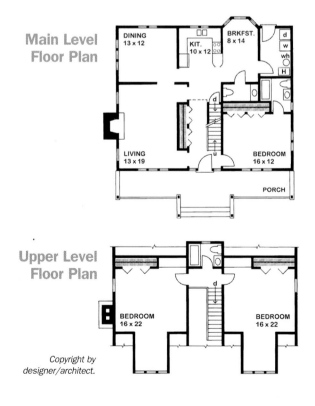

Main Level Floor Plan

DINING 13 x 12

KIT. 10 x 12

BRKFST. 8 x 14

d

w

wh

H

LIVING 13 x 19

BEDROOM 16 x 12

PORCH

Images provided by designer/architect.

Upper Level Floor Plan

BEDROOM 16 x 22

BEDROOM 16 x 22

Copyright by designer/architect.

Plan #381005

Dimensions: 43' W x 40' D
Levels: 2
Square Footage: 2,030
Main Level Sq. Ft.: 1,295
Upper Level Sq. Ft.: 735
Bedrooms: 3
Bathrooms: 2½
Foundation: Basement
Materials List Available: Yes
Price Category: D

Main Level Floor Plan

Breakfast 14' x 11'2"
Hearth Room 17' x 14'10"
Great Room 16' x 19'6"
Dressing
walk-in closet
Kitchen
Foyer
Laun.
Master Bedroom 14' x 14'1"
Porch
Dining Room 12' x 13'10"
Two-car Garage 21' x 20'4"
Sitting Area 11'2" x 9'4"
48'
63'4"

Images provided by designer/architect.

Plan #161041

Dimensions: 63'4" W x 48' D
Levels: 2
Square Footage: 2,738
Main Level Sq. Ft.: 1,915
Upper Level Sq. Ft.: 823
Bedrooms: 4
Bathrooms: 3½
Foundation: Basement
Materials List Available: Yes
Price Category: F

Upper Level Floor Plan

Great Room Below
Bedroom 17' x 12'6"
Balcony
Bedroom 10' x 13'10"
Bath
Bedroom 12' x 10'6"
slope ceiling

Rear Elevation

Copyright by designer/architect.

Plan #361017

Dimensions: 56' W x 46' D
Levels: 2
Square Footage: 2,116
Main Level Sq. Ft.: 1,643
Upper Level Sq. Ft.: 473
Bedrooms: 3
Bathrooms: 2½
Foundation: Crawl space
Materials List Available: No
Price Category: D

Images provided by designer/architect.

CAD FILE AVAILABLE

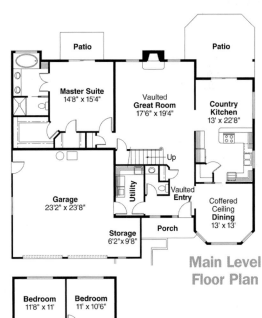

Patio
Patio
Master Suite 14'8" x 15'4"
Vaulted Great Room 17'6" x 19'4"
Country Kitchen 13' x 22'8"
Up
Garage 23'2" x 23'8"
Utility
Vaulted Entry
Coffered Ceiling Dining 13' x 13'
Storage 6'2" x 9'8"
Porch

Main Level Floor Plan

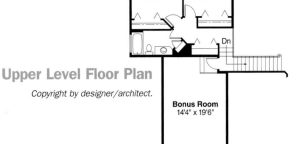

Bedroom 11'8" x 11'
Bedroom 11' x 10'6"
Dn

Upper Level Floor Plan

Copyright by designer/architect.

Bonus Room 14'4" x 19'6"

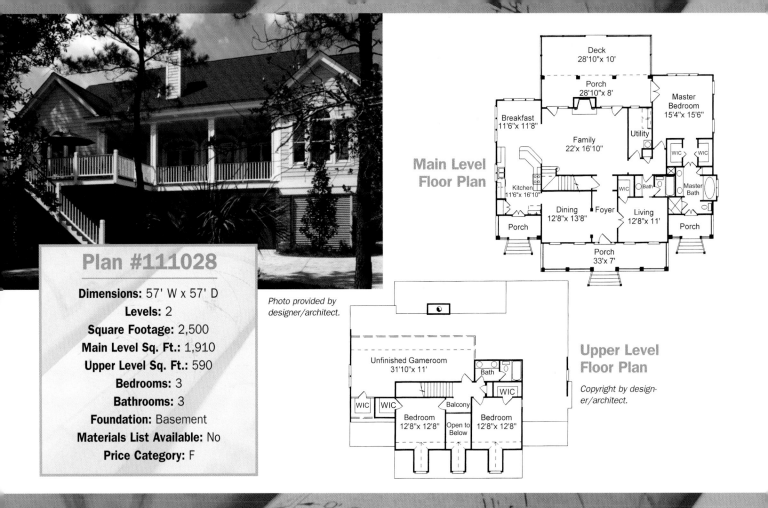

Plan #111028

Dimensions: 57' W x 57' D
Levels: 2
Square Footage: 2,500
Main Level Sq. Ft.: 1,910
Upper Level Sq. Ft.: 590
Bedrooms: 3
Bathrooms: 3
Foundation: Basement
Materials List Available: No
Price Category: F

Photo provided by designer/architect.

Main Level Floor Plan

Deck 28'10"x 10'
Porch 28'10"x 8'
Master Bedroom 15'4"x 15'6"
Breakfast 11'6"x 11'8"
Family 22'x 16'10"
Utility
WIC
WIC
Kitchen 11'6"x 16'10"
WIC
Bath
Master Bath
Dining 12'8"x 13'8"
Foyer
Living 12'8"x 11'
Porch
Porch
Porch 33'x 7'

Upper Level Floor Plan

Copyright by designer/architect.

Unfinished Gameroom 31'10"x 11'
Bath
WIC
WIC
WIC
Balcony
Bedroom 12'8"x 12'8"
Open to Below
Bedroom 12'8"x 12'8"

Plan #111044

Dimensions: 43' W x 47' D
Levels: 2
Square Footage: 1,819
Main Level Sq. Ft.: 1,242
Upper Level Sq. Ft.: 577
Bedrooms: 3
Bathrooms: 2½
Foundation: Pier
Materials List Available: No
Price Category: E

Photos provided by designer/architect.

Deck
Breakfast 10'10"x 16'
Dining 13'x 12'
Kitchen 14'6"x 10'2"
Utility
Bath
Main Level Floor Plan
Copyright by designer/architect.
WIC
1/2 Bath
Living 13'x 20'
Bedroom 12'x 15'
Porch

Upper Level Floor Plan
WIC
Bath
WIC
Bedroom 13'x 11'
Bedroom 12'x 11'
Open to Below

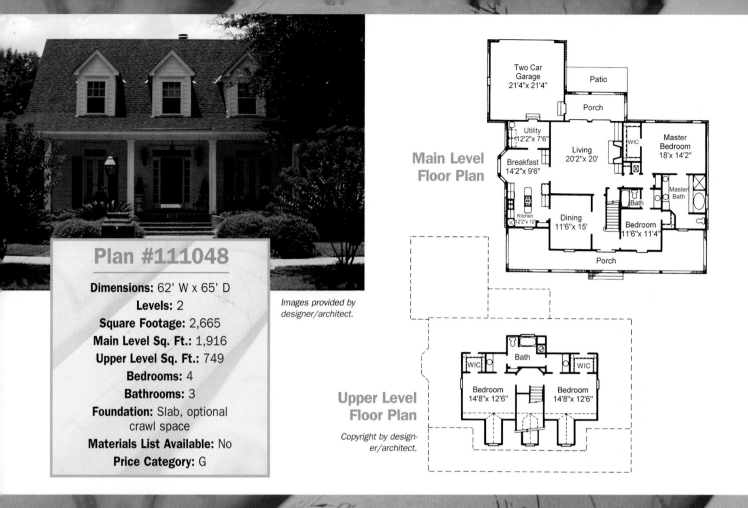

Plan #111048

Dimensions: 62' W x 65' D
Levels: 2
Square Footage: 2,665
Main Level Sq. Ft.: 1,916
Upper Level Sq. Ft.: 749
Bedrooms: 4
Bathrooms: 3
Foundation: Slab, optional crawl space
Materials List Available: No
Price Category: G

Images provided by designer/architect.

Main Level Floor Plan

Two Car Garage 21'4"x 21'4"
Patio
Porch
Utility 12'2"x 7'6"
Breakfast 14'2"x 9'6"
Living 20'2"x 20'
WIC
Master Bedroom 18'x 14'2"
Kitchen 12'2"x 12'
Bath
Master Bath
Dining 11'6'x 15'
Bedroom 11'6"x 11'4"
Porch

Upper Level Floor Plan

Copyright by designer/architect.

WIC
Bath
WIC
Bedroom 14'8"x 12'6"
Bedroom 14'8"x 12'6"

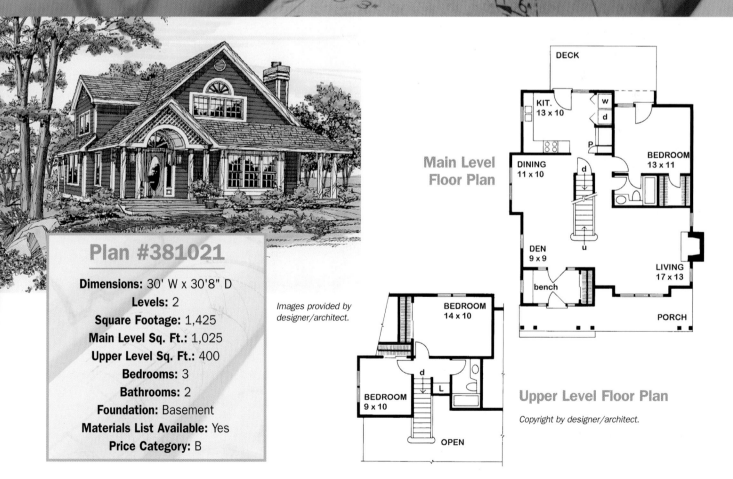

Plan #381021

Dimensions: 30' W x 30'8" D
Levels: 2
Square Footage: 1,425
Main Level Sq. Ft.: 1,025
Upper Level Sq. Ft.: 400
Bedrooms: 3
Bathrooms: 2
Foundation: Basement
Materials List Available: Yes
Price Category: B

Images provided by designer/architect.

Main Level Floor Plan

DECK
KIT. 13 x 10
w
d
DINING 11 x 10
BEDROOM 13 x 11
DEN 9 x 9
bench
LIVING 17 x 13
PORCH

Upper Level Floor Plan

Copyright by designer/architect.

BEDROOM 14 x 10
BEDROOM 9 x 10
OPEN

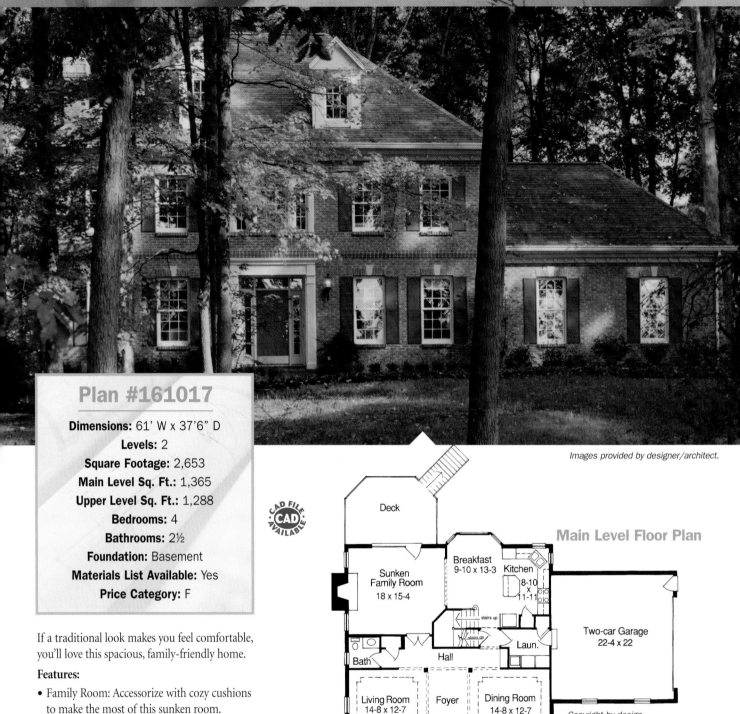

Plan #161017

Dimensions: 61' W x 37'6" D

Levels: 2

Square Footage: 2,653

Main Level Sq. Ft.: 1,365

Upper Level Sq. Ft.: 1,288

Bedrooms: 4

Bathrooms: 2½

Foundation: Basement

Materials List Available: Yes

Price Category: F

If a traditional look makes you feel comfortable, you'll love this spacious, family-friendly home.

Features:

- **Family Room:** Accessorize with cozy cushions to make the most of this sunken room. Windows flank the fireplace, adding warm, natural light. Doors leading to the rear deck make this room a family "headquarters."

- **Living and Dining Rooms:** These formal rooms open to each other, so you'll love hosting gatherings in this home.

- **Kitchen:** A handy pantry fits well with the traditional feeling of this home, and an island adds contemporary convenience.

- **Master Suite:** Relax in the whirlpool tub in your bath and enjoy the storage space in the two walk-in closets in the bedroom.

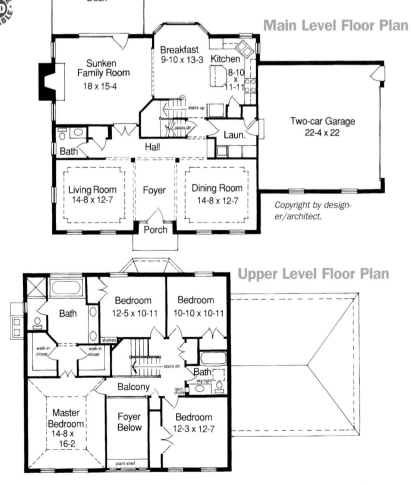

Main Level Floor Plan

Deck

Sunken Family Room 18 x 15-4

Breakfast 9-10 x 13-3

Kitchen 8-10 x 11-11

stairs up

stairs dn

Laun.

Two-car Garage 22-4 x 22

Bath

Hall

Living Room 14-8 x 12-7

Foyer

Dining Room 14-8 x 12-7

Porch

Copyright by designer/architect.

Upper Level Floor Plan

Bath

shelves

walk-in closet

walk-in closet

Bedroom 12-5 x 10-11

Bedroom 10-10 x 10-11

stairs dn

Bath

sky-light

laun. chute

Balcony

Master Bedroom 14-8 x 16-2

Foyer Below

Bedroom 12-3 x 12-7

plant shelf

Plan #271010

Dimensions: 46'8" W x 43' D
Levels: 2
Square Footage: 1,724
Main Level Sq. Ft.: 922
Upper Level Sq. Ft.: 802
Bedrooms: 3
Bathrooms: 2½
Foundation: Basement
Materials List Available: Yes
Price Category: C

Photo provided by designer/architect.

This traditional home features a wide assortment of windows that flood the interior with light and accentuate the open, airy atmosphere.

Features:

- Entry: A beautiful Palladian window enlivens this two-story-high space.

- Great Room: A second Palladian window brightens this primary gathering area, which is topped by a vaulted ceiling.

- Dining Room: Sliding glass doors connect this formal area to a large backyard deck.

- Kitchen: Centrally located, this kitchen includes a boxed-out window over the sink, providing a nice area for plants.

- Family/Breakfast Area: Smartly joined, this open space hosts a snack bar and a wet bar, in addition to a warming fireplace.

- Master Suite: Located on the upper floor, the master bedroom boasts corner windows, a large walk-in closet, and a split bath with a dual-sink vanity.

Main Level Floor Plan

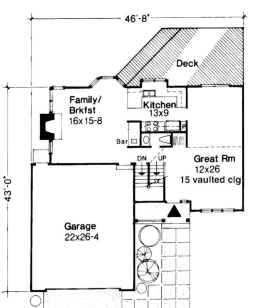

Upper Level Floor Plan

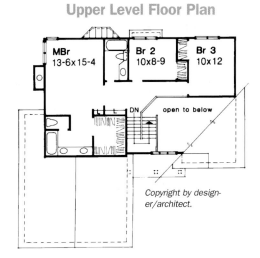

Copyright by designer/architect.

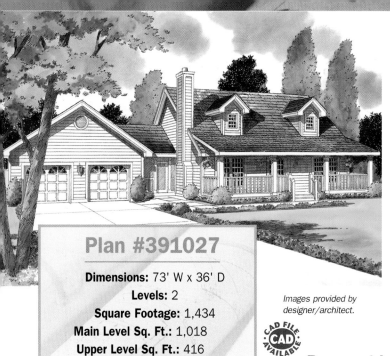

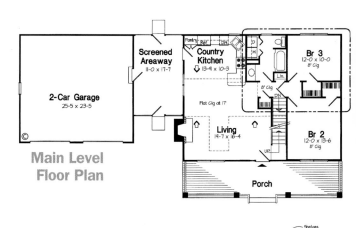

Main Level Floor Plan

Screened Areaway 11-0 x 17-7

Country Kitchen 13-4 x 10-3

2-Car Garage 25-5 x 23-5

Living 14-7 x 16-4

Br 3 12-0 x 10-0 8' Clg

Br 2 12-0 x 13-6 8' Clg

Flat Clg at 11'

Porch

Plan #391027

Dimensions: 73' W x 36' D

Levels: 2

Square Footage: 1,434

Main Level Sq. Ft.: 1,018

Upper Level Sq. Ft.: 416

Bedrooms: 3

Bathrooms: 2

Foundation: Crawl space, slab, basement

Materials List Available: Yes

Price Category: B

Images provided by designer/architect.

CAD FILE CAD AVAILABLE

Upper Level Floor Plan

Copyright by designer/architect.

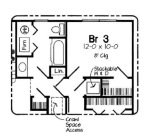

Basement Level Floor Plan

Br 3 12-0 x 10-0 8' Clg

Crawl Space Access

Alternate Foundation Plan

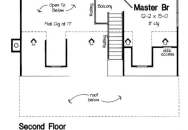

Master Br 12-2 x 15-0 8' Clg

Open To Below

Balcony

Flat Clg at 11'

roof below

attic access

Second Floor

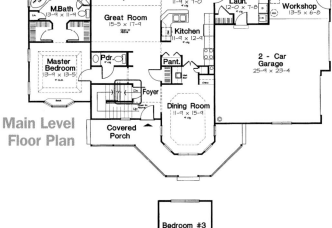

Sun Terrace

Deck

M.Bath 13-4 x 11-4

Great Room 15-5 x 17-9

Breakfast 11-9 x 7-0

Laun. 12-0 x 7-8

Workshop 13-5 x 6-8

Master Bedroom 13-4 x 13-5

Pdr.

Kitchen 11-9 x 12-4

Pant.

2 - Car Garage 25-4 x 23-4

Foyer

Dining Room 11-9 x 15-9

Covered Porch

Main Level Floor Plan

Plan #391048

Dimensions: 68' W x 47' D

Levels: 2

Square Footage: 2,044

Main Level Sq. Ft.: 1,403

Upper Level Sq. Ft.: 641

Bedrooms: 3

Bathrooms: 2½

Foundation: Crawl space, slab, or basement

Materials List Available: Yes

Price Category: D

Images provided by designer/architect.

Upper Level Floor Plan

Copyright by designer/architect.

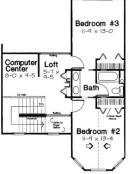

Bedroom #3 11-9 x 13-0

Computer Center 8-0 x 9-5

Loft 5-7 x 9-5

Bath

Bedroom #2 11-9 x 13-4

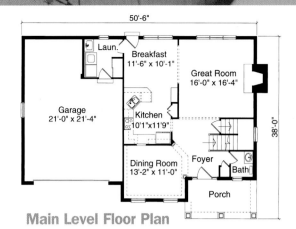

Main Level Floor Plan

Rear Elevation

Images provided by designer/architect.

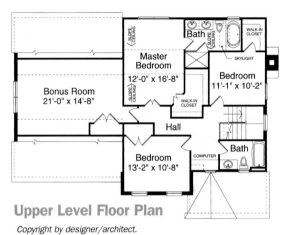

Upper Level Floor Plan

Copyright by designer/architect.

Plan #161043

Dimensions: 50'6" W x 38' D
Levels: 2
Square Footage: 1,856
Main Level Sq. Ft.: 980
Upper Level Sq. Ft.: 876
Bedrooms: 3
Bathrooms: 2½
Foundation: Basement
Materials List Available: Yes
Price Category: D

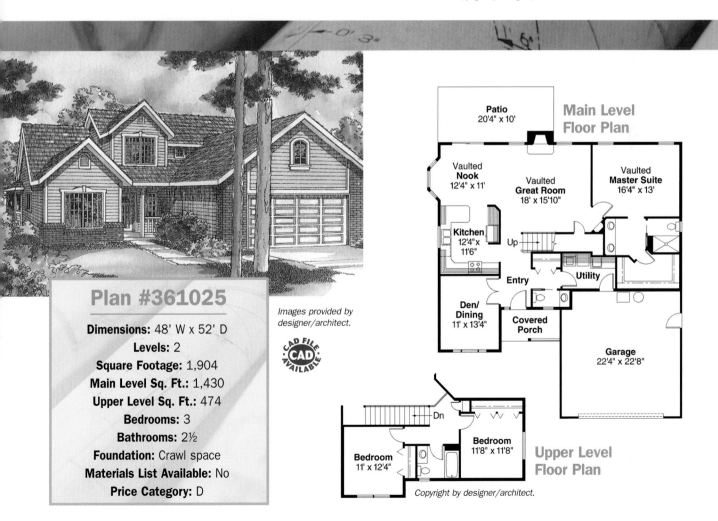

Plan #361025

Dimensions: 48' W x 52' D
Levels: 2
Square Footage: 1,904
Main Level Sq. Ft.: 1,430
Upper Level Sq. Ft.: 474
Bedrooms: 3
Bathrooms: 2½
Foundation: Crawl space
Materials List Available: No
Price Category: D

Images provided by designer/architect.

CAD FILE AVAILABLE

Copyright by designer/architect.

Main Level Floor Plan

MBR.
TRAY CEILING
13'8" X 15'6"

DIN.
VAULTED
18'4" X 9'4"

KIT.
VAULTED

LIV.
VAULTED CEILING
18'4" X 15'8"

LAUNDRY CHUTE

BR. #2
10'4" X 10'0"

BR. #3
10'4" X 13'0"

E.

Images provided by designer/architect.

CAD FILE AVAILABLE

Plan #221024

Dimensions: 43' W x 40' D

Levels: 2

Square Footage: 1,732

Main Level Sq. Ft.: 745

Upper Level Sq. Ft.: 544

Lower Level Sq. Ft.: 443

Bedrooms: 3

Bathrooms: 2½

Foundation: Basement

Materials List Available: No

Price Category: C

Upper Level Floor Plan

Copyright by designer/architect.

FAM. RM.
21'0" X 13'6"

UNFINISHED
18'0" X 29'8"

W. D.

W.H.

FURN

2 CAR GAR.
21'8" X 19'4"

40'-0"

43'-0"

Plan #161021

Dimensions: 48' W x 38' D

Levels: 2

Square Footage: 1,897

Main Level Sq. Ft.: 1,036

Upper Level Sq. Ft.: 861

Bedrooms: 3

Bathrooms: 2½

Foundation: Basement

Materials List Available: No

Price Category: D

Images provided by designer/architect.

Rear Elevation

Laun.
hanging space

Bath

Breakfast
10'8" x 11'

Great Room
14'10" x 17'1"

French doors
w/ arched window above

high ceiling

Kitchen
10'6" x 13'6"

pantry

wood rail

Foyer

stairs up

stairs dn

Two-car Garage
20' x 21'

furniture alcove

Dining Room
11' x 13'7"

38'

48'

Main Level Floor Plan

walk-in closet

Master Bedroom
12' x 14'11"

Bedroom
10'6" x 11'2"

Great Room Below

Bath

Bath

computer desk

Balcony

Bedroom
11' x 12'

stairs dn

window seat

Upper Level Floor Plan

Copyright by designer/architect.

Plan #161039

Dimensions: 61' W x 41'8" D

Levels: 2

Square Footage: 2,320

Main Level Sq. Ft.: 1,595

Upper Level Sq. Ft.: 725

Bedrooms: 4

Bathrooms: 2½

Foundation: Basement

Materials List Available: Yes

Price Category: E

Images provided by designer/architect.

Upper Level Floor Plan

Copyright by designer/architect.

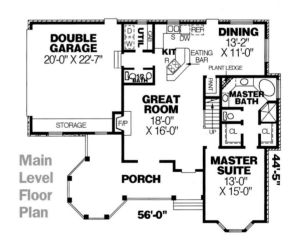

Plan #241010

Dimensions: 56' W x 44'5" D

Levels: 2

Square Footage: 2,044

Main Level Sq. Ft.: 1,203

Upper Level Sq. Ft.: 841

Bedrooms: 3

Bathrooms: 2½

Foundation: Slab

Materials List Available: No

Price Category: D

Images provided by designer/architect.

Main Level Floor Plan

Upper Level Floor Plan

Copyright by designer/architect.

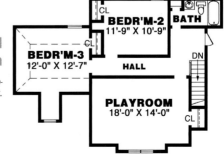

Plan #271012

Dimensions: 48' W x 29'1" D
Levels: 2
Square Footage: 1,359
Main Level Sq. Ft.: 668
Upper Level Sq. Ft.: 691
Bedrooms: 3
Bathrooms: 2½
Foundation: Basement
Materials List Available: Yes
Price Category: B

This home, as shown in the photograph, may differ from the actual blueprints. For more detailed information, please check the floor plans carefully.

Images provided by designer/arch

This traditional home blends an updated exterior with a thoroughly modern interior.

Features:

• Living Room: This sunny, vaulted gathering room offers a handsome fireplace and open access to the adjoining dining room.

• Dining Room: Equally suited to intimate family gatherings and larger dinner parties, this space includes access to a spacious backyard deck.

• Kitchen/Breakfast Nook: Smartly joined, these two rooms are just perfect for speedy weekday mornings and lazy weekend breakfasts.

• Master Suite: A skylighted staircase leads to this upper-floor masterpiece, which include a private bath, a walk-in closet, and bright, boxed-out window arrangement.

• Secondary Bedrooms: One of these is actually a loft/bedroom conversion, which makes it suitable for expansion space as you family grows.

Main Level Floor Plan

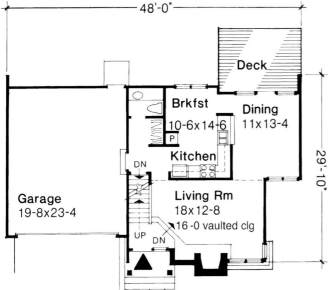

Upper Level Floor Plan

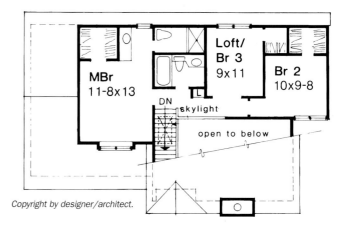

Copyright by designer/architect.

Plan #271027

Dimensions: 61' W x 44' D
Levels: 2
Square Footage: 2,463
Main Level Sq. Ft.: 1,380
Upper Level Sq. Ft.: 1,083
Bedrooms: 4
Bathrooms: 2½
Foundation: Basement
Materials List Available: Yes
Price Category: D

This post-modern design uses half-round transom windows and a barrel-vaulted porch to lend elegance to its facade.

Features:

- **Living Room:** A vaulted ceiling and a striking fireplace enhance this formal gathering space.

- **Dining Room:** Introduced from the living room by square columns, this formal dining room is just steps from the kitchen.

- **Kitchen:** Thoroughly modern in its design, this walk-through kitchen includes an island cooktop and a large pantry. Nearby, a sunny, bayed breakfast area offers sliding-glass-door access to an angled backyard deck.

- **Family Room:** Columns provide an elegant preface to this fun gathering spot, which sports a vaulted ceiling and easy access to the deck.

- **Master suite:** A vaulted ceiling crowns this luxurious space, which includes a private bath and bright windows.

Main Level Floor Plan

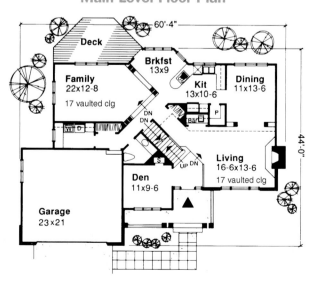

Upper Level Floor Plan

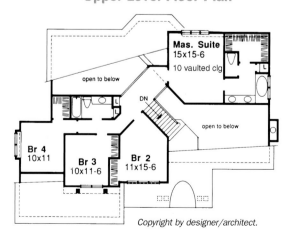

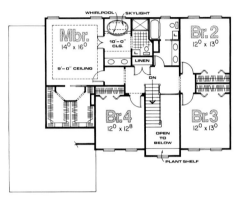

Main Level Floor Plan

Plan #121028

Dimensions: 54'8" W x 42' D

Levels: 2

Square Footage: 2,644

Main Level Sq. Ft.: 1,366

Upper Level Sq. Ft.: 1,278

Bedrooms: 4

Bathrooms: 2½

Foundation: Basement

Materials List Available: Yes

Price Category: F

Photo provided by designer/architect.

Upper Level Floor Plan

Copyright by designer/architect.

Main Level Floor Plan

Plan #121030

Dimensions: 58' W x 45' D

Levels: 2

Square Footage: 2,613

Main Level Sq. Ft.: 1,333

Upper Level Sq. Ft.: 1,280

Bedrooms: 4

Bathrooms: 2½

Foundation: Basement

Materials List Available: Yes

Price Category: F

Photo provided by designer/architect.

Upper Level Floor Plan

Copyright by designer/architect.

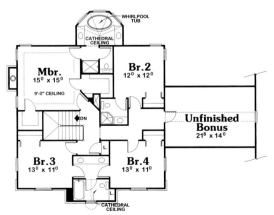

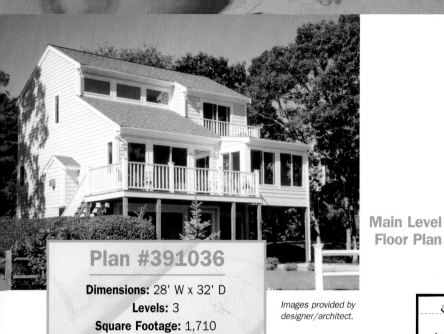

Plan #391036

Dimensions: 28' W x 32' D
Levels: 3
Square Footage: 1,710
Main Level Sq. Ft.: 728
Upper Level Sq. Ft.: 573
Lower Level Sq. Ft.: 409
Bedrooms: 3
Bathrooms: 2
Foundation: Full basement
Materials List Available: Yes
Price Category: C

Images provided by designer/architect.

Main Level Floor Plan

Upper Level Floor Plan

Copyright by designer/architect.

Lower Level Floor Plan

Plan #391032

Dimensions: 56' W x 38' D
Levels: 2
Square Footage: 2,129
Main Level Sq. Ft.: 1,136
Upper Level Sq. Ft.: 993
Bedrooms: 3
Bathrooms: 2½
Foundation: Full basement
Materials List Available: Yes
Price Category: D

Images provided by designer/architect.

CAD FILE CAD AVAILABLE

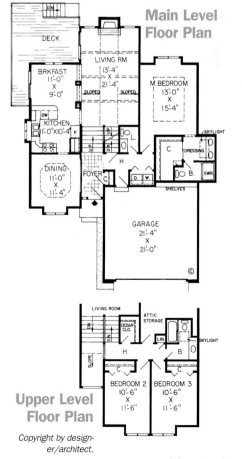

Main Level Floor Plan

Upper Level Floor Plan

Copyright by designer/architect.

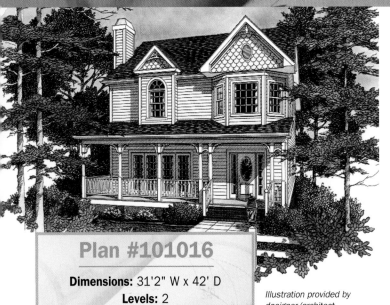

Plan #101016

Dimensions: 31'2" W x 42' D

Levels: 2

Square Footage: 1,985

Main Level Sq. Ft.: 1,009

Upper Level Sq. Ft.: 976

Bedrooms: 3

Bathrooms: 2½

Foundation: Slab, crawl space, or basement

Materials List Available: No

Price Category: D

Illustration provided by designer/architect.

Main Level Floor Plan

DECK
30'-6" x 11'-7"

BRKFST

KITCHEN
15'-0" x 17'-0"

DINING
14'-8" x 12'-8"

42'-0"

UP

ENTRY
7'-11" x 15'-6"

FAMILY
18'-8" x 16'-0"

PORCH
30'-6" x 7'-7"

31'-2"

Upper Level Floor Plan

Copyright by designer/architect.

TRAY CEILING

MASTER BDRM
16'-4" x 15'-0"

DN

BEDROOM 2
12'-0" x 12'-8"

BEDROOM 3
12'-8" x 12'-0"

WINDOW SEAT

Plan #131050

Dimensions: 72'8" W x 47' D

Levels: 2

Square Footage: 2,874

Main Level Sq. Ft.: 2,146

Upper Level Sq. Ft.: 728

Bedrooms: 4

Bathrooms: 3

Foundation: Crawl space, slab, or basement

Materials List Available: Yes

Price Category: G

Illustration provided by designer/architect.

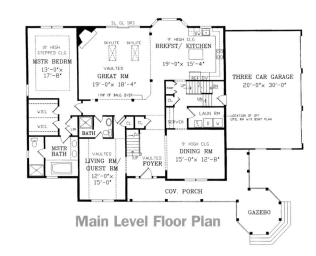

SL GL DRS

SKYLITE   SKYLITE

9' HIGH CLG
BRKFST/ KITCHEN
19'-0" x 15'-4"

10' HIGH
STEPPED CLG
MSTR BEDRM
13'-0" x 17'-8"

VAULTED
GREAT RM
19'-0" x 18'-4"

THREE CAR GARAGE
20'-0" x 30'-0"

WICL

WICL

BATH

LAUN RM

LOCATION OF OPT
UTIL RM W/O BSMT PLAN

MSTR
BATH

VAULTED
LIVING RM/
GUEST RM
12'-0" x 15'-0"

SERVER

VAULTED
FOYER

9' HIGH CLG
DINING RM
15'-0" x 12'-8"

COV. PORCH

GAZEBO

Main Level Floor Plan

Upper Level Floor Plan

Copyright by designer/architect.

BEDRM #2
15'-0" x 13'-4"

UPPER
GREAT RM

VAULTED
UNFIN. LOFT
19'-0" x 16'-0"

LIN

RAIL

BALCONY

UNFIN
ATTIC

BATH

UPPER
FOYER

VAULTED
BEDRM #3
15'-0" x 13'-0"

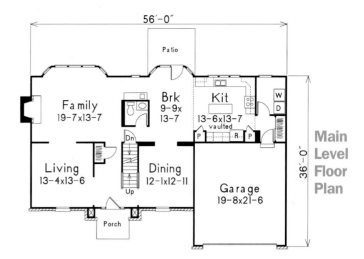

Main Level Floor Plan

Family 19-7x13-7
Brk 9-9x 13-7
Kit 13-6x13-7 vaulted
Living 13-4x13-6
Dining 12-1x12-11
Garage 19-8x21-6
Porch
Patio
56'-0"
36'-0"

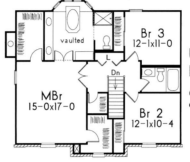

Images provided by designer/architect.

CAD FILE AVAILABLE

Plan #321043

Dimensions: 56' W x 36' D
Levels: 2
Square Footage: 2,401
Main Level Sq. Ft.: 1,355
Upper Level Sq. Ft.: 1,046
Bedrooms: 3
Bathrooms: 2½
Foundation: Basement
Materials List Available: Yes
Price Category: E

Upper Level Floor Plan

Copyright by designer/architect.

Br 3 12-1x11-0
MBr 15-0x17-0
Br 2 12-1x10-4
vaulted

Plan #321056

Dimensions: 40' W x 57'4" D
Levels: 2
Square Footage: 2,050
Main Level Sq. Ft.: 1,028
Upper Level Sq. Ft.: 1,022
Bedrooms: 3
Bathrooms: 2½
Foundation: Basement
Materials List Available: Yes
Price Category: D

Images provided by designer/architect.

CAD FILE AVAILABLE

Main Level Floor Plan

Garage 23-5x23-8
Kit 11-5x13-5
Din 10-0x13-5
Family 17-5x13-5
Living 11-8x19-0
Porch
raised ceiling
Furn.
Foyer
Porch
40'-0"
57'-4"

Upper Level Floor Plan

Copyright by designer/architect.

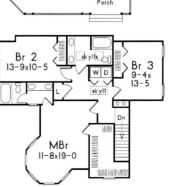

Br 2 13-9x10-5
skylts
Br 3 9-4x 13-5
W D
MBr 11-8x19-0

Plan #131032

Dimensions: 69'2" W x 46' D
Levels: 2
Square Footage: 2,455
Main Level Sq. Ft.: 1,499
Upper Level Sq. Ft.: 956
Bedrooms: 4
Bathrooms: 3
Foundation: Crawl space, slab, or basement
Materials List Available: Yes
Price Category: F

Photos provided by designer/architect.

If you love Victorian styling, you'll be charmed by the ornate, rounded front porch and the two-story bay that distinguish this home.

Features:

- Living Room: You'll love the 13-ft. ceiling in this room, as well as the panoramic view it gives of the front porch and yard.
- Kitchen: Sunlight streams into this room, where an angled island with a cooktop eases both prepping and cooking.
- Breakfast Room: This room shares an eating bar with the kitchen, making it easy for the family to congregate while the family chef is cooking.
- Guest Room: Use this lovely room on the first level as a home office or study if you wish.
- Master Suite: The dramatic bayed sitting area with a high ceiling has an octagonal shape that you'll adore, and the amenities in the private bath will soothe you at the end of a busy day.

Rear View

Upper Level Floor Plan

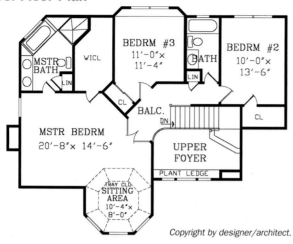

MSTR BATH

WICL

LIN

BEDRM #3
11'-0"×
11'-4"

BATH

LIN

BEDRM #2
10'-0"×
13'-6"

CL

CL

MSTR BEDRM
20'-8"× 14'-6"

BALC.

DN

UPPER FOYER

PLANT LEDGE

TRAY CLG.
SITTING AREA
10'-4"×
8'-0"

Copyright by designer/architect.

Main Level Floor Plan

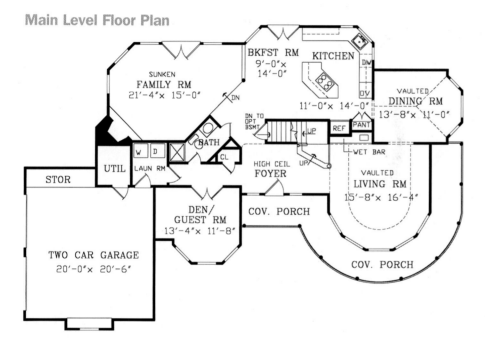

SUNKEN
FAMILY RM
21'-4"× 15'-0"

BKFST RM
9'-0"×
14'-0"

KITCHEN

DW

OV

11'-0"× 14'-0"

VAULTED
DINING RM
13'-8"× 11'-0"

DN

DN TO OPT BSMT

REF

PANT

BATH

W   D

CL

HIGH CEIL
FOYER

UP

UP

WET BAR

VAULTED
LIVING RM
15'-8"× 16'-4"

STOR

UTIL

LAUN RM

DEN/
GUEST RM
13'-4"× 11'-8"

COV. PORCH

COV. PORCH

TWO CAR GARAGE
20'-0"× 20'-6"

Dining Room

Living Room

Kitchen

Breakfast

Foyer

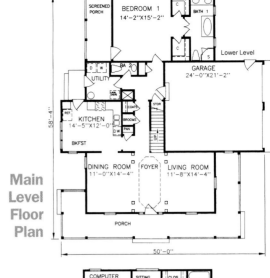

Main Level Floor Plan

Images provided by designer/architect.

Upper Level Floor Plan

Copyright by designer/architect.

Upper Level

Plan #341011

Dimensions: 50' W x 58'4" D

Levels: 2

Square Footage: 2,560

Main Level Sq. Ft.: 1,387

Upper Level Sq. Ft.: 1,173

Bedrooms: 4

Bathrooms: 3½

Foundation: Crawl space; slab or basement for fee

Materials List Available: Yes

Price Category: E

CAD FILE AVAILABLE

Main Level Floor Plan

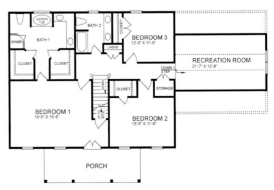

Upper Level Floor Plan

Copyright by designer/architect.

Images provided by designer/architect.

Plan #341020

Dimensions: 62' W x 44'6" D

Levels: 2

Square Footage: 2,614

Main Level Sq. Ft.: 1,334

Upper Level Sq. Ft.: 1,280

Bedrooms: 3

Bathrooms: 2½

Foundation: Crawl space; slab or basement for fee

Materials List Available: Yes

Price Category: F

CAD FILE AVAILABLE

Plan #271083

Dimensions: 28' W x 54' D
Levels: 2
Square Footage: 1,690
Main Level Sq. Ft.: 810
Upper Level Sq. Ft.: 880
Bedrooms: 3
Bathrooms: 2½
Foundation: Crawl space
Materials List Available: Yes
Price Category: C

Images provided by designer/architect.

CAD FILE AVAILABLE — CAD

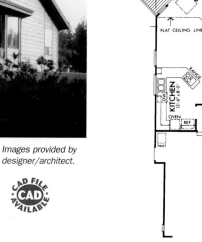

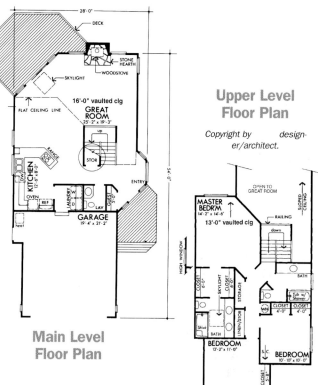

Upper Level Floor Plan

Copyright by designer/architect.

Main Level Floor Plan

Plan #341016

Dimensions: 61'6" W x 37'10" D
Levels: 2
Square Footage: 2,630
Main Level Sq. Ft.: 1,124
Upper Level Sq. Ft.: 1,506
Bedrooms: 3
Bathrooms: 2½
Foundation: Crawl space; slab or basement for fee
Materials List Available: Yes
Price Category: F

Images provided by designer/architect.

Main Level Floor Plan

Upper Level Floor Plan

Copyright by designer/architect.

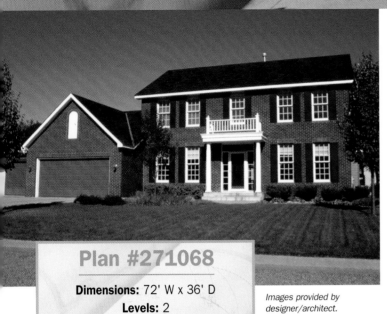

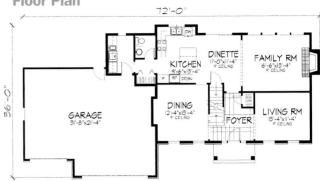

72'-0"

36'-0"

GARAGE
31'-8"x21'-4"

KITCHEN
9'-6"x13'-4"

DINETTE
11'-0"x11'-4"
8' CEILING

FAMILY RM
16'-6"x13'-4"
8' CEILING

DINING
12'-4"x13'-4"
8' CEILING

FOYER

LIVING RM
13'-4"x11'-4"
8' CEILING

*Images provided by
designer/architect.*

BEDRM 3
12'-4"x11'-0"
8' CEILING

BEDRM 4
11'-8"x9'-4"
8' CEILING

BEDRM 2
9'-0"x10'-4"
8' CEILING

MSTR SUITE
16'-4"x12'-4"
9'-4" TRAY CLG

**Upper Level
Floor Plan**

*Copyright by design-
er/architect.*

Plan #271068

Dimensions: 72' W x 36' D
Levels: 2
Square Footage: 2,214
Main Level Sq. Ft.: 1,150
Upper Level Sq. Ft.: 1,064
Bedrooms: 4
Bathrooms: 2½
Foundation: Basement
Materials List Available: No
Price Category: E

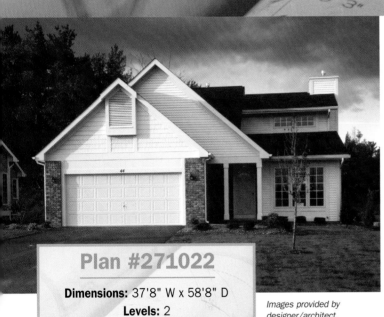

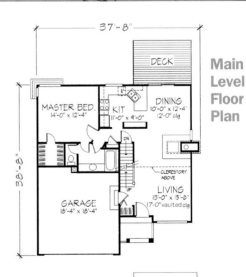

37'-8"

38'-8"

DECK

MASTER BED.
14'-0" x 12'-4"

KIT
11'-0" x 9'-0"

DINING
10'-0" x 12'-4"
12'-0" clg

CLERESTORY
ABOVE

GARAGE
18'-4" x 18'-4"

LIVING
13'-0" x 15'-8"
17'-0" vaulted clg

**Main
Level
Floor
Plan**

*Images provided by
designer/architect.*

LOFT/
BDRM 3
12'-0" x 12'-4"

BDRM 2
9'-8" x 12'-8"

OPEN TO BELOW

**Upper Level
Floor Plan**

*Copyright by design-
er/architect.*

Plan #271022

Dimensions: 37'8" W x 58'8" D
Levels: 2
Square Footage: 1,317
Main Level Sq. Ft.: 894
Upper Level Sq. Ft.: 423
Bedrooms: 2
Bathrooms: 2
Foundation: Basement
Materials List Available: Yes
Price Category: B

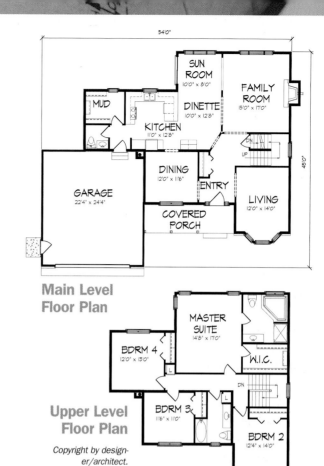

Main Level Floor Plan

Images provided by designer/architect.

Upper Level Floor Plan

Copyright by designer/architect.

Plan #271062

Dimensions: 54' W x 45' D
Levels: 2
Square Footage: 2,356
Main Level Sq. Ft.: 1,222
Upper Level Sq. Ft.: 1,134
Bedrooms: 4
Bathrooms: 2½
Foundation: Daylight basement
Materials List Available: No
Price Category: E

Main Level Floor Plan

Images provided by designer/architect.

Upper Level Floor Plan

Copyright by designer/architect.

Plan #271066

Dimensions: 72'10" W x 38'2" D
Levels: 2
Square Footage: 2,249
Main Level Sq. Ft.: 1,209
Upper Level Sq. Ft.: 1,040
Bedrooms: 4
Bathrooms: 2½
Foundation: Basement or crawl space
Materials List Available: No
Price Category: E

Plan #271030

Dimensions: 56' W x 45' D
Levels: 2
Square Footage: 1,926
Main Level Sq. Ft.: 1,490
Upper Level Sq. Ft.: 436
Bedrooms: 3
Bathrooms: 2½
Foundation: Crawl space or basement
Materials List Available: Yes
Price Category: D

Photo provided by designer/architect.

This traditional home's main-floor master suite is hard to resist, with its inviting window seat and delightful bath.

Features:

• Master Suite: Just off from the entry foyer, this luxurious oasis is entered through double doors, and offers an airy vaulted ceiling, plus a private bath that includes a separate tub and shower, dual-sink vanity, and walk-in closet.

• Great Room: This space does it all in style, with a breathtaking wall of windows and a charming fireplace.

• Kitchen: A cooktop island makes dinnertime tasks a breeze. You'll also love the roomy pantry. The adjoining breakfast room, with its deck access and built-in desk, is sure to be a popular hangout for the teens.

• Secondary Bedrooms: Two additional bedrooms reside on the upper floor and allow the younger family members a measure of desired—and necessary—privacy.

CAD FILE AVAILABLE

Main Level Floor Plan

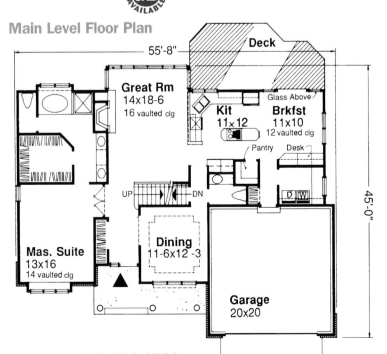

Upper Level Floor Plan

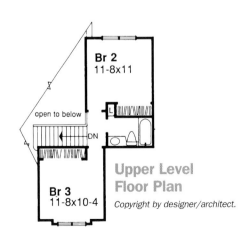

Copyright by designer/architect.

Plan #311003

Dimensions: 70'10" W x 65'4" D
Levels: 2
Square Footage: 2,428
Main Level Sq. Ft.: 2,348
Upper Level Sq. Ft.: 80
Bedrooms: 3
Bathrooms: 2½
Foundation: Slab, crawl space, or basement
Materials List Available: Yes
Price Category: E

If you admire the gracious colonnaded porch, curved brick steps, and stunning front windows, you'll fall in love with the interior of this home.

Features:

- **Great Room:** Enjoy the vaulted ceiling, balcony from the upper level, and fireplace with flanking windows that let you look out to the patio.

- **Dining Room:** Columns define this formal room, which is adjacent to the breakfast room.

- **Kitchen:** A bayed sink area and extensive curved bar provide visual interest in this well-designed kitchen, which every cook will love.

- **Breakfast Room:** Huge windows let the sun shine into this room, which is open to the kitchen.

- **Master Suite:** The sitting area is open to the rear porch for a special touch in this gorgeous suite. Two walk-in closets and a vaulted ceiling and double vanity in the bath will make you feel completely pampered.

Main Level Floor Plan

- Bath 16-2x16-1
- Patio
- Garage 24-6x21-2
- Sitting 12-10x9-8
- Porch 20-2x10-0
- Owner's Bedroom 16-2x15-3
- Greatroom 18-0x17-2
- Laun. 7-3x6-0
- Kitchen 17-0x11-8
- Bedroom 11-3x14-3
- Bedroom 11-7x12-3
- Foyer
- Dining 14-0x12-6
- Brkfst 11-3x10-0
- Porch 36-0x8-2

Copyright by designer/architect.

Upper Level Floor Plan

- Future 21-8x12-0
- Open to Below
- Future 13-5x12-0
- Balcony
- Future 35-5x11-4

Plan #141019

Dimensions: 57' W x 41' D
Levels: 2
Square Footage: 2,826
Main Level Sq. Ft.: 1,258
Second Level Sq. Ft.: 1,568
Bedrooms: 5
Bathrooms: 3
Foundation: Basement
Materials List Available: Yes
Price Category: F

Images provided by designer/architect.

Main Level Floor Plan

Patio / Deck
Office / Bdrm.5 11^0 x 11^4
Bth.3
Cubby Holes
Command Center
Living Area 15^0 x 19^2 11' Ceil. Boxed Tray
Brkfst. 13^4 x 10^0
Kit. 13^4 x 11^6
Dw.
Pant.
Double Garage 21^4 x 21^8
Two Story Foyer 7^0 x 5^{10}
Dining 13^4 x 11^6
Up

Upper Level Floor Plan

Copyright by designer/architect.

Seat
Bdrm.2 11^0 x 13^4
Lin.
Bth.2
Children's Den / Media Room 15^0 x 17^4
Seat
Master Bdrm. 13^6 x 17^4 Stepped Ceil.
Bdrm.3 12^8 x 11^8
Opt. Tray w/ Plant Shelf
W / D
Laund.
Up
M. Bath Tray Ceil. Plant Shelf Above
Balcony
Sh.
Opt. Tray w/ Plant Shelf
Linen
Dn
Two Story Foyer
Seat W/ Drawers
Bdrm.4 11^4 x 11^2

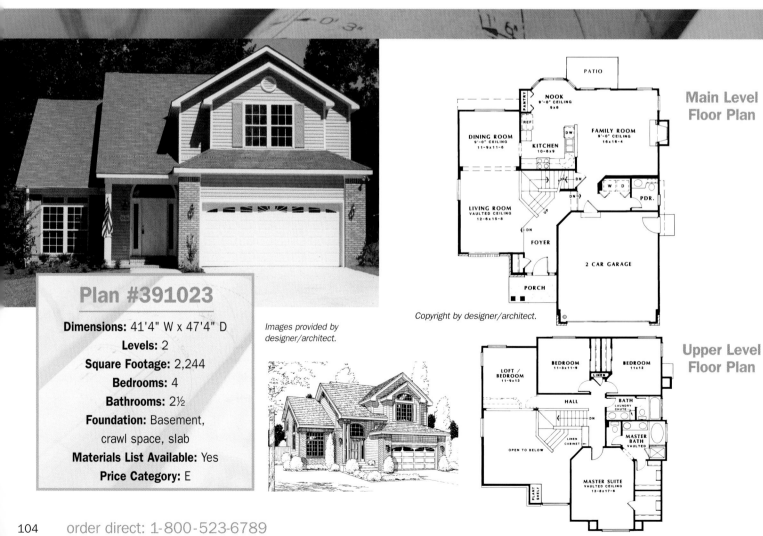

Plan #391023

Dimensions: 41'4" W x 47'4" D
Levels: 2
Square Footage: 2,244
Bedrooms: 4
Bathrooms: 2½
Foundation: Basement, crawl space, slab
Materials List Available: Yes
Price Category: E

Images provided by designer/architect.

Main Level Floor Plan

PATIO
NOOK 9'-0" CEILING 9x8
PANTRY
REF.
DINING ROOM 9'-0" CEILING 11-9x11-6
KITCHEN 10-6x9
DW
FAMILY ROOM 9'-0" CEILING 16x16-4
LIVING ROOM VAULTED CEILING 12-6x15-8
UP
DN
DN
W D
PDR.
FOYER
2 CAR GARAGE
PORCH

Copyright by designer/architect.

Upper Level Floor Plan

LOFT / BEDROOM 11-9x11
BEDROOM 11-3x11-9
LINEN
BEDROOM 11x12
HALL
BATH LAUNDRY CHUTE
DN
OPEN TO BELOW
LINEN CABINET
MASTER BATH VAULTED
PLANT SHELF
MASTER SUITE VAULTED CEILING 13-8x17-6

Main Level Floor Plan

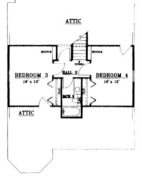

Upper Level Floor Plan

Copyright by designer/architect.

Images provided by designer/architect.

Plan #171005

Dimensions: 56' W x 58' D
Levels: 2
Square Footage: 2,276
Main Level Sq. Ft.: 1,748
Upper Level Sq. Ft.: 528
Bedrooms: 4
Bathrooms: 3
Foundation: Slab, crawl space
Materials List Available: Yes
Price Category: E

Main Level Floor Plan

Upper Level Floor Plan
Copyright by designer/architect.

Images provided by designer/architect.

Plan #171014

Dimensions: 47' W x 52' D
Levels: 2
Square Footage: 1,815
Main Level Sq. Ft.: 1,257
Upper Level Sq. Ft.: 558
Bedrooms: 3
Bathrooms: 2½
Foundation: Slab, crawl space
Materials List Available: Yes
Price Category: D

Plan #271069

Dimensions: 63'5" W x 51'8" D

Levels: 2

Square Footage: 2,376

Main Level Sq. Ft.: 1,248

Upper Level Sq. Ft.: 1,128

Bedrooms: 4

Bathrooms: 2½

Foundation: Basement, crawl space

Materials List Available: No

Price Category: E

Images provided by designer/architect.

This home's Federal-style facade has a simple elegance that is still popular among today's homeowners.

Features:

- Living Room: This formal space is perfect for serious conversation or thoughtful reflection. Optional double doors would open directly into the family room beyond.

- Dining Room: You won't find a more elegant room than this for hosting holiday feasts.

- Kitchen: This room has everything the cook could hope for—a central island, a handy pantry, and a menu desk. Sliding glass doors in the dinette let you step outside for some fresh air with your cup of coffee.

- Family Room: Here's the spot to spend a cold winter evening. Have hot chocolate in front of a crackling fire!

- Master Suite: With an optional vaulted ceiling, the sleeping chamber is bright and spacious. The private bath showcases a splashy whirlpool tub.

Main Level Floor Plan

Upper Level Floor Plan

Copyright by designer/architect.

Plan #161015

Dimensions: 55'4" W x 40'4" D
Levels: 2
Square Footage: 1,768
Main Level Sq. Ft.: 960
Upper Level Sq. Ft.: 808
Bedrooms: 3
Bathrooms: 2½
Foundation: Basement
Materials List Available: No
Price Category: C

One look at this dramatic exterior—a 12-ft. high entry with a transom and sidelights, multiple gables, and an impressive box window—you'll fall in love with this home.

Features:

• **Foyer:** This 2-story area announces the grace of this home to everyone who enters it.

• **Great Room:** A natural gathering spot, this room is sunken to set it off from the rest of the house. The 12-ft. ceiling adds a spacious feeling, and the access to the rear porch makes it ideal for friends and family.

• **Kitchen:** The kids will enjoy the snack bar and you'll love the adjoining breakfast room with its access to the rear porch.

• **Master Suite:** A whirlpool in the master bath and walk-in closets in the bedroom spell luxury.

• **Laundry Area:** Two large closets are so handy that you'll wonder how you ever did without them.

Images provided by designer/architect.

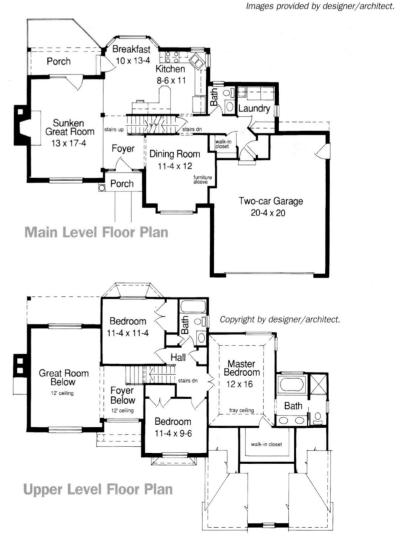

Main Level Floor Plan

Copyright by designer/architect.

Upper Level Floor Plan

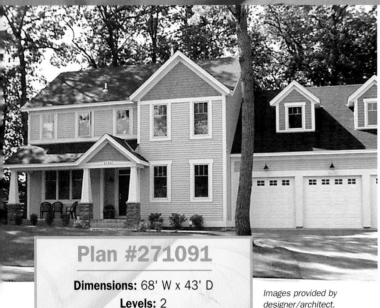

Main Level Floor Plan

Images provided by designer/architect.

Upper Level Floor Plan

Copyright by designer/architect.

DINING 19' X 11'

GREAT RM 16' X 16'

KITCHEN 19' X 13'

GARAGE 32' X 24'

STUDY 11' X 11'

ENTRY

MUD RM

BATH

LAUN

BATH

OWNER'S SUITE 15' X 15'

BED RM 11' X 13'

BONUS RM 28' X 14'

BATH

W.I.C.

BED RM 15' X 13'

Plan #271091

Dimensions: 68' W x 43' D

Levels: 2

Square Footage: 2,854

Main Level Sq. Ft.: 1,219

Upper Level Sq. Ft.: 1,635

Bedrooms: 3

Bathrooms: 2½

Foundation: Daylight basement

Materials List Available: No

Price Category: F

Main Level Floor Plan

Images provided by designer/architect.

CAD FILE AVAILABLE

Upper Level Floor Plan

Copyright by designer/architect.

GREAT RM 21' X 18'

DINING 21' X 10'

KITCHEN 15' X 14'

STUDY 11' X 13'

MUD RM

PORCH

GARAGE 40' X 24'

BED RM 10' X 14'

BED RM 10' X 14'

BATH

OWNER'S SUITE 14' X 18'

LAUN

BATH

BED RM 11' X 13'

BED RM 11' X 13'

W.I.C.

Plan #271094

Dimensions: 71' W x 70' D

Levels: 2

Square Footage: 3,242

Main Level Sq. Ft.: 1,552

Upper Level Sq. Ft.: 1,690

Bedrooms: 5

Bathrooms: 2½

Foundation: Full basement

Materials List Available: No

Price Category: G

Main Level Floor Plan

Images provided by designer/architect.

Upper Level Floor Plan

Copyright by designer/architect.

Plan #271090

Dimensions: 78' W x 49' D
Levels: 2
Square Footage: 2,708
Main Level Sq. Ft.: 1,430
Upper Level Sq. Ft.: 1,278
Bedrooms: 3
Bathrooms: 2½
Foundation: Daylight basement
Materials List Available: No
Price Category: F

Main Level Floor Plan

Images provided by designer/architect.

CAD FILE AVAILABLE

Upper Level Floor Plan

Copyright by designer/architect.

Plan #271089

Dimensions: 66' W x 51' D
Levels: 2
Square Footage: 2,476
Main Level Sq. Ft.: 1,266
Upper Level Sq. Ft.: 1,210
Bedrooms: 3
Bathrooms: 2½
Foundation: Daylight basement
Materials List Available: No
Price Category: E

Main Level Floor Plan

Plan #341001

Dimensions: 47'8" W x 53' D

Levels: 2

Square Footage: 2,867

Main Level Sq. Ft.: 1,306

Upper Level Sq. Ft.: 1,561

Bedrooms: 4

Bathrooms: 2½

Foundation: Crawl space; slab or basement for fee

Materials List Available: Yes

Price Category: F

Images provided by designer/architect.

CAD FILE AVAILABLE

Upper Level Floor Plan

Copyright by designer/architect.

Upper Level Floor Plan

Copyright by designer/architect.

Plan #341006

Dimensions: 86'3" W x 35'4" D

Levels: 2

Square Footage: 2,588

Main Level Sq. Ft.: 1,660

Upper Level Sq. Ft.: 928

Bedrooms: 4

Bathrooms: 3½

Foundation: Crawl space; slab or basement for fee

Materials List Available: Yes

Price Category: E

Images provided by designer/architect.

Main Level Floor Plan

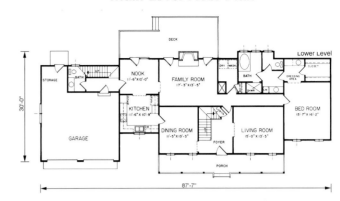

Main Level Floor Plan

Images provided by designer/architect.

CAD FILE AVAILABLE

Upper Level Floor Plan

Copyright by designer/architect.

Plan #341007

Dimensions: 87'7" W x 30' D

Levels: 2

Square Footage: 4,068

Main Level Sq. Ft.: 3,218

Upper Level Sq. Ft.: 850

Bedrooms: 4

Bathrooms: 2½

Foundation: Crawl space; slab or basement for fee

Materials List Available: Yes

Price Category: I

Plan #271095

Dimensions: 70' W x 75' D

Levels: 2

Square Footage: 3,220

Main Level Sq. Ft.: 2,040

Upper Level Sq. Ft.: 1,180

Bedrooms: 3

Bathrooms: 3½

Foundation: Crawl space, slab

Materials List Available: No

Price Category: G

Main Level Floor Plan

Images provided by designer/architect.

Upper Level Floor Plan

Copyright by designer/architect.

Images provided by designer/architect.

Plan #161018

Dimensions: 74'4" W x 69'11" D
Levels: 2
Square Footage: 2,816
+ 325 Sq. Ft. bonus room
Main Level Sq. Ft.: 2,231
Upper Level Sq. Ft.: 624
Bedrooms: 3
Bathrooms: 3 full, 2 half
Foundation: Basement
Materials List Available: No
Price Category: F

If you love classic European designs, look closely at this home with its multiple gables and countless conveniences and luxuries.

Features:

• Foyer: Open to the great room, the 2-story foyer offers a view all the way to the rear windows.

• Great Room: A fireplace makes this room cozy in any kind of weather.

• Kitchen: This large room features an island with a sink, and an angled wall with French doors to the back yard.

• Dining Room: The furniture alcove and raised ceiling make this room both formal and practical.

• Master Suite: You'll love the quiet in the bedroom and the luxuries—a whirlpool tub, separate shower, and double vanities—in the bath.

• Basement: The door from the basement to the side yard adds convenience to outdoor work.

Rear View

Main Level Floor Plan

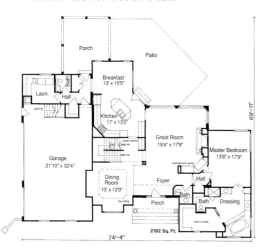

Upper Level Floor Plan

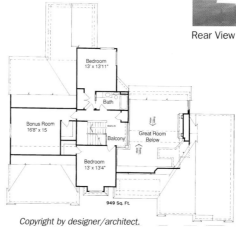

Copyright by designer/architect.

Foyer/Dining Room

Plan #161022

Dimensions: 52'10" W x 38'2" D
Levels: 2
Square Footage: 1,898
Main Level Sq. Ft.: 1,065
Upper Level Sq. Ft.: 833
Bedrooms: 3
Bathrooms: 2½
Foundation: Basement
Materials List Available: No
Price Category: D

A covered porch and boxed window add to the charm of the stone exterior of this home.

Features:

- **Great Room:** This sunken room can be warmed by a fireplace on winter days and chilly evenings, and lit by natural light flowing through the bank of windows on the rear wall.

- **Kitchen:** You'll love the companionship that the snack bar in the kitchen naturally encourages. A large pantry in this area gives you ample storage space and helps to keep you organized.

- **Breakfast Room:** Quiet elegance marks this room with its sloped ceiling and arched windows that look out into the rear yard.

- **Master Suite:** Enjoy the vaulted ceiling and bath with a whirlpool tub.

- **Extra Spaces:** A loft on the second floor and a bonus room allow endless possibilities in this comfortable home.

Rear Elevation

Main Level Floor Plan

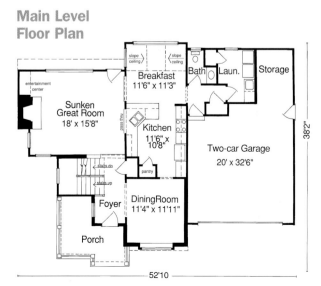

Upper Level Floor Plan

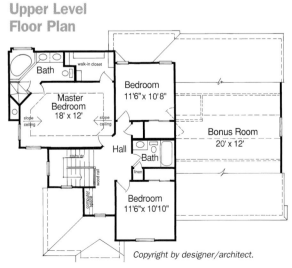

Copyright by designer/architect.

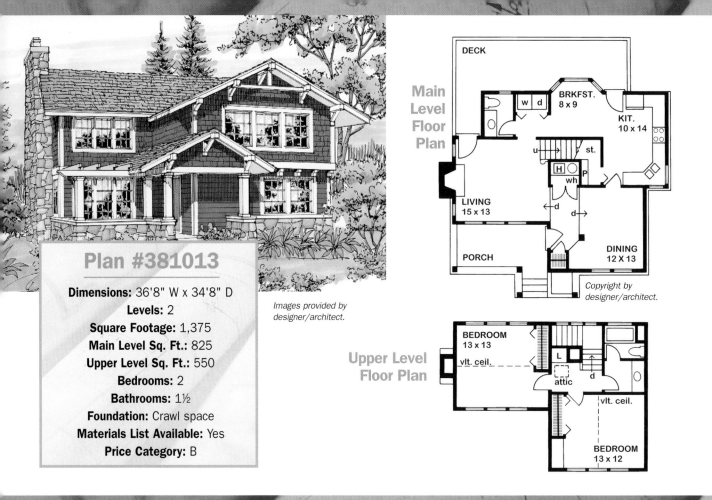

DECK

Main Level Floor Plan

BRKFST. 8 x 9

w | d

KIT. 10 x 14

u | st.

H | P

wh

LIVING 15 x 13

d | d

PORCH

DINING 12 X 13

Copyright by designer/architect.

Plan #381013

Dimensions: 36'8" W x 34'8" D

Levels: 2

Square Footage: 1,375

Main Level Sq. Ft.: 825

Upper Level Sq. Ft.: 550

Bedrooms: 2

Bathrooms: 1½

Foundation: Crawl space

Materials List Available: Yes

Price Category: B

Images provided by designer/architect.

Upper Level Floor Plan

BEDROOM 13 x 13

vlt. ceil.

L

d

attic

vlt. ceil.

BEDROOM 13 x 12

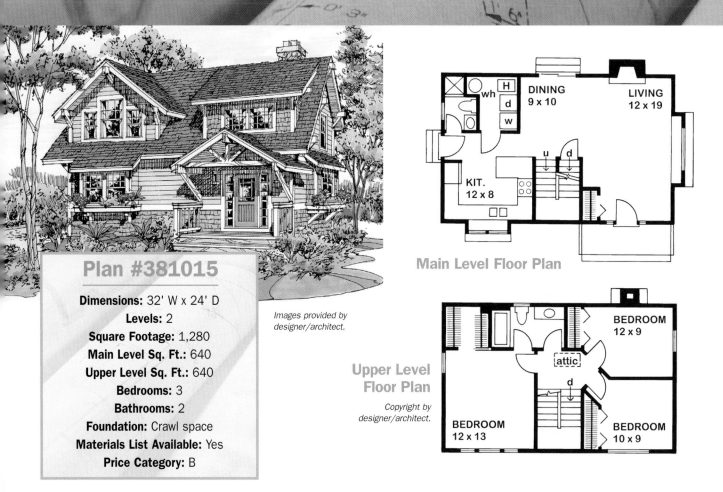

DINING 9 x 10

wh | H

d

w

LIVING 12 x 19

u | d

KIT. 12 x 8

Main Level Floor Plan

Plan #381015

Dimensions: 32' W x 24' D

Levels: 2

Square Footage: 1,280

Main Level Sq. Ft.: 640

Upper Level Sq. Ft.: 640

Bedrooms: 3

Bathrooms: 2

Foundation: Crawl space

Materials List Available: Yes

Price Category: B

Images provided by designer/architect.

Upper Level Floor Plan

Copyright by designer/architect.

BEDROOM 12 x 9

attic

d

BEDROOM 12 x 13

BEDROOM 10 x 9

Main Level Floor Plan

Patio
20' x 12'

Kitchen

Family
15' x 17'

Nook
8' x 15'

Dining
10'6" x 14'

Living
12'2" x 16'8"

Garage
23'4" x 41'4"

Up
2-Story
Foyer

Covered Porch

Images provided by designer/architect.

CAD FILE AVAILABLE CAD

Upper Level Floor Plan

Copyright by designer/architect.

Bedroom
12 x 11

Bedroom
11'8" x 11'

Dn

Master
Suite
12'2" x 16'8"

Utility

Open to
Foyer
Below

Plan #361024

Dimensions: 54' W x 42' D
Levels: 2
Square Footage: 2,296
Main Level Sq. Ft.: 1,186
Upper Level Sq. Ft.: 1,110
Bedrooms: 3
Bathrooms: 2½
Foundation: Crawl space
Materials List Available: No
Price Category: E

Main Level Floor Plan

BEDROOM
12 x 12

w d

LIVING
16 x 13

KIT. / DINING
13 x 17

PORCH

Images provided by designer/architect.

Plan #381017

Dimensions: 30' W x 38'8" D
Levels: 2
Square Footage: 1,540
Main Level Sq. Ft.: 910
Upper Level Sq. Ft.: 630
Bedrooms: 3
Bathrooms: 2
Foundation: Basement
Materials List Available: Yes
Price Category: C

Upper Level Floor Plan

BEDROOM
13 x 12

H

attic

d

OPEN

BEDROOM
12 x 11

sto.

DECK

Copyright by designer/architect.

Plan #161024

Dimensions: 54'4" W x 26'8" D
Levels: 2
Square Footage: 1,698
Main Level Sq. Ft.: 868
Upper Level Sq. Ft.: 830
Bonus Space Sq. Ft.: 269
Bedrooms: 3
Bathrooms: 2½
Foundation: Basement
Materials List Available: No
Price Category: C

The covered porch, dormers, and center gable that grace the exterior let you know how comfortable your family will be in this home.

Features:

- Great Room: Walk from windows overlooking the front porch to a door into the rear yard in this spacious room, which runs the width of the house.

- Dining Room: Adjacent to the great room, the dining area gives your family space to spread out and makes it easy to entertain a large group.

- Kitchen: Designed for efficiency, the kitchen area includes a large pantry.

- Master Suite: Tucked away on the second floor, the master suite features a walk-in closet in the bedroom and a luxurious attached bathroom.

- Bonus Room: Finish the 269-sq.-ft. area over the 2-bay garage as a guest room, study, or getaway for the kids.

Main Level Floor Plan

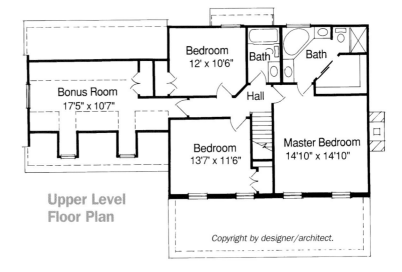

Upper Level Floor Plan

Plan #161025

Dimensions: 63'4" W x 48' D
Levels: 2
Square Footage: 2,738
Main Level Sq. Ft.: 1,915
Upper Level Sq. Ft.: 823
Bedrooms: 4
Bathrooms: 3½
Foundation: Basement
Materials List Available: No
Price Category: F

This home, as shown in the photograph, may differ from the actual blueprints. For more detailed informtaion, please check the floor plans carefully.

Images provided by designer/architect.

One look at the octagonal tower, boxed window, and wood-and-stone trim, and you'll know how much your family will love this home.

Features:

- Foyer: View the high windows across the rear wall, a fireplace, and open stairs as you come in.

- Great Room: Gather in this two-story-high area.

- Hearth Room: Open to the breakfast room, it's close to both the kitchen and dining room.

- Kitchen: A snack bar and an island make the kitchen ideal for family living.

- Master Suite: You'll love the 9-ft. ceiling in the bedroom and 11-ft. ceiling in the sitting area. The bath has a whirlpool tub, double-bowl vanity, and walk-in closet.

- Upper Level: A balcony leads to a bedroom with a private bath and 2 other rooms with private access to a shared bath.

Main Level Floor Plan

Upper Level Floor Plan

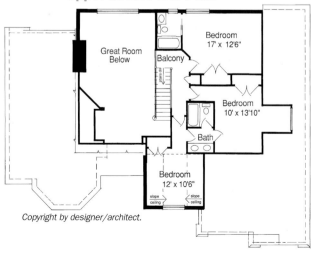

Copyright by designer/architect.

Main Level Floor Plan

Patio

Covered Porch

Breakfast 10'6" x 13'6"

Kitchen 8'7" x 11'6"

Great Room 12'9" x 17'10" 12' ceiling

Bath

Laun.

Foyer

WALK-IN CLOSET

CLOSET

Dining Room 11'6" x 12'

FURNITURE ALCOVE

Porch

Two-Car Garage 21' x 25'

42'-4"

57'-10"

Plan #161052

Dimensions: 57'10" W x 42'4" D
Levels: 2
Square Footage: 1,727
Main Level Sq. Ft.: 941
Upper Level Sq. Ft.: 786
Bedrooms: 3
Bathrooms: 2½
Foundation: Basement
Materials List Available: Yes
Price Category: E

Images provided by designer/architect.

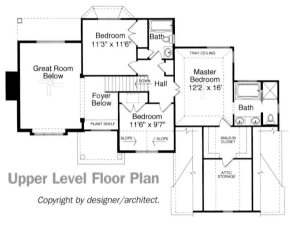

Bedroom 11'3" x 11'6"

Bath

TRAY CEILING

Great Room Below

DOWN

Hall

Master Bedroom 12'2" x 16'

Foyer Below

Bath

PLANT SHELF

Bedroom 11'6" x 9'7"

SLOPE

SLOPE

WALK-IN CLOSET

ATTIC STORAGE

Upper Level Floor Plan

Rear Elevation

Copyright by designer/architect.

Main Level Floor Plan

Porch

Hearth Room 21' x 19'6"

Breakfast 13'6" x 11'

Porch

Sitting Area

Kitchen 21'3" x 15'

Great Room 22'2" x 18'2"

Master Bedroom 25'6" x 24'6" ireg.

Hall

Dressing

BATH

Three Car Garage 22' x 40'9"

Laun.

Dining Room 12'9" x 14'7"

Foyer

Library 13'1" x 15'1"

Porch

90'6"

78'9"

Plan #161044

Dimensions: 90'6" W x 78'9" D
Levels: 2
Square Footage: 4,652
Main Level Sq. Ft.: 3,414
Upper Level Sq. Ft.: 1,238
Bedrooms: 4
Bathrooms: 3½
Foundation: Basement
Materials List Available: Yes
Price Category: I

Images provided by designer/architect.

Upper Level Floor Plan

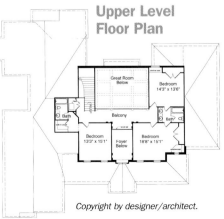

Great Room Below

Bedroom 14'3" x 13'6"

Bath

Balcony

Bath

Bedroom 13'3" x 15'1"

Foyer Below

Bedroom 18'8" x 15'1"

Rear Elevation

Copyright by designer/architect.

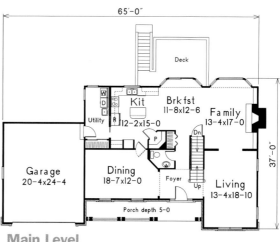

Main Level Floor Plan

Deck

65'-0"

Kit 12-2x15-0
Brk fst 11-8x12-6
Family 13-4x17-0
Utility
W D
Dining 18-7x12-0
Garage 20-4x24-4
Foyer
Dn
Up
Living 13-4x18-10
37'-0"
Porch depth 5-0

Images provided by designer/architect.

CAD FILE AVAILABLE

Plan #321059

Dimensions: 65' W x 37' D
Levels: 2
Square Footage: 2,521
Main Level Sq. Ft.: 1,375
Upper Level Sq. Ft.: 1,146
Bedrooms: 4
Bathrooms: 2½
Foundation: Basement
Materials List Available: Yes
Price Category: E

Upper Level Floor Plan
Copyright by designer/architect.

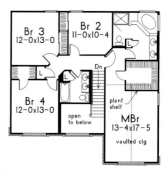

Br 3 12-0x13-0
Br 2 11-0x10-4
Dn
Br 4 12-0x13-0
open to below
plant shelf
MBr 13-4x17-5
vaulted clg

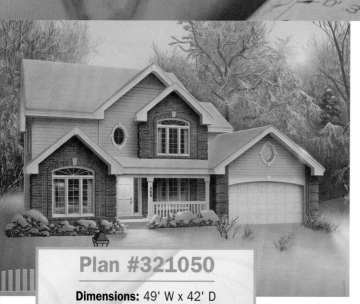

Main Level Floor Plan

Family 20-2x16-8
Brk 10-0x16-8
Kitchen 10-8x11-6
W D
Dn
Up
Living 11-0x14-8 Sunken
vaulted
Dining 10-6x13-3
Entry
Up
Garage 19-4x21-4
Porch 17-4x5-0
42'-0"
49'-0"

Images provided by designer/architect.

CAD FILE AVAILABLE

Plan #321050

Dimensions: 49' W x 42' D
Levels: 2
Square Footage: 2,336
Main Level Sq. Ft.: 1,291
Upper Level Sq. Ft.: 1,045
Bedrooms: 4
Bathrooms: 2½
Foundation: Basement
Materials List Available: Yes
Price Category: E

Upper Level Floor Plan
Copyright by designer/architect.

Br 2 11-0x10-0
MBr 13-0x17-8 vaulted
L
Dn
Dn
Br 3 11-0x11-0
open to below
Br 4 10-6x11-0
vaulted

Plan #121108

Dimensions: 67'4" W x 66' D
Levels: 2
Square Footage: 3,806
Main Level Sq. Ft.: 2,126
Basement Level Sq. Ft.: 1,680
Bedrooms: 4
Bathrooms: 2½
Foundation: Basement
Materials List Available: Yes
Price Category: H

Images provided by designer/architect.

Elegant architecture and stylish details define this home.

Features:

- Master Suite: This room will become your oasis with its large bedroom area, beautiful ceiling details, spacious walk-in closet, his-and-her sinks, and a large whirlpool bath surrounded by windows for a truly relaxing experience.

- Hearth Room: This roomy hearth room features an entertainment center, open access to the kitchen, and a two-way fireplace shared with the great room.

- Kitchen: You'll love the elegant details in this kitchen, with its walk-in pantry and snack bar. The brightly-lit connecting breakfast area is a perfect place for your morning cup of coffee.

Main Level Floor Plan

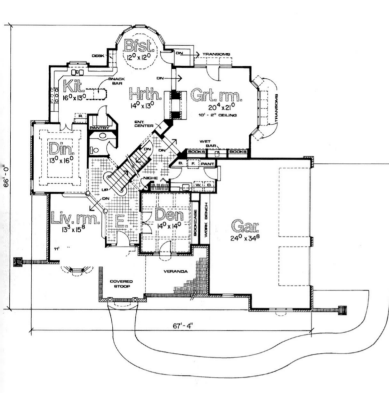

Upper Level Floor Plan

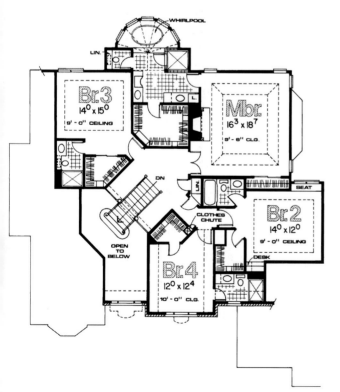

Hearth

Kitchen

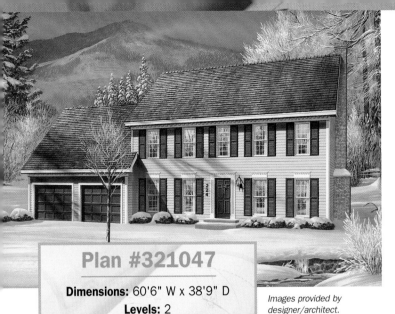

Main Level Floor Plan

38'-9"

Garage
21-5x25-5

Kit
11-0x10-2

Brk
9-6x
14-5

Family
20-4x16-10

Dining
14-6x14-3

Living
13-0x14-3

Porch

60'-6"

Images provided by designer/architect.

Upper Level Floor Plan

Copyright by designer/architect.

Br 4
12-2x11-1

Br 3
13-0x11-1

MBr
18-4x14-3

Br 2
13-0x12-2

Plan #321047

Dimensions: 60'6" W x 38'9" D
Levels: 2
Square Footage: 2,461
Main Level Sq. Ft.: 1,252
Upper Level Sq. Ft.: 1,209
Bedrooms: 4
Bathrooms: 2½
Foundation: Basement
Materials List Available: Yes
Price Category: E

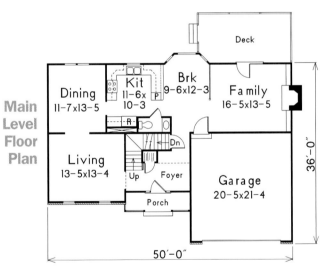

Deck

Main Level Floor Plan

Dining
11-7x13-5

Kit
11-6x
10-3

Brk
9-6x12-3

Family
16-5x13-5

Living
13-5x13-4

Foyer

Garage
20-5x21-4

Porch

36'-0"

50'-0"

Images provided by designer/architect.

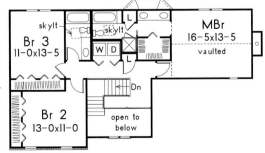

Upper Level Floor Plan

Copyright by designer/architect.

skylt   skylt

Br 3
11-0x13-5

MBr
16-5x13-5
vaulted

Br 2
13-0x11-0

open to below

Plan #321045

Dimensions: 50' W x 36' D
Levels: 2
Square Footage: 2,058
Main Level Sq. Ft.: 1,098
Upper Level Sq. Ft.: 960
Bedrooms: 3
Bathrooms: 2½
Foundation: Basement
Materials List Available: Yes
Price Category: D

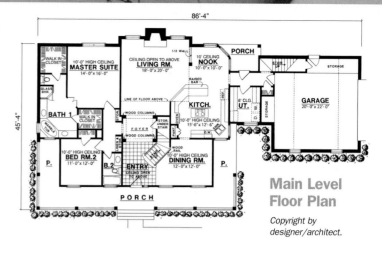

Main Level Floor Plan

Copyright by designer/architect.

Images provided by designer/architect.

Plan #371008

Dimensions: 86'4" W x 45'4" D

Levels: 2

Square Footage: 2,656

Main Level Sq. Ft: 1,969

Upper Level Sq. Ft.: 687

Bedrooms: 4

Bathrooms: 3

Foundation: Slab
(crawl space option for fee)

Materials List Available: No

Price Category: F

Upper Level Floor Plan

Main Level Floor Plan

Plan #131049

Dimensions: 88'8" W x 59'2" D

Levels: 2

Square Footage: 2,837

Main Level Sq. Ft.: 2,152

Upper Level Sq. Ft.: 685

Bedrooms: 3

Bathrooms: 3

Foundation: Crawl space, slab, or basement

Materials List Available: Yes

Price Category: G

Images provided by designer/architect.

Upper Level Floor Plan

Copyright by designer/architect.

Plan #161034

Dimensions: 56' W x 53' D
Levels: 2
Square Footage: 2,156
Main Level Sq. Ft.: 1,605
Upper Level Sq. Ft.: 551
Bedrooms: 3
Bathrooms: 2½
Foundation: Basement
Materials List Available: No
Price Category: D

Multiple gables, a covered porch, and circle-topped windows combine to enhance the attractiveness of this exciting home.

Features:

• Great Room: A raised foyer introduces this open combined great room and dining room. Enjoy the efficiency of a dual-sided fireplace that warms both the great room and kitchen.

• Kitchen: The kitchen, designed for easy traffic patterns, offers an abundance of counter space and features a cooktop island.

• Master Suite: This first-floor master suite, separated for privacy, includes twin vanities and a walk-in closet. A deluxe corner bath and walk-in shower complete its luxurious detail.

• Additional Rooms: Two additional bedrooms lead to the second-floor balcony, which overlooks the great room. You can use the optional bonus room as a den or office.

Copyright by designer/architect.

Main Level Floor Plan

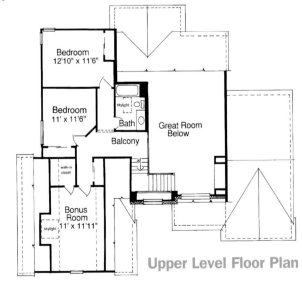

Upper Level Floor Plan

Plan #151014

Dimensions: 70'2" W x 51'4" D
Levels: 1.5
Square Footage: 2,698
Main Level Sq. Ft.: 1,813
Upper Level Sq. Ft.: 885
Bedrooms: 5
Bathrooms: 3
Foundation: Crawl space, slab, optional basement for fee
Price Category: D
CompleteCost List Available: Yes
Price Catagory: F

Images provided by designer/architect.

CAD FILE AVAILABLE

A comfortable front porch welcomes you into this home that features a balcony over the great room, a study, and a kitchen designed for gourmet cooks.

Features:

- Ceiling Height: 9 ft.
- Front Porch: Stately 12-in.-wide pillars form the entryway.
- Foyer: Open to upper story.
- Great Room: A fireplace, vaulted 9-ft. ceiling, and balcony from the second floor add character to this lovely room.
- Dining Room: Open to the kitchen for convenience.
- Kitchen: A large walk-in pantry, well-designed work areas, and eat-in bar make this room a treasure.

- Breakfast Room: Enjoy this spot that opens to both the kitchen and a large covered porch at the rear of the house.
- Study: This quiet room has French doors leading to the yard.
- Master Suite: This spacious area has cozy window seats as well as his and her walk-in closets. The master bathroom is fitted with a whirlpool tub, a glass shower, and his and her sinks.

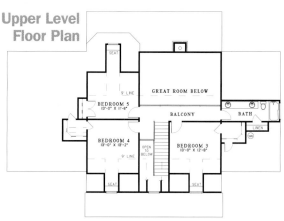

Upper Level Floor Plan

Main Level Floor Plan

Copyright by designer/architect.

Plan #161051

Dimensions: 57'8" W x 58' D

Levels: 2

Square Footage: 2,484

Main Level Sq. Ft.: 1,710

Upper Level Sq. Ft.: 774

Bedrooms: 4

Bathrooms: 3½

Foundation: Basement
Optional crawl space
available for extra fee

Materials List Available: Yes

Price Category: E

Images provided by designer/architect.

Upper Level Floor Plan

Bedroom 14'2" x 11'
Great Room Below
Bath
Bedroom 13' x 11'2"
Balcony
WOOD RAIL
Foyer Below
Bedroom 11'6" x 12'1"
Bath

Main Level Floor Plan

Copyright by designer/architect.

Porch
Master Bedroom 15' x 13'1"
Breakfast 11'5" x 11'3"
Office 8'3" x 5'2"
Great Room 18'4" x 18'10"
Bath
Laun. 8'3" X 9'6"
Kitchen 13'7" x 12'1"
Dressing
Dining Room 11'6" x 14'6"
Foyer
Two-Car Garage 21' x 24'
Porch
58'-0"
57'-8'"

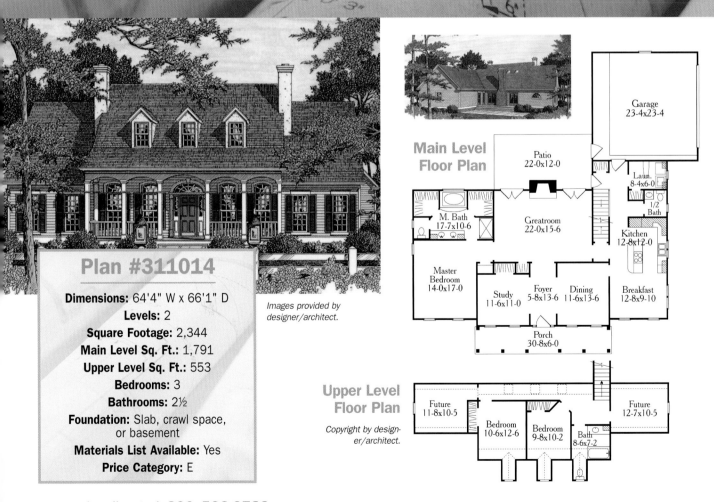

Plan #311014

Dimensions: 64'4" W x 66'1" D

Levels: 2

Square Footage: 2,344

Main Level Sq. Ft.: 1,791

Upper Level Sq. Ft.: 553

Bedrooms: 3

Bathrooms: 2½

Foundation: Slab, crawl space,
or basement

Materials List Available: Yes

Price Category: E

Images provided by designer/architect.

Main Level Floor Plan

Garage 23-4x23-4
Patio 22-0x12-0
Laun. 8-4x6-0
1/2 Bath
M. Bath 17-7x10-6
Greatroom 22-0x15-6
Kitchen 12-8x12-0
Master Bedroom 14-0x17-0
Study 11-6x11-0
Foyer 5-8x13-6
Dining 11-6x13-6
Breakfast 12-8x9-10
Porch 30-8x6-0

Upper Level Floor Plan

Copyright by designer/architect.

Future 11-8x10-5
Bedroom 10-6x12-6
Bedroom 9-8x10-2
Bath 8-6x7-2
Future 12-7x10-5

Plan #271064

Dimensions: 76' W x 54' D

Levels: 2

Square Footage: 2,864

Main Level Sq. Ft.: 1,610

Upper Level Sq. Ft.: 1,254

Bedrooms: 4

Bathrooms: 2½

Foundation: Daylight basement

Materials List Available: No

Price Category: E

Images provided by designer/architect.

Main Level Floor Plan

Upper Level Floor Plan

Copyright by designer/architect.

Plan #391043

Dimensions: 48' W x 36' D

Levels: 2

Square Footage: 2,143

Main Level Sq. Ft.: 1,086

Upper Level Sq. Ft.: 1,057

Bedrooms: 4

Bathrooms: 2½

Foundation: Basement, crawl space, slab

Materials List Available: Yes

Price Category: D

Images provided by designer/architect.

Main Level Floor Plan

First Floor

Upper Level Floor Plan

Copyright by designer/architect.

Main Level Floor Plan

Plan #151015

Dimensions: 72'4" W x 48'4" D

Levels: 2

Square Footage: 2,789

Main Level Sq. Ft.: 1,977

Upper Level Sq. Ft.: 812

Bedrooms: 4

Bathrooms: 3

Foundation: Basement, crawl space, or slab

CompleteCost List Available: Yes

Price Category: F

Images provided by designer/architect.

Upper Level Floor Plan

Copyright by designer/architect.

Plan #151025

Dimensions: 71' W x 55' D

Levels: 2

Square Footage: 3,914

Main Level Sq. Ft.: 2,291

Upper Level Sq. Ft.: 1,623

Bedrooms: 3

Bathrooms: 3

Foundation: Crawl space or slab; basement or walk out for fee

CompleteCost List Available: Yes

Price Category: H

Images provided by designer/architect.

Main Level Floor Plan

Upper Level Floor Plan

Copyright by designer/architect.

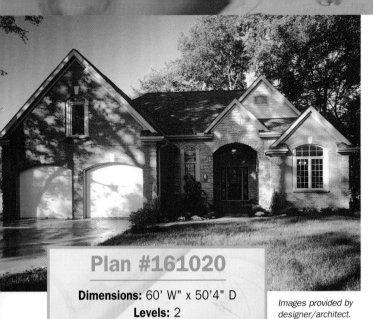

Upper Level Floor Plan

Bedroom 11'1" x 13'3"
Bedroom 11'5" x 12'0"
Bath
bookshelves
computer desk
Balcony
Foyer Below
Bonus Room 11'0" x 22'0"

Master Bedroom 13'6" x 15'1"
Bath
Bath
Great Room 17'4" x 21'2"
Dining Room 10'10" x 14'0"
walk-in closet
Laun.
hanging space
Kitchen 12'4" x 11'6"
Foyer
Breakfast 11' x 9'4"
Two-car Garage 22'9" x 22'0"

Main Level Floor Plan

60'

50'4"

Images provided by designer/architect.

Copyright by design-

Plan #161020

Dimensions: 60' W" x 50'4" D
Levels: 2
Square Footage: 2,082; 2,349 with bonus space
Main Level Sq. Ft.: 1,524
Upper Level Sq. Ft.: 558
Bedrooms: 3
Bathrooms: 2
Foundation: Basement
Materials List Available: Yes
Price Category: D

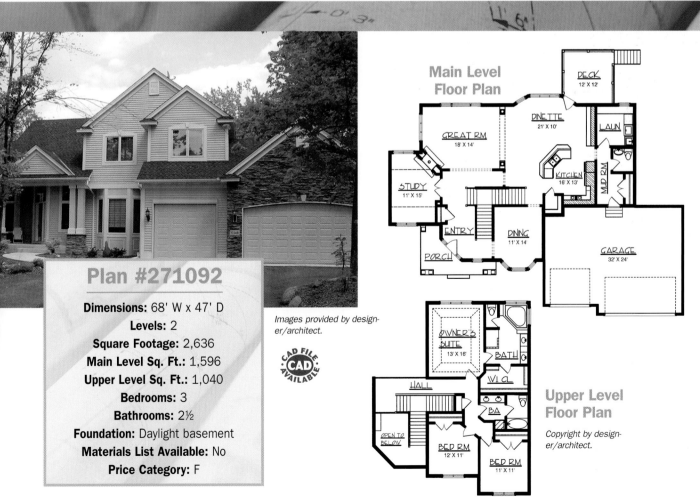

Main Level Floor Plan

DECK 12' X 12'
GREAT RM 18' X 14'
DINETTE 21' X 10'
LAUN
STUDY 11' X 15'
KITCHEN 16' X 13'
MUD RM
ENTRY
DINING 11' X 14'
GARAGE 32' X 24'
PORCH

OWNER'S SUITE 13' X 16'
BATH
HALL
W.I.CL
BA
OPEN TO BELOW
BED RM 12' X 11'
BED RM 11' X 11'

Upper Level Floor Plan

Images provided by designer/architect.

Copyright by designer/architect.

Plan #271092

Dimensions: 68' W x 47' D
Levels: 2
Square Footage: 2,636
Main Level Sq. Ft.: 1,596
Upper Level Sq. Ft.: 1,040
Bedrooms: 3
Bathrooms: 2½
Foundation: Daylight basement
Materials List Available: No
Price Category: F

Plan #211108

Dimensions: 66' W x 66' D
Levels: 2
Square Footage: 2,954
First Level Sq. Ft.: 1,984
Second Level Sq. Ft.: 970
Bedrooms: 4
Bathrooms: 3½
Foundation: Slab, crawl space, or basement
Materials List Available: Yes
Price Category: F

This home is designed with the feel of a European cottage and will nestle nicely in any neighborhood.

Features:

- Ceiling Height: 8 ft.

- Living Room: This formal living room offers plenty of space for all kinds of entertaining and family activities.

- Eating Area: This eating area adjacent to the kitchen is the perfect spot for informal family meals, with its panoramic view of an intimate private courtyard through a graceful Palladian-style window.

- Family Room: Relax with the family in this cozy family room, which opens to the rear covered porch and the formal living room and dining room via pairs of French doors.

- Wet Bar: This small wet bar is conveniently located between the kitchen and the family room.

- Master Suite: Retreat to this master suite, which features a gracious bath and a small sitting area.

Illustration provided by designer/architect.

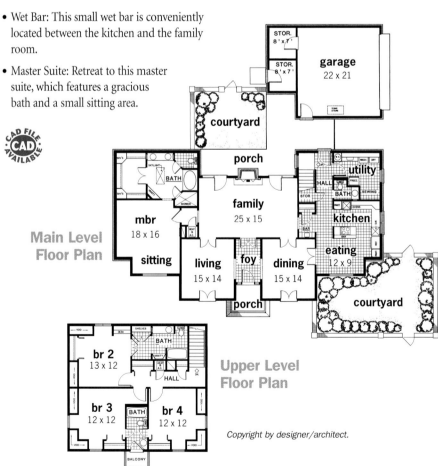

Main Level Floor Plan

Upper Level Floor Plan

Copyright by designer/architect.

Plan #281001

Dimensions: 54' W x 47' D
Levels: 2
Square Footage: 2,423
Main Level Sq. Ft.: 1,388
Second Level Sq. Ft.: 1,035
Bedrooms: 3
Bathrooms: 2½
Foundation: Basement
Materials List Available: Yes
Price Category: E

This stately manor appears larger than it is and is filled with amenities for comfortable living.

Features:

- Ceiling Height: 8 ft. unless otherwise noted.
- Foyer: The grand entrance porch leads into this spacious two-story foyer, with an open staircase and architecturally interesting angles.

- Balcony: This second story has a balcony that overlooks the foyer.
- Living Room: This delightful living room seems even more spacious, thanks to its sloped vaulted ceiling.
- Dining Room: This elegant dining room shares the living room's sloped vaulted ceiling.
- Kitchen: This beautiful kitchen will be a real pleasure in which to cook. You'll love lingering over morning coffee in the breakfast nook, which is located on the sunny full-bayed wall.
- Family Room: Relax in this roomy family room, with its 9-ft. ceiling.

Photo and Illustration provided by designer/architect.

Main Level Floor Plan

Upper Level Floor Plan

Copyright by designer/architect.

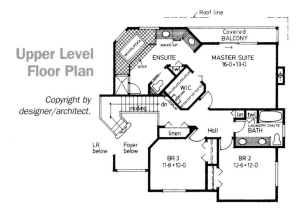

Flooring

Selecting a flooring material is one of the most important decisions you will make when decorating a room. The right material can enhance the color scheme and the overall look of the room, and flooring provides a unique tactile component to the design.

If you are are acting as your own designer, one of the first things you should do is learn about the various types of flooring—from wood to stone to vinyl—on today's market. The choices are myriad and innovations in technology have widened the range of finishes.

Choices in Wood

In bygone eras, a wood floor was simply one that was created by laying wide wood planks side by side. Later, as the milling of lumber improved, homeowners were able to choose narrower planks that look more refined than rustic. Parquet floors were created by woodcrafters with a flair for the dramatic and an appreciation of the artistic richness of wood grains set in nonlinear patterns.

Today's manufacturers have made it possible to have it all. The wood floor, factory- or custom-stained to suit a particular style or mood in a room, is still a traditional favorite. It's readily available in strips of 1 to 2¼ inches wide, or in country-style planks of 3 to 8 inches wide. The formal, sophisticated look of a parquet floor is unparalleled for richness of visual texture.

Types of Wood Flooring

Wood varieties available as a surface material are vast, and cost varies widely, depending on the type and grade of wood and on the choice of design.

Softwoods, like pine and fir, are often used to make simple tongue-and-groove floorboards. These floors are less expensive than hardwoods but also less durable. The hardwoods—maple, birch, oak, ash—are far less likely to mar with normal use. A hardwood floor is not indestructible; however, it will stand up to demanding use.

Both hardwoods and softwoods are graded according to their color, grain, and imperfections. The top of the line is known as clear, followed by select, No. 1 common, and No. 2 common. In addition to budget considerations, the decision whether to pay top dollar for clear wood or to economize with a lesser grade depends on use factors and on the design objectives. For example, if you plan to install a wood floor in a small room and then cover most of it with an area rug, the No. 2 common grade may be a good choice; lesser grades are also fine for informal rooms where a few defects just enhance a lived-in look. If your design calls for larger areas of rich wood grain that will be exposed, with scatter rugs used for color accents, a clear or select grade will make an attractive choice.

Finishing Options

Color stains—reds, blues, and greens—may work in settings where a casual or rustic feeling is desired. This, however, is a departure from the traditional use of

Wood flooring, below, fits well in both formal and informal spaces.

Laminate flooring, opposite, can mimic the look of real wood or natural stone.

Laminate Flooring

Laminate flooring is the great pretender among flooring materials. When your creative side tells you to install wood but your practical side knows it just won't hold up in the traffic-heavy location for which you're considering it, a wood floor look-alike might be just the thing. Faux wood and faux stone laminate floors provide you with the look you want, tempered with physical wear and care properties that you and your family can live with. Laminate is particularly suited to rooms where floors are likely to see heavy duty—kitchens, family rooms, hallways, and children's bedrooms and playrooms—anywhere stain and scratch resistance and easy cleanup count. Prolonged exposure to moisture will damage some laminate products, but many can now be used in wet areas. Manufacturers of laminate offer warranties against staining, scratching, cracking, and peeling for up to 25 years.

Laminate is made from paper impregnated with melamine, an organic resin, and bonded to a core of particleboard, fiberboard, or other wood by-products. It can be laid over virtually any subflooring surface, including wood and concrete. It can also be applied on top of an existing wood, ceramic, or vinyl tile, as well as vinyl or other sheet flooring. You can even install it over certain types of carpeting, but check the manufacturer's guidelines before doing so.

Installation and Care

The installation of laminate flooring is a reasonably quick and relatively easy do-it-yourself project. It requires sheets of a special foam underlayment followed by the careful placement, cutting, and gluing of the laminate.

Laminate is available in sheets that are ideal when your design calls for a uniform look, such as monotone stone, or a linear design that mimics strip or plank wood flooring. Laminate planks, squares, and blocks offer added design flexibility: with them, you can design your own tile patterns, lay strips of wood-look planks with alternating "stain" finishes, or border your floor with a contrasting color.

wood. Wood is not typically used to deliver color impact; instead it blends with and subtly enhances its surroundings. Natural wood stains range from light ash tones to deep, coffee-like colors. Generally, lighter stains make a room feel less formal, and darker, richer stains suggest a stately atmosphere. As with lighter colors, lighter stains create a feeling of openness; darker stains foster a more intimate feeling and can reduce the visual vastness of a large space.

Installation

If the design plan calls for the laying of unfinished wood strips, factor the cost of hiring a skilled professional into your budget. Many manufacturers offer products with installation kits that make wood flooring a do-it-yourself option for those whose skills are good but don't necessarily approach a professional carpenter's level. Some make strips or planks already finished and sealed. Most parquet tiles come finished and sealed as well.

Vinyl Sheet & Tile Flooring

Like laminate, resilient flooring is also available in design-friendly sheet or tile form. Resilient floors can be made from a variety of materials, including linoleum, asphalt, cork, or rubber. However, the most commonly used material in manufacturing today's resilient floors for homes is vinyl.

Price, durability, and easy maintenance make resilient flooring an attractive and popular choice. Do-it-yourself installation, an option even for those who are not particularly skilled, can mean further savings.

Sheet versus Tiles

Resilient flooring comes in an enormous array of colors and patterns, plus many of the flooring styles have a textured surface. With the tiles, you can combine color and pattern in limitless ways. Even the sheet form of resilient flooring can be customized with inlay strips.

Cushioned sheet vinyl offers the most resilience. It provides excellent stain resistance; it's comfortable and quiet underfoot and easy to maintain, with no-wax and never-wax finishes often available. These features make the floor especially attractive for areas with lots of kid traffic. Beware though: only the more expensive grades show an acceptable degree of resistance to nicking and denting. In rooms where furniture is often moved around, this could be a problem. Although the range of colors, patterns, and surface textures is wide, sheet floor-

Vinyl sheet flooring, left, is a good choice for high-traffic areas, such as kitchens, family rooms, and playrooms. Most products have a no-wax finish that is easy to maintain.

Vinyl flooring, above, comes in a variety of styles and colors. Tiles and sheet flooring can look like ceramic tiles and natural stone.

Ceramic tile, opposite, offers a number of possibilities—from simple patterns to more elaborate designs that feature borders and inlays.

ing is not as flexible as vinyl tile when it comes to customizing your look.

Regular sheet vinyl is less expensive than the cushioned types, but it carries the same disadvantages and is slightly less resilient. Except for the availability of no-wax finishes, a vinyl tile floor is as stain resistant and as easy to maintain as the sheet-vinyl products. Increased design possibilities are the trade-off.

Here, as with other flooring materials, one possible way out of the choice maze is to take the unconventional step of mixing flooring materials. For example, use a durable cushioned sheet vinyl in more trafficked areas, but frame it with a pretty vinyl tile or laminate border.

Ceramic Choices

Ceramic tile—actually fired clay—is an excellent choice for areas subject to a lot of traffic and in rooms where resistance to moisture and stains is needed. These features, combined with easy cleanup, have made ceramic tile a centuries-old tradition for flooring, walls, and ceilings in bathrooms and kitchens. Color, texture, and pattern choices available today make ceramic tile the most versatile flooring option in terms of design possibilities.

Tile Options

Some handcrafted ceramic tiles are very costly, but manufacturers have created a market full of design and style options.

Tiles come in a variety of sizes, beginning with 1-inch-square mosaic tiles up to large 16 x 16-inch squares. Other shapes, such as triangles, diamonds, and rectangles, are also available. Tile textures range from shiny to matte-finished and from glass-smooth to ripple-surfaced. Tiles are available either glazed or unglazed. Glazed tiles have a hard, often colored, surface that is applied during the firing process; the resulting finish can range from glossy to matte. Unglazed tiles, such as terra-cotta or quarry tiles, have a matte finish, are porous, and need to be sealed to prevent staining.

Consider using accent borders to create unique designs, such as a faux area rug, that visually separate sections of a room or separate one room from another. When added in a random pattern, embossed accent tiles add interest, variety, and elegance to an expanse of single-colored tiles.

Alas, no surfacing material is perfect. Ceramic tile offers long-lasting beauty, design versatility, and simplicity of maintenance, but it also has some hard-to-live-with features. Tile is cold underfoot, noisy when someone walks across it in hard-soled shoes, and not at all resilient—always expect the worst when something breakable falls on a tile floor. If you have infants and toddlers around, it may be best to wait a few years for your tiled floor.

Natural Stone

Like ceramic tile, stone and marble are classified as "non-resilients." Like tile, these materials offer richness of color, durability, moisture and stain resistance, and ease of maintenance. They also share with tile the drawbacks of being cold to the touch, noisy to walk on, and unforgivingly hard.

Stone and marble floors are clearly, unmistakably natural. As remarkably good as some faux surfaces look, no product manufactured today actually matches the rustic irregularity and random color variation of natural stone.

Picking a Flooring Material

Now that you've got the facts about each floor surface option, picking the right one for your design will be much less confusing. The following steps can make it downright simple.

Step 1: Make a "Use/Abuse" Analysis. Begin by asking yourself the most important question: How will this room used? Your answer should tell you just what kind of traffic the future floor surface will endure. With a relatively expensive investment like a floor, it's best not to guess. Instead, use this system to arrive at an accurate use/abuse analysis.

On a piece of paper, make columns headed "Who" and "Activities," and then list who in the family will use the room and what activities will occur there. Will the kids play with toys on the floor? Will they do arts and crafts projects with paint, glue, and glitter? Will the family gather on Saturday afternoons and snack while watching a football game on television? Is it a formal living room where you will entertain your friends and business clients? Is it a busy kitchen? Does the hallway extend from your front entrance or from a busier back door where the kids will drop off their hockey skates?

The answers to these questions will help you to determine how durable and resilient a flooring surface needs to be, whether warmth and softness are requirements, and how much maintenance will be necessary to keep the surface clean.

Step 2: Determine Your Design Objectives. Your choices are limited by the other elements in the room. Your color choices can enhance the color palette you are planning. Because you will be starting from scratch—including walls, furniture, and accessories—you have more flexibility, although your job is a bit more complex and involves more decisions.

Once you've determined your design objectives, compare your use/abuse analysis

High-traffic areas, below left, require flooring that can stand up to abuse.

Laminate flooring, below right, is a good choice for a variety of rooms.

to the types of flooring that meet both your style and use needs. From the list of options that are left, you can narrow down your choices even more.

Step 3: Draw and Use a Floor Plan.

After you have completed the use/abuse analysis and the list of design objectives, draw up a floor plan—a separate one for experimenting with your flooring ideas. Follow these guidelines: measure the length and width of the room, and plot it on graph paper, using a scale of 1 inch to 1 foot. If your room is larger than 8 x 10 feet, you can tape two pieces of 8½- x 11-inch graph paper together. Measure and mark the locations of entryways and any permanent features in the room, such as cabinets, fixtures, or appliances.

Make several photocopies of your floor plan. Reserve one copy as a template. Use the other copies for previewing pattern ideas for flooring that comes in tiles (ceramic, vinyl, or carpeting tiles). Buy multicolored pencils, and fill in your grid. You'll be able to determine not only how the pattern will look but also how many tiles of various colors you'll need to buy to complete the project. Don't forget to include such items as borders and inlays.

Step 4: Convert Your Overall Budget to Cost per Square Foot.

After you've completed the use/abuse analysis, determined your design objectives, and created a floor plan, the next step is determining cost.

Most flooring is priced in terms of square feet. To determine how many square feet are in your room, round the measurements up to the next foot. Then simply multiply the length by the width. For example, for a room measuring 10 feet 4 inches x 12 feet 6 inches, round the figures to 11 x 13 feet. Multiply 11 x 13 feet (that's 143 square feet). You will end up with extra flooring, but it is better to have more than less.

Some flooring—like carpeting—is priced in terms of square yards. To determine the number of square yards in your room, divide the number of square feet by nine. In our example, there are just under 16 square yards in 143 square feet.

Let's say you have a budget of $850 to purchase tile for your 10-foot-4-inch x 12-foot-6-inch room. For the sake of the illustration, let's assume your subflooring is adequate, you have the tools, and the cost of adhesive and grout for your room is about $75. That leaves you with $775. To determine how much you can spend per tile, divide the remainder by the number of square feet in the room. In our example, $775 divided by 143 square feet equals about $5.40 per square foot of tile.

Light colors, below left, make a room feel more open than darker colors.

Consider the rest of the room, below, when selecting flooring.

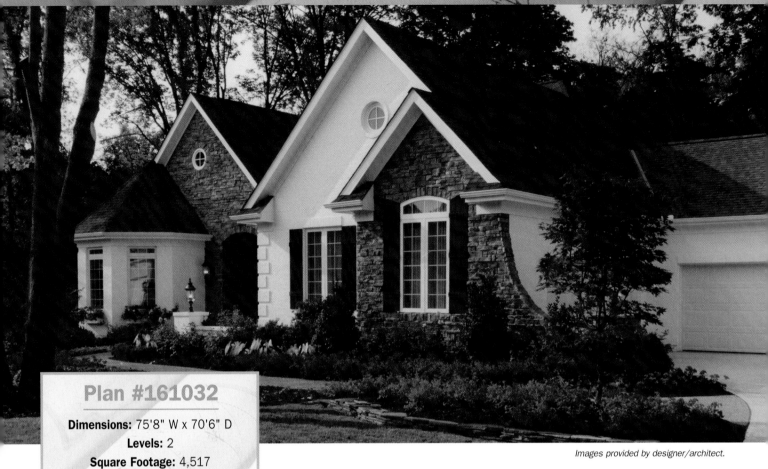

Plan #161032

Dimensions: 75'8" W x 70'6" D
Levels: 2
Square Footage: 4,517
Main Level Sq. Ft.: 2,562
Finished Lower Level Sq. Ft.: 1,955
Bedrooms: 3
Full Baths: 2
Half Baths: 3
Foundation: Basement
Materials List Available: Yes
Price Category: I

SMARTtip

Art Underfoot

Make a simple geometric pattern with your flooring materials. Create a focal point in a courtyard or a small area of a patio by fashioning an intricate mosaic with tile, stone, or colored concrete. By combining elements and colors, a simple garden room floor becomes a wonderful work of art. Whether you commission a craftsman or do it yourself, you'll have a permanent art installation right in your own backyard.

Images provided by designer/architect.

The brick-and-stone exterior, a recessed entry, and a tower containing a large library combine to convey the strength and character of this enchanting house.

Features:

- Hearth Room: Your family or guests will enjoy this large, comfortable hearth room, which has a gas fireplace and access to the rear deck, perfect for friendly gatherings.

- Kitchen: This spacious kitchen features a walk-in pantry and a center island.

- Master Suite: Designed for privacy, this master suite includes a sloped ceiling and opens to the rear deck. It also features a deluxe whirlpool bath, walk-in shower, separate his and her vanities, and a walk-in closet.

- Lower Level: This lower level includes a separate wine room, exercise room, sauna, two bedrooms, and enough space for a huge recreation room.

Rear View

Main Level
Floor Plan

Deck

Deck

Hearth Room
19'10" x 17'7"
10' ceiling height

Master Bedroom
15'4" x 18'9"

Breakfast
11'7" x 9'6"
irregular

9' ceiling height

stairs down

Great Room
17'9" x 17'10"
11' ceiling height

Kitchen
15'5" x 13'10"
irregular

Dressing

Bath

Laun.

Garage
13'8" x 20'

walk-in closet

Pantry

Library
13' x 14'7"

Foyer

Dining Room
12' x 15'

Porch

Two Car Garage
23' x 30'6"

Basement Level
Floor Plan

Bedroom
15' x 12'

Rec. Room
15' x 17'2"

stairs up

Bath

walk-in closet

cabinets

Rec. Room
34'5" x 19'6"

Bedroom
16'6" x 13'

Bath

walk-in closet

Wine Room

Sauna

Exercise Room
9'7" x 15'3"

Unexcavated

Basement

Unexcavated

Copyright by designer/architect.

Rear Elevation

Kitchen

Kitchen

Living Room

Plan #661066

Dimensions: 52' W x 36'8" D
Levels: 2
Square Footage: 1,995
Main Level Sq. Ft.: 1,073
Upper Level Sq. Ft.: 922
Bedrooms: 4
Bathrooms: 2½
Foundation: Slab
Materials List Available: No
Price Category: D

Illustration provided by designer/architect.

Main Level Floor Plan

Upper Level Floor Plan

Copyright by designer/architect.

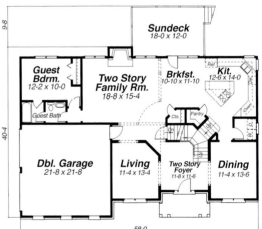

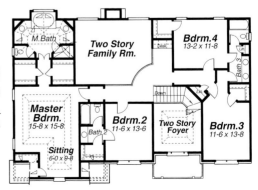

Plan #141020

Dimensions: 58' W x 40'4" D
Levels: 2
Square Footage: 3,140
Main Level Sq. Ft.: 1,553
Upper Level Sq. Ft.: 1,587
Bedrooms: 5
Bathrooms: 4½
Foundation: Basement
Materials List Available: Yes
Price Category: G

Illustration provided by designer/architect.

Main Level Floor Plan

Upper Level Floor Plan

Copyright by designer/architect.

Plan #151121

Dimensions: 66'8" W x 60'4" D
Levels: 2
Square Footage: 3,108
Main Level Sq. Ft.: 2,107
Upper Level Sq. Ft.: 1,001
Bedrooms: 3
Bathrooms: 2½
Foundation: Crawl space, slab
(basement option for fee)
CompleteCost List Available: Yes
Price Category: G

Illustration provided by designer/architect.

This home, as shown in the photograph, may differ from the actual blueprints. For more detailed information, please check the floor plans carefully.

Upper Level Floor Plan

Main Level Floor Plan

Copyright by designer/architect.

Plan #231030

Dimensions: 76' W x 81' D
Levels: 3
Square Footage: 4,200
Finished Basement Sq. Ft.: 377
Main Level Sq. Ft.: 2,120
Upper Level Sq. Ft.: 1,520
Third Floor Sq. Ft.: 183
Bedrooms: 5
Bathrooms: 4 full, 2 half
Foundation: Slab, crawl space, or basement
Materials List Available: No
Price Category: I

Illustration provided by designer/architect.

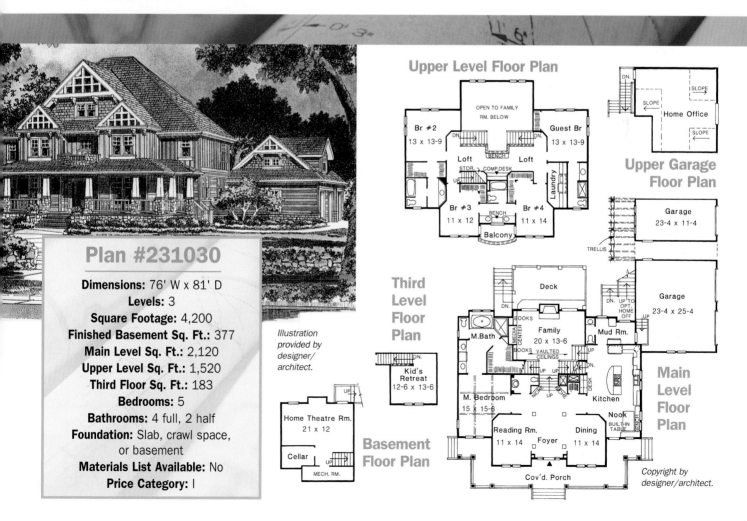

Upper Level Floor Plan

Upper Garage Floor Plan

Third Level Floor Plan

Basement Floor Plan

Main Level Floor Plan

Copyright by designer/architect.

Plan #331005

Dimensions: 85'11" W x 55'7" D

Levels: 2

Square Footage: 3,585

Main Level Sq. Ft.: 2,691

Upper Level Sq. Ft.: 894

Bedrooms: 4

Bathrooms: 3½

Foundation: Basement, crawl space, or slab

Materials List Available: No

Price Category: H

Images provided by designer/architect.

Features:

- Foyer: The highlight of this spacious area is the curved stairway to the balcony overhead.

- Family Room: The two-story ceiling and second-floor balcony overlooking this room add to its spacious feeling, but you can decorate around the fireplace to create a cozy, intimate area.

- Study: Use this versatile room as a guest room, home office or media room.

- Kitchen: Designed for the modern cook, this kitchen features a step-saving design, an island for added work space, and ample storage space.

- Master Suite: Step out to the rear deck from the bedroom to admire the moonlit scenery or bask in the morning sun. The luxurious bath makes an ideal place to relax in privacy.

You'll love the stately, traditional exterior design and the contemporary, casual interior layout as they are combined in this elegant home.

Rear View

Copyright by designer/architect.

Main Level Floor Plan

Upper Level Floor Plan

Plan #391002

Dimensions: 76'4" W x 45'10" D
Levels: 2
Square Footage: 2,281
Bedrooms: 3
Bathrooms: 2½
Foundation: Crawl space, slab, basement
Materials List Available: Yes
Price Category: E

The luxurious amenities in this compact, well designed home are sure to delight everyone in the family.

Features:

- Ceiling Height: 9-ft. ceilings add to the spacious feeling created by the open design.

- Family Room: A vaulted ceiling and large window area add elegance to this comfortable room, which will be the heart of this home.

- Dining Area: Adjoining the kitchen, this room features a large bayed area as well as French doors that open onto the back deck.

- Kitchen: This step-saving design will make cooking a joy for everyone in the family.

- Utility Room: Near the kitchen, this room includes cabinets and shelves for extra storage space.

- Master Suite: A triple window, tray ceiling, walk-in closet, and luxurious bath make this area a treat.

Images provided by designer/architect.

Main Level Floor Plan

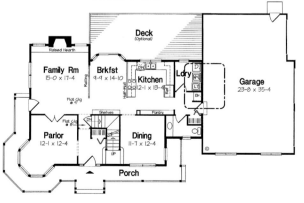

Upper Level Floor Plan

Copyright by designer/architect.

Plan #131031

Dimensions: 69'8" W x 48'4" D
Levels: 2
Square Footage: 4,027
Main Level Sq. Ft.: 2,198
Upper Level Sq. Ft.: 1,829
Bedrooms: 5
Bathrooms: 4½
Foundation: Crawl space, basement
Materials List Available: Yes
Price Category: I

Photos provided by designer/architect.

If you love dramatic lines and contemporary design, you'll be thrilled by this lovely home.

Features:

- Foyer: A gorgeous vaulted ceiling sets the stage for a curved staircase flanked by a formal living room and dining room.

- Living Room: The foyer ceiling continues in this room, giving it an unusual presence.

- Family Room: This sunken family room features a fireplace and a wall of windows that look out to the backyard. It's open to the living room, making it an ideal spot for entertaining.

- Kitchen: With a large island, this kitchen flows into the breakfast room.

- Master Suite: The luxurious bedroom has a dramatic tray ceiling and includes two-walk-in closets. The dressing room is fitted with a sink, and the spa bath is sumptuous.

Foyer

Breakfast Area

Main Level Floor Plan

SL GL DRS

9' CLG
MAID'S RM
10'-0"×
12'-8"

CL

KITCHEN BKFST RM
10'-0"×
19'-4"

9' CLG
SUNKEN
FAMILY RM
24'-0"× 19'-4"

9'-7" CLG

LOW WALL

BATH

LAUN RM

ISLAND

10'-8"×
17'-4"

FREZ

CL

DN

DN

CL

PANT

BUT'L PANT

LAV

DN

9' CLG
LIVING RM
17'-8"× 19'-8"

THREE CAR GARAGE
20'-0"× 30'-0"

DINING RM
16'-0"× 14'-0"

9' CLG

FOYER

CL

CL

PORCH

Butler's Pantry

Upper Level Floor Plan

Copyright by designer/architect.

BEDRM #2
12'-0"×
15'-0"

13'-0"
CEIL

WICL WICL

10'-8" HIGH
TRAY CEIL
MSTR BEDRM
21'-0"× 19'-4"

ATTIC

BATH

MSTR BATH

DRESSING

WICL

WICL

ATTIC

CL

BALC.

UPPER
LIVING RM
CEILING

BEDRM #3
13'-8"× 15'-0"

LIN

WICL

BATH

11'-6" HIGH
VAULTED
BEDRM #4
16'-0"×
13'-8"

UPPER
FOYER
CEILING

Kitchen

Master Bedroom

Master Bathroom

Plan #181079

Dimensions: 60' W x 47'8" D
Levels: 2
Square Footage: 3,016
Main Level Sq. Ft.: 1,716
Upper Level Sq. Ft.: 1,300
Bedrooms: 6
Bathrooms: 4½
Foundation: Crawl space
Materials List Available: Yes
Price Category: G

Images provided by designer/architect.

CAD FILE AVAILABLE

Main Level Floor Plan

Upper Level Floor Plan

Copyright by designer/architect.

Plan #371003

Dimensions: 61' W x 57'4" D
Levels: 2
Square Footage: 2,297
Main Level Sq. Ft.: 1,752
Upper Level Sq. Ft.: 545
Bedrooms: 3
Bathrooms: 3
Foundation: Slab
(crawl space option for fee)
Materials List Available: No
Price Category: E

Images provided by designer/architect.

CAD FILE AVAILABLE

Main Level Floor Plan

Upper Level Floor Plan

Copyright by designer/architect.

Plan #211125

Dimensions: 94' W x 92' D

Levels: 2

Square Footage: 4,440

Main Level Sq. Ft.: 3,465

Upper Level Sq. Ft.: 975

Bedrooms: 4

Bathrooms: 5½

Foundation: Crawl space

Materials List Available: Yes

Price Category: I

Images provided by designer/architect.

CAD FILE AVAILABLE · CAD

Main Level Floor Plan

porch 40 x 10

family 23 x 20

books / books+ / books

built in entertainment center and library

mbr 20 x 16

kit & den 35 x 17

util

wet bar

gallery

clo / clo

sto

phone niche

bar

dining 18 x 12

study 18 x 12

foy

br 2 13 x 12

clo / lin

golf cart & sto 18 x 17

garage 22 x 22

work bench

Upper Level Floor Plan

DOWN

open to lower level

future space 36 x 12

library

attic

br 3 18 x 12

br 4 18 x 12

open to lower level

books / desk / desk / books

Bonus Area Floor Plan

Copyright by designer/architect.

Plan #661056

Dimensions: 38' W x 53'6" D

Levels: 2

Square Footage: 1,879

Main Level Sq. Ft.: 1,230

Upper Level Sq. Ft.: 649

Bedrooms: 4

Bathrooms: 2½

Foundation: Slab

Materials List Available: No

Price Category: D

Illustration provided by designer/architect.

Main Level Floor Plan

Covered Patio

Living Room volume ceiling 13' · 18'

Master Bedroom 13' · 14'

Dining vaulted ceiling 10' · 12'

storage

Bath

w.i.c.

Foyer

Utility

niche

Kitchen vaulted ceiling

Entry

Breakfast volume ceiling

Double Garage

opt. door

Upper Level Floor Plan

Copyright by designer/architect.

Open To Below

Loft 13' · 11'

half wall

Balcony

shelves

half wall

Bedroom 2 10' · 11'

plant shelf

w.i.c.

Bath

Bedroom 3 12' · 11'

Plan #131025

Dimensions: 62'4" W x 65'10" D
Levels: 1½
Square Footage: 3,204
Main Level Sq. Ft.: 2,196
Upper Level Sq. Ft.: 1,008
Bedrooms: 4
Bathrooms: 4
Foundation: Basement, crawl space, or slab
Materials List Available: Yes
Price Category: H

Photo provided by designer/architect.

You'll appreciate the flowing layout that's designed for entertaining but also suits an active family.

Features:

- Ceiling Height: 8 ft.
- Great Room: Decorative columns serve as the entryway to the great room that's made for entertaining. A fireplace makes it warm in winter; built-in shelves give a classic appearance; and the serving counter it shares with the kitchen is both practical and attractive.
- Kitchen: A door into the backyard makes outdoor entertaining easy, and the full bathroom near the door adds convenience.
- Master Suite: Enjoy the sunny sitting area that's a feature of this suite. A tray ceiling adds character to the room, and a huge walk-in closet is easy to organize. The bathroom features a corner spa tub.
- Bedrooms: Each of the additional 3 bedrooms is bright and cheery.

Main Level Floor Plan

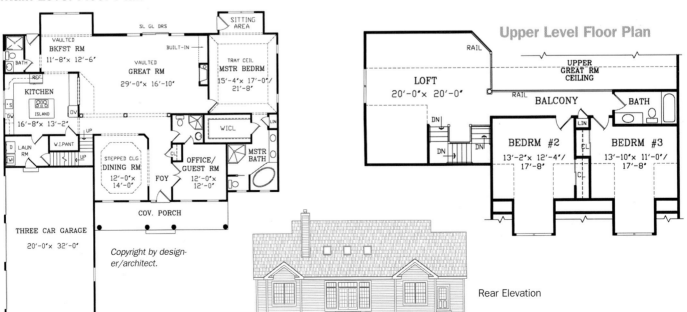

Copyright by designer/architect.

Upper Level Floor Plan

Rear Elevation

Plan #121026

Dimensions: 66'8" W x 76' D
Levels: 2
Square Footage: 3,926
Main Level Sq. Ft.: 2,351
Upper Level Sq. Ft.: 1,575
Bedrooms: 4
Bathrooms: 3 full, 2 half
Foundation: Basement
Materials List Available: Yes
Price Category: H

Photo provided by designer/architect.

Plenty of space and architectural detail make this a comfortable and gracious home.

Features:

- Ceiling Height: 8 ft. unless otherwise noted.

- Great Room: A soaring cathedral ceiling makes this great room seem even more spacious than it is, while the fireplace framed by windows lends warmth and comfort.

- Eating Area: There's a dining room for more formal entertaining, but this informal eating area to the left of the great room will get plenty

of daily use. It features a built-in desk for compiling shopping lists and recipes and access to the backyard.

- Kitchen: Next door to the eating area, this kitchen is designed to make food preparation a pleasure. It features a center cooktop, a recycling area, and a corner pantry.

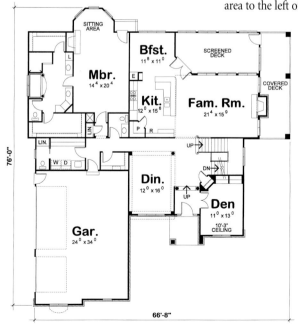

Main Level Floor Plan

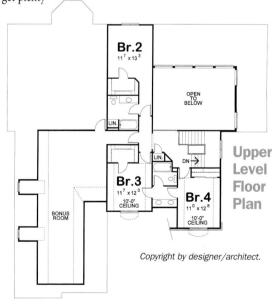

Upper Level Floor Plan

Copyright by designer/architect.

Plan #481035

Dimensions: 99' W x 64' D
Levels: 2
Square Footage: 3,204
Main Level Sq. Ft.: 1,701
Upper Level Sq. Ft.: 1,503
Bedrooms: 3
Full Bathrooms: 2½
Foundation: Walk-out basement
Materials List Available: No
Price Category: G

Distinctive design details set this home apart from others in the neighborhood.

Features:

•Foyer: This large foyer welcomes you home and provides a view through the home and into the family room. The adjoining study can double as a home office.

•Family Room: This two-story gathering space features a fireplace flanked by built-in cabinets. The full-height windows on the rear wall allow natural light to flood the space.

•Kitchen: This island kitchen flows into the nearby family room, allowing mingling between both spaces when friends or family are visiting. The adjacent dinette is available for daily meals.

•Master Suite: This private retreat waits for you to arrive home. The tray ceiling in the sleeping area adds elegant style to the area.

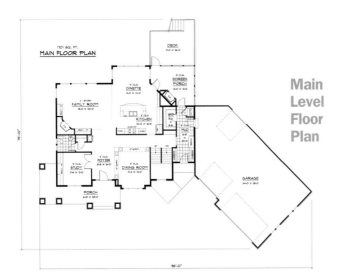

Main Level Floor Plan

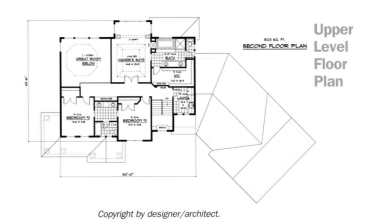

Upper Level Floor Plan

Great Room

Kitchen

Office

Interior

Plan #291013

Dimensions: 72' W x 75' D
Levels: 2
Square Footage: 3,553
Main Level Sq. Ft.: 1,830
Upper Level Sq. Ft.: 1,723
Bedrooms: 4
Bathrooms: 2½
Foundation: Basement
Materials List Available: No
Price Category: H

Illustrations provided by designer/architect.

Copyright by designer/architect.

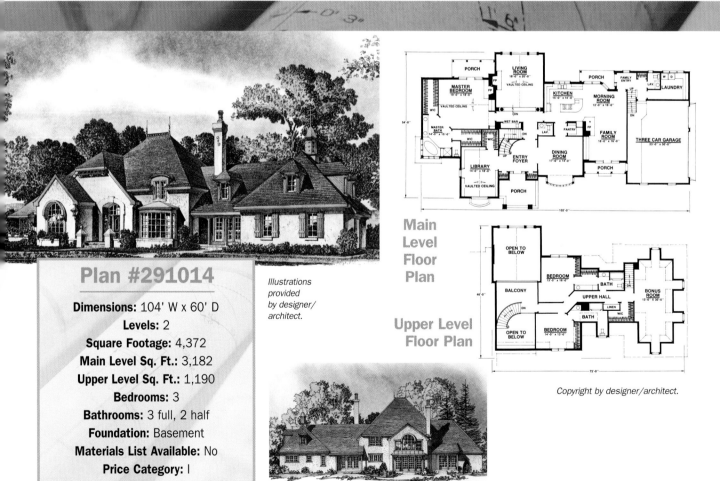

Plan #291014

Dimensions: 104' W x 60' D
Levels: 2
Square Footage: 4,372
Main Level Sq. Ft.: 3,182
Upper Level Sq. Ft.: 1,190
Bedrooms: 3
Bathrooms: 3 full, 2 half
Foundation: Basement
Materials List Available: No
Price Category: I

Illustrations provided by designer/ architect.

Copyright by designer/architect.

Illustration provided by designer/architect.

Plan #611048

Dimensions: 55' W x 60' D
Levels: 2
Square Footage: 4,073
Main Level Sq. Ft.: 2,291
Upper Level Sq. Ft.: 1,782
Bedrooms: 4
Bathrooms: 4½
Foundation: Slab
Materials List Available: No
Price Category: I

Upper Level Floor Plan

Copyright by designer/architect.

Main Level Floor Plan

Illustration provided by designer/architect.

Plan #271032

Dimensions: 78' W x 40' D
Levels: 2
Square Footage: 3,195
Main Level Sq. Ft.: 1,758
Upper Level Sq. Ft.: 1,437
Bedrooms: 4
Bathrooms: 2½
Foundation: Basement
Materials List Available: No
Price Category: E

Upper Level Floor Plan

Copyright by designer/architect.

Plan #111011

Dimensions: 68' W x 49' D

Levels: 2

Square Footage: 3,292

Main Level Sq. Ft.: 2,862

Upper Level Sq. Ft.: 430

Bedrooms: 4

Bathrooms: 3½

Foundation: Crawl space, slab

Price Category: H

Materials List Available: No

If you're looking for a home where you can create a lovely and memorable lifestyle, this could be it.

Features:

- Ceiling Height: 10 ft.

- Foyer: This large area opens to the dining room and living room.

- Dining Room: You can decorate to enhance the slightly formal feeling of this room or give it a more casual atmosphere.

- Living Room: High ceilings and a fireplace make this room comfortable all year.

- Office: Use this office for a home business or as a place where family members can retreat for quiet time or solitary activities.

- Kitchen: This well-designed area has lots of counter space, an eating bar, and a door to the rear porch from the breakfast area.

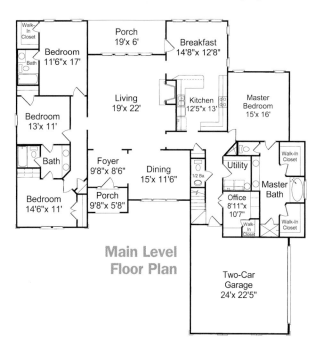

Main Level Floor Plan

Upper Level Floor Plan

Copyright by designer/architect.

Dining Room

Living Room

Rear Elevation

SMARTtip

Lead in Paint

Prior to the 1970s most paint contained lead, which is toxic to humans.

Lead poisoning symptoms include headaches, fatigue, disorientation, and in extreme cases, brain damage. Lead in paint has been banned, but many buildings still contain lead paint. Lead-paint-testing kits are available in many home centers. If you detect lead paint in your home, you should remove it. Because preparation for new painting work involves sanding and scraping, dangerous lead-laced chips and dust can be spread through the air and into your lungs. You should take the following common-sense precautions:

- Use drop cloths to catch paint chips, and then dispose of the chips. Vacuum and damp-mop the floor at the end of each workday.

- Wear a mask designed to filter out lead dust.

- Remove and wash work clothes every day. Shower and change before eating.

Children and fetuses are particularly susceptible to lead poisoning. You should keep children and pregnant women away from the work area until the work is completed. Have your children tested for lead levels, whether or not you are working with lead paint.

Plan #211111

Dimensions: 66' W x 74' D

Levels: 2

Square Footage: 3,035

Main Level Sq. Ft.: 2,008

Upper Level Sq. Ft.: 1,027

Bedrooms: 4

Bathrooms: 3½

Foundation: Crawl space

Materials List Available: Yes

Price Category: G

Kids can be kids without disturbing the adults, thanks to the rear stair in this large family house.

Features:

- Ceiling Height: 9 ft. unless otherwise noted.

- Formal Living Room: This large formal living room is connected to the formal dining room and to the family room by a pair of French doors, making this an ideal home for entertaining.

- Wet Bar: This wet bar is neatly placed between the kitchen and the family room, adding to the entertainment amenities.

- Deck: Step out of the family room onto a covered porch that leads to this spacious deck and a breezeway.

- Master Suite: This master suite is isolated for privacy. The master bath is flooded with natural light from sky windows in the sloped ceiling, and it has a dressing vanity with surrounding mirrors.

- Secondary Bedrooms: All secondary bedrooms have bath access and dual closets.

Illustration provided by designer/architect.

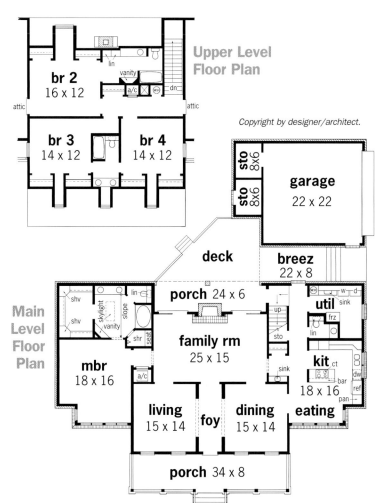

Copyright by designer/architect.

Plan #221025

Dimensions: 69'8" W x 72' D

Levels: 2

Square Footage: 3,009

Main Level Sq. Ft.: 2,039

Upper Level Sq. Ft.: 970

Bedrooms: 4

Bathrooms: 2½

Foundation: Basement

Materials List Available: No

Price Category: G

Illustration provided by designer/architect.

Designed to resemble a country home in France, this two-story beauty will delight you with its good looks and luxurious amenities.

Features:

- **Great Room:** You'll look into this great room as soon as you enter the two-story foyer. A fireplace flanked by built-in bookcases and large windows looking out to the deck highlight this room.

- **Dining Room:** This formal room is located just off the entry for the convenience of your guests.

- **Kitchen:** A huge central island and large pantry make this kitchen a delight for any cook. The large nook looks onto the deck and opens to the lovely three-season porch.

- **Master Suite:** You'll love this suite, with its charming bay shape, great windows, walk-in closet, luxurious bath, and door to the deck.

- **Upper Level:** Everyone will love the two bedrooms, large bath, and huge game.

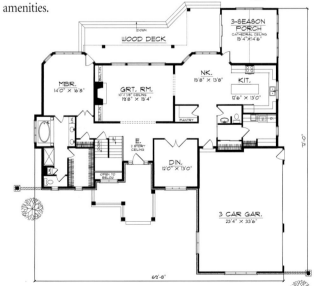

Main Level Floor Plan

Upper Level Floor Plan

Copyright by designer/architect.

Plan #161029

Dimensions: 87' W x 82' D
Levels: 2
Square Footage: 4,470
Main Level Sq. Ft.: 3,300
Upper Level Sq. Ft.: 1,170
Bedrooms: 4
Bathrooms: 3 Full; 2 Half
Foundation: Basement
Materials List Available: Yes
Price Category: I

Images provided by designer/architect.

This gracious home is so impressive—inside and out—that it suits the most discriminating tastes.

Features:

• Foyer: A balcony overlooks this gracious area decorated by tall columns.

• Hearth Room: Visually open to the kitchen and the breakfast area, this room is ideal for any sort of gathering.

• Great Room: Colonial columns also form the entry here, and a magnificent window treatment that includes French doors leads to the terrace.

• Library: Built-in shelving adds practicality to this quiet retreat.

• Kitchen: Spread out on the oversized island with a cooktop and seating.

• Additional Bedrooms: Walk-in closets and private access to a bath define each bedroom.

Main Level Floor Plan

Copyright by designer/architect.

Upper Level Floor Plan

Rear View

Living Room

Living Room/Kitchen

Ideas for Entertaining

Whether an everyday family meal or a big party for 50, make it memorable and fun. With a world of options, it's easier than you think. Be imaginative with food and decoration. Although it is true that great hamburgers and hot dogs will taste good even if served on plain white paper plates, make the meal more fun by following a theme of some sort—color, occasion, or seasonal activity, for example. Be inventive with the basic elements as well as the extraneous touches, such as flowers and lighting. Here are some examples to get you started.

- For an all-American barbecue, set a picnic table with a patchwork quilt having red, white, and blue in it. Use similar colors for the napkins, and perhaps even bandannas. Include a star-studded centerpiece.

- Make a children-size dining set using an old door propped up on crates, and surround it with appropriate-size benches or chairs. Cover the table with brightly colored, easy-to-clean waxed or vinyl-covered fabric.

- If you're planning an elegant dinner party, move your dining room table outside and set it with your best linens, china, silver, and crystal. Add romantic lighting with candles in fabulous candelabras, and set a beautiful but small floral arrangement at each place setting.

- Design a centerpiece showcasing the flowers from your garden. Begin the arrangement with a base of purchased flowers, and fill in with some of your homegrown blooms. That way your flower beds will still be full of blossoms when the guests arrive.

- Base your party theme on the vegetables growing in your yard, and let them be the inspiration for the menu. When your zucchini plants are flowering, wow your family or guests by serving steamed squash blossoms. Or if the vegetables are starting to develop, lightly grill them with other young veggies—they have a much more delicate flavor than mature vegetables do.

- During berry season, host an elegant berry brunch. Serve mixed-berry crepes on your prettiest plates.

Plan #161045

Dimensions: 57' W x 49'8" D

Levels: 2

Square Footage: 2,077

Main Level Sq. Ft.: 1,532

Upper Level Sq. Ft.: 545

Bedrooms: 3

Bathrooms: 2½

Foundation: Basement; crawl space for fee

Materials List Available: Yes

Price Category: D

Images provided by designer/architect.

Multiple gables, arched windows, and the stone accents that adorn the exterior of this lovely two-story home create a dramatic first impression.

Features:

- **Great Room:** With multiple windows to light your way, grand openings, varied ceiling treatments, and angled walls let you flow from room to room. Enjoy the warmth of a gas fireplace in both this great room and the dining area.

- **Master Suite:** Experience the luxurious atmosphere of this master suite, with its coffered ceiling and deluxe bath.

- **Additional Bedrooms:** Angled stairs lead to a balcony with writing desk and to two additional bedrooms.

- **Porch:** Exit two sets of French doors to the rear yard and a covered porch, perfect for relaxing in comfortable weather.

Copyright by designer/architect.

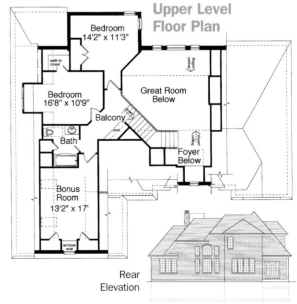

Plan #261001

Dimensions: 77'8" W x 49' D

Levels: 2

Square Footage: 3,746

Main Level Sq. Ft.: 1,965

Upper Level Sq. Ft.: 1,781

Bedrooms: 4

Bathrooms: 3½

Foundation: Basement

Materials List Available: No

Price Category: H

If contemporary designs appeal to you, you're sure to love this stunning home.

Features:

- **Foyer:** A volume ceiling here announces the spaciousness of this gracious home.

- **Family Room:** Also with a volume ceiling, this great room features a fireplace where you can create a cozy sitting area.

- **Kitchen:** Designed for the pleasure of the family cooks, this room features a large pantry, ample counter and cabinet space, and a dining bar.

- **Dinette:** Serve the family in style, or host casual, informal dinners for friends in this dinette with its gracious volume ceiling.

- **Master Suite:** A fireplace makes this suite a welcome retreat on cool nights, but even in warm weather you'll love its spaciousness and the walk-in closet. The bath features dual vanities, a whirlpool tub, and a separate shower.

Images provided by designer/architect.

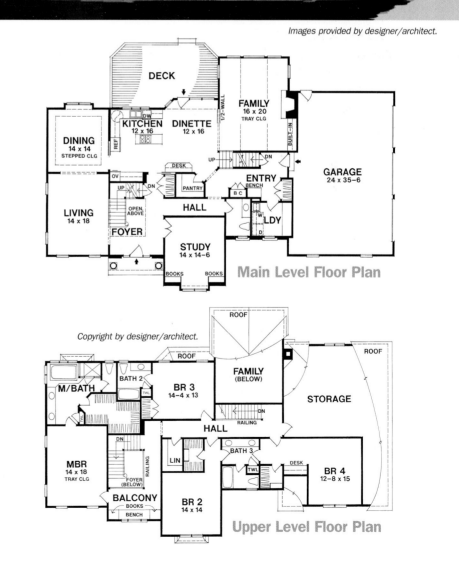

Copyright by designer/architect.

Main Level Floor Plan

Upper Level Floor Plan

Plan #151031

Dimensions: 60'2" W x 60'2" D
Levels: 2
Square Footage: 3,130
Main Level Sq. Ft.: 1,600
Upper Level Sq. Ft.: 1,530
Bedrooms: 3
Bathrooms: 3½
Foundation: Crawl space, slab
CompleteCost List Available: Yes
Price Category: F

If you love traditional Southern plantation homes, you'll want this house with its wraparound porches that are graced with boxed columns.

Features:

- Great Room: Use the gas fireplace for warmth in this comfortable room, which is open to the kitchen.

- Living Room: 8-in. columns add formality as you enter this living and dining room.

- Kitchen: You'll love the island bar with a sink. An elevator here can take you to the other floors.

- Master Suite: A gas fireplace warms this area, and the bath is luxurious.

- Bedrooms: Each has a private bath and built-in bookshelves for easy organizing.

- Optional Features: Choose a 2,559-sq.-ft. basement and add a kitchen to it, or finish the 1,744-sq.-ft. bonus room and add a spiral staircase and a bath.

Main Level Floor Plan

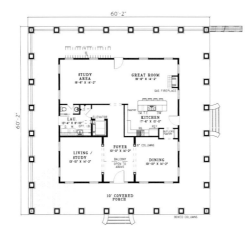

Upper Level Floor Plan

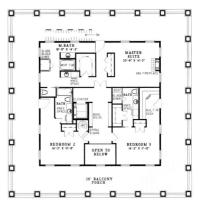

Basement Level Floor Plan

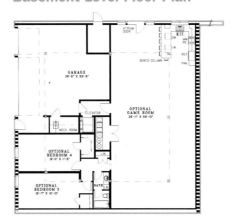

Optional Upper Level Floor Plan

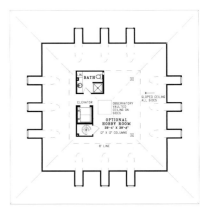

Plan #151020

Dimensions: 96'10" W x 75'10" D
Levels: 2
Square Footage: 4,532
Main Level Sq. Ft.: 3,732
Upper Level Sq. Ft.: 800
Bedrooms: 3
Bathrooms: 3
Foundation: Crawl space or slab;
optional full basement plan available
for extra fee
CompleteCost List Available: Yes
Price Category: I

From the arched entry to the lanai and exercise
and game rooms, this elegant home is a delight.

CAD FILE AVAILABLE

Photos provided by designer/architect.

Features:

• **Foyer:** This spacious foyer with 12-ft. ceilings sets an open-air feeling for this home.

• **Hearth Room:** This cozy hearth room shares a 3-sided fireplace with the breakfast room. French doors open to the rear lanai.

• **Dining Room:** Entertain in this majestic dining room, with its arched entry and 12-ft. ceilings.

• **Master Suite:** This stunning suite includes a sitting room and access to the lanai. The bath

features two walk-in closets, a step-up whirlpool tub with 8-in. columns, and glass-block shower.

• **Upper Level:** You'll find an exercise room, a game room, and attic storage space upstairs.

Rear View

Main Level Floor Plan

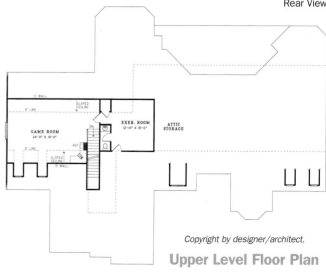

Copyright by designer/architect.

Upper Level Floor Plan

Plan #161036

Dimensions: 74'10" W x 65' D
Levels: 2
Square Footage: 3,664
Main Level Sq. Ft.: 2,497
Upper Level Sq. Ft.: 1,167
Bedrooms: 4
Bathrooms: 2½
Foundation: Basement
Materials List Available: No
Price Category: H

Images provided by designer/architect.

The traditional European brick-and-stone facade on the exterior of this comfortable home will thrill you and make your guests feel welcome.

Features:

- **Pub:** The beamed ceiling lends a casual feeling to this pub and informal dining area between the kitchen and the great room.
- **Dining Room:** Columns set off this formal dining room, from which you can see the fireplace in the expansive great room.
- **Library:** Close to the master suite, this room lends itself to quiet reading or work.
- **Master Suite:** The ceiling treatment makes the bedroom luxurious, while the whirlpool tub, double-bowl vanity, and large walk-in closet make the bath a pleasure.
- **Upper Level:** Each of the three bedrooms features a large closet and easy access to a convenient bathroom.

Main Level Floor Plan

Upper Level Floor Plan

Copyright by designer/architect.

Rear Elevation

Left Elevation

Right Elevation

Kitchen

Dining Room

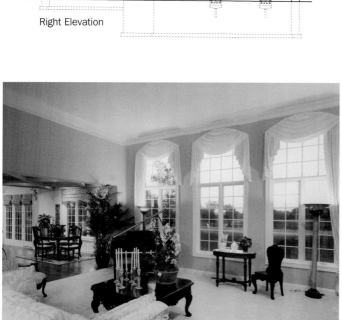

Living Room

Living Room

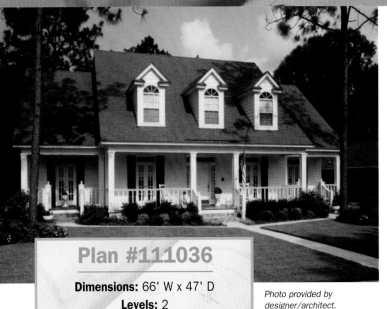

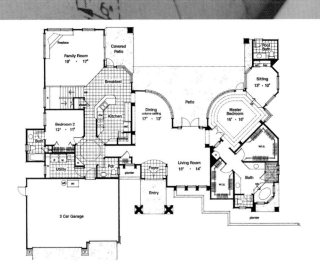

Main Level Floor Plan

Plan #111036

Dimensions: 66' W x 47' D
Levels: 2
Square Footage: 3,149
Main Level Sq. Ft.: 2,033
Upper Level Sq. Ft.: 1,116
Bedrooms: 4
Bathrooms: 3½
Foundation: Pier
Materials List Available: No
Price Category: H

Photo provided by designer/architect.

Upper Level Floor Plan

Copyright by designer/architect.

Plan #661205

Dimensions: 82'4" W x 70' D
Levels: 2
Square Footage: 3,200
Main Level Sq. Ft.: 2,531
Upper Level Sq. Ft.: 669
Bedrooms: 4
Bathrooms: 3 full, 2 half
Foundation: Slab
Materials List Available: No
Price Category: G

Photo provided by designer/architect.

Main Level Floor Plan

Upper Level Floor Plan

Copyright by designer/architect.

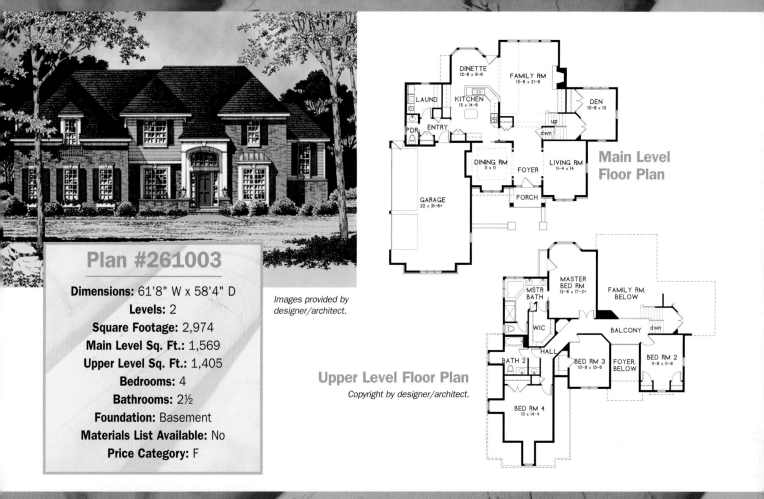

Plan #261003

Dimensions: 61'8" W x 58'4" D

Levels: 2

Square Footage: 2,974

Main Level Sq. Ft.: 1,569

Upper Level Sq. Ft.: 1,405

Bedrooms: 4

Bathrooms: 2½

Foundation: Basement

Materials List Available: No

Price Category: F

Images provided by designer/architect.

Main Level Floor Plan

Upper Level Floor Plan

Copyright by designer/architect.

Plan #261008

Dimensions: 68'W x 64'6" D

Levels: 2

Square Footage: 2,226

Main Level Sq. Ft.: 1,689

Upper Level Sq. Ft.: 537

Bedrooms: 4

Bathrooms: 3

Foundation: Basement

Materials List Available: No

Price Category: E

Images provided by designer/architect.

Main Level Floor Plan

Upper Level Floor Plan

Copyright by designer/architect.

Plan #211074

Dimensions: 64' W x 89' D
Levels: 2
Square Footage: 3,486
Main Level Sq. Ft.: 2,575
Upper Level Sq. Ft.: 911
Bedrooms: 4
Bathrooms: 3
Foundation: Crawl space
Materials List Available: Yes
Price Category: G

Photo provided by designer/architect.

This plantation-style home may have an old-fashioned charm, but the energy-efficient design and many amenities inside make it thoroughly contemporary.

Features:

- Ceiling Height: 9 ft.
- Porches: This wraparound front porch is fully 10 ft. wide, so you can group rockers, occasional tables, and even a swing here and save the rear porch for grilling and alfresco dining.

- Entry: A two-story ceiling here sets an elegant tone for the rest of the home.
- Living Room: Somewhat isolated, this room is an ideal spot for quiet entertaining. It has built-in bookshelves and a nearby wet bar.
- Kitchen: You'll love the large counter areas and roomy storage space in this lovely kitchen, where both friends and family are sure to congregate.
- Master Suite: It's easy to pamper yourself in this comfortable bedroom and luxurious bath.

Main Level Floor Plan

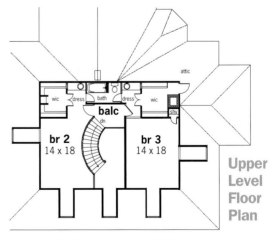

Upper Level Floor Plan

Copyright by designer/architect.

Plan #121061

Dimensions: 56' W x 52' D
Levels: 2
Square Footage: 3,025
Main Level Sq. Ft.: 1,583
Upper Level Sq. Ft.: 1,442
Bedrooms: 4
Bathrooms: 3½
Foundation: Basement
Materials List Available: Yes
Price Category: G

This large home with a contemporary feeling is ideal for the family looking for comfort and amenities.

Features:

• **Entry:** Stacked windows bring sunlight into this two-story entry, with its stylish curved staircase.

• **Library:** French doors off the entry lead to this room, with its built-in bookcases flanking a large, picturesque window.

• **Family Room:** Located in the rear of the home, this family room is sunken to set it apart. A spider-beamed ceiling gives it a contemporary feeling, and a bay window, wet bar, and pass-through fireplace add to this impression.

• **Kitchen:** The island in this kitchen makes working here a pleasure. The corner pantry joins a breakfast area and hearth room to this space.

Main Level Floor Plan

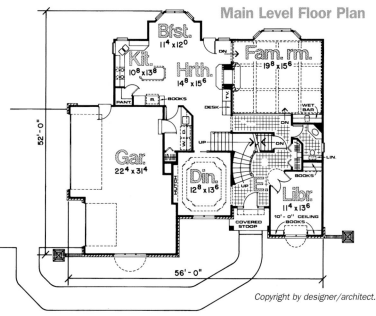

Copyright by designer/architect.

Upper Level Floor Plan

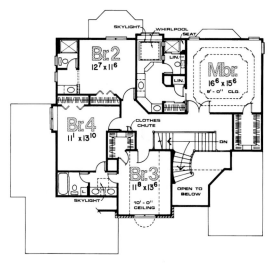

Plan #161035

Dimensions: 75' W x 64'11" D
Levels: 2
Square Footage: 3,688
Main Level Sq. Ft.: 2,702
Upper Level Sq. Ft.: 986
Bedrooms: 4
Bathrooms: 3½
Foundation: Basement
Materials List Available: No
Price Category: H

Images provided by designer/architect.

You'll appreciate the style of the stone, brick, and cedar shake exterior of this contemporary home.

Features:

• Hearth Room: Positioned for an easy flow for guests and family, this hearth room features a bank of windows that integrate it with the yard.

• Breakfast Room: Move through the sliding doors here to the rear porch on sunny days.

• Kitchen: Outfitted for a gourmet cook, this kitchen is also ideal for friends and family who can perch at the island or serve themselves at the bar.

• Master Suite: A stepped ceiling, crown moldings, and boxed window make the bedroom easy to decorate, while the two walk-in closets, lavish dressing area, and whirlpool tub in the bath make this area comfortable and luxurious.

Main Level Floor Plan

Upper Level Floor Plan

Copyright by designer/architect.

Left Elevation

Right Elevation

Kitchen

SMARTtip

How to Arrange Seating Around Your Fireplace

When the TV is near or on the same wall as the fireplace, you can arrange seating that places you at the best advantage to enjoy both. Position sofas and chairs in front of the fire, and remember that the distance between you and the TV should be at least three times the size of the screen.

Dining Room

Living Room

Master Bathroom

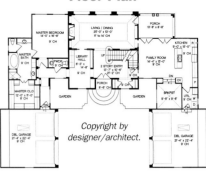

Main Level Floor Plan

Rear Elevation

This home, as shown in the photograph, may differ from the actual blueprints. For more detailed information, please check the floor plans carefully.

Photo provided by designer/architect.

Plan #121049

Dimensions: 82' W x 60'8" D

Levels: 2

Square Footage: 3,335

Main Level Sq. Ft.: 2,054

Upper Level Sq. Ft.: 1,281

Bedrooms: 4

Bathrooms: 3½

Foundation: Slab

Materials List Available: Yes

Price Category: G

Copyright by designer/architect.

Upper Level Floor Plan

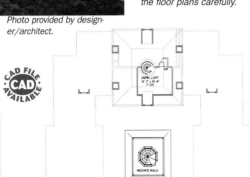

CAD FILE AVAILABLE

Plan #611126

Dimensions: 61'11" W x 59'2" D

Levels: 2

Square Footage: 2,543

Main Level Sq. Ft.: 2,098

Upper Level Sq. Ft.: 445

Bedrooms: 4

Bathrooms: 3

Foundation: Slab

Materials List Available: No

Price Category: E

Photo provided by designer/architect.

CAD FILE AVAILABLE

Main Level Floor Plan

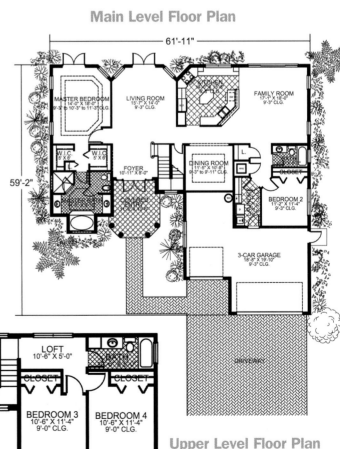

Upper Level Floor Plan

Copyright by designer/architect.

Plan #611044

Dimensions: 54'9" W x 74'9" D
Levels: 2
Square Footage: 3,715
Main Level Sq. Ft.: 3,026
Upper Level Sq. Ft.: 689
Bedrooms: 4
Bathrooms: 3½
Foundation: Slab
Materials List Available: No
Price Category: H

Photo provided by designer/architect.

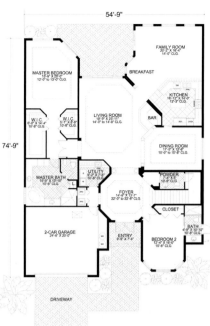

Main Level Floor Plan

Upper Level Floor Plan

Copyright by designer/architect.

Plan #111039

Dimensions: 59' W x 64' D
Levels: 2
Square Footage: 3,335
Main Level Sq. Ft.: 2,129
Upper Level Sq. Ft.: 1,206
Bedrooms: 4
Bathrooms: 4
Foundation: Basement
Materials List Available: No
Price Category: H

Photo provided by designer/architect.

Main Level Floor Plan

Copyright by designer/architect.

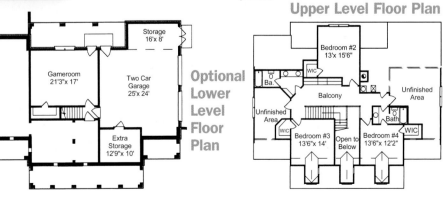

Optional Lower Level Floor Plan

Upper Level Floor Plan

Plan #121076

Dimensions: 64' W x 60'8" D
Levels: 2
Square Footage: 3,067
Main Level Sq. Ft.: 2,169
Upper Level Sq. Ft.: 898
Bedrooms: 4
Bathrooms: 2½
Foundation: Basement
Materials List Available: Yes
Price Category: G

You'll love the combination of formal features and casual, family-friendly areas in this spacious home with an elegant exterior.

Features:

- **Entry:** The elegant windows in this two-story area are complemented by the unusual staircase.
- **Family Room:** This family room features an 11-ft. ceiling, wet bar, fireplace, and trio of windows that look out to the covered porch.

- **Living Room:** Columns set off both this room and the dining room. Decorate to accentuate their formality, or make them blend into a more casual atmosphere.
- **Master Suite:** Columns in this suite highlight a bayed sitting room where you'll be happy to relax at the end of the day or on weekend mornings.
- **Bedrooms:** Bedroom 2 has a private bath, making it an ideal guest room, and you'll find private vanities in bedrooms 3 and 4.

Main Level Floor Plan

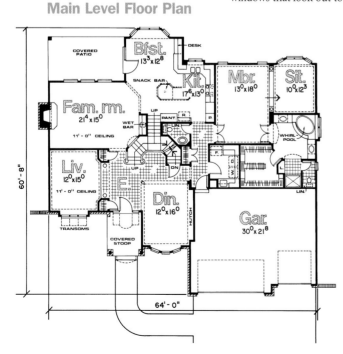

Upper Level Floor Plan

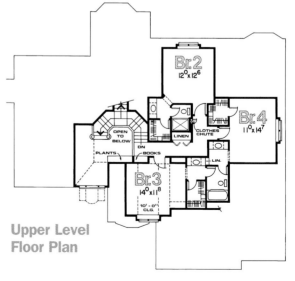

Copyright by designer/architect.

Plan #121081

Dimensions: 76'8" W x 68' D
Levels: 2
Square Footage: 3,623
Main Level Sq. Ft.: 2,603
Upper Level Sq. Ft.: 1,020
Bedrooms: 4
Bathrooms: 4½
Foundation: Basement
Materials List Available: Yes
Price Category: G

You'll love this impressive home if you're looking for perfect spot for entertaining as well as a home for comfortable family living.

Features:

- Entry: Walk into this grand two-story entryway through double doors, and be greeted by the sight of a graceful curved staircase.

- Great Room: This two-story room features stacked windows, a fireplace flanked by an entertainment center, a bookcase, and a wet bar.

- Dining Room: A corner column adds formality to this room, which is just off the entryway for the convenience of your guests.

- Hearth Room: Connected to the great room by a lovely set of French doors, this room features another fireplace as well as a convenient pantry.

Main Level Floor Plan

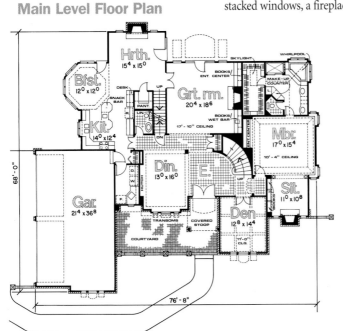

Upper Level Floor Plan

Copyright by designer/architect.

Plan #221023

Dimensions: 90'3" W x 65'8" D
Levels: 2
Square Footage: 3,511
Main Level Sq. Ft.: 1,931
Upper Level Sq. Ft.: 1,580
Bedrooms: 4
Bathrooms: 3½
Foundation: Basement
Materials List Available: No
Price Category: H

Images provided by designer/architect.

The curb appeal of this traditional two-story home, with its brick-and-stucco facade, is well matched by the luxuriousness you'll find inside.

Features:

- Ceiling Height: 9 ft.

- Family Room: This large room is open to the kitchen and the dining nook, making it an ideal spot in which to entertain.

- Living Room: The high ceiling in this room contributes to its somewhat formal feeling, and the fireplace and built-in bookcase allow you to decorate for a classic atmosphere.

- Master Suite: The bedroom in this suite has a luxurious feeling, partially because of the double French doors that are flanked by niches for displaying small art pieces or collectables. The bathroom here is unusually large and features a walk-in closet.

- Upper Level: You'll find four bedrooms, three bathrooms, and a large bonus room to use as a study or play room on this floor.

Main Level Floor Plan

FAM.RM.
22'4" × 17'0"

NK.
VAULT CEILING
11'0" × 10'0"

KIT.
18'8" × 13'6"

LIV.
10'-1 1/8" CEILING
14'4" × 18'6"

DEN
10'-1 1/8" CEILING
11'4" × 19'0"

STOR.

BUTLER'S PANTRY

DIN.
13'0" × 15'0"

E.
2 STORY

3 CAR GAR.
22'0" × 43'4"

90'-3"

65'-8"

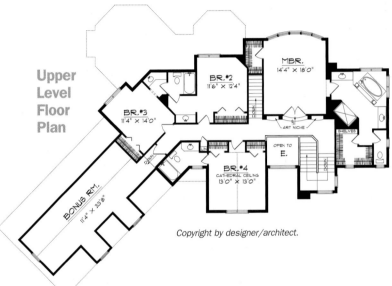

Upper Level Floor Plan

BR.#3
11'4" × 14'0"

BR.#2
11'6" × 12'4"

MBR.
14'4" × 18'0"

ART NICHE

SHELVES

OPEN TO E.

BR.#4
CATHEDRAL CEILING
13'0" × 13'0"

BONUS RM.
11'4" × 39'8"

Copyright by designer/architect.

SMARTtip
Competing Interests- Fireplace, Media Center, and Windows

What should you do if the only place for the television is next to the fireplace? If the TV is small enough to keep on a cart that you can wheel away when the set is not in use, that's ideal. But with cable hookups, VCRs, DVDs, and large-screen TVs, that might be impractical. A cabinet that lets you store the all of this equipment behind closed doors may be the answer, especially if the storage unit is part of a large built-in paneled wall system that incorporates the fireplace into its overall design.

When large windows or glass doors share the wall with a fireplace, easy-to-adjust window treatments are essential: drapery panels on a traverse rod or suspended from rings on a pole, or shutters, shades, or blinds are options that can help with glare when viewing a TV during the daytime. But by all means, make certain your selection allows the sun shine in during the day when appropriate.

Also be aware that a pleasant window view by day just becomes a large dark hole at night. So in the evening, close the curtains while the fire sets the mood, whether you're entertaining or relaxing alone.

Rear Elevation

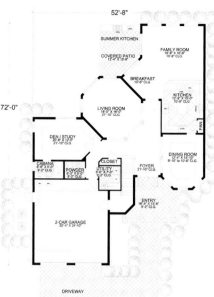

Main Level
Floor Plan

52'-8"

SUMMER KITCHEN

COVERED PATIO
12'-4" CLG.

FAMILY ROOM
18'-6" X 16'-0"
10'-6" CLG.

BREAKFAST
10'-6" CLG.

KITCHEN
12'-8" X 13'-6"
10'-0" CLG.

PAN.

Copyright by designer/architect.

72'-0"

LIVING ROOM
18'-6" X 16'-0"
21'-10" CLG.

DEN / STUDY
20'-6" X 12'-0"
21'-10" CLG.

DINING ROOM
12'-4" X 15'-10"
9'-10" to 10'-6" CLG.

CABANA
9'-2" CLG.

POWDER
6'-2" CLG.

UTILITY
6'-6" X 8'-0"
8'-2" CLG.

CLOSET

FOYER
21'-10" CLG.

ENTRY
16'-4" X 13'-6"
9'-2" CLG.

2-CAR GARAGE
22'-4" X 24'-10"

DRIVEWAY

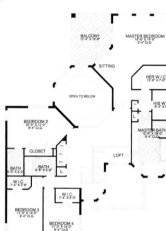

BALCONY
12'-6" X 5'-0"

MASTER BEDROOM
18'-6" X 16'-9"
9'-4" CLG.

SITTING

HER W.I.C.
12'-6" X 7'-0"

OPEN TO BELOW

HIS W.I.C.
6'-4" X 7'-0"

BEDROOM 2
20'-6" X 12'-0"
9'-4" CLG.

CLOSET

BATH
6'-0" X 5'-0"

BATH
9'-6" X 6'-6"

W.I.C.
7'-4" X 5'-0"

LOFT

MASTER BATH
12'-8" X 18'-0"
9'-4" CLG.

W.I.C.
7'-4" X 6'-0"

BEDROOM 3
11'-0" X 14'-0"
9'-4" CLG.

BEDROOM 4
11'-0" X 14'-0"
9'-4" CLG.

Upper Level
Floor Plan

Plan #611045

Dimensions: 52'8" W x 72' D

Levels: 2

Square Footage: 3,869

Main Level Sq. Ft.: 1,863

Upper Level Sq. Ft.: 2,006

Bedrooms: 4

Bathrooms: 3½

Foundation: Slab

Materials List Available: No

Price Category: H

Photos provided by designer/architect.

CAD FILE AVAILABLE

Plan #111035

Dimensions: 68'6" W x 74'7" D

Levels: 2

Square Footage: 3,064

Main Level Sq. Ft.: 2,143

Upper Level Sq. Ft.: 921

Bedrooms: 4

Bathroom: 3½

Foundation: Slab

Materials List Available: No

Price Category: H

Photo provided by designer/architect.

Main Level
Floor Plan

Garage
22'6"x 24'6"

Covered Porch

Master Bedroom
17'2"x 16'4"

Living
22'2"x 18'

Gameroom
13'6"x 15'6"

Bedroom
11'2"x 10'6"

Dining
11'6"x 14'

Breakfast
12'6"x 10'

Upper Level Floor Plan

Copyright by designer/architect.

Bedroom
12'x 11'

Bedroom
11'x 16'

Bedroom
11'x 16'

Open to Below

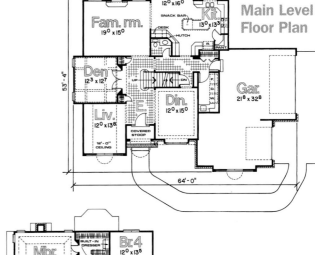

Main Level Floor Plan

Upper Level Floor Plan

Copyright by designer/architect.

Images provided by designer/architect.

Plan #121072

Dimensions: 64' W x 53'4" D
Levels: 2
Square Footage: 3,031
Main Level Sq. Ft.: 1,640
Upper Level Sq. Ft.: 1,391
Bedrooms: 4
Bathrooms: 3½
Foundation: Basement
Materials List Available: Yes
Price Category: G

Main Level Floor Plan

Upper Level Floor Plan

Copyright by designer/architect.

Images provided by designer/architect.

Plan #261006

Dimensions: 73'10" W x 60' D
Levels: 2
Square Footage: 4,583
Main Level Sq. Ft.: 2,575
Upper Level Sq. Ft.: 2,008
Bedrooms: 4
Bathrooms: 3 full, 2 half
Foundation: Basement
Materials List Available: No
Price Category: I

Plan #211076

Dimensions: 95' W x 90' D
Levels: 2
Square Footage: 4,242
Main Level Sq. Ft.: 3,439
Upper Level Sq. Ft.: 803
Bedrooms: 4
Bathrooms: 4 full, 3 half
Foundation: Raised slab
Materials List Available: Yes
Price Category: I

Photos and illustration provided by designer/architect.

Build this country manor home on a large lot with a breathtaking view to complement its beauty.

CAD FILE AVAILABLE

Features:

- Foyer: You'll love the two-story ceiling here.

- Living Room: A sunken floor, two-story ceiling, large fireplace, and generous balcony above combine to create an unusually beautiful room.

- Kitchen: Use the breakfast bar at any time of the day. The layout guarantees ample working space, and the pantry gives room for extra storage.

- Master Suite: A sunken floor, wood-burning fireplace, and 200-sq.-ft. sitting area work in concert to create a restful space.

- Bedrooms: The guest room is on the main floor, and bedrooms 2 and 3, both with built-in desks in special study areas, are on the upper level.

- Outdoor Grilling Area: Fitted with a bar, this area makes it a pleasure to host a large group.

Kitchen

Kitchen

Main Level Floor Plan

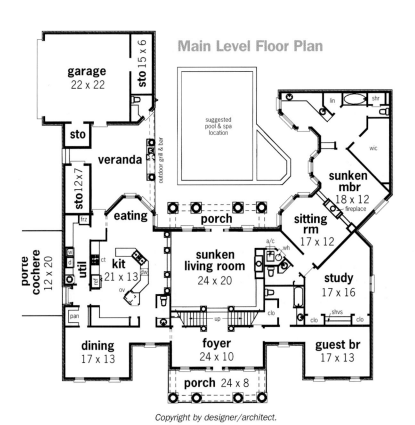

garage 22 x 22

sto 15 x 6

sto

veranda

sto 12 x 7

outdoor grill & bar

suggested pool & spa location

eating

frz

porte cochere 12 x 20

w
d
ct
ref
ov
dw

util

kit 21 x 13

pan

dining 17 x 13

porch

sunken living room 24 x 20

a/c
wh

up
clo

foyer 24 x 10

porch 24 x 8

lin
shr

wic

sunken mbr 18 x 12
fireplace

sitting rm 17 x 12

study 17 x 16

clo
shvs
clo

guest br 17 x 13

Copyright by designer/architect.

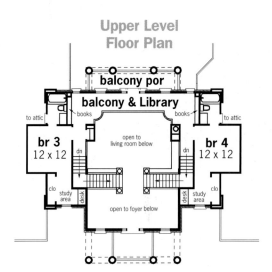

Master Bathroom

Upper Level Floor Plan

balcony por

balcony & Library

to attic
books

open to living room below

books
to attic

br 3 12 x 12

dn

dn

br 4 12 x 12

clo
study area
desk

open to foyer below

desk
study area
clo

Dining Room

Living Room

Plan #211077

Dimensions: 94' W x 68' D
Levels: 2
Square Footage: 5,560
Main Level Sq. Ft.: 4,208
Upper Level Sq. Ft.: 1,352
Bedrooms: 4
Bathrooms: 4 full, 2 half
Foundation: Slab, or crawl space
Materials List Available: No
Price Category: I

This palatial home has a two-story veranda and offers room and amenities for a large family.

Features:

- Ceiling Height: 10 ft.

- Library: Teach your children the importance of quiet reflection in this library, which boasts a full wall of built-in bookshelves.

- Master Suite: Escape the pressures of a busy day in this truly royal master suite. Curl up in front of your own fireplace. Or take a long, soothing soak in the private bath, with his and her sinks and closets.

- Kitchen: This room offers many modern comforts and amenities, and free-flowing traffic patterns.

Photo provided by designer/architect.

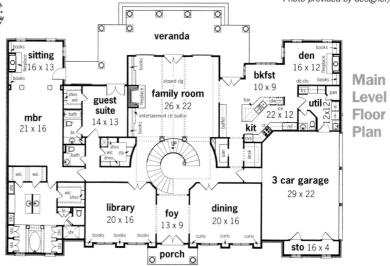

Main Level Floor Plan

Copyright by designer/architect.

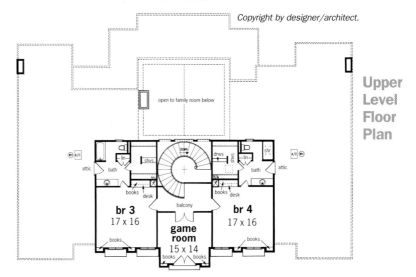

Upper Level Floor Plan

Plan #211075

Dimensions: 80' W x 84' D
Levels: 2
Square Footage: 3,568
Main Level Sq. Ft.: 2,330
Upper Level Sq. Ft.: 1,238
Bedrooms: 4
Bathrooms: 3½
Foundation: Crawl space
Materials List Available: Yes
Price Category: H

Photo provided by designer/architect.

The porte-cochere — or covered passage over a driveway — announces the quality and beauty of this spacious country home.

Features:

- Front Porch: Spot groups of potted plants on this 779-sq.-ft. porch, and add a glider and some rocking chairs to take advantage of its comfort.

- Family Room: Let this family room become the heart of the home. With a fireplace to make it cozy and a wet bar for easy serving, it's a natural for entertaining.

- Game Room: Expect a crowd in this room, no matter what the weather.

- Kitchen: A cooktop island and a pantry are just two features of this fully appointed kitchen.

- Master Suite: The bedroom is as luxurious as you'd expect, but the quarter-circle raised tub in the master bath might surprise you. Two walk-in closets and two vanities add a practical touch.

Main Level Floor Plan

Upper Level Floor Plan

Copyright by designer/architect.

Plan #161033

Dimensions: 78'2" W x 74'6" D
Levels: 2
Square Footage: 3,809
Main Level Sq. Ft.: 2,782
Upper Level Sq. Ft.: 1,027
Optional Basement Sq. Ft.: 1,316
Bedrooms: 4
Bathrooms: 3½
Foundation: Basement
Materials List Available: Yes
Price Category: I

Images provided by designer/architect.

The dramatic design of this home, combined with its comfort and luxuries, suit those with discriminating tastes.

Features:

- Great Room: Let the fireplace and 14-ft. ceilings in this room set the stage for all sorts of gatherings, from causal to formal.

- Dining Room: Adjacent to the great room and kitchen fit for a gourmet, the dining room allows you to entertain with ease.

- Music Room: Give your music the space it deserves in this specially-designed room.

- Library: Use this room as an office, or reserve it for quiet reading and studying.

- Master Suite: You'll love the separate dressing area and walk-in closet in the bedroom.

- Lower Level: A bar and recreational area give even more space for entertaining.

Rear View

Main Level Floor Plan

Copyright by designer/architect.

Patio
22' x 18'

Dining Room
15'3" x 15'3"
9' ceiling ht.

Kitchen
20' x 15'4"

Master
Bedroom
14'6" x 15'4"

Great Room
21'5" x 27'8"
14' ceiling ht.

Library
15'6" x 15'2" irr.

Dressing

Laun.

Hall

Foyer
9' ceiling ht.

Music Room
14'9" x 12'2"
11' ceiling ht.

Porch

Three Car Garage
21' x 28'9"

Upper Level Floor Plan

Bedroom
12'10" x 12'10"

Bedroom
14'4" x 12'

Balcony
10'2" x 6'4"

Bath

Bedroom
17' x 12'

Sitting
Area
8'8" x 11'7"

**Optional Basement
Level Floor Plan**

Media
Room
12'7" x 15'

Billiards
19'6" x 22'3'

Hobby Room
14' x 16'5"

Bar
12' x 11'6"

Bath

Basement

Basement

Unexcavated

Unexcavated

SMARTtip
Color Wheel Combinations

The color wheel is the designer's most useful tool for pairing colors. Basically, it presents the spectrum of pigment hues as a circle. The primary colors (yellow, blue, and red) are combined in the remaining hues (orange, green, and purple). The following are the most often used configurations for creating color schemes.

Dining Room

Living Room

Plan #161023

Dimensions: 71'8" W x 38'10" D
Levels: 2
Square Footage: 3,445
Main Level Sq. Ft.: 1,666
Mid Level Sq. Ft.: 743
Upper Level Sq. Ft.: 1,036
Bedrooms: 4
Bathrooms: 3½
Foundation: Basement
Materials List Available: No
Price Category: G

You'll love the versatility that the mixture of formal and informal spaces gives to this home.

Features:

- Dining Room: Let guests move from the formal dining room into the adjoining cozy hearth room.

- Hearth Room: Also situated close to the kitchen and breakfast room, the hearth room is a true center of this home. The fireplace, wood ceiling, and a recessed entertainment center add charm.

- Mid Level Wing: A computer area and 2 bedrooms highlight this separate space.

- Master Suite: A sitting area, fireplace, and dressing room attached to the master bath make this area a dream come true.

- Guest Room: This area includes a private bath and walk-in closet.

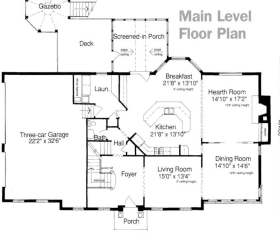

Main Level Floor Plan

Upper Level Floor Plan

Copyright by designer/architect.

Living Room

Kitchen

Dining Room

Plan #151021

Dimensions: 75'2" W x 89'6" D
Levels: 2
Square Footage: 3,385
Main Level Sq. Ft.: 2,633
Upper Level Sq. Ft.: 752
Bedrooms: 4
Bathrooms: 4
Foundation: Crawl space, or slab
CompleteCost List Available: Yes
Price Category: F

From the fireplace in the master suite to the well-equipped game room, the amenities in this home will surprise and delight you.

Features:

• **Great Room:** A bank of windows on the far wall lets sunlight stream into this large room. The fireplace is located across the room and is flanked by the built-in media center and built-in bookshelves. Gracious brick arches create an entry into the breakfast area and kitchen.

• **Breakfast Room:** Move easily between this room with 10-foot ceiling either into the kitchen or onto the rear covered porch.

• **Game Room:** An icemaker and refrigerator make entertaining a snap in this room.

• **Master Suite:** A 10-ft. boxed ceiling, fireplace, and access to the rear porch give romance, while the built-ins in the closet, whirlpool tub with glass blocks, and glass shower give practicality.

Main Level Floor Plan

Upper Level Floor Plan

Copyright by designer/architect.

Color

No other decorating component has more power and greater effect at such little cost than color. It can fill a space and make furnishings look fresh and new. Color can also show off fine architectural details or downplay a room's structural flaws. A particular color can make a cold room cozy, while another hue can cool down a sunny cooker. And color comes cheap, giving a tremendous impact for your decorating dollar: elbow grease, supplies, prep work, and paint will all cost pretty much the same if you choose a gorgeous hue over plain white.

But finding the color—the right color—isn't easy. Where do you begin to look? Like the economy, color has leading indicators. You have a market basket full of choices, and there are lots of signposts to direct you where to go.

The Lay of the Land

For the past 200 years, white has been the most popular choice for American home exteriors. And it still is, followed by tan, brown, and beige. You can play it safe and follow the leader. But you should also think about the architecture of your house and where you live when you're considering exterior color. For example, traditional Colonials have a color-combination range of about two that look appropriate: white with black or green shutters and gray with white trim. Mediterranean-style houses typically pick up the colors of terra-cotta and the tile that are indigenous to the regions that developed the architecture—France, Italy, and Spain. A ranch-style house shouldn't be overdone—it is, after all, usually a modest structure. On the other hand, a cottage can be fanciful. Whimsical colors also look charming on Victorian houses in San Francisco, but they would be out of place in conservative Scarsdale, New York, where you must

check with the local building board even when you want to change the exterior color of your house.

How's the Weather?

Like exteriors, interiors often take their color cues from their environs and local traditions. In the rainy and often chilly Pacific Northwest, cozy blanket plaids in strong reds and black abound. In the hot-and-arid climate of the West, indigo or brown ticking-stripes and faded denim look appropriately casual and cool. Subtle grays and neutrals, reflecting steel, limestone, and concrete, look apropos for sophisticated city life. In extremely warm southern climates, the brilliant sun tends to overpower lighter colors. That explains the popularity of strong hues in tropical, sun-drenched locales.

Natural Light. That's the one you don't pay for. Its direction and intensity greatly affects color. A room with a window that faces trees will look markedly different in summer, when warm white sunlight is filtered through the leaves, than in winter, when the trees are bare and the color of natural light takes on a cool blue cast. Time of day affects color, too. Yellow walls that are pleasant and cheerful in the early morning can be stifling and blinding in the afternoon. That's because afternoon

The yellow-colored wall, above, complements the antique painted dresser.

Warm neutral-color walls, opposite, and touches of red make this bedroom cozy.

sun is stronger than morning sun.

When you're choosing a color for an interior, always view it at different times of day, but especially during the hours in which you will inhabit the room.

Artificial Light. Because artificial light affects color rendition as much as natural light, don't judge a color in the typically chilly fluorescence of a hardware store. The very same color chip will look completely different when you bring it home, which is why it's so important to test out a paint color in your own home. Most fluorescent light is bluish and distorts colors. It depresses red and exaggerates green, for example. A romantic faded rose on your dining room walls will just wash out in the kitchen if your use a fluorescent light there. Incandescent light, the type produced by the standard bulbs you probably use in your chandelier and in most of your home's light fixtures, is warm but slightly yellow. Halogen light, which comes from another newer type of incandescent bulb, is white and the closest to natural sunlight. Of all three types of bulbs, halogen is truest in rendering color.

red

RED is powerful, dramatic, motivating. Red is also hospitable, and it stimulates the appetite, which makes it a favorite choice for dining rooms. Some studies have indicated that a red room actually makes people feel warmer.

order direct: 1-800-523-6789

yellow

YELLOW illuminates the colors it surrounds. It warms rooms that receive northern light but can be too bright in a sunny room. It's best for daytime rooms, not bedrooms. It has a short range, which means as white is added to yellow, it disappears. Yellow highlights and calls attention to features—think of bright taxicabs.

green

GREEN is tranquil, nurturing, rejuvenating. It is a psychological primary, and because it is mixed from yellow and blue, it can appear both warm and cool. Time seems to pass more quickly in green rooms. Perhaps that's why waiting rooms off-stage are called "green rooms."

neutrals

GRAY goes with all colors—it is a good neighbor. Various tones of gray range from dark charcoal to pale oyster.

BLACK (technically the absence of color) enhances and brightens other colors, making for livelier decorating schemes when used as an accent.

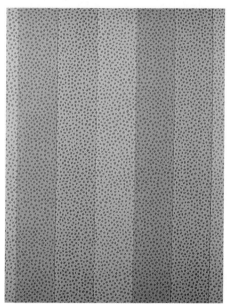

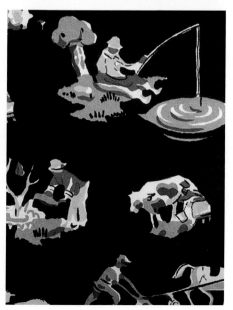

 **pink**

PINK is perceived as outgoing and active. It's also a color that flatters skin tones. Hot shades are invigorating, while soft, toned-down versions can be relaxed and charming.

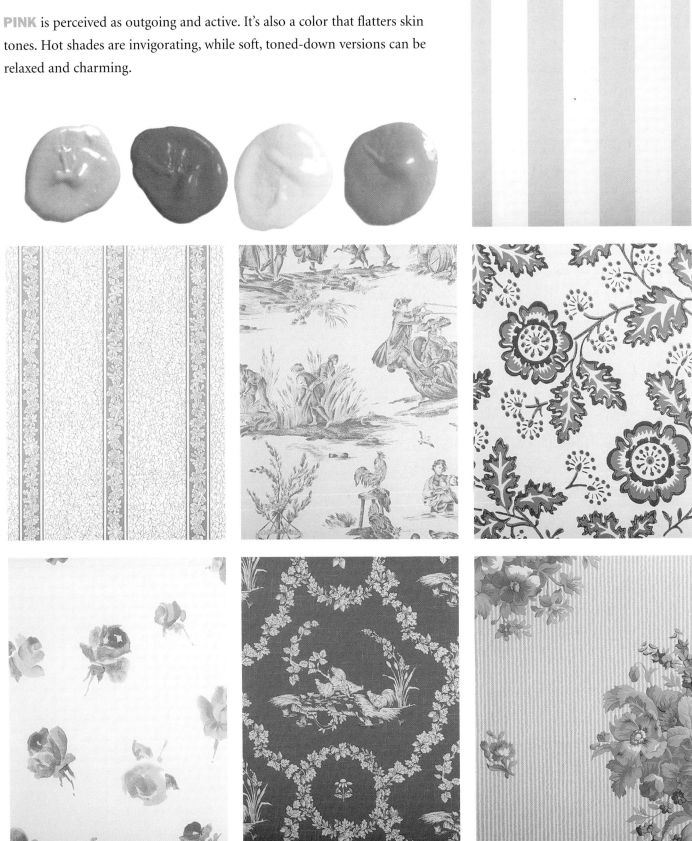

order direct: 1-800-523-6789

 # blue

BLUE, with its associations of sea and sky, offers serenity, which is why it is a favorite in bedrooms. Studies have shown that people think better in blue rooms. Perhaps that explains the popularity of the navy blue suit. Cooler blues show this color's melancholy side, however.

Plan #151026

Dimensions: 34' W x 66'8" D
Levels: 2
Square Footage: 1,574
Main Level Sq. Ft.: 1,131
Upper Level Sq. Ft.: 443
Bedrooms: 3
Bathrooms: 2
Foundation: Crawl space, slab; optional full basement plan available for extra fee
CompleteCost List Available: Yes
Price Category: C

This French Country home gives space for entertaining and offers privacy.

Features:

- **Great Room:** Move through the gracious foyer framed by wooden columns into the great room with its lofty 10-ft. ceilings and gas fireplace.

- **Dining Room:** Set off by 8-in. columns, the dining room opens to the kitchen, both with 9-foot ceilings.

- **Master Suite:** Enjoy relaxing in the bedroom with its 10-ft. boxed ceiling and well-placed windows. Atrium doors open to the backyard, where you can make a secluded garden. A glass-bricked corner whirlpool tub, corner shower, and double vanity make the master bath luxurious.

- **Bedrooms:** Upstairs, two large bedrooms with a walk-through bath provide plenty of room as well as privacy for kids or guests.

Main Level Floor Plan

Upper Level Floor Plan

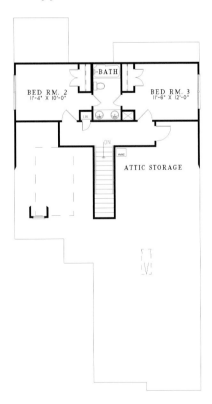

Copyright by designer/architect.

Plan #271025

Dimensions: 62' W x 57' D
Levels: 2
Square Footage: 2,223
Main Level Sq. Ft.: 1,689
Upper Level Sq. Ft.: 534
Bedrooms: 3
Bathrooms: 2½
Foundation: Basement
Materials List Available: Yes
Price Category: E

This traditional home's unique design combines a dynamic, exciting exterior with a fantastic floor plan.

Features:

- Living Room: To the left of the column-lined, barrel-vaulted entry, this inviting space features a curved wall and corner windows.

- Dining Room: A tray ceiling enhances this formal meal room.

- Kitchen: This island-equipped kitchen includes a corner pantry and a built-in desk. Nearby, the sunny breakfast room opens onto a backyard deck via sliding glass doors.

- Family Room: A corner bank of windows provides a glassy backdrop for this room's handsome fireplace. Munchies may be served on the snack bar from the breakfast nook.

- Master Suite: This main-floor retreat is simply stunning, and includes a vaulted ceiling, access to a private courtyard, and of course, a sumptuous bath with every creature comfort.

Main Level Floor Plan

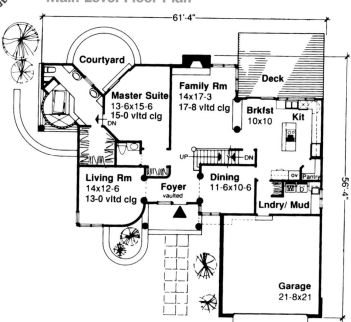

Upper Level Floor Plan

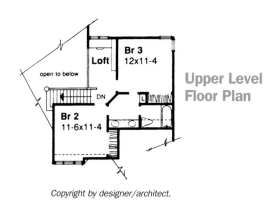

Plan #161031

Dimensions: 99'8" W x 68'8" D
Levels: 2
Square Footage: 2,776
Main Level Sq. Ft.: 2,776
Opt. Lower Level Sq. Ft.: 1,588
Bedrooms: 4
Bathrooms: 3½
Foundation: Basement
Materials List Available: Yes
Price Category: F

This home, as shown in the photograph, may differ from the actual blueprints. For more detailed information, please check the floor plans carefully. Images provided by designer/architect.

If you're looking for a compatible mixture of formal and informal areas in a home, look no further!

Features:

• Great Room: Columns at the entry to this room and the formal dining room set a gracious tone that is easy around which to decorate.

• Library: Set up an office or just a cozy reading area in this quiet room.

• Hearth Room: Spacious and inviting, this hearth room is positioned so that friends and family can flow from here to the breakfast area and kitchen.

• Master Suite: The luxury of this area is capped by the access it gives to the rear yard.

• Lower Level: Enjoy the 9-ft.-tall ceilings as you walk out to the rear yard from this area.

Entry

Rear View

Main Level Floor Plan

Bedroom
16'8" x 12'

Bath

Hall

Bedroom
16'8" x 12'

Laun.

Hearth Room

Breakfast
23' x 16' irr.

Bath

Kitchen
17'7" x 14'8"

Deck

Great Room
16' x 21'6"

Sloped Ceiling

Sloped Ceiling

Master Bedroom
15'8" x 22"

Dressing

walk-in closet

Three Car
Garage
20' x 33'4"

Dining Room
13'6" x 15'3" irr.

Foyer

Porch

Library
12'4" x 16'2" irr.

walk-in closet

Main Level Floor Plan

Copyright by designer/architect.

Optional Lower Level Floor Plan

Bedroom
12' x 10'

Bath

Rec Room
44'1" x 31'2" Irreg.

Bar

Unfinished Basement

Optional Lower Level Floor Plan

Dining Room

Rear Elevation

Left Elevation

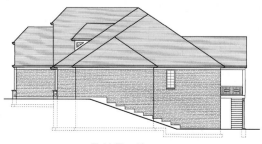

Right Elevation

Plan #181039

Dimensions: 38' W x 36' D

Levels: 2

Square Footage: 1,661

Main Level Sq. Ft.: 923

Upper Level Sq. Ft.: 738

Bedrooms: 3

Bathrooms: 1½

Foundation: Full basement

Materials List Available: Yes

Price Category: C

Illustration provided by designer/architect.

CAD FILE AVAILABLE

Main Level Floor Plan

9'-8" X 6'-6"
2,90 X 1,95

12'-4" X 13'-0"
3,70 X 3,90

10'-8" X 11'-0"
3,20 X 3,30

14'-0" X 17'-4"
4,20 X 5,20

14'-4" X 20'-8"
4,30 X 6,20

36'-0"
10,8 m

38'-0"
11,4 m

Upper Level Floor Plan

Copyright by designer/architect.

10'-4" X 9'-8"
3,10 X 2,90

10'-0" X 13'-0"
3,00 X 3,90

14'-8" X 12'-0"
4,40 X 3,60

Plan #231020

Dimensions: 58' W x 35' D

Levels: 2

Square Footage: 2,166

Main Level Sq. Ft.: 1,538

Upper Level Sq. Ft.: 628

Bedrooms: 3

Bathrooms: 2½

Foundation: Slab, basement

Materials List Available: No

Price Category: D

Illustration provided by designer/architect.

Main Level Floor Plan

Br #2
11 x 11

Util.

BRM.

Deck

Kit.

Great Rm.
18 x 21

Br #3
10 x 11

Dining
13 x 11

Foyer

Deck

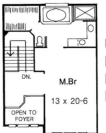

Upper Level Floor Plan

M.Br
13 x 20-6

OPEN TO FOYER

DN.

Garage Level Floor Plan

Shop
13 x 13

Garage
31 x 27

Unfin. Stor.
13 x 15

Unfin.Stor.
9-6 x 9

Copyright by designer/architect.

Plan #161027

Dimensions: 59'10" W x 37'4" D
Levels: 2
Square Footage: 2,388
Main Level Sq. Ft.: 1,207
Upper Level Sq. Ft.: 1,181
Bedrooms: 4
Bathrooms: 2½
Foundation: Basement
Materials List Available: No
Price Category: E

Images provided by designer/architect.

Double gables, wood trim, an arched window, and sidelights at the entry give elegance to this family-friendly home.

Features:

- Foyer: Friends and family will see the angled stairs, formal dining room, living room, and library from this foyer.

- Family Room: A fireplace makes this room cozy in the evenings on those chilly days, and multiple windows let natural light stream into it.

- Kitchen: You'll love the island and the ample counter space here as well as the butler's pantry. A breakfast nook makes a comfortable place to snack or just curl up and talk to the cook.

- Master Suite: Tucked away on the upper level, this master suite provides both privacy and luxury.

- Additional Bedrooms: These three additional bedrooms make this home ideal for any family.

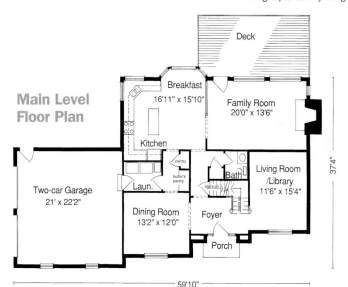

Main Level Floor Plan

Upper Level Floor Plan

Copyright by designer/architect.

Photo provided by designer/architect.

Plan #121024

Dimensions: 60' W x 58' D
Levels: 2
Square Footage: 3,057
Main Level Sq. Ft.: 1,631
Second Level Sq. Ft.: 1,426
Bedrooms: 4
Bathrooms: 2½
Foundation: Basement
Materials List Available: Yes
Price Category: G

This distinctive home offers plenty of space and is designed for gracious and convenient living.

Features:

• Ceiling Height: 8 ft. unless otherwise noted.

• Foyer: A curved staircase in this elegant entry will greet your guests.

• Living Room: This room invites you with a volume ceiling flanked by transom-topped windows that flood the room with sunlight.

• Screened Veranda: On warm summer nights, throw open the French doors in the living

room and enjoy a breeze on the huge screened veranda.

• Dining Room: This distinctive room is overlooked by the veranda.

• Family Room: At the back of the home is this comfortable family retreat with its soaring cathedral ceiling and handsome fireplace flanked by bookcases.

• Master Bedroom: This bayed bedroom features a 10-ft. vaulted ceiling.

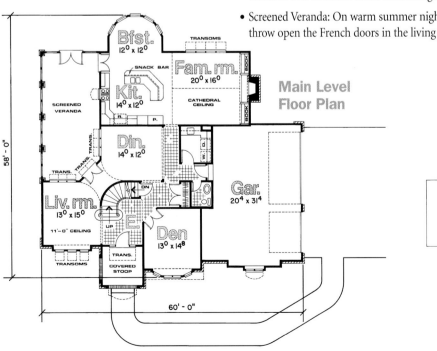

Main Level Floor Plan

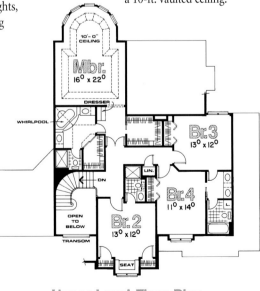

Upper Level Floor Plan

Copyright by designer/architect.

Plan #121020

Dimensions: 64' W x 46' D
Levels: 2
Square Footage: 2,480
Main Level Sq. Ft.: 1,369
Upper Level Sq. Ft.: 1,111
Bedrooms: 4
Bathrooms: 3
Foundation: Basement
Materials List Available: Yes
Price Category: E

Photo provided by designer/architect.

Tapered columns and an angled stairway give this home a classical style.

Features:

- **Ceiling Height:** 8 ft.

- **Living Room:** Just off the dramatic two-story entry is this distinctive living room, with its tapered columns, transom-topped windows, and boxed ceiling.

- **Formal Dining Room:** The tapered columns, transom-topped windows, and boxed ceiling found in the living room continue into this gracious dining space.

- **Family Room:** Located on the opposite side of the house from the living room and dining room, the family room features a beamed ceiling and fireplace framed by windows.

- **Kitchen:** An island is the centerpiece of this convenient kitchen.

- **Master Suite:** Upstairs, a tiered ceiling and corner windows enhance the master bedroom, which is served by a pampering bath.

Main Level Floor Plan

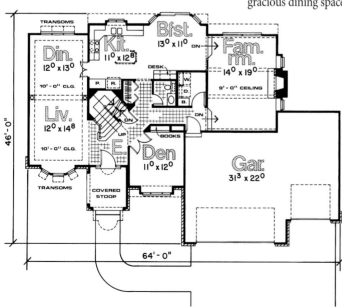

Upper Level Floor Plan

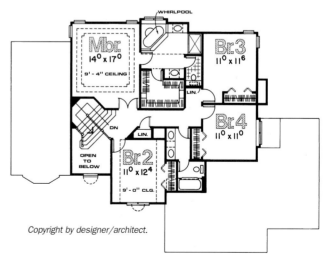

Copyright by designer/architect.

Plan #131033

Dimensions: 84'10" W x 48' D
Levels: 1.5
Square Footage: 2,813
Main Level Sq. Ft.: 1,890
Upper Level Sq. Ft.: 923
Bedrooms: 5
Bathrooms: 3½
Foundation: Crawl space, slab, or basement
Materials List Available: Yes
Price Category: G

Contemporary styling, luxurious amenities, and the classics that make a house a home are all available here.

Features:

• **Family Room:** A sloped ceiling with skylight and a railed overlook to make this large space totally up to date.

• **Living Room:** Sunken for comfort and with a cathedral ceiling for style, this room features a fireplace flanked by windows and sliding glass doors.

• **Master Suite:** Unwind in this room, with its cathedral ceiling, with a skylight, walk-in closet, and private access to the den.

• **Upper Level:** A bridge overlooks the living room and foyer and leads through the family room to three bedrooms and a bath.

• **Optional Guest Suite:** 500 sq. ft. above the master suite and den provides total comfort.

Images provided by designer/architect.

Main Level Floor Plan

Copyright by designer/architect.

Upper Level Floor Plan

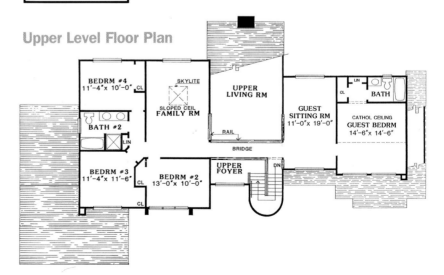

Living Room / Foyer

Entry

Living Room

Rear View

Plan #121015

Dimensions: 52' W x 47'4" D

Levels: 2

Square Footage: 1,999

Main Level Sq. Ft.: 1,421

Upper Level Sq. Ft.: 578

Bedrooms: 3

Bathrooms: 3

Foundation: Basement

Materials List Available: Yes

Price Category: D

This home, as shown in the photograph, may differ from the actual blueprints. For more detailed information, please check the floor plans carefully. *Photo provided by designer/architect.*

Hipped roofs and a trio of gables bring distinction to this plan.

Features:

• **Ceiling Height:** 8 ft.

• **Open Floor Plan:** The rooms flow into each other and are flanked by an abundance of windows. The result is a light and airy space that seems much larger than it really is.

• **Formal Dining Room:** Here is the perfect room for elegant entertaining.

• **Breakfast Nook:** This bright, bayed nook is the perfect place to start the day. It's also great for intimate get-togethers.

• **Great Room:** The family will enjoy gathering in this spacious area.

• **Bedrooms:** This large master bedroom, along with three secondary bedrooms and an extra room, provides plenty of room for a growing family.

• **Attached Garage:** The garage provides two bays of parking plus plenty of storage space.

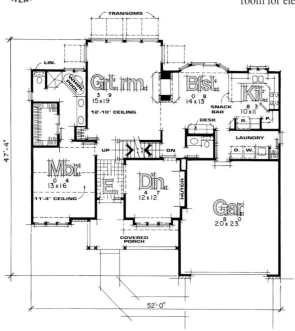

Main Level Floor Plan

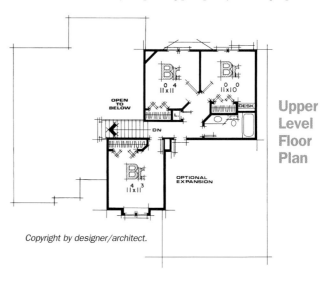

Upper Level Floor Plan

Copyright by designer/architect.

Plan #121031

Dimensions: 52' W x 51'4" D
Levels: 2
Square Footage: 1,772
Main Level Sq. Ft.: 1,314
Upper Level Sq. Ft.: 458
Bedrooms: 3
Bathrooms: 2½
Foundation: Basement
Materials List Available: Yes
Price Category: C

This home features architectural details reminiscence of earlier fine homes.

Features:

- Ceiling Height: 8 ft. unless otherwise noted.

- Foyer: This grand entry soars two-stories high. The U-shaped staircase with window leads to a second-story balcony.

- Great Room: You'll be drawn to the impressive views through the triple-arch windows at the front and rear of this room.

- Kitchen: Designed for maximum efficiency, this kitchen is a pleasure to be in. It features a center island, a full pantry, and a desk for added convenience.

- Breakfast Area: This area adjoins the kitchen. Both rooms are flooded with sunlight streaming from a shared bay window.

- Master Suite: The stylish bedroom includes a walk-in closet. Luxuriate in the whirlpool tub at the end of a long day .

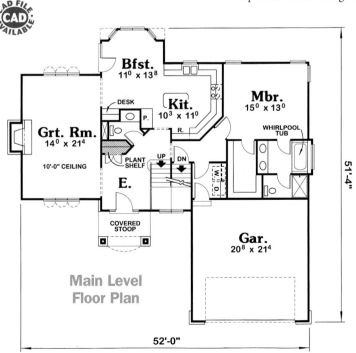

Main Level Floor Plan

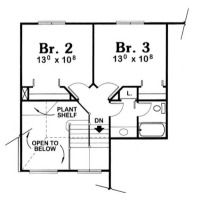

Upper Level Floor Plan

Plan #321051

Dimensions: 69'8" W x 46' D

Levels: 2

Square Footage: 2,624

Main Level Sq. Ft.: 1,774

Upper Level Sq. Ft.: 850

Bedrooms: 4

Bathrooms: 2½

Foundation: Basement

Materials List Available: Yes

Price Category: F

If you're looking for a home that deserves to be called "grand" and "elegant," you will love this spacious beauty.

This home, as shown in the photograph, may differ from the actual blueprints. For more detailed information, please check the floor plans carefully.

Images provided by designer/architect.

Features:

- **Entryway:** Two stories high, this area sets the tone for the whole house.

- **Great Room:** The 18-ft. ceiling in this room gives a bright and airy feeling that the three magnificent Palladian windows surely enhance.

- **Dining Room:** A classic colonnade forms the entry to this lovely bayed room.

- **Kitchen:** Designed for gourmet cooks who love efficient work spaces, this kitchen will delight the whole family.

- **Master Suite:** Relax in the comfort of this luxurious suite at the end of the day. You'll find walk-in closets, a large bay window, and plant shelves in the bedroom, as well as a sunken tub in the bathroom.

Master Bath

Main Level Floor Plan

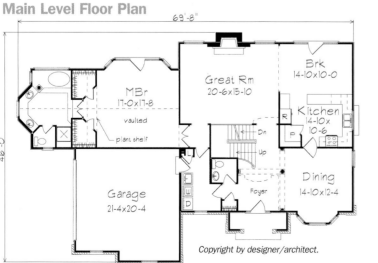

Copyright by designer/architect.

Upper Level Floor Plan

Main Level Floor Plan

Illustration provided by designer/architect.

CAD FILE AVAILABLE

53'-0"
15,9 m

15'-4" X 16'-8"
4,60 X 5,00

15'-0" X 8'-4"
4,50 X 2,50

15'-8" X 13'-4"
4,70 X 4,00

13'-0" X 15'-8"
3,80 X 4,70

23'-4" X 24'-0"
7,00 X 7,20

9'-0" X 10'-4"
2,70 X 3,10

12'-0" X 14'-4"
3,60 X 4,30

70'-0"
21,0 m

Upper Level Floor Plan

Copyright by designer/architect.

Plan #181056

Dimensions: 70' W x 53' D

Levels: 2

Square Footage: 2,889

Main Level Sq. Ft.: 1,927

Upper Level Sq. Ft.: 962

Bedrooms: 4

Bathrooms: 3½

Foundation: Basement

Materials List Available: Yes

Price Category: F

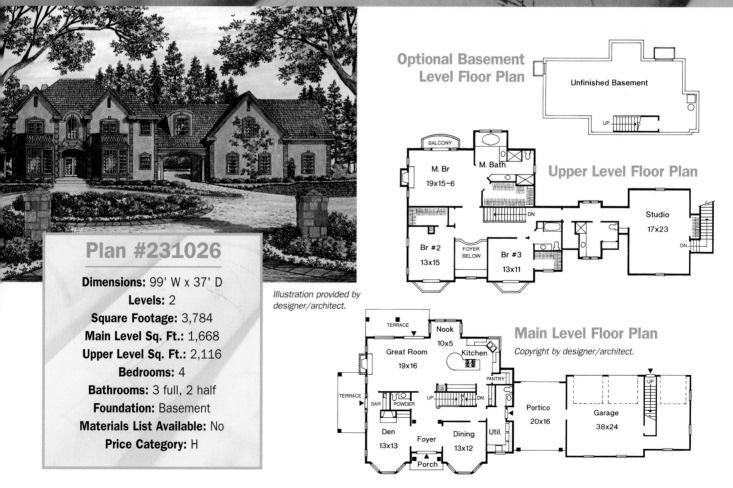

Optional Basement Level Floor Plan

Unfinished Basement

UP

Upper Level Floor Plan

BALCONY

M. Br
19x15-6

M. Bath

Studio
17x23

Br #2
13x15

FOYER
BELOW

Br #3
13x11

DN.

DN.

Main Level Floor Plan

Copyright by designer/architect.

TERRACE

Nook
10x5

Great Room
19x16

Kitchen

PANTRY

TERRACE

BAR   POWDER

UP

DN.

Portico
20x16

Garage
38x24

UP

Den
13x13

Foyer

Dining
13x12

Util.

Porch

Illustration provided by designer/architect.

Plan #231026

Dimensions: 99' W x 37' D

Levels: 2

Square Footage: 3,784

Main Level Sq. Ft.: 1,668

Upper Level Sq. Ft.: 2,116

Bedrooms: 4

Bathrooms: 3 full, 2 half

Foundation: Basement

Materials List Available: No

Price Category: H

Plan #121029

Dimensions: 58'8" W x 54' D
Levels: 2
Square Footage: 2,576
Main Level Sq. Ft.: 1,735
Upper Level Sq. Ft.: 841
Bedrooms: 4
Bathrooms: 2½
Foundation: Basement
Materials List Available: Yes
Price Category: E

Photo provided by designer/architect.

This gracious home is designed with the contemporary lifestyle in mind.

Features:

- Ceiling Height: 8 ft. unless otherwise noted.

- Great Room: This room features a fireplace and entertainment center. It's equally suited for family gatherings and formal entertaining.

- Breakfast Area: The fireplace is two-sided so it shares its warmth with this breakfast area — the perfect spot for informal family meals.

- Master Suite: Halfway up the staircase you'll find double-doors into this truly distinctive suite featuring a barrel-vault ceiling, built-in bookcases, and his and her walk-in closets. Unwind at the end of the day by stretching out in the oval whirlpool tub.

- Computer Loft: This loft overlooks the great room. It is designed as a home office with a built-in desk for your computer.

- Garage: Two bays provide plenty of storage in addition to parking space.

Main Level Floor Plan

CAD FILE AVAILABLE

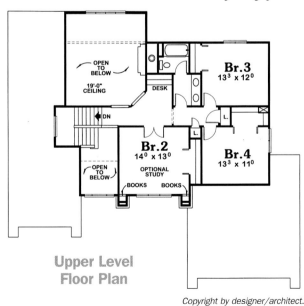

Upper Level Floor Plan

Copyright by designer/architect.

Plan #121025

Dimensions: 60' W x 59'4" D
Levels: 2
Square Footage: 2,562
Main Level Sq. Ft.: 1,875
Upper Level Square Footage: 687
Bedrooms: 4
Bathrooms: 2½
Foundation: Basement
Materials List Available: Yes
Price Category: F

Dramatic arches are the reoccurring architectural theme in this distinctive home.

Features:

- Ceiling Height: 8 ft. unless otherwise noted.
- Foyer: This is a grand two-story entrance. Plants will thrive on the plant shelf thanks to light streaming through the arched window.
- Great Room: The foyer flows into the great room through dramatic 15-ft.-high arched openings.
- Kitchen: An island is the centerpiece of this highly functional kitchen that includes a separate breakfast area.
- Office: French doors open into this versatile office that features a 10-ft. ceiling and transom-topped windows.
- Master Suite: The master suite features a volume ceiling, built-in dresser, and two closets. You'll unwind in the beautiful corner whirlpool bath with its elegant window treatment.

Main Level Floor Plan

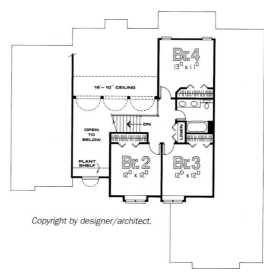

Upper Level Floor Plan

Plan #121017

Dimensions: 54' W x 50' D
Levels: 2
Square Footage: 2,353
Main Level Sq. Ft.: 1,653
Upper Level Sq. Ft.: 700
Bedrooms: 4
Bathrooms: 3
Foundation: Basement
Materials List Available: Yes
Price Category: E

The dramatic two-story entry with bent staircase is the first sign that this is a gracious home.

Features:

• Ceiling Height: 8 ft. except as noted.

• Great Room: A row of transom-topped windows and a tall, beamed ceiling add a sense of spaciousness to this family gathering area.

• Formal Dining Room: The bayed window helps make this an inviting place to entertain.

• See-through Fireplace: This feature spreads warmth and coziness throughout the informal areas of the home.

• Breakfast Area: This sunny area shares a see-through fireplace with the great room. It's the perfect place to start the day.

• Master Suite: Here are all the features you expect to find in large luxury homes. Wake up to tall, sloped ceilings, and enjoy the corner whirlpool, separate shower, and vanity. A large walk-in closet provides plenty of wardrobe storage.

Main Level Floor Plan

CAD FILE AVAILABLE CAD

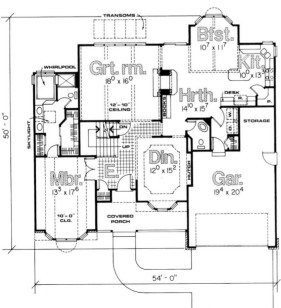

Upper Level Floor Plan

Copyright by designer/architect.

Plan #321060

Dimensions: 36' W x 46'8" D
Levels: 2
Square Footage: 1,575
Main Level Sq. Ft.: 802
Upper Level Sq. Ft.: 773
Bedrooms: 3
Bathrooms: 2½
Foundation: Basement
Materials List Available: Yes
Price Category: C

Images provided by designer/architect.

CAD FILE AVAILABLE

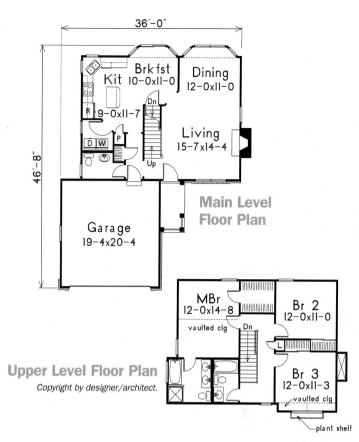

Main Level Floor Plan

Upper Level Floor Plan

Copyright by designer/architect.

Plan #321058

Dimensions: 39' W x 42'8" D
Levels: 2
Square Footage: 1,700
Main Level Sq. Ft.: 896
Upper Level Sq. Ft.: 804
Bedrooms: 4
Bathrooms: 2½
Foundation: Basement
Materials List Available: Yes
Price Category: C

Images provided by designer/architect.

CAD FILE AVAILABLE

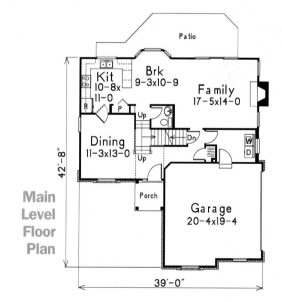

Main Level Floor Plan

Upper Level Floor Plan

Copyright by designer/architect.

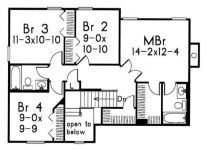

38'-0"

Patio

Living
17-8x12-0

MBr
12-4x15-4

Main Level Floor Plan

P
R

Kit
10-6x
10-6

Dn

39'-4"

Dining
10-6x9-10

Up

Garage
19-4x20-4

Porch

Images provided by designer/architect.

CAD FILE AVAILABLE

Br 2
17-8x12-0

Upper Level Floor Plan

Copyright by designer/architect.

Dn

Br 3
10-6x13-0

open to below

Plan #321057

Dimensions: 38' W x 39'4" D

Levels: 2

Square Footage: 1,524

Main Level Sq. Ft.: 951

Upper Level Sq. Ft.: 573

Bedrooms: 3

Bathrooms: 2½

Foundation: Basement

Materials List Available: Yes

Price Category: C

Main Level Floor Plan

23'-2" X 21'-0"
6.90 X 6.30

53'-2"
16.95 m

13'-8" X 10'-0"
4.10 X 3.00

15'-0" X 17'-8"
3.90 X 6.30

7'-0" X 10'-0"
2.10 X 3.00

15'-0" X 17'-8"
3.90 X 6.30

12'-0" X 14'-0"
3.60 X 4.20

10'-0" X 10'-4"
3.00 X 3.10

6'-4" X 13'-4"
1.90 X 4.00

12'-0" X 12'-0"
3.90 X 3.50

56'-0"
16.8 m

Upper Level Floor Plan

Bonus room/Espace boni
20'-4" X 14'-0"
6.10 X 4.20

10'-8" X 8'-8"
3.20 X 2.30

10'-0" X 12'-0"
3.00 X 3.60

open to below

Copyright by designer/ architect.

Plan #181061

Dimensions: 56' W x 53'2" D

Levels: 2

Square Footage: 2,111

Main Level Sq. Ft.: 1,545

Upper Level Sq. Ft.: 566

Bedrooms: 2

Bathrooms: 2½

Foundation: Basement or crawl space

Materials List Available: Yes

Price Category: D

Images provided by designer/architect.

CAD FILE AVAILABLE

Plan #121021

Dimensions: 46' W x 48' D

Levels: 2

Square Footage: 2,270

Main Level Sq. Ft.: 1,150

Upper Level Sq. Ft.: 1,120

Bedrooms: 4

Bathrooms: 3

Foundation: Basement

Materials List Available: Yes

Price Category: E

With its wraparound porch, this home evokes the charm of a traditional home.

Features:

- Ceiling Height: 8 ft.

- Foyer: The dramatic two-story entry enjoys views of the formal dining room and great room. A second floor balcony overlooks the entry and a plant shelf.

- Formal Dining Room: This gracious room is perfect for family holiday gatherings and for more formal dinner parties.

- Great Room: All the family will want to gather in this comfortable, informal room which features bay windows, an entertainment center, and a see-through fireplace.

- Breakfast Area: Conveniently located just off the great room, the bayed breakfast area features a built-in desk for household bills and access to the backyard.

- Kitchen: An island is the centerpiece of this kitchen. Its intelligent design makes food preparation a pleasure.

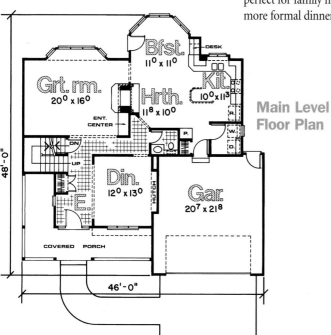

Main Level Floor Plan

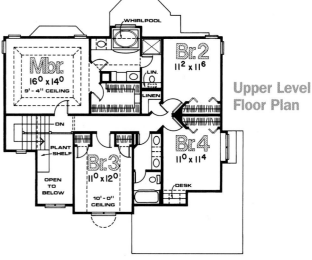

Upper Level Floor Plan

Photo provided by designer/architect.

Plan #121045

Dimensions: 40' W x 48' D
Levels: 2
Square Footage: 1,575
Main Level Sq. Ft.: 787
Upper Level Sq. Ft.: 788
Bedrooms: 3
Bathrooms: 2½
Foundation: Basement
Materials List Available: Yes
Price Category: C

This home, as shown in the photograph, may differ from the actual blueprints. For more detailed information, please check the floor plans carefully.

This home is carefully laid out to provide the convenience demanded by busy family life.

Features:

- Ceiling Height: 8 ft.
- Family Room: This charming family room, with its fireplace and built-in cabinetry, will become the central gathering place for family and friends.
- Kitchen: This kitchen offers a central island that makes food preparation more convenient and doubles

as a snack bar for a quick bite on the run. The breakfast area features a pantry and planning desk.

- Computer Loft: The second-floor landing includes this loft designed to accommodate the family computer.
- Room to Grow: Also on the second-floor landing you will find a large unfinished area waiting to accommodate the growing family.

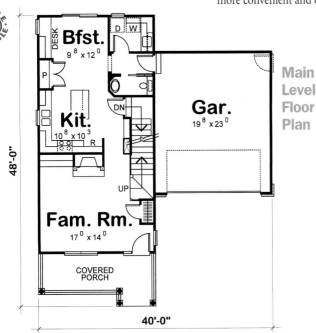

Main Level Floor Plan

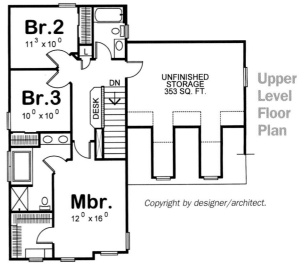

Upper Level Floor Plan

Copyright by designer/architect.

Photo provided by designer/architect.

Plan #121035

Dimensions: 45'4" W x 38' D

Levels: 2

Square Footage: 1,471

Main Level Sq. Ft.: 716

Upper Level Sq. Ft.: 755

Bedrooms: 3

Bathrooms: 2½

Foundation: Basement

Materials List Available: Yes

Price Category: B

This convenient and elegant home is designed to expand as the family does.

Features:

- Ceiling Height: 8 ft. unless otherwise noted.

- Family Room: An open staircase to the second level visually expands this room where a built-in entertainment center maximizes the floor space. The whole family will be drawn to the warmth from the handsome fireplace.

- Kitchen: Cooking will be a pleasure in this

bright and efficient kitchen that features an island and a corner pantry. A snack bar offers a convenient spot for informal family meals.

- Dining Area: This lovely bayed area adjoins the kitchen.

- Room to Expand: Upstairs is 258 sq. ft. of unfinished area offering plenty of space for expansion as the family grows.

- Garage: This two-bay garage offers plenty of storage space in addition to parking for cars.

Main Level Floor Plan CAD FILE AVAILABLE

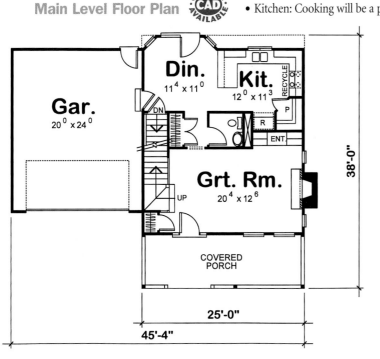

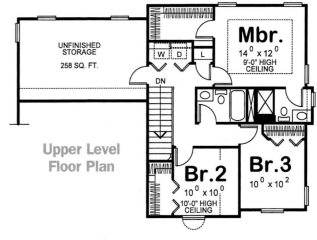

Upper Level Floor Plan

Copyright by designer/architect.

Plan #131030

Dimensions: 51' W x 41'10" D
Levels: 2
Square Footage: 2,470
Main Level Sq. Ft.: 1,290
Upper Level Sq. Ft.: 1,180
Bedrooms: 4
Bathrooms: 2½
Foundation: Crawl space, slab, basement, or walk-out basement
Materials List Available: Yes
Price Category: F

This home, as shown in the photograph, may differ from the actual blueprints. For more detailed information, please check the floor plans carefully.

Photos provided by designer/architect.

Master Bedroom

Master Bathroom

Entry

If high ceilings and spacious rooms make you happy, you'll love this gorgeous home.

Features:

- **Family Room:** An 18-ft. vaulted ceiling that's open to the balcony above, a corner fireplace, and a wall of windows make this room feel special.

- **Dining Room:** This formal room, which flows into the living room, also opens to the front porch and optional backyard deck.

- **Kitchen:** A bright breakfast room joins with this kitchen and opens to the backyard deck.

- **Master Suite:** You'll smile when you see the 11-ft. vaulted ceiling, stunning arched window, and two walk-in closets in the bedroom. A skylight lets natural light into the private bath, with its spa tub, separate shower, and dual-sink vanity.

- **Bedrooms:** To reach these three charming bedrooms, you'll admire the view into the family room below as you walk along the balcony hall.

Main Level Floor Plan

OPT WOOD DECK

BKFST RM

FAMILY RM
VAULTED CLG
18'-0" x 15'-0"

9' HIGH CLG
DINING RM
12'-0" x 13'-4"

9' HIGH CLG
KITCHEN
18'-8" x 16'-0"

REF

LAV

W D

LAUN RM

PANT

DN

STOR

9' HIGH CLG
LIVING RM
13'-0" x 16'-6"

UP

2 STORY
HIGH
FOYER

CL

TWO CAR GARAGE
21'-8" x 20'-0"

COVERED PORCH

UP

Upper Level Floor Plan

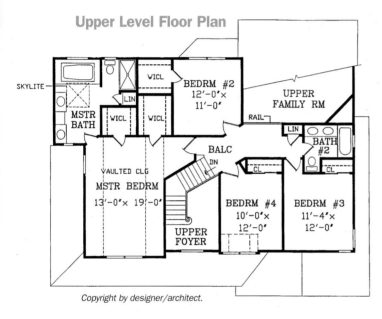

SKYLITE

WICL

LIN

BEDRM #2
12'-0" x
11'-0"

UPPER
FAMILY RM

RAIL

MSTR
BATH

WICL

WICL

LIN

BATH
#2

BALC

DN

CL

CL

VAULTED CLG
MSTR BEDRM
13'-0" x 19'-0"

UPPER
FOYER

BEDRM #4
10'-0" x
12'-0"

BEDRM #3
11'-4" x
12'-0"

Copyright by designer/architect.

Kitchen/Breakfast Area

Dining Room

Living Room

Kitchen/Breakfast Area

Plan #141014

Dimensions: 72' W x 38' D

Levels: 2

Square Footage: 2,091

Main Level Sq. Ft.: 1,362

Upper Level Sq. Ft.: 729

Bedrooms: 3

Bathrooms: 2½

Foundation: Basement

Materials List Available: Yes

Price Category: D

Images provided by designer/architect.

The wraparound front porch and front dormers evoke an old-fashioned country home.

Features:

- Ceiling Height: 8 ft. unless otherwise noted.

- Living Room: This spacious area has an open flow to the dining room, so you can graciously usher guests when it is time to eat.

- Dining Room: This elegant dining room has a bay that opens to the sun deck.

- Kitchen: This warm and inviting kitchen looks out to the front porch. Its bayed breakfast area is perfect for informal family meals.

- Master Suite: The bedroom enjoys a view through the front porch and features a master bath with all the amenities.

- Flexible Room: A room above the two-bay garage offers plenty of space that can be used for anything from a home office to a teen suite.

- Study Room: The two second-floor bedrooms share a study that is perfect for homework.

Main Level Floor Plan

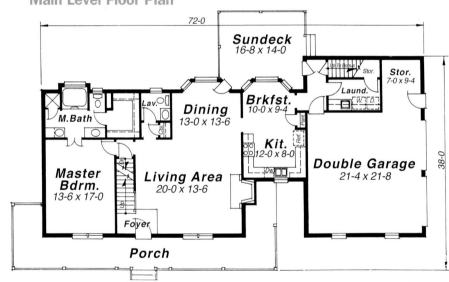

Upper Level Floor Plan

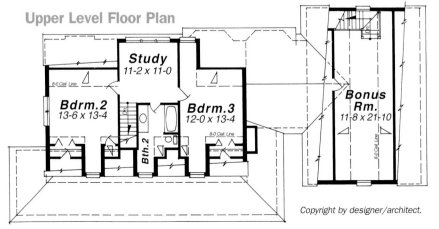

Copyright by designer/architect.

Plan #131041

Dimensions: 42' W x 45' D
Levels: 2
Square Footage: 1,679
Main Level Sq. Ft.: 1,134
Upper Level Sq. Ft.: 545
Bedrooms: 3
Bathrooms: 2½
Foundation: Crawl space, slab, or basement
Materials List Available: Yes
Price Category: D

Illustrations provided by designer/architect.

This rustic-looking two-story cottage includes contemporary amenities for your total comfort.

Features:

• Great Room: With a 9-ft.-4-in.-high ceiling, this large room makes everyone feel at home. A fireplace with raised hearth and built-in niche for a TV will encourage the whole family to gather here on cool evenings, and sliding glass doors leading to

the rear covered porch make it an ideal entertaining area in mild weather.

• Kitchen: When people aren't in the great room, you're likely to find them here, because the convenient serving bar welcomes casual dining, and this room also opens to the p porch.

• Master Suite: Relax at the end of the day in this room, with its 9-ft.-4-in.-high ceiling and walk-in closet, or luxuriate in the private bath with whirlpool tub and dual-sink vanity.

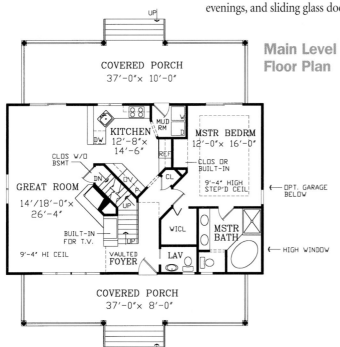

Main Level Floor Plan

Upper Level Floor Plan

Copyright by designer/architect.

Great Room

Plan #121036

Dimensions: 42' W x 43' D
Levels: 2
Square Footage: 1,297
Main Level Sq. Ft.: 603
Upper Level Sq. Ft.: 694
Bedrooms: 3
Bathrooms: 2½
Foundation: Basement
Materials List Available: Yes
Price Category: B

This bright and cheery home offers the growing family plenty of room to expand.

Features:

• Ceiling Height: 8 ft. unless otherwise noted.

• Living Room: Family and friends will be drawn to this delightful living room. A double window at the front and windows framing the fireplace bring lots of sunlight that adds to the appeal.

• Dining Room: From the living room, you'll usher guests into this large and inviting dining room.

• Kitchen: A center island is the highlight of this attractive and well-designed kitchen.

• Three-Season Porch: This appealing enclosed porch is accessible from the dining room.

• Master Bedroom: A dramatic angled ceiling highlights a picturesque window in this bedroom.

• Bonus Area: With 354 sq. ft. of unfinished area, you'll never run out of space to expand.

CAD FILE AVAILABLE

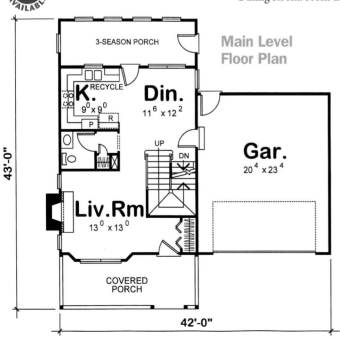

Main Level Floor Plan

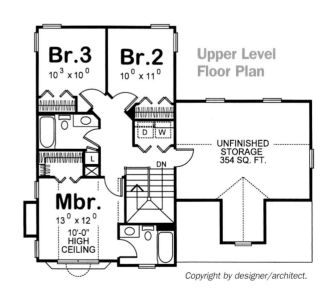

Upper Level Floor Plan

Plan #151028

Dimensions: 36' W X 69' D

Levels: 2

Square Footage: 2,252

Main Level Sq. Ft.: 1,694

Upper Level Sq. Ft.: 558

Bedrooms: 3

Bathrooms: 3

Foundation: Crawl space, slab; optional basement plan available for extra fee

CompleteCost List Available: Yes

Price Category: E

You'll love entertaining in this elegant home with its large covered front porch, grilling porch off the kitchen and breakfast room, and great room with a gas fireplace and media center.

Features:

- **Foyer:** A wonderful open staircase from the foyer leads you to the second floor.

- **Guest Room/Study:** A private bath makes this room truly versatile.

- **Dining Room:** Attached to the great room, this dining room features 8-in. wooden columns that you can highlight for a formal atmosphere.

- **Kitchen:** This cleverly laid-out kitchen with access to the breakfast room is ideal for informal gatherings as well as family meals.

- **Master Suite:** French doors here open to the bath, with its large walk-in closet, double vanities, corner whirlpool tub, and corner shower.

Main Level Floor Plan

Upper Level Floor Plan

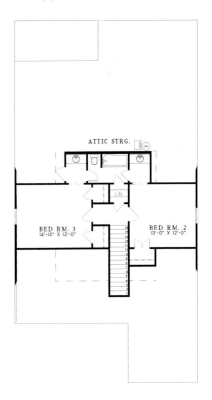

Plan #641001

Dimensions: 61'6" W x 56' D
Levels: 2
Square Footage: 3,034
Main Level Sq. Ft.: 1,323
Upper Level Sq. Ft.: 1,711
Bedrooms: 4
Bathrooms: 2½
Foundation: Basement
Materials List Available: No
Price Category: G

Images provided by designer/architect.

Main Level Floor Plan

Copyright by designer/architect.

Upper Level Floor Plan

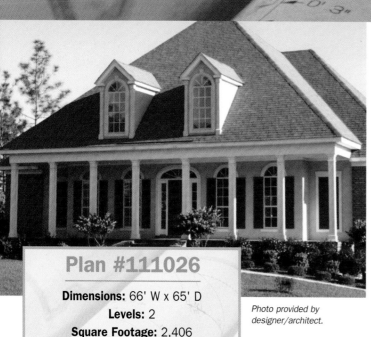

Plan #111026

Dimensions: 66' W x 65' D
Levels: 2
Square Footage: 2,406
Main Level Sq. Ft.: 1,796
Upper Level Sq. Ft.: 610
Bedrooms: 4
Bathrooms: 4
Foundation: Crawlspace
Materials List Available: No
Price Category: F

Photo provided by designer/architect.

Main Level Floor Plan

Upper Level Floor Plan

Copyright by designer/architect.

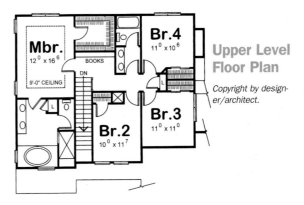

Main Level Floor Plan

Kit. 9⁸ x 12³
Bfst. 10⁰ x 12³
Fam. Rm. 16⁷ x 16⁰
Din. 12⁰ x 11⁰
Liv. Rm. 12⁰ x 12⁰
Gar. 22⁰ x 23⁰
COVERED PORCH

40'-0"
49'-0"

Plan #121039

Dimensions: 46' W x 47'10" D
Levels: 2
Square Footage: 2,292
Main Level Sq. Ft.: 1,158
Upper Level Sq. Ft.: 1,134
Bedrooms: 4
Bathrooms: 2½
Foundation: Basement
Materials List Available: Yes
Price Category: E

Photo provided by designer/architect.

Mbr. 12⁰ x 16⁶
9'-0" CEILING
BOOKS
Br. 4 11⁰ x 10⁶
Br. 2 10⁰ x 11⁷
Br. 3 11⁰ x 11⁰

Upper Level Floor Plan

Copyright by designer/architect.

Mbr. 15⁰ x 13⁰
10'-0" CEIL.
Fam. Rm. 14⁸ x 15⁴
Bfst. 9⁴ x 11⁰
Kit. 13³ x 11²
Gar. 19⁸ x 20⁴
Den 10⁰ x 10⁶
COVERED PORCH

47'-8"
40'-0"

Main Level Floor Plan

Plan #121099

Dimensions: 40' W x 47'8" D
Levels: 2
Square Footage: 1,699
Main Level Sq. Ft.: 1,268
Upper Level Sq. Ft.: 431
Bedrooms: 3
Bathrooms: 2½
Foundation: Basement
Materials List Available: Yes
Price Category: C

Photo provided by designer/architect.

This home, as shown in the photograph, may differ from the actual blueprints. For more detailed information, please check the floor plans carefully.

OPTIONAL EXPANSION
COMP. AREA
Br. 3 10⁰ x 10⁰
Br. 2 10⁰ x 10⁶

Upper Level Floor Plan

Copyright by designer/architect.

Plan #181151

Dimensions: 50' W x 46' D
Levels: 2
Square Footage: 2,283
Main Level Sq. Ft.: 1,274
Second Level Sq. Ft.: 1,009
Bedrooms: 3
Bathrooms: 2½
Foundation: Basement
Materials List Available: Yes
Price Category: F

- **Kitchen:** This efficient and well-designed kitchen has double sinks and offers a separate eating area for those impromptu family meals.

- **Master Suite:** This master retreat has a walk-in closet and its own sumptuous bath.

- **Home Office:** Whether you work at home or just need a place for the family computer and keeping track of family finances, this home office fills the bill.

Multiple porches, stately columns, and arched multi-paned windows adorn this country home.

Features:

- Ceiling Height: 8 ft. unless otherwise noted.

- **Great Room:** The second-floor mezzanine overlooks this great room. With its soaring ceiling, this dramatic room is the centerpiece of a spacious and flowing design that is just as suited to entertaining as it is to family life.

- **Dining Area:** Guests will naturally flow into this dining area when it is time to eat. After dinner they can step directly out onto the porch to enjoy coffee and dessert when the weather is fair.

Main Level Floor Plan

21'-0" X 20'-8"
6,30 X 6,20

17'-0" X 11'-8"
5,10 X 3,50

9'-8" X 8'-8"
2,90 X 2,60

9'-0" X 10'-0"
2,70 X 3,00

10'-0" X 12'-0"
3,00 X 3,60

9'-8" X 9'-4"
2,90 X 2,80

12'-0" X 20'-8"
3,60 X 6,20

46'-0"
13,8 m

50'-0"
15,0 m

Upper Level Floor Plan

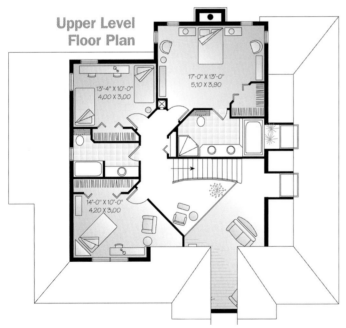

13'-4" X 10'-0"
4,00 X 3,00

17'-0" X 13'-0"
5,10 X 3,90

14'-0" X 10'-0"
4,20 X 3,00

Copyright by designer/architect.

SMARTtip

Coping Chair Rails

If the teeth of your rasp tend to break out thin edges of the cope, try wrapping the rasp with sandpaper to make fine adjustments.

Dining Room

Living Room

Master Bath

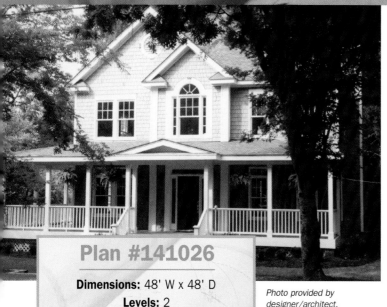

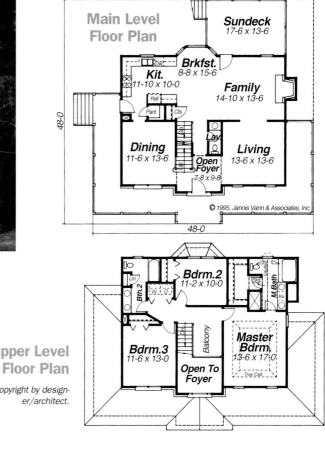

Main Level Floor Plan

Sundeck 17-6 x 13-6

Brkfst. 8-8 x 15-6

Kit. 11-10 x 10-0

Family 14-10 x 13-6

Pant.

Cts.

Lav

Dining 11-6 x 13-6

Open Foyer 7-8 x 9-8

Living 13-6 x 13-6

48-0

48-0

© 1995, Jannis Vann & Associates, Inc.

Photo provided by designer/architect.

Plan #141026

Dimensions: 48' W x 48' D
Levels: 2
Square Footage: 1,993
Main Level Sq. Ft.: 1,038
Upper Level Sq. Ft.: 955
Bedrooms: 3
Bathrooms: 2½
Foundation: Basement
Materials List Available: Yes
Price Category: D

Lin.

Bdrm.2 11-2 x 10-0

Bth.2

W.I.C.

M.Bath

Bdrm.3 11-6 x 13-0

Balcony

Open To Foyer

Master Bdrm. 13-6 x 17-0

Tray Ceil.

Upper Level Floor Plan

Copyright by designer/architect.

Wood Deck 12'6"x 8'

Covered Porch 12'2"x 10'

Ext. Storage

Master Bath

WIC

Breakfast 11'10"x 9'6'

Utility

Master Bedroom 12'6"x 15'6"

1/2 Ba.

Kitchen 10'x 11'6"

Living 14'4"x 17'6"

Dining 13'x 12'

Main Level Floor Plan

Porch 32'x 5'

Plan #111046

Dimensions: 37' W x 57' D
Levels: 2
Square Footage: 1,768
Main Level Sq. Ft.: 1,247
Upper Level Sq. Ft.: 521
Bedrooms: 3
Bathrooms: 2½
Foundation: Crawl space
Materials List Available: No
Price Category: D

Photo provided by designer/architect.

Bedroom 12'6"x 14'

Bedroom 10'6"x 13'2"

Balcony

Upper Level Floor Plan

Copyright by designer/architect.

Plan #151016

Dimensions: 60'2" W x 39'10" D

Levels: 2

Square Footage: 1,783;
2,107 with bonus

Main Level Sq. Ft.: 1,124

Upper Level Sq. Ft.: 659

Bedrooms: 3

Bathrooms: 2½

Foundation: Basement, crawl space,
or slab

Complete Cost List Available: Yes

Price Category: C

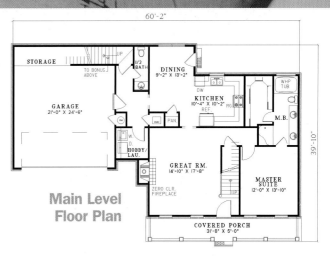

**Main Level
Floor Plan**

*Images provided by
designer/architect.*

CAD FILE AVAILABLE

**Upper Level
Floor Plan**

*Copyright by design-
er/architect.*

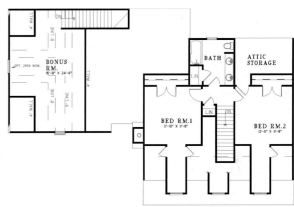

Plan #131043

Dimensions: 65'8" W x 43'10" D

Levels: 1.5

Square Footage: 1,945

Main Level Sq. Ft.: 1,375

Upper Level Sq. Ft.: 570

Bedrooms: 3

Bathrooms: 2½

Foundation: Crawl space, slab,
or basement

Materials List Available: Yes

Price Category: E

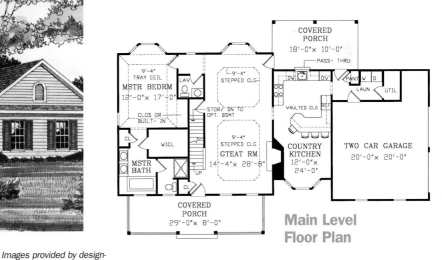

*Images provided by design-
er/architect.*

**Main Level
Floor Plan**

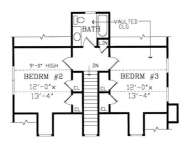

**Upper Level
Floor Plan**

*Copyright by design-
er/architect.*

Plan #131021

Dimensions: 60'0" W x 52'4" D
Levels: 2
Square Footage: 3,110
Main Level Sq. Ft.: 1,818
Upper Level Sq. Ft.: 1,292
Bedrooms: 5
Bathrooms: 2½
Foundation: Basement, crawl space, or slab
Materials List Available: Yes
Price Category: H

This home, as shown in the photograph, may differ from the actual blueprints. For more detailed information, please check the floor plans carefully.

Photo provided by designer/architect.

Features:

- Ceiling Height: 8 ft.

- Foyer: This two-story high foyer is breathtaking.

- Family Room: Roomy with open views of the kitchen, the family room has a vaulted ceiling and boasts a functional fireplace and a built-in entertainment center.

- Dining Room: Formal yet comfortable, this spacious dining room is perfect for entertaining family and friends.

- Kitchen: Perfectly located with access to a breakfast room and the family room, this U-shaped kitchen with large center island is charming as well as efficient.

- Master Suite: Enjoy this sizable room with a vaulted ceiling, two large walk-in closets, and a lovely compartmented bath.

Rear Elevation

Amenities abound in this luxurious two-story beauty with a cozy gazebo on one corner of the spectacular wraparound front porch. Comfort, functionality, and spaciousness characterize this home.

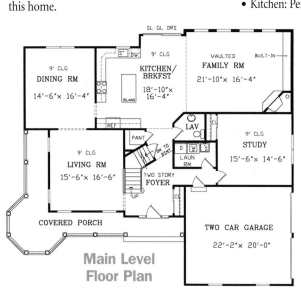

Main Level Floor Plan

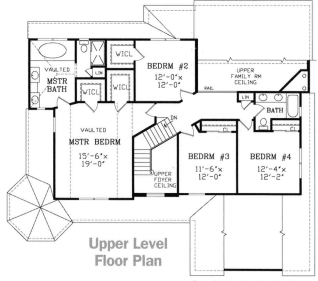

Upper Level Floor Plan

Copyright by designer/architect.

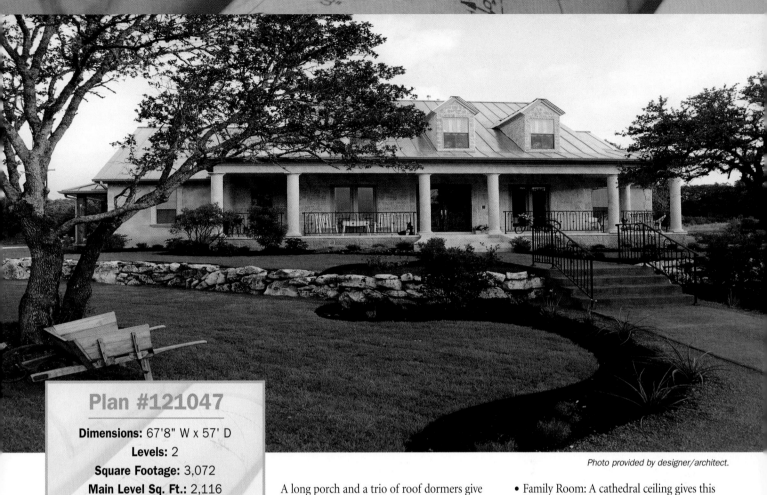

Plan #121047

Dimensions: 67'8" W x 57' D
Levels: 2
Square Footage: 3,072
Main Level Sq. Ft.: 2,116
Upper Level Sq. Ft.: 956
Bedrooms: 4
Bathrooms: 3½
Foundation: Slab
Materials List Available: Yes
Price Category: G

Photo provided by designer/architect.

A long porch and a trio of roof dormers give this gracious home a sophisticated country look.

Features:

• Ceiling Height: 8 ft. unless otherwise noted.

• Balcony: This balcony overlooks the entry and the staircase hall.

• Dining Room: Columns and a cased opening lend elegance, making this the perfect venue for stylish dinner parties.

• Family Room: A cathedral ceiling gives this room a light and airy feel. The handsome fireplace framed by windows is sure to become a favorite family gathering place.

• Master Suite: This architecturally distinctive bedroom features a bayed sitting area and a tray ceiling.

• Bedrooms: One of the bedrooms enjoys a private bath, making it a perfect guest room. Other bedrooms feature walk-in closets.

CAD FILE AVAILABLE

Main Level Floor Plan

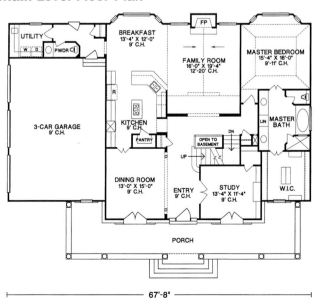

Upper Level Floor Plan

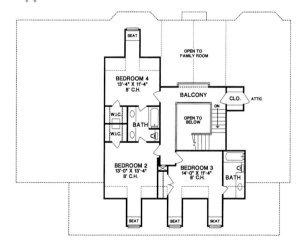

Copyright by designer/architect.

Plan #171017

Dimensions: 84' W x 54' D
Levels: 2
Square Footage: 2,558
Main Level Sq. Ft.: 1,577
Upper Level Sq. Ft.: 981
Bedrooms: 4
Bathrooms: 2½
Foundation: Slab, crawl space
Materials List Available: Yes
Price Category: E

Illustration provided by designer/architect.

Main Level Floor Plan

Upper Level Floor Plan

Copyright by designer/architect.

Plan #281003

Dimensions: 71' W x 35' D
Levels: 2
Square Footage: 2,370
Main Level Sq. Ft.: 1,252
Upper Level Sq. Ft.: 1,118
Bedrooms: 4
Bathrooms: 2½
Foundation: Full basement
Materials List Available: Yes
Price Category: E

Illustration provided by designer/architect.

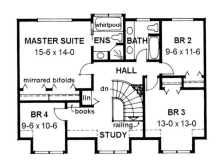

Upper Level Floor Plan

Copyright by designer/architect.

Main Level Floor Plan

Main Level Floor Plan ▲ ▼

44'-0"
13,2 m

11'-8" X 16'-4"
3,50 X 4,90

20'-4" X 21'-4"
6,10 X 6,40

26'-0" X 15'-0"
7,80 X 4,50

12'-4" X 14'-0"
3,70 X 4,20

18'-4" X 20'-0"
5,50 X 6,00

◄ 60'-0" ►
18,0 m

Plan #181034

Dimensions: 60' W x 44' D

Levels: 2

Square Footage: 2,687

Main Level Sq. Ft.: 1,297

Upper Level Sq. Ft.: 1,390

Bedrooms: 3

Bathrooms: 2½

Foundation: Full basement

Materials List Available: Yes

Price Category: F

Images provided by designer/architect.

Upper Level Floor Plan

11'-0" X 11'-0"
3,30 X 3,30

11'-8" X 16'-4"
3,50 X 4,90

18'-0" X 15'-0"
5,40 X 4,50

12'-4" X 15'-4"
3,70 X 4,00

12'-4" X 14'-0"
3,70 X 4,20

12'-0" X 21'-4"
3,60 X 6,40

11'-8" X 9'-6"
3,50 X 2,90

Copyright by designer/architect.

Main Level Floor Plan

DECK

BRKFST.
10 x 7

FAMILY
14 x 20

d w

KIT.
12 x 15

GARAGE
24 x 27

LIVING
14 x 12

DINING
12 x 14

PORCH

Plan #381002

Dimensions: 68'4" W x 42'4" D

Levels: 2

Square Footage: 2,225

Main Level Sq. Ft.: 1,125

Upper Level Sq. Ft.: 1,100

Bedrooms: 3

Bathrooms: 2½

Foundation: Basement, crawl space

Materials List Available: Yes

Price Category: E

Images provided by designer/architect.

Upper Level Floor Plan

BEDROOM
12 x 13

STUDY
17 x 11

BEDROOM
14 x 21

BEDROOM
12 x 16

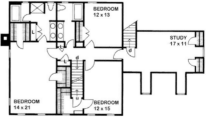

Copyright by designer/architect.

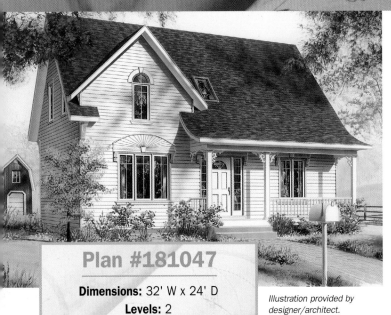

Main Level Floor Plan

24'-0"
7,2 m

32'-0"
9,6 m

15'-0" X 11'-0"
4,50 X 3,30

12'-0" X 14'-0"
3,60 X 4,20

12'-0" X 11'-0"
3,60 X 3,30

Plan #181047

Dimensions: 32' W x 24' D

Levels: 2

Square Footage: 1,458

Main Level Sq. Ft.: 768

Upper Level Sq. Ft.: 690

Bedrooms: 3

Bathrooms: 2½

Foundation: Full basement

Materials List Available: Yes

Price Category: B

Illustration provided by designer/architect.

CAD FILE AVAILABLE

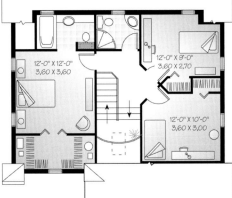

Upper Level Floor Plan

Copyright by designer/architect.

12'-0" X 12'-0"
3,60 X 3,60

12'-0" X 9'-0"
3,60 X 2,70

12'-0" X 10'-0"
3,60 X 3,00

Main Level Floor Plan

40'-0"
12,0 m

42'-0"
12,6 m

20'-8" X 11'-4"
6,20 X 3,40

17'-0" X 11'-0"
5,10 X 3,30

15'-4" X 22'-8"
4,60 X 6,80

12'-8" X 15'-8"
3,80 X 4,70

Plan #181074

Dimensions: 42' W x 40' D

Levels: 2

Square Footage: 1,760

Main Level Sq. Ft.: 880

Upper Level Sq. Ft.: 880

Bedrooms: 4

Full Baths: 2½

Foundation: Full basement

Materials List Available: Yes

Price Category: D

Illustration provided by designer/architect.

CAD FILE AVAILABLE

Upper Level Floor Plan

Copyright by designer/architect.

13'-4" X 9'-0"
4,00 X 2,70

11'-0" X 11'-0"
3,30 X 3,30

15'-8" X 15'-4"
4,70 X 4,60

12'-8" X 15'-8"
3,80 X 4,70

Plan #121014

Dimensions: 52' W x 47'4" D
Levels: 2
Square Footage: 1,869
Main Level Sq. Ft.: 1,421
Upper Level Sq. Ft.: 448
Bedrooms: 3
Bathrooms: 2
Foundation: Basement; crawl space or slab for fee
Materials List Available: Yes
Price Category: D

Photo provided by designer/architect.

This compact home is packed with all the amenities you'll need for a gracious lifestyle.

Features:

• Ceiling Height: 8 ft. except as noted.

• Great Room: A soaring ceiling and six tall transom-topped windows make this a light and airy spot for entertaining.

• Formal Dining Room: This elegant room is ideal for entertaining dinner guests.

• Breakfast Area: This sunny area shares a see-through fireplace with the great room. It's the perfect place to start the day.

• Master Suite: Here are all the features you expect to find in large luxury homes. Wake up to tall, sloped ceilings, and enjoy the corner whirlpool, separate shower, and vanity. A large walk-in closet provides plenty of wardrobe storage.

• Attached Garage: The garage provides two bays of parking plus plenty of storage space.

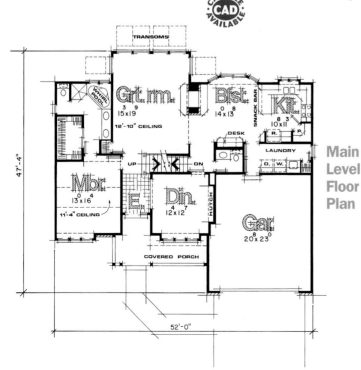

Main Level Floor Plan

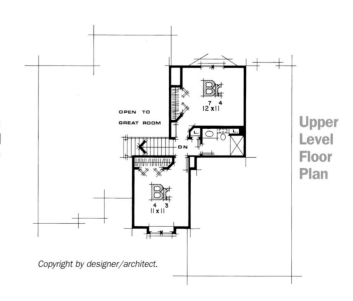

Upper Level Floor Plan

Copyright by designer/architect.

Plan #131029

Dimensions: 56'4" W x 46'6" D
Levels: 2
Square Footage: 2,936
Main Level Sq. Ft.: 1,680
Upper Level Sq. Ft.: 1,256
Bedrooms: 4
Bathrooms: 2½
Foundation: Crawl space, slab, or basement
Materials List Available: Yes
Price Category: G

This home, as shown in the photograph, may differ from the actual blueprints. For more detailed information, please check the floor plans carefully.

Photos provided by designer/arch

This home is ideal if you love the look of a country-style farmhouse.

Features:

- **Foyer:** Walk across the large wraparound porch that defines this home to enter this two-story foyer.

- **Living Room:** French doors from the foyer lead into this living room.

- **Family Room:** The whole family will love this room, with its vaulted ceiling, fireplace, and sliding glass doors that open to the wooden rear deck.

- **Kitchen:** A beautiful sit-down center island opens to the family room. There's also a breakfast nook with a lovely bay window.

- **Master Suite:** Luxury abounds with vaulted ceilings, walk-in closets, private bath with whirlpool tub, separate shower, and dual sinks.

- **Loft:** A special place with vaulted ceiling and view into the family room below.

Main Level Floor Plan

Copyright by designer/architect.

Dining Room

Breakfast Area

Kitchen Island

Kitchen

Master Bathroom

Plan #181085

Dimensions: 56'4" W x 44' D
Levels: 2
Square Footage: 2,183
Main Level Sq. Ft.: 1,232
Second Level Sq. Ft.: 951
Bedrooms: 3
Bathrooms: 2½
Foundation: Basement
Materials List Available: Yes
Price Category: E

This country home features an inviting front porch and a layout designed for modern living.

Illustration provided by designer/architect.

CAD FILE AVAILABLE

Features:

- Ceiling Height: 8 ft.
- Solarium: Sunlight streams through the windows of this solarium at the front of the house.
- Living Room: Walk through French doors, and you will enter this inviting living room. Family and friends will be drawn to the corner fireplace.
- Formal Dining Room: Usher your guests directly from the living room into this formal dining room. The kitchen is located on the other side of the dining room for convenient service.
- Kitchen: This generously sized kitchen is a delight, it offers a center island, separate eat-in area, and access to the back deck.
- Bonus Room: This room just off the entry hall can become a family room, a bedroom, or an office.
- Master Suite: Curl up by the corner fireplace in this master retreat, with its walk-in closet and lavish bath with separate shower and tub.

Main Level Floor Plan

Upper Level Floor Plan

Copyright by designer/architect.

Plan #251008

Dimensions: 44'4" W x 73' 2" D

Levels: 2

Square Footage: 1,808

Main Level Sq. Ft.: 1,271

Upper Level Sq. Ft.: 537

Bedrooms: 3

Bathrooms: 2½

Foundation: Basement

Materials List Available: Yes

Price Category: D

Illustration provided by designer/architect.

An elegant front dormer adds distinction to this country home and brings light into the foyer.

Features:

• Ceiling Height: 9 ft. unless otherwise noted

• Front Porch: A full-length front porch adds to the country charm and provides a relaxing place to sit.

• Foyer: This impressive foyer soars to two stories thanks to the front dormer.

• Dining Room: This dining room has ample space for entertaining. After dinner, guests can step out of the dining room directly onto the rear deck.

• Kitchen: This well-designed kitchen has a double sink. It features a snack bar with plenty of room for impromptu meals.

• Master Bedroom: This distinctive master bedroom features a large-walk-in closet.

• Master Bath: This master bath features walk-in closets in addition to a double vanity and a deluxe tub.

CAD FILE AVAILABLE

Main Level Floor Plan

Copyright by designer/architect.

Upper Level Floor Plan

Plan #391026

Dimensions: 35' W x 42' D
Levels: 2
Square Footage: 1,470
Main Level Sq. Ft.: 1,035
Upper Level Sq. Ft.: 435
Bedrooms: 3
Bathrooms: 2
Foundation: Basement, crawl space, slab
Materials List Available: Yes
Price Category: B

Images provided by designer/architect.

Main Level Floor Plan

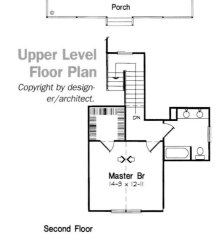

Deck

Brkfst
9-0 x 6-0

flat clg.

Kit.
11-6 x 9-8

Br #2
12-2 x 9-11

UP

Foyer
flat clg.

DN

Utility

Living Rm
18-11 x 12-11

Br #3
12-2 x 9-3

Porch

Upper Level Floor Plan

Copyright by designer/architect.

DN

Master Br
14-3 x 12-11

Second Floor

Plan #181094

Dimensions: 50' W x 39' D
Levels: 2
Square Footage: 2,099
Main Level Sq. Ft.: 1,060
Upper Level Sq. Ft.: 1,039
Bedrooms: 4
Bathrooms: 2½
Foundation: Full basement
Materials List Available: Yes
Price Category: D

Images provided by designer/architect.

CAD FILE AVAILABLE

Main Level Floor Plan

39'-0"
11,7 m

12'-4" X 12'-0"
3,70 X 3,60

11'-0" X 13'-4"
3,30 X 4,00

11'-6" X 14'-8"
3,50 X 4,40

20'-0" X 22'-0"
6,00 X 6,60

12'-0" X 14'-8"
3,60 X 4,40

50'-0"
15,0 m

Upper Level Floor Plan

Copyright by designer/architect.

12'-8" X 11'-4"
3,80 X 3,40

11'-0" X 10'-0"
3,30 X 3,00

11'-0" X 10'-0"
3,30 X 3,00

12'-0" X 14'-8"
3,60 X 4,40

Plan #241012

Dimensions: 63'9" W x 56'3" D
Levels: 2
Square Footage: 2,743
Main Level Sq. Ft.: 2,153
Upper Level Sq. Ft.: 590
Bedrooms: 3
Bathrooms: 2½
Foundation: Slab
Materials List Available: No
Price Category: E

Images provided by designer/architect.

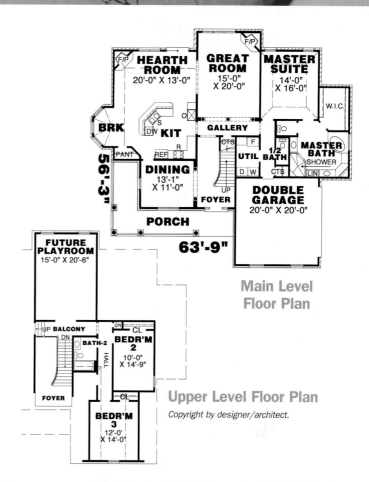

Main Level Floor Plan

Upper Level Floor Plan

Copyright by designer/architect.

Plan #241014

Dimensions: 66'6" W x 55'6" D
Levels: 2
Square Footage: 3,046
Main Level Sq. Ft.: 2,292
Upper Level Sq. Ft.: 754
Bedrooms: 4
Bathrooms: 3
Foundation: Slab
Materials List Available: No
Price Category: G

Images provided by designer/architect.

Main Level Floor Plan

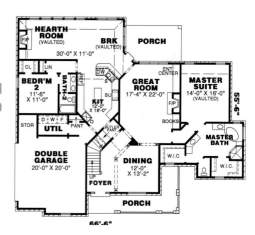

Upper Level Floor Plan

Copyright by designer/architect.

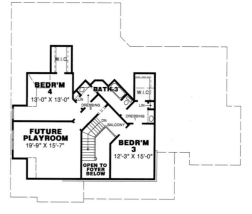

Plan #121016

Dimensions: 56' W x 48' D
Levels: 2
Square Footage: 2,594
Main Level Sq. Ft.: 1,322
Upper Level Sq. Ft.: 1,272
Bedrooms: 4
Bathrooms: 3
Foundation: Basement
Materials List Available: Yes
Price Category: E

A huge wraparound porch gives this home warmth and charm.

Features:

- Ceiling Height: 8 ft. except as noted.
- Family Room: This informal sunken room's beamed ceiling and fireplace flanked by windows makes it the perfect place for family gatherings.
- Formal Dining Room: Guests will enjoy gathering in this large elegant room.

- Master Suite: The second-floor master bedroom features its own luxurious bathroom.
- Compartmented Full Bath: This large bathroom serves the three secondary bedrooms on the second floor.
- Optional Play Area: This special space, included in one of the bedrooms, features a cathedral ceiling.
- Kitchen: A large island is the centerpiece of this modern kitchen's well-designed food-preparation area.

Main Level Floor Plan

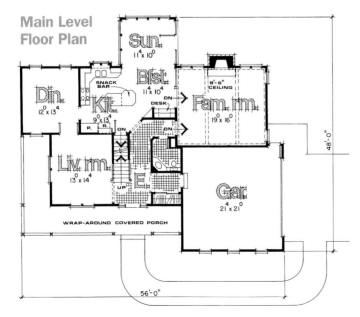

Upper Level Floor Plan

Plan #121044

Dimensions: 40' W x 55'8" D

Levels: 2

Square Footage: 1,923

Main Level Sq. Ft.: 1,351

Upper Level Sq. Ft.: 572

Bedrooms: 3

Bathrooms: 3

Foundation: Basement

Materials List Available: Yes

Price Category: D

Photo provided by designer/architect.

The layout of this gracious home is designed with the contemporary family in mind.

Features:

• Ceiling Height: 8 ft. unless otherwise noted.

• Foyer: This elegant entry is graced with an open stairway that enhances the sense of spaciousness.

• Kitchen: Located just beyond the entry, this convenient kitchen features a center island that doubles as a snack bar.

• Breakfast Area: A sloped ceiling unites this area with the family room. Here you will find a planning desk for compiling menus and shopping lists.

• Master Bedroom: This bedroom has a distinctively contemporary appeal, with its cathedral ceiling and triple window.

• Computer Loft: Designed to house a computer, this loft overlooks the family room.

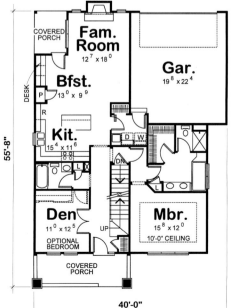

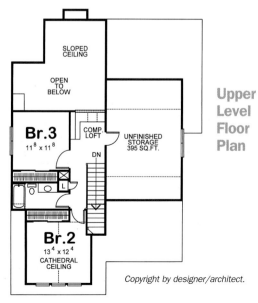

Copyright by designer/architect.

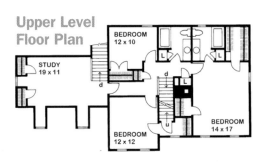

DECK

BRKFST.
10 x 9

KIT.
12 x 11

GARAGE
22 x 25

DINING
12 x 14

LIVING
14 x 25

PORCH

*Images provided by
designer/architect.*

**Upper Level
Floor Plan**

STUDY
19 x 11

BEDROOM
12 x 10

BEDROOM
12 x 12

BEDROOM
14 x 17

Copyright by designer/architect.

Plan #381003

Dimensions: 63' W x 38'8" D
Levels: 2
Square Footage: 1,925
Main Level Sq. Ft.: 1,000
Upper Level Sq. Ft.: 925
Bedrooms: 3
Bathrooms: 2½
Foundation: Basement, crawl space
Materials List Available: Yes
Price Category: D

DECK

BEDROOM
14 x 15

KIT.
13 x 13

DINING
11 x 15

LIVING
14 x 15

**Main Level
Floor Plan**

PORCH

Copyright by designer/architect.

*Images provided by
designer/architect.*

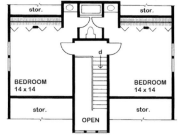

**Upper Level
Floor Plan**

stor.

stor.

BEDROOM
14 x 14

BEDROOM
14 x 14

stor.

stor.

OPEN

Plan #381004

Dimensions: 44' W x 48' D
Levels: 2
Square Footage: 1,860
Main Level Sq. Ft.: 1,155
Upper Level Sq. Ft.: 705
Bedrooms: 3
Bathrooms: 2½
Foundation: Basement
Materials List Available: Yes
Price Category: D

Plan #211072

Dimensions: 62' W x 86' D
Levels: 2
Square Footage: 3,012
Main Level Sq. Ft.: 2,202
Upper Level Sq. Ft.: 810
Bedrooms: 4
Bathrooms: 3½
Foundation: Crawl space, optional basement
Materials List Available: Yes
Price Category: G

Photo provided by designer/architect.

CAD FILE AVAILABLE

Main Level Floor Plan

Upper Level Floor Plan

Copyright by designer/architect.

Plan #211073

Dimensions: 66' W x 80' D
Levels: 1½
Square Footage: 3,119
Main Level Sq. Ft.: 2,092
Upper Level Sq. Ft.: 1,027
Bedrooms: 4
Bathrooms: 3½
Foundation: Foundation: Crawl space, optional basement
Materials List Available: Yes
Price Category: G

Photo provided by designer/architect.

CAD FILE AVAILABLE

Main Level Floor Plan

Upper Level Floor Plan

Copyright by designer/architect.

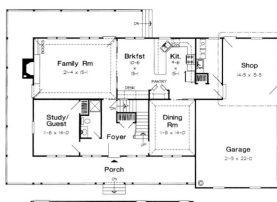

Main Level Floor Plan

Images provided by designer/architect.

Upper Level Floor Plan

Copyright by designer/architect.

Plan #391024

Dimensions: 71' W x 45' D
Levels: 2
Square Footage: 2,647
Main Level Sq. Ft.: 1,378
Upper Level Sq. Ft.: 1,269
Bedrooms: 4
Bathrooms: 2¾
Foundation: Crawl space, basement, slab
Materials List Available: No
Price Category: F

Main Level Floor Plan

Images provided by designer/architect.

Upper Level Floor Plan

Copyright by designer/architect.

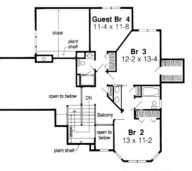

Second Floor

Plan #391041

Dimensions: 41' W x 50' D
Levels: 2
Square Footage: 1,880
Main Level Sq. Ft.: 1,244
Upper Level Sq. Ft.: 636
Bedrooms: 3
Bathrooms: 2½
Foundation: Slab
Materials List Available: No
Price Category: D

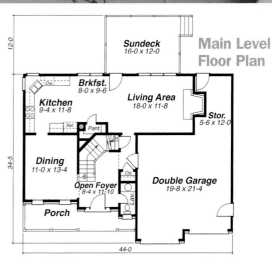

Main Level Floor Plan

Sundeck
16-0 x 12-0

Brkfst.
8-0 x 9-6

Kitchen
9-4 x 11-8

Living Area
18-0 x 11-8

Stor.
5-6 x 12-0

Dining
11-0 x 13-4

Open Foyer
8-4 x 11-10

Double Garage
19-8 x 21-4

Porch

12-0
34-5
44-0

Plan #141009

Dimensions: 44' W x 34'5" D

Levels: 2

Square Footage: 1,683

Main Level Sq. Ft.: 797

Upper Level Sq. Ft.: 886

Bedrooms: 3

Bathrooms: 2½

Foundation: Basement, crawl space or slab

Materials List Available: No

Price Category: C

Images provided by designer/architect.

Upper Level Floor Plan

M.Bath

Bdrm. 3
13-0 x 9-6

Master Bdrm.
15-6 x 11-0

Open Foyer

Bdrm. 2
13-0 x 9-6

Bth. 2

Copyright by designer/architect.

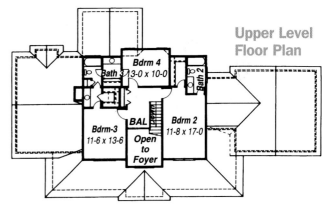

Upper Level Floor Plan

Bath 3

Bdrm 4
13-0 x 10-0

Bath 2

Bdrm-3
11-6 x 13-6

BAL

Open to Foyer

Bdrm 2
11-8 x 17-0

Copyright by designer/architect.

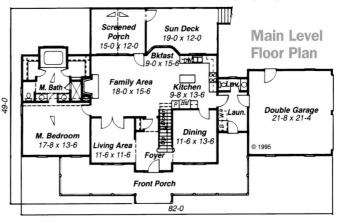

Main Level Floor Plan

Screened Porch
15-0 x 12-0

Sun Deck
19-0 x 12-0

Bkfast
9-0 x 15-6

M. Bath

Family Area
18-0 x 15-6

Kitchen
9-8 x 13-6

Lav.

M. Bedroom
17-8 x 13-6

Living Area
11-6 x 11-6

Foyer

Dining
11-6 x 13-6

Laun.

Double Garage
21-8 x 21-4

© 1995

Front Porch

49-0
82-0

Plan #141017

Dimensions: 82' W x 49' D

Levels: 2

Square Footage: 2,480

Main Level Sq. Ft.: 1,581

Upper Level Sq. Ft.: 899

Bedrooms: 4

Bathrooms: 3½

Foundation: Basement, crawl space, or slab

Materials List Available: Yes

Price Category: E

Images provided by designer/architect.

Plan #151027

Dimensions: 37' W x 73' D
Levels: 2
Square Footage: 2,332
Main Level Sq. Ft.: 1,713
Upper Level Sq. Ft.: 619
Bedrooms: 3
Bathrooms: 3
Foundation: Crawl space, slab; optional basement plan available for extra fee
CompleteCost List Available: Yes
Price Category: E

A traditional design with a covered front porch and high ceilings in many rooms gives this home all the space and comfort you'll ever need.

Features:

- Foyer: A formal foyer with 8-in. wood columns will lead you to an elegant dining area.

- Great Room: This wonderful gathering room has 10-ft. boxed ceilings, a built-in media center, and an atrium door leading to a rear grilling porch.

- Kitchen: Functional yet cozy, this kitchen opens to the breakfast area with built-in computer desk and is open to the great room as well.

- Master Suite: Pamper yourself in this luxurious bedroom with 10-ft. boxed ceilings, large walk-in closets, and a bath area with a whirlpool tub, shower, and double vanity.

- Second Level: A game room and two bedrooms with walk-thru baths make this floor special.

Main Level Floor Plan

Upper Level Floor Plan

Copyright by designer/architect.

Plan #151029

Dimensions: 59'4" W x 74'2" D

Levels: 1½

Square Footage: 2,777

Main Level Sq. Ft.: 2,082

Upper Level Sq. Ft.: 695

Bedrooms: 4

Bathrooms: 2

Foundation: Crawl space, slab; optional basement plan available for extra fee

CompleteCost List Available: Yes

Price Category: F

Photo provided by designer/architect.

This grand home combines historic Southern charm with modern technology and design. A two-car garage and covered front porch allow for optimum convenience.

Features:

- **Foyer:** This marvelous foyer leads directly to an elegant dining room and comfortable great room.

- **Great Room:** With high ceilings, a built-in media center, and a fireplace, this will be your favorite room during the chilly fall months.

- **Kitchen:** An eat-in-bar with an optional island, computer area, and adjoining breakfast room with a bay window make a perfect layout.

- **Master Suite:** Relax in comfort with a corner whirlpool tub, a separate glass shower, double vanities, and large walk-in closets.

- **Upper Level Bedrooms:** 2 and 3 both have window seats.

CAD FILE AVAILABLE

Copyright by designer/architect.

Main Level Floor Plan

Upper Level Floor Plan

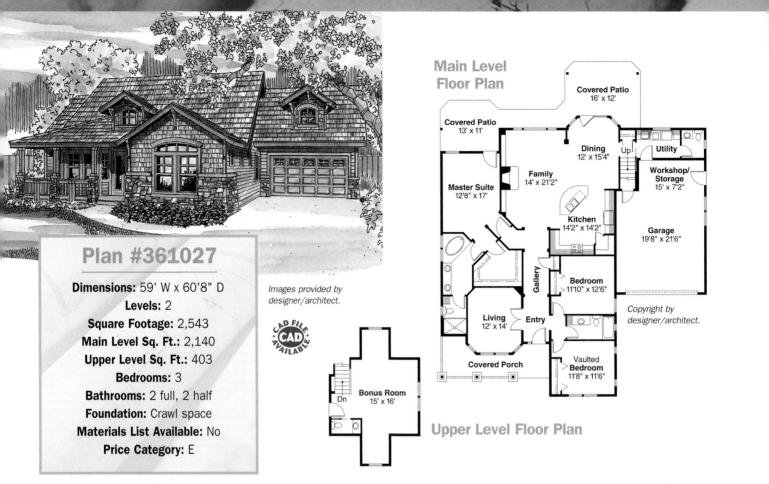

Plan #361027

Dimensions: 59' W x 60'8" D
Levels: 2
Square Footage: 2,543
Main Level Sq. Ft.: 2,140
Upper Level Sq. Ft.: 403
Bedrooms: 3
Bathrooms: 2 full, 2 half
Foundation: Crawl space
Materials List Available: No
Price Category: E

Images provided by designer/architect.

CAD FILE AVAILABLE

Main Level Floor Plan

Covered Patio 16' x 12'
Covered Patio 13' x 11'
Dining 12' x 15'4"
Family 14' x 21'2"
Master Suite 12'8" x 17'
Utility
Workshop/Storage 15' x 7'2"
Kitchen 14'2" x 14'2"
Garage 19'8" x 21'6"
Gallery
Bedroom 11'10" x 12'6"
Living 12' x 14'
Entry
Bonus Room 15' x 16'
Covered Porch
Vaulted Bedroom 11'8" x 11'6"

Copyright by designer/architect.

Upper Level Floor Plan

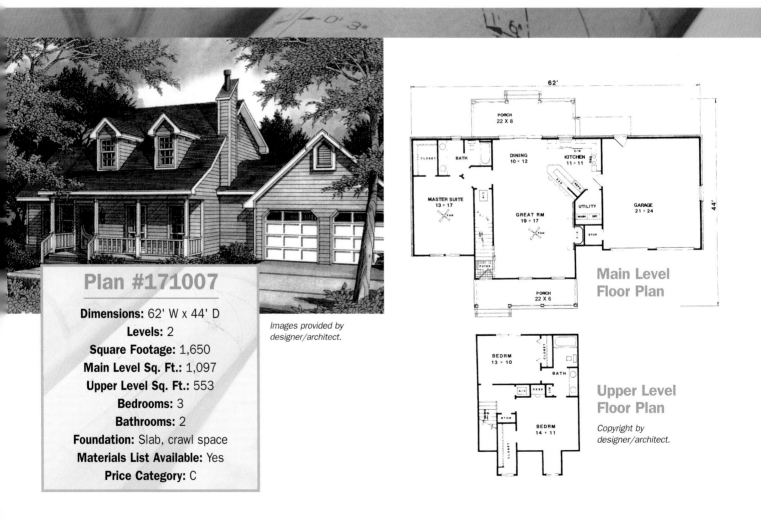

Plan #171007

Dimensions: 62' W x 44' D
Levels: 2
Square Footage: 1,650
Main Level Sq. Ft.: 1,097
Upper Level Sq. Ft.: 553
Bedrooms: 3
Bathrooms: 2
Foundation: Slab, crawl space
Materials List Available: Yes
Price Category: C

Images provided by designer/architect.

62'
PORCH 22 X 8
CLOSET
BATH
DINING 10 x 12
KITCHEN 11 x 11
MASTER SUITE 13 x 17
GREAT RM 19 x 17
UTILITY
GARAGE 21 x 24
FOYER
44'
PORCH 22 X 6

Main Level Floor Plan

BEDRM 13 x 10
CLOSET
BATH
A/C DESK
BEDRM 14 x 11
CLOSET

Upper Level Floor Plan

Copyright by designer/architect.

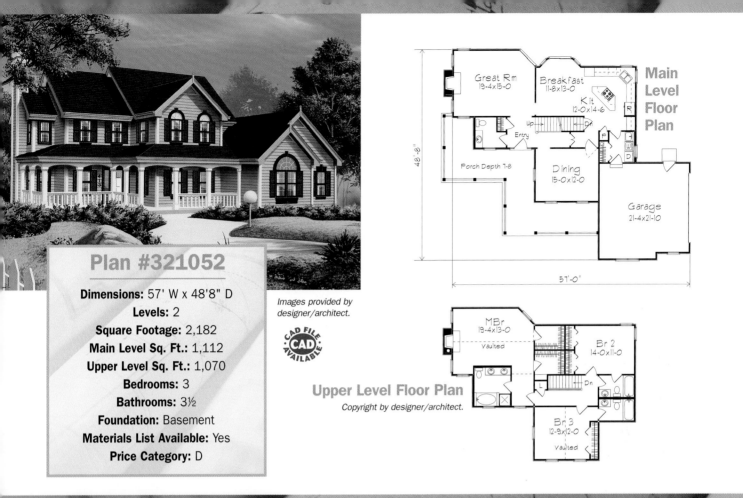

Plan #321052

Dimensions: 57' W x 48'8" D

Levels: 2

Square Footage: 2,182

Main Level Sq. Ft.: 1,112

Upper Level Sq. Ft.: 1,070

Bedrooms: 3

Bathrooms: 3½

Foundation: Basement

Materials List Available: Yes

Price Category: D

Main Level Floor Plan

Images provided by designer/architect.

CAD FILE AVAILABLE

Upper Level Floor Plan

Copyright by designer/architect.

Plan #141012

Dimensions: 44'4" W x 38' D

Levels: 2

Square Footage: 1,870

Main Level Sq. Ft.: 1,159

Upper Level Sq. Ft.: 711

Bedrooms: 3

Bathrooms: 2½

Foundation: Basement

Materials List Available: Yes

Price Category: D

Main Level Floor Plan

Images provided by designer/architect.

Upper Level Floor Plan

Copyright by designer/architect.

Plan #131027

Dimensions: 62'4" W x 53'6" D
Levels: 1.5
Square Footage: 2,567
Main Level Sq. Ft.: 2,017
Upper Level Sq. Ft.: 550
Bedrooms: 4
Bathrooms: 3
Foundation: Crawl space, slab, or basement
Materials List Available: Yes
Price Category: F

This home, as shown in the photograph, may differ from the actual blueprints. For more detailed information, please check the floor plans carefully.

Images provided by designer/archit

The features of this home are so good that you may have trouble imagining all of them at once.

Features:

- Great Room: Imagine a stepped ceiling, corner fireplace, built-media center, and wall of windows with a glass door to the backyard—in one room.

- Dining Room: A stepped ceiling and server with a sink add to the elegance of this formal room.

- Breakfast Room: Eat at the bar this room shares with the island kitchen, and admire the 12-ft. cathedral ceiling and bayed group of

8- and 9-ft. windows. Or go through the sliding glass door to the covered side porch.

- Master Suite: The bedroom has a tray ceiling and cozy sitting area, and a whirlpool tub, shower, and walk-in closet are in the skylighted bath.

- Optional Study: The private bath in bedroom 2 makes it ideal for a study or home office.

Breakfast Nook

Rear View

Great Room

Main Level Floor Plan

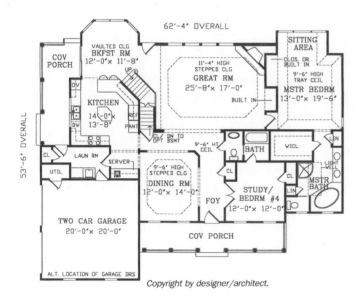

Copyright by designer/architect.

Upper Level Floor Plan

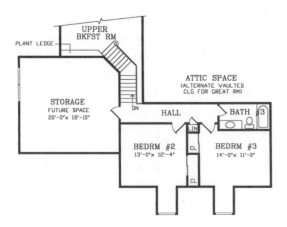

Painting Tips

As with any skill, there is a right and a wrong way to paint. There is a right way to hold a brush, a right way to maneuver a roller, a right way to spray a wall, etc. Follow these basic professional tips:

Brushing vs. Rolling. Some painters insist that only a brush-painted job looks right. However, most painters will "cut in" the edges with a brush, and then finish the main body of a wall or ceiling using a roller. Brushing alone can be time-consuming, and it is typically reserved for architectural woodwork.

Using the Right Brush. Use the largest brush with which you are comfortable. Professional painters seldom pick up anything smaller than a 4-inch brush. Most homeowners will achieve good results using a 4-inch brush for "cutting in" and for large surfaces, and an angled 2½- to 3-inch sash brush for trim around windows and doors. Be sure, also, to use brushes that are appropriate for the type of paint being applied. Oil-based paints require a natural bristle (also called "China bristles"), while water-based paints are applied with a synthetic bristle brush.

Handling a Brush. Many people grip a paintbrush as if they were shaking someone's hand. It is better to grip a brush more like a pencil, with the fingers and thumb wrapped around the metal ferrule. This grip provides the hand and wrist with a wider range of motion and therefore greater speed and precision. If your hand cramps, switch hands or switch temporarily to the handshake grip.

Wiping Rags. Before you begin painting, put a dust rag in your pocket. This is helpful for clearing away cobwebs and dust before painting. It is also handy for wiping off paint drips before they have a chance to dry.

Paint Hooks. When working on a ladder, use a good-quality paint hook to secure the paint bucket to your ladder. Avoid makeshift hooks made with wire or coat hangers. Paint hooks are inexpensive and available at virtually all paint and hardware stores.

Plan #131046

Dimensions: 68' W x 57'6" D
Levels: 2
Square Footage: 2,245
Main Level Sq. Ft.: 1,720
Upper Level Sq. Ft.: 525
Bedrooms: 3
Bathrooms: 2½
Foundation: Crawl space, slab, or basement
Materials List Available: Yes
Price Category: F

You'll love the mixture of country charm and contemporary amenities in this lovely home.

Features:

- **Porch:** The covered wraparound porch spells comfort, and the arched windows spell style.

- **Great Room:** Look up at the 18-ft. vaulted ceiling and the balcony that looks over this room from the upper level, and then notice the wall of windows and the fireplace that's set into a media wall for decorating ease.

- **Kitchen:** This roomy kitchen is also designed for convenience, thanks to its ample counter space and work island.

- **Breakfast Room:** The kitchen looks out to this lovely room, with its vaulted ceiling and sliding French doors that open to the rear covered porch.

- **Master Bedroom:** A 10-ft-ceiling and a dramatic bay window give character to this charming room.

Main Level Floor Plan

Upper Level Floor Plan

Plan #101014

Dimensions: 52' W x 28' D
Levels: 2
Square Footage: 1,598
Main Level Sq. Ft.: 812
Upper Level Sq. Ft.: 786
Bedrooms: 3
Bathrooms: 2½
Foundation: Slab, crawl space
Materials List Available: No
Price Category: D

This lovely Victorian home has a perfect balance of ornamental features and modern amenities.

Features:

- Ceiling Height: 8 ft. unless otherwise noted.

- Foyer: An impressive beveled glass-front door invites you into this roomy foyer.

- Kitchen: This bright and open kitchen offers an abundance of counter space to make cooking a pleasure.

- Breakfast Room: You'll enjoy plenty of informal family meals in this sunny and open spot next to the kitchen.

- Family Room: The whole family will be attracted to this handsome room. A full-width bay window adds to the Victorian charm.

- Master Suite: This dramatic suite features a multi-faceted vaulted ceiling and his and her closets and vanities. A separate shower and 6-ft. garden tub complete the lavish appointments.

Main Level Floor Plan

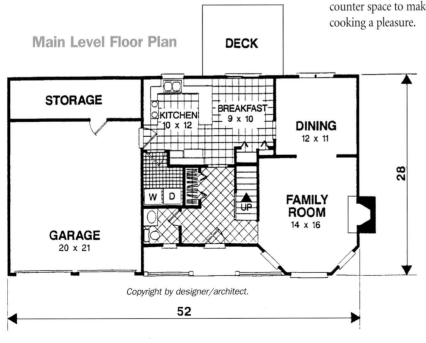

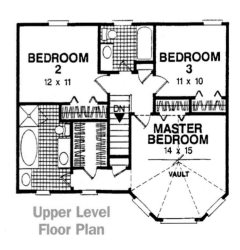

Upper Level Floor Plan

Plan #141023

Dimensions: 38' W x 40' D

Levels: 2

Square Footage: 1,715

Main Level Sq. Ft.: 1,046

Upper Level Sq. Ft.: 669

Bedrooms: 3

Bathrooms: 2½

Foundation: Basement

Materials List Available: Yes

Price Category: C

Photo provided by designer/architect.

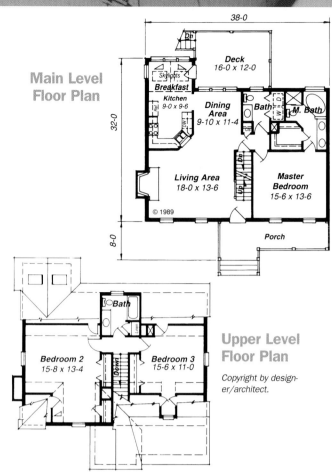

Main Level Floor Plan

Deck 16-0 x 12-0

Breakfast

Kitchen 9-0 x 9-6

Dining Area 9-10 x 11-4

Bath

M. Bath

Living Area 18-0 x 13-6

Master Bedroom 15-6 x 13-6

© 1989

Porch

38-0

32-0

8-0

Upper Level Floor Plan

Bath

Bedroom 2 15-8 x 13-4

Bedroom 3 15-6 x 11-0

Copyright by designer/architect.

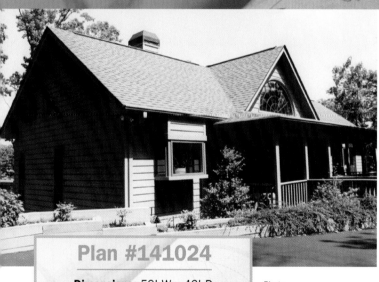

Plan #141024

Dimensions: 59' W x 46' D

Levels: 2

Square Footage: 1,732

Main Level Sq. Ft.: 1,128

Lower Level Sq. Ft.: 604

Bedrooms: 3

Bathrooms: 2½

Foundation: Basement

Materials List Available: Yes

Price Category: C

Photo provided by designer/architect.

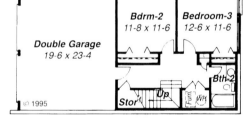

Double Garage 19-6 x 23-4

Bdrm-2 11-8 x 11-6

Bedroom-3 12-6 x 11-6

Bth-2

Stor

Up

Furn

WH

© 1995

Lower Level Floor Plan

Copyright by designer/architect.

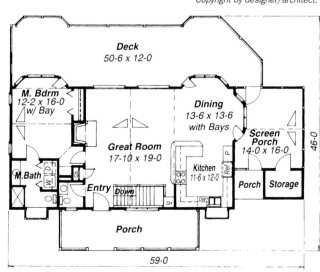

Main Level Floor Plan

Deck 50-6 x 12-0

M. Bdrm 12-2 x 16-0 w/ Bay

Dining 13-6 x 13-6 with Bays

Screen Porch 14-0 x 16-0

Great Room 17-10 x 19-0

Kitchen 11-6 x 12-0

Porch

Storage

M. Bath

Entry

Down

Porch

59-0

46-0

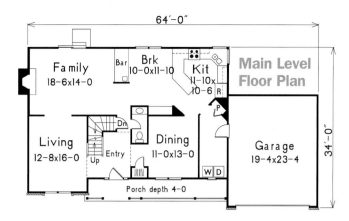

Main Level Floor Plan

64'-0"

34'-0"

Family 18-6x14-0
Bar
Brk 10-0x11-10
Kit 11-10x 10-6
Living 12-8x16-0
Dn
Up
Entry
Dining 11-0x13-0
Garage 19-4x23-4
W D
Porch depth 4-0

Plan #321041

Dimensions: 64' W x 34' D
Levels: 2
Square Footage: 2,286
Main Level Sq. Ft.: 1,283
Upper Level Sq. Ft.: 1,003
Bedrooms: 4
Bathrooms: 2½
Foundation: Basement
Materials List Available: Yes
Price Category: E

Images provided by designer/architect.

Copyright by designer/architect.

Upper Level Floor Plan

Br 4 10-2x 10-8
Br 3 11-7x10-8
MBr 12-8x15-11 vaulted
Dn L
open to below
Br 2 12-4x10-8

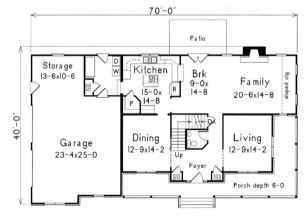

Main Level Floor Plan

70'-0"

40'-0"

Patio
Storage 13-6x10-6
D W
Kitchen 15-0x 14-8
Brk 9-0x 14-8
Family 20-6x14-8
sloped clg
P
Garage 23-4x25-0
Dining 12-9x14-2
Up
Dn
Living 12-9x14-2
Foyer
Porch depth 6-0

Plan #321055

Dimensions: 70' W x 40' D
Levels: 2
Square Footage: 2,505
Main Level Sq. Ft.: 1,436
Upper Level Sq. Ft.: 1,069
Bedrooms: 3
Bathrooms: 2½
Foundation: Basement
Materials List Available: Yes
Price Category: E

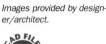

Images provided by designer/architect.

Upper Level Floor Plan

Copyright by designer/architect.

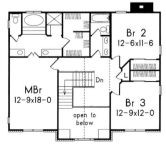

Br 2 12-6x11-6
MBr 12-9x18-0
Dn L
open to below
Br 3 12-9x12-0

Plan #131051

Dimensions: 64'4" W x 53'4" D
Levels: 3
Square Footage: 2,431
Main Level Sq. Ft.: 1,293
Upper Level Sq. Ft.: 1,138
Optional Third Level Sq. Ft.: 575
Bedrooms: 4
Bathrooms: 2½
Foundation: Basement, crawl space, or slab
Materials List Available: Yes
Price Category: F

Gracious and charming with a wraparound front porch and a backyard terrace, this home also has a ready-to-finish third floor all-purpose room and a full bath.

Features:

• Main Level Ceiling Height: 8 ft.

• Family Room: A comfortable space for the entire family to gather, this delightful room can be warmed by a heat-circulating fireplace.

• Dining Room: A cozy dinette boasts a sliding glass door with access to a gorgeous backyard terrace with an optional calm reflecting pool.

• Kitchen: Adjoining the dining area, the kitchen offers plenty of storage and counter space. The laundry room and half-bath are nearby for convenience.

• Garage: The garage is tucked way back to keep it from intruding into the traditional facade.

Main Level Floor Plan

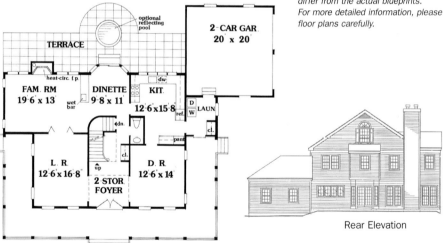

Photo provided by designer/architect.

This home, as shown in the photograph, may differ from the actual blueprints.
For more detailed information, please check the floor plans carefully.

Rear Elevation

Upper Level Floor Plan

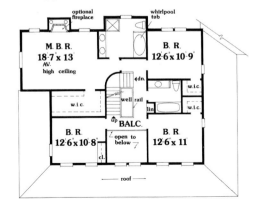

Optional 3rd Level Floor Plan

Copyright by designer/architect.

Plan #131024

Dimensions: 36' W by 54'4" D
Levels: 2
Square Footage: 1,635
Main Level Sq. Ft.: 880
Upper Level Sq. Ft.: 755
Bedrooms: 3
Bathrooms: 2½
Foundation: Basement, crawl space, or slab
Materials List Available: Yes
Price Category: D

Photo provided by designer/architect.

You'll love the combination of early-American detailing on the outside and the contemporary, open layout of the interior.

Features:

• Ceiling Height: 8 ft.

• Front Porch: Use this wraparound front porch as an extra room when the weather's fine.

• Living Room: Separated only by columns, the open arrangement of the living and dining rooms enhances the spacious feeling in this home.

• Family Room/Kitchen: This combination family room/country kitchen includes a large work island and snack bar for convenience.

• Master Suite: A tray ceiling creates a contemporary look in the spacious master bedroom, and three closets make it practical. A compartmented full bath completes the suite.

• Bedrooms: Two additional bedrooms share a second full bath.

• Attic: Finish the attic space that's over the garage for even more living space.

Main Level Floor Plan

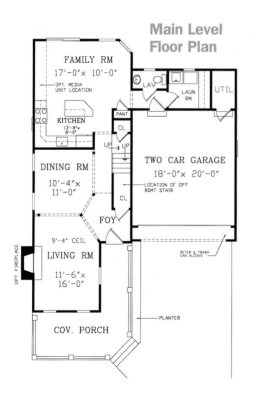

Upper Level Floor Plan

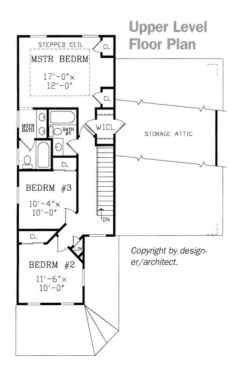

Copyright by designer/architect.

Rear Elevation

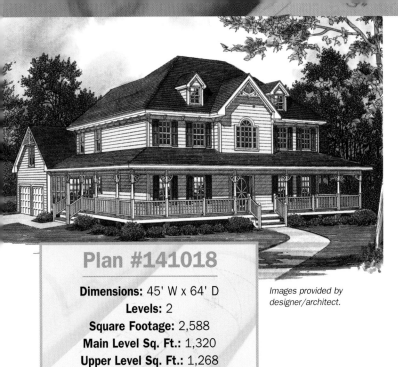

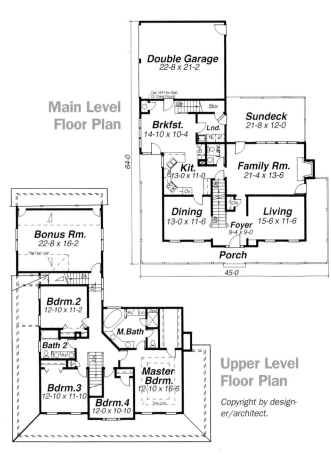

Plan #141018

Dimensions: 45' W x 64' D

Levels: 2

Square Footage: 2,588

Main Level Sq. Ft.: 1,320

Upper Level Sq. Ft.: 1,268

Bedrooms: 4

Bathrooms: 2½

Foundation: Basement, crawl space, or slab

Materials List Available: Yes

Price Category: E

Images provided by designer/architect.

Main Level Floor Plan

Double Garage
22-8 x 21-2

Opt. W/H for Slab Or Crawl Found.

Brkfst.
14-10 x 10-4

Sundeck
21-8 x 12-0

Kit.
13-0 x 11-0

Family Rm.
21-4 x 13-6

Dining
13-0 x 11-6

Living
15-6 x 11-6

Foyer
9-4 x 9-0

Porch

64-0

45-0

Bonus Rm.
22-8 x 16-2

Upper Level Floor Plan

Copyright by designer/architect.

Bdrm.2
12-10 x 11-2

M.Bath

Bath 2

Bdrm.3
12-10 x 11-10

Master Bdrm.
12-10 x 16-6

Bdrm.4
12-0 x 10-10

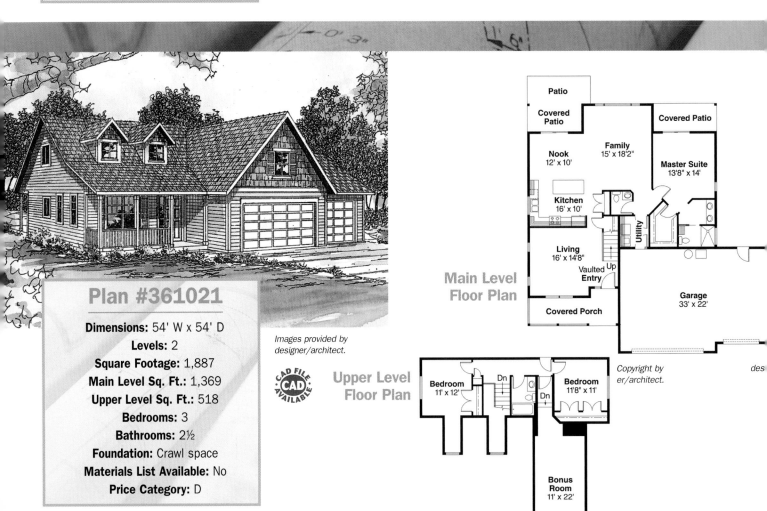

Plan #361021

Dimensions: 54' W x 54' D

Levels: 2

Square Footage: 1,887

Main Level Sq. Ft.: 1,369

Upper Level Sq. Ft.: 518

Bedrooms: 3

Bathrooms: 2½

Foundation: Crawl space

Materials List Available: No

Price Category: D

Images provided by designer/architect.

CAD FILE AVAILABLE

Main Level Floor Plan

Patio

Covered Patio

Covered Patio

Nook
12' x 10'

Family
15' x 18'2"

Master Suite
13'8" x 14'

Kitchen
16' x 10'

Utility

Living
16' x 14'8"

Vaulted Entry

Garage
33' x 22'

Covered Porch

Upper Level Floor Plan

Copyright by designer/architect.

Bedroom
11' x 12'

Dn

Bedroom
11'8" x 11'

Dn

Bonus Room
11' x 22'

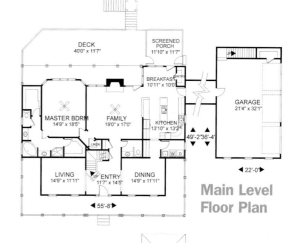

Main Level Floor Plan

Images provided by designer/architect.

CAD FILE AVAILABLE
CAD

Plan #101020

Dimensions: 55'8" W x 49'2" D
Levels: 2
Square Footage: 2,972
Main Level Sq. Ft.: 1,986
Upper Level Sq. Ft.: 986
Bedrooms: 4
Bathrooms: 3½
Foundation: Basement
Materials List Available: No
Price Category: F

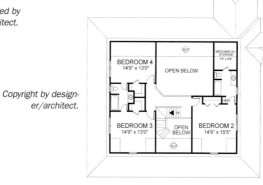

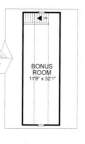

Copyright by designer/architect.

Upper Level Floor Plan

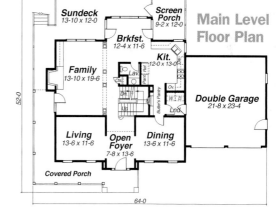

Main Level Floor Plan

Illustration provided by designer/architect.

Plan #141016

Dimensions: 64' W x 52' D
Levels: 2
Square Footage: 2,416
Main Level Sq. Ft.: 1,250
Upper Level Sq. Ft.: 1,166
Bedrooms: 4
Bathrooms: 2½
Foundation: Basement
Materials List Available: Yes
Price Category: E

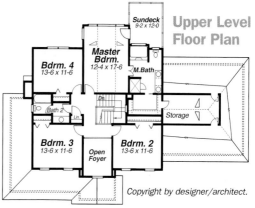

Upper Level Floor Plan

Copyright by designer/architect.

Photo provided by designer/architect.

Plan #121037

Dimensions: 46' W x 47'10" D

Levels: 2

Square Footage: 2,292

Main Level Sq. Ft.: 1,158

Upper Level Sq. Ft.: 1,134

Bedrooms: 4

Bathrooms: 2½

Foundation: Basement

Materials List Available: Yes

Price Category: E

This convenient and comfortable home is filled with architectural features that set it apart.

Features:

- Ceiling Height: 8 ft. unless otherwise noted.

- Foyer: You'll know you have arrived when you enter this two-story area highlighted by a decorative plant shelf and a balcony.

- Great Room: Just beyond the entry is the great room where the warmth of the two-sided fireplace will attract family and friends to gather. A bay window offers a more intimate place to sit and converse.

- Hearth Room: At the other side of the fireplace, the hearth offers a cozy spot for smaller gatherings or a place to sit alone and enjoy a book by the fire.

- Breakfast Area: With sunlight streaming into its bay window, the breakfast area offers the perfect spot for informal family meals.

- Master Suite: This private retreat is made more convenient by a walk-in closet. It features its own tub and shower.

CAD FILE AVAILABLE · CAD

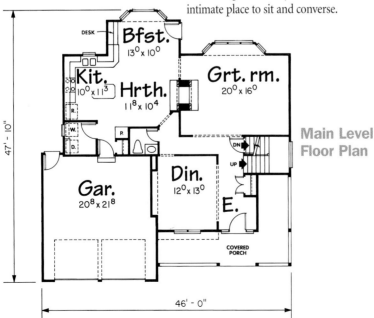

Main Level Floor Plan

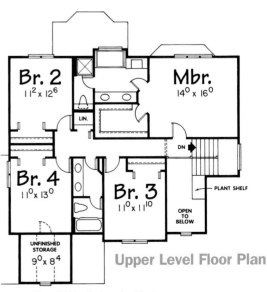

Upper Level Floor Plan

Copyright by designer/architect.

262   order direct: 1-800-523-6789

Plan #121083

Dimensions: 72' W x 45'4" D
Levels: 2
Square Footage: 2,695
Main Level Sq. Ft.: 1,881
Upper Level Sq. Ft.: 814
Bedrooms: 4
Bathrooms: 3½
Foundation: Basement
Materials List Available: Yes
Price Category: F

Photo provided by designer/architect.

You'll love this home for its soaring entryway ceiling and well-designed layout.

Features:

- **Entry:** A balcony from the upper level looks down into this two-story entry, which features a decorative plant shelf.

- **Great Room:** Comfort is guaranteed in this large room, with its built-in bookcases framing a lovely fireplace and trio of transom-topped windows along one wall.

- **Living Room:** Save both this formal room and the formal dining room, both of which flank the entry, for guests and special occasions.

- **Kitchen:** This convenient work space includes a gazebo-shaped breakfast area where friends and family will gather at any time of day.

Main Level Floor Plan

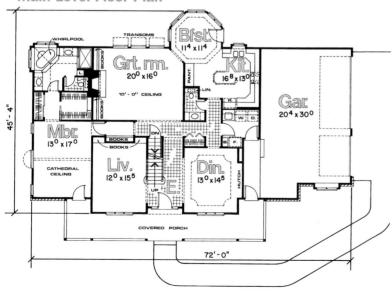

Upper Level Floor Plan

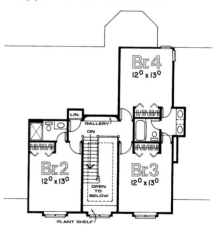

Copyright by designer/architect.

Plan #211069

Dimensions: 58' W x 42' D
Levels: 1½
Square Footage: 1,600
Main Level Sq. Ft.: 1,136
Upper Level Sq. Ft.: 464
Bedrooms: 3
Bathrooms: 2
Foundation: Crawl space
Materials List Available: Yes
Price Category: C

Photo provided by designer/architect.

Enjoy the large front porch on this traditionally styled home when it's too sunny for the bugs, and use the screened back porch at dusk and dawn.

Features:

• Living Room: Call this the family room if you wish, but no matter what you call it, expect friends and family to gather here, especially when the fireplace gives welcome warmth.

• Kitchen: You'll love the practical layout that pleases everyone from gourmet chefs to beginning cooks.

• Master Suite: Positioned on the main floor to give it privacy, this suite has two entrances for convenience. You'll find a large walk-in closet here as well as a dressing room that includes a separate vanity and mirror makeup counter.

• Storage Space: The 462-sq.-ft. garage is roomy enough to hold two cars and still have space to store tools, out-of-season clothing, or whatever else that needs a dry, protected spot.

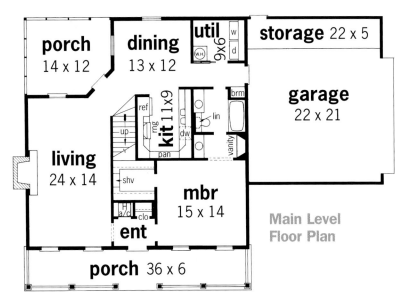

Main Level Floor Plan

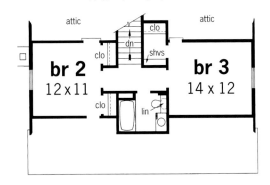

Upper Level Floor Plan

Copyright by designer/architect.

Plan #121038

Dimensions: 54' W x 52' D
Levels: 2
Square Footage: 2,332
Main Level Sq. Ft.: 1,597
Upper Level Sq. Ft.: 735
Bedrooms: 4
Bathrooms: 2½
Foundation: Basement
Materials List Available: Yes
Price Category: E

CAD FILE AVAILABLE

Offering plenty of architectural style, this home is designed with the busy modern lifestyle in mind.

Features:

- Ceiling Height: 8 ft. unless otherwise noted.

- Family Room: The visual spaciousness of this stylish family room is enhanced by a cathedral ceiling and light streaming through stacked windows.

- Kitchen: This is sure to be a popular informal gathering place. The kitchen features a convenient center island with a snack bar, pantry, and planning desk. The breakfast area is perfect for quick family meals.

- Master Suite: This peaceful retreat is thoughtfully located apart from the rest of the house. It includes a walk-in closet and a private bath.

- Bedrooms: Bedroom 2 has its own walk-in closet and private bath. Bedrooms 3 and 4 share a full bath.

Main Level Floor Plan

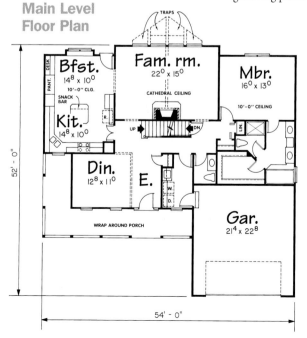

Upper Level Floor Plan

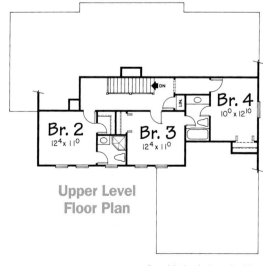

Plan #121040

Dimensions: 50' W x 48' D
Levels: 2
Square Footage: 1,818
Main Level Sq. Ft.: 1,302
Upper Level Sq. Ft.: 516
Bedrooms: 3
Bathrooms: 2½
Foundation: Basement
Materials List Available: Yes
Price Category: D

Offering plenty of architectural style, this home is designed with the busy modern lifestyle in mind.

Features:

- Ceiling Height: 8 ft. unless otherwise noted.

- Great Room: This is sure to be the central gathering place of the home with its volume ceiling, abundance of windows, and its handsome fireplace.

- Kitchen: This convenient and attractive kitchen offers plenty of storage. It includes a snack bar that will get lots of use for impromptu family meals.

- Breakfast Area: Joined to the kitchen by the snack bar, this breakfast area will invite you to linger over morning coffee. It includes a pantry and access to the backyard.

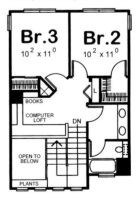

Upper Level Floor Plan

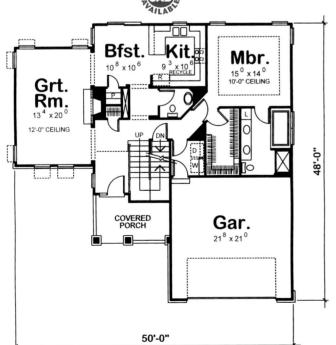

Main Level Floor Plan

- Master Bedroom: This private retreat offers the convenience of a walk-in closet and the luxury of its own whirlpool bath and shower.

- Computer Loft: Designed with the family computer in mind, this loft overlooks a two-story entry.

The Right Light

Lighting is one of the most important design elements in any home. Coordinating all of your artificial lighting sources—lamps, recessed or track lighting, sconces, ceiling-mounted fixtures, even pendants—can make the difference between a place that is warm and welcoming or one that is dark and depressing. In addition, light can be used in more focused ways—whether that be illuminating your desk in a home office or minimizing reflection as you watch a DVD on your big-screen television.

Light even has the power to visually reconfigure space, making rooms seem larger or smaller than they are. Lastly, the smart use of lighting can shine attention on architectural high points while obscuring less desirable details.

Lighting Plans

The rooms in your new home will combine the three types of lighting: ambient, task, and accent light. How you plan to use the room will determine the amount and type of lighting you will need. Although there are some general rules and an actual formula to determine how many watts of light to use for every square foot of space in your house, you must be the ultimate judge of your lighting needs.

General Lighting

Ambient Light. Because this is the soft diffused overall light that fills a room, ambient lighting is also called general lighting. Obviously, it is critical to the mood of a room. Aside from natural light, there are numerous artificial sources of ambient light. You can use all or some of them for your home.

Ceiling Fixtures. Standard ceiling-mounted fixtures, such as pendants and chandeliers, and recessed canisters are good sources of general lighting.

Sconces and Torcheres. Wall fixtures usually direct light upward, where it washes the wall and is reflected back into the room. Other possible sources of good general lighting are lamps with opaque shades. But the important thing to remember is that ambient light is inconspicuous. Although you know the source of the light, the glow is diffused. Of course, never use an exposed bulb, which is much too harsh.

How bright you should make the rooms in your new home depends on the way and the time of day the room will be used. To create the precise level of light, wire ambient light sources to dimmer switches. This puts you in control and allows you to easily

Recessed accent lighting highlights the painting and the shelves of collectibles.

adjust the light level. For example, in a family room you may want subdued lighting for watching a movie, and stronger, more cheerful lighting when you're hosting a kid's birthday party.

Task Lighting

Task lighting focuses on a specific area. It illuminates the work surface—whether it be the kitchen counter or the top of your desk in a home office. Metal architects' lamps, under-cabinet lights, reading lamps, and desk lamps are all excellent examples

Wall sconces, above left, placed on both sides of a bathroom mirror are good sources of light for applying makeup and general grooming.

Track-mounted spotlights, above right, serve a number of lighting needs. Here some provide general lighting while others accentuate the wall of art.

Use light to set off a collection, left, of personal objects. Here the items alone draw attention, but the lighting makes this area a focal point of the room.

of task lighting. Optimally, task lights should be angled between you and the work. A reading lamp functions best, after all, when it is positioned behind you and over your shoulder. Aiming light directly on a surface creates glare, which causes eye strain.

In bathrooms include task lights for grooming. Sconces on either side of the mirror are preferable to a strip of light above the mirror because the latter will cast shadows. If the room is small, the sconces may serve as general lighting as well.

Accent Lighting

Designers like to use accent lighting because it is decorative and often dramatic. Accent lighting draws attention to a favorite work of art, a recessed niche on a stairway landing, or a tall plant at the end of a long room, for example. Designers agree that when you want to highlight something special, be sure the light source is concealed in order not to detract from the object you are spotlighting.

Room-by-Room Guide to Lighting

With lighting, one size doesn't fit all. Each room presents its own lighting challenges and solutions. Think outside of the box. Recessed lighting, for example, can be tucked away under bookshelves, not just in the ceiling; track lighting can be installed in a circular pattern to mirror a room with sweeping curves rather than in straight strips. Here are some other strategies for lighting each of your new rooms.

Family/Play Room. Pendants or chandeliers are obvious choices here if headroom is not an issue. Add recessed lighting in the corners or near doors and windows. Or if the room is designed for active play, install recessed lighting throughout. Use lamps or track lighting for areas that will be used for reading or hobbies. And don't forget about accent lighting to highlight wall-hung photographs or paintings.

Media/TV Room. No light should be brighter than the TV screen. Instead of one bright light source, try several low-level lights—recessed lighting, lamps, and lighting under shelves. Three-way bulbs or dimmers are often the best solution. Remember: light should be behind you, not between you and the screen.

Home Office. A good lighting arrangement combines indirect overhead illumination with table lamps. Indirect light means that the light is softy diffused throughout the home office, not shining down on you. Use a desktop lamp, preferably an adjustable fixture, to focus light on the task at hand and to deflect glare from the computer screen. Install unobtrusive light fixtures in a hutch above the work surface or create a light bridge, a horizontal strip of wood with a light built into it, fastened to the underside of two upper cabinets.

In media room, try to keep the lighting levels below that of the TV.

Light home offices, left, using indirect general lighting combined with desk-mounted task lighting.

Kitchens, below, require overhead ambient lighting and concentrated task lighting over work surfaces.

For workshops, bottom, install overhead lights that won't cast shadows on the work.

Bedrooms. Any number of lighting combinations could work in this room, but generally an overhead fixture that you flip on when you first enter the room is practical and, depending on your choice of fixture, stylish. For a more intimate mood, wiring bedside lamps to a light switch will also work. A must-have is a swing-arm reading lamp with a narrow beam of light that enables you to finish your novel while your spouse catches up on shuteye. These types of reading lamps are responsible for saving more than one marriage.

Bathrooms. As with a home office, you need ambient (general) light that helps you find your way to the toilet or shower without tripping and task lighting for personal grooming. The ideal task lighting should come from both sides of the mirror at eye level.

Kitchens. Team up general illumination—recessed or ceiling-mounted fixtures installed about 12 to 15 inches from the front of the upper cabinets is a good choice and a fixture or two over the sink—with under-the-cabinet task lighting for food preparation. Install decorative wood trim to hide the light strips.

Home Workshop. A workable solution that has stood the test of time is fluorescent fixtures at regular intervals along the ceiling and work lights for specific tasks. Installing a strip of outlets along the length of a worktable and plugging in lights, either portable ones or those attached to the underside of the cabinet, provides illumination on demand.

Staircase. Sufficient light is critical around staircases, where one false step can lead to injury. As a rule, figure you will need at least one 60-watt fixture per 10 feet of running stairs. Try recessed lighting in the ceiling, or for a more dramatic look, install lighting in several recessed niches along the staircase wall that won't invade the stair area.

Images provided by designer/architect.

Plan #321061

Dimensions: 55' W x 49'4" D
Levels: 2
Square Footage: 3,169
Main Level Sq. Ft.: 1,679
Upper Level Sq. Ft.: 1,490
Bedrooms: 4
Bathrooms: 2½
Foundation: Basement
Materials List Available: Yes
Price Category: G

This spacious home combines a truly elegant appearance with family-oriented, comfortable design elements.

CAD FILE AVAILABLE

Features:

- Entryway: This large area features a hand crafted stairway to the upper floor, French doors leading to the living room, and an adjacent powder room.

- Living Room: This lovely room is ideal for quiet times or lively entertaining.

- Family Room: You'll enjoy all the amenities in this large room, with its lovely bay window, handsome fireplace, and walk-in wet bar.

- Dining Area: This area is open to the living room but is visually set apart by a gracious tray ceiling.

- Study: Adjacent to the front bedroom on the main floor, this study provides a place for quiet times.

- Master Suite: Located on the second floor for privacy, this area is luxurious in every respect.

Main Level Floor Plan

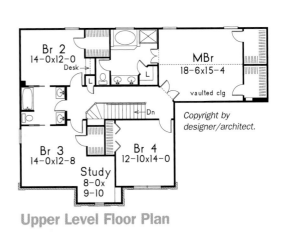

Upper Level Floor Plan

Copyright by designer/architect.

Plan #121062

Dimensions: 70' W x 62' D
Levels: 2
Square Footage: 3,448
Main Level Sq. Ft.: 2,375
Upper Level Sq. Ft.: 1,073
Bedrooms: 4
Bathrooms: 3½
Foundation: Basement
Materials List Available: Yes
Price Category: G

Photo provided by designer/architect.

You'll love this design if you're looking for a comfortable home with dimensions and details that create a sense of grandeur.

Features:

• Entry: A soaring ceiling, curved staircase, and balcony that overlooks a tall plant shelf combine to create your first impression of grandeur in this home.

• Great Room: A transom-topped bowed window highlights this room, with its 11-ft., beamed ceiling, built-in wet bar, and see-through fireplace.

• Kitchen: Designed for the gourmet cook, this kitchen has every amenity you could desire.

• Breakfast Room: Adjacent to the great room and the kitchen, this gazebo-shaped breakfast area lights both the kitchen and hearth room.

Main Level Floor Plan

Upper Level Floor Plan

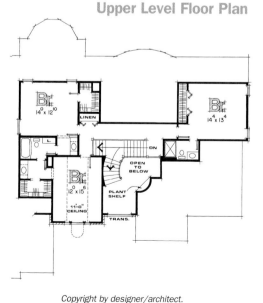

Copyright by designer/architect.

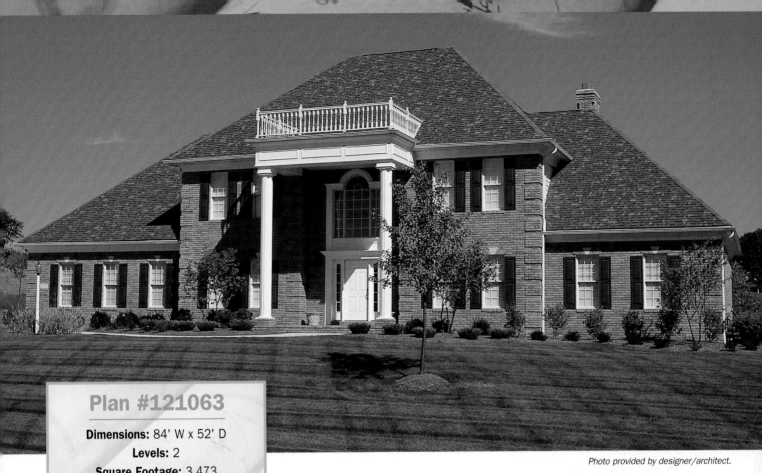

Photo provided by designer/architect.

Plan #121063

Dimensions: 84' W x 52' D

Levels: 2

Square Footage: 3,473

Main Level Sq. Ft.: 2,500

Upper Level Sq. Ft.: 973

Bedrooms: 4

Bathrooms: 3½

Foundation: Basement

Materials List Available: Yes

Price Category: G

Enjoy the many amenities in this well-designed and gracious home.

Features:

- **Entry:** A large sparkling window and a tapering split staircase distinguish this lovely entryway.

- **Great Room:** This spacious great room will be the heart of your new home. It has a 14-ft. spider-beamed ceiling that serves to highlight its built-in bookcase, built-in entertainment center, raised hearth fireplace, wet bar, and lovely arched windows topped with transoms.

- **Kitchen:** Anyone who walks into this kitchen will realize that it's designed for both convenience and efficiency.

- **Master Suite:** The tiered ceiling in the bedroom gives an elegant touch, and the bay window adds to it. The two large walk-in closets and the spacious bath, with columns setting off the whirlpool tub and two vanities, complete this dream of a suite.

Main Level Floor Plan

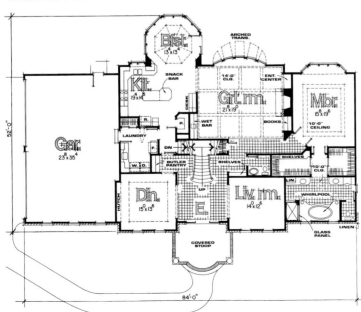

Upper Level Floor Plan

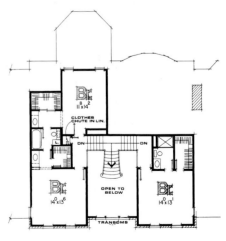

Copyright by designer/architect.

Plan #121065

Dimensions: 62' W x 55'4" D

Levels: 2

Square Footage: 3,407

Main Level Sq. Ft.: 1,719

Upper Level Sq. Ft.: 1,688

Bedrooms: 4

Bathrooms: 2½

Foundation: Basement

Materials List Available: Yes

Price Category: G

If you love contemporary design, the unusual shapes of the rooms in this home will delight you.

Features:

• **Entry:** You'll see a balcony from the upper level that overlooks this entryway, as well as the lovely curved staircase to this floor.

• **Great Room:** This room is sunken to set it apart. A fireplace, wet bar, spider-beamed ceiling, and row of arched windows give it character.

• **Dining Room:** Columns define this lovely octagon room, where you'll love to entertain guests or create lavish family dinners.

• **Master Suite:** A multi-tiered ceiling adds a note of grace, while the fireplace and private library create a real retreat. The gracious bath features a gazebo ceiling and a skylight.

Main Level Floor Plan

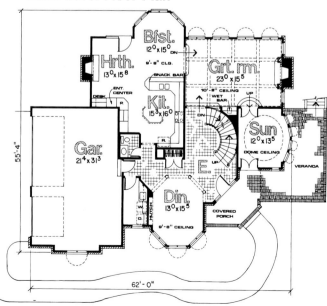

Upper Level Floor Plan

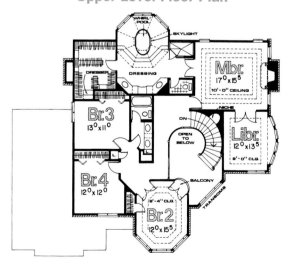

Plan #121067

Dimensions: 56' W x 59'4" D
Levels: 2
Square Footage: 2,708
Main Level Sq. Ft.: 1,860
Upper Level Sq. Ft.: 848
Bedrooms: 4
Bathrooms: 3½
Foundation: Basement
Materials List Available: Yes
Price Category: F

Photo provided by designer/architect.

You'll love this home because it is such a perfect setting for a family and still has room for guests.

Features:

• Family Room: Expect everyone to gather in this room, near the built-in entertainment centers that flank the lovely fireplace.

• Living Room: The other side of the see-through fireplace looks out into this living room, making it an equally welcoming spot in chilly weather.

• Kitchen: This room has a large center island, a corner pantry, and a built-in desk. It also features a breakfast area where friends and family will congregate all day long.

• Master Suite: Enjoy the oversized walk-in closet and bath with a bayed whirlpool tub, double vanity, and separate shower.

Main Level Floor Plan

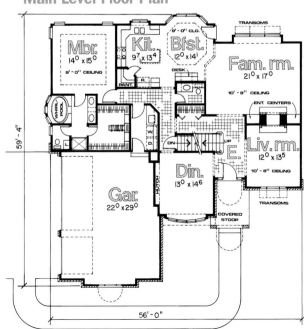

Upper Level Floor Plan

Copyright by designer/architect.

Plan #111029

Dimensions: 65' W x 77' D
Levels: 1½
Square Footage: 2,781
Main Level Sq. Ft.: 2,781
Upper Level Sq. Ft.: 319
Bedrooms: 4
Bathrooms: 3
Foundation: Crawl space
Materials List Available: No
Price Category: G

Photo provided by designer/architect.

Copyright by designer/architect.

Upper Level Floor Plan

Main Level Floor Plan

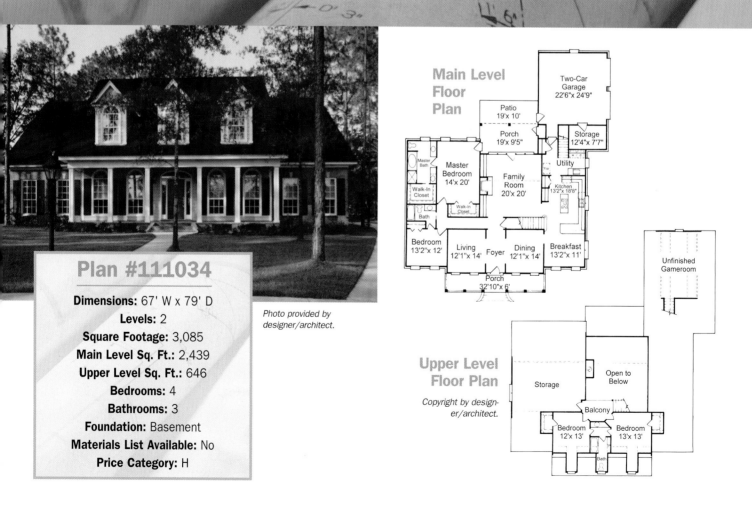

Plan #111034

Dimensions: 67' W x 79' D
Levels: 2
Square Footage: 3,085
Main Level Sq. Ft.: 2,439
Upper Level Sq. Ft.: 646
Bedrooms: 4
Bathrooms: 3
Foundation: Basement
Materials List Available: No
Price Category: H

Photo provided by designer/architect.

Copyright by designer/architect.

Main Level Floor Plan

Upper Level Floor Plan

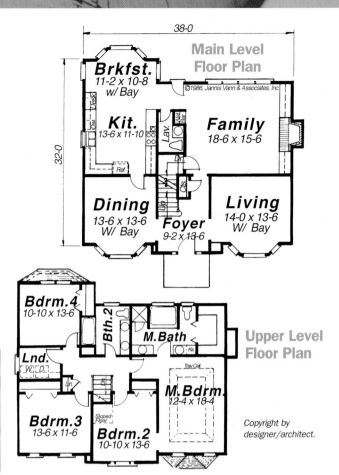

Main Level Floor Plan

38-0

©1986, Jannis Vann & Associates, Inc.

Brkfst. 11-2 x 10-8 w/ Bay

Kit. 13-6 x 11-10

Lav.

Wet Bar

32-0

Family 18-6 x 15-6

Ref.

Dn.

Cls.

Up

Dining 13-6 x 13-6 W/ Bay

Foyer 9-2 x 13-6

Living 14-0 x 13-6 W/ Bay

Upper Level Floor Plan

Bdrm.4 10-10 x 13-6

Bth.2

M.Bath

Lnd. W/D

Ks.

Tray Ceil.

M.Bdrm. 12-4 x 18-4

Bdrm.3 13-6 x 11-6

Sloped Floor

Bdrm.2 10-10 x 13-6

Copyright by designer/architect.

Plan #141030

Dimensions: 38' W x 32' D
Levels: 2
Square Footage: 2,323
Main Level Sq. Ft.: 1,179
Upper Level Sq. Ft.: 1,144
Bedrooms: 4
Bathrooms: 2½
Foundation: Basement
Materials List Available: Yes
Price Category: E

Photo provided by designer/architect.

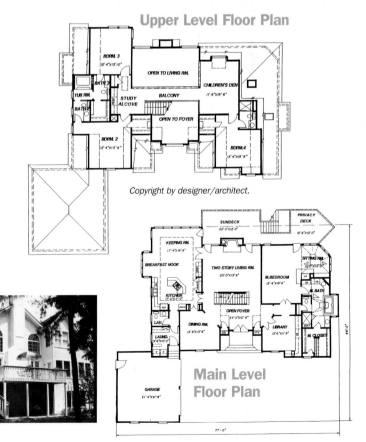

Upper Level Floor Plan

BDRM. 3 16'-4"x13'-10"

OPEN TO LIVING RM.

CHILDREN'S DEN 11'-6"x15'-6"

BATH 3

TUB RM.

BATH 2

STUDY ALCOVE

BALCONY

OPEN TO FOYER

BDRM. 2 16'-4"x13'-6"

BDRM. 4 15'-4"x15'-6"

Copyright by designer/architect.

SUNDECK 20'-0"x12'-0"

PRIVACY DECK 15'-6"x12'-0"

KEEPING RM. 17'-4"x16'-6"

SITTING RM.

BREAKFAST NOOK

TWO STORY LIVING RM. 20'-0"x15'-6"

M. BEDROOM 15'-6"x19'-6"

KITCHEN

M. BATH

LAV.

OPEN FOYER

DINING RM. 14'-6"x13'-6"

LIBRARY 13'-6"x10'-0"

LAUND.

M. CLOSET

GARAGE 21'-4"x21'-8"

Main Level Floor Plan

77'-0"

Plan #141034

Dimensions: 77' W x 66' D
Levels: 2
Square Footage: 3,588
Main Level Sq. Ft.: 2,329
Upper Level Sq. Ft.: 1,259
Bedrooms: 4
Bathrooms: 3 full, 2 half
Foundation: Basement
Materials List Available: Yes
Price Category: H

Photo provided by designer/architect.

Plan #221022

Dimensions: 79' W x 55' D

Levels: 2

Square Footage: 3,382

Main Level Sq. Ft.: 2,376

Upper Level Sq. Ft.: 1,006

Bedrooms: 4

Bathrooms: 3½

Foundation: Basement

Materials List Available: No

Price Category: G

This home, as shown in the photograph, may differ from the actual blueprints.
For more detailed information, please check the floor plans carefully.

Images provided by designer/architect.

- Master Suite: Located on the main floor for privacy, this area includes a walk-in closet and a deluxe full bathroom.

- Upper Level: Look into the great room and entryway as you climb the stairs to the three large bedrooms and a full bath on this floor.

The traditional-looking facade of stone, brick, and siding opens into a home you'll love for its spaciousness, comfort, and great natural lighting.

Features:

- Ceiling Height: 9 ft.

- Great Room: The two-story ceiling here emphasizes the dimensions of this large room, and the huge windows make it bright and cheery.

- Sunroom: Use this area as a den or an indoor conservatory, where you can relax in the midst of health-promoting and beautiful plants.

- Kitchen: This well-planned kitchen features a snacking island and opens into a generous dining nook where everyone will gather.

Main Level Floor Plan

SMARTtip

Clearing the Canvas- Arranging Furniture

If you are having trouble creating a pleasing arrangement of furniture in a room, it can help to remove all of the contents and start from scratch. This is a good idea if you have trouble picturing things on paper or if you aren't going to buy a lot of new furniture and just need a fresh start. If at all possible, strip the room down completely, removing all of the furnishings, including window treatments, rugs, wall art, and accessories. This way you can observe the true architectural nature of the space without distractions that influence your perceptions. For example, minus the trappings of curtains, you can see that two windows may be slightly different sizes or installed too close to a corner. Other things you may notice might be odd corners, uneven walls, radiators or heating registers that are conspicuously located, or any other quirky features that are unique to your home.

Don't be in a rush to start filling up the room again. Live with it empty for a few days so that you can really get a sense of the space. Then slowly begin to bring things back inside, starting with the largest objects. You'll know immediately when you've crossed the line with something that doesn't belong. But you have to be willing to pull back and pare down.

OPEN TO
FAM.RM.

BR.#4
11'8" × 12'4"

LINEN

LIN.

BR.#2
13'4" × 12'8"

OPEN TO
E.

BR.#3
11'8" × 12'6"

**Upper Level
Floor Plan**

Rear
Elevation

Plan #121069

Dimensions: 58' W x 59'4" D

Levels: 2

Square Footage: 2,914

Main Level Sq. Ft.: 1,583

Upper Level Sq. Ft.: 1,331

Bedrooms: 4

Bathrooms: 3½

Foundation: Basement

Materials List Available: Yes

Price Category: F

Photo provided by designer/architect.

You'll love this design if you're looking for a home to complement a site with a lovely rear view.

Features:

• Family Room: A trio of lovely windows looks out to the rear entry of this home.

• Kitchen: Designed to suit a gourmet cook, this kitchen includes a roomy pantry and an island with a snack bar.

• Breakfast Area: The boxed window here is perfect for houseplants or a collection of

culinary herbs. A door leads to the rear porch, where you'll love to dine in good weather.

• Master Suite: On the upper level, the bedroom features a cathedral ceiling and two walk-in closets, and a window seat. The bath also has a cathedral ceiling and includes dual lavatories, a large dressing area, and a sunlit whirlpool tub.

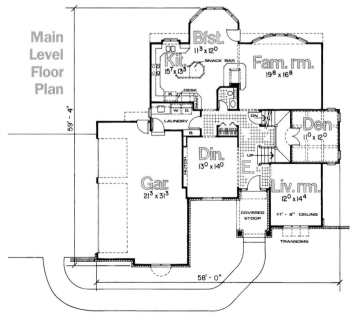

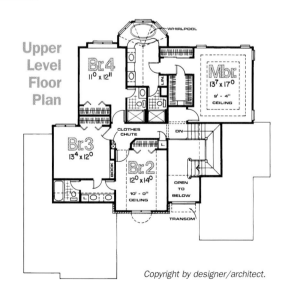

Copyright by designer/architect.

Plan #121073

Dimensions: 70' W x 52' D
Levels: 2
Square Footage: 2,579
Main Level Sq. Ft.: 1,933
Upper Level Sq. Ft.: 646
Bedrooms: 4
Bathrooms: 2½
Foundation: Basement
Materials List Available: Yes
Price Category: E

Luxury will surround you in this home with contemporary styling and up-to-date amenities at every turn.

Features:

• Great Room: This large room shares both a see-through fireplace and a wet bar with the adjacent hearth room. Transom-topped windows add both light and architectural interest to this room.

• Den: Transom-topped windows add visual interest to this private area.

• Kitchen: A center island and corner pantry add convenience to this well-planned kitchen, and a lovely ceiling treatment adds beauty to the bayed breakfast area.

• Master Suite: A built-in bookcase adds to the ambiance of this luxury-filled area, where you're sure to find a retreat at the end of the day.

Main Level Floor Plan

Upper Level Floor Plan

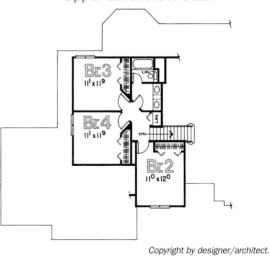

Plan #121074

Dimensions: 68'8" W x 47'8" D
Levels: 2
Square Footage: 2,486
Main Level Sq. Ft.: 1,829
Upper Level Sq. Ft.: 657
Bedrooms: 4
Bathrooms: 2½
Foundation: Basement
Materials List Available: Yes
Price Category: E

Photo provided by designer/architect.

Enjoy the natural light that streams through the many lovely windows in this well-designed home.

Features:

- Living Room: This room is sure to be your family's headquarters, thanks to the lovely 15-ft. ceiling, stacked windows, central location, and cozy fireplace.

- Dining Room: A boxed ceiling adds formality to this well-positioned room.

- Kitchen: The island cooktop in this kitchen is so large that it includes a snack bar area. A pantry gives ample storage space, and a built-in desk—where you can set up a computer station or a record-keeping area—adds efficiency.

- Master Suite: For the sake of privacy, this master suite is located on the opposite side of the home from the other living areas. You'll love the roomy bedroom and luxuriate in the private bath with its many amenities.

Main Level Floor Plan

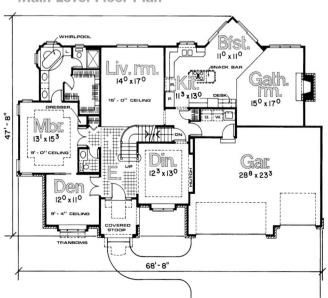

Upper Level Floor Plan

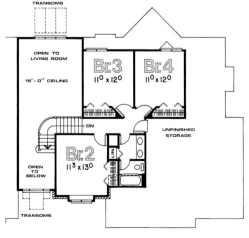

Copyright by designer/architect.

Plan #661229

Dimensions: 105'6" W x 100'4" D

Levels: 1

Square Footage: 5,420

Main Level Sq. Ft.: 4,431

Upper Level Sq. Ft.: 939

Bedrooms: 5

Bathrooms: 5 full, 2 half

Foundation: Slab

Materials List Available: No

Price Category: J

Photo provided by designer/architect.

This unique luxury home hs an intimate feel throughout its beautiful interior and exterior.

Features:

• Master Suite: This beautiful master suite comes complete with a "see through" shower placed behind the garden tub, which lines up a perfect view from the arched opening over the tub through to an outside garden wall fountatin.

• Dining Room: Long spanning wood beams are the highlight in this room, which opens into a large game room perfect for leisure entertaining.

• Loft Area: This loft area is perfect for children's activities, with its close proximity to the secondary bedrooms and home theatre.

Main Level Floor Plan

Upper Level Floor Plan

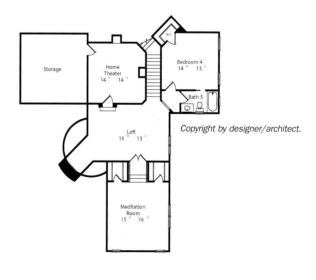

Copyright by designer/architect.

Plan #161030

Dimensions: 96'6" W x 61'5" D
Levels: 2
Square Footage: 4,575
Main Level Sq. Ft.: 3,393
Upper Level Sq. Ft.: 1,182
Bedrooms: 4
Bathrooms: 3½
Foundation: Basement
Materials List Available: Yes
Price Category: I

You'll be charmed by this impressive home, with its stone-and-brick exterior.

Features:

- Great Room: The two-story ceiling here adds even more dimension to this expansive space.

- Hearth Room: A tray ceiling and molding help to create a cozy feeling in this room, which is located so your guests will naturally gravitate to it.

- Dining Room: This formal room features columns at the entry and a butler's pantry for entertaining.

- Master Suite: A walk-in closet, platform whirlpool tub, and 2-person shower are only a few of the luxuries in the private bath, and tray ceilings and moldings give extra presence to the bedroom.

- Upper Level: A balcony offers a spectacular view of the great room and leads to three large bedrooms, each with a private bath.

Images provided by designer/architect.

Main Level Floor Plan

Upper Level Floor Plan

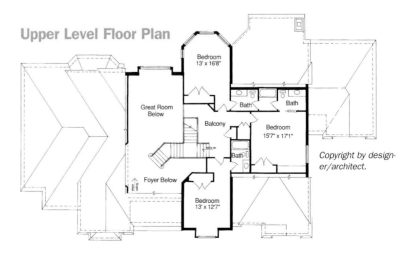

Copyright by designer/architect.

Plan #121082

Dimensions: 68'8" W x 60' D
Levels: 2
Square Footage: 2,932
Main Level Sq. Ft.: 2,084
Upper Level Sq. Ft.: 848
Bedrooms: 4
Bathrooms: 3½
Foundation: Basement
Materials List Available: Yes
Price Category: F

Enjoy the spacious covered veranda that gives this house so much added charm.

Features:

• Great Room: A volume ceiling enhances the spacious feeling in this room, making it a natural gathering spot for friends and family. Transom-topped windows look onto the veranda, and French doors open to it.

• Den: French doors from the entry lead to this room, with its unusual ceiling detail, gracious fireplace, and transom-topped windows.

• Hearth Room: Three skylights punctuate the cathedral ceiling in this room, giving it an extra measure of light and warmth.

• Kitchen: This kitchen is a delight, thanks to its generous working and storage space.

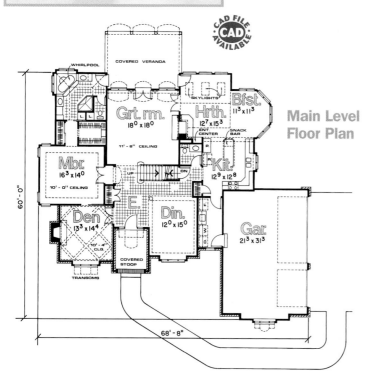

Main Level Floor Plan

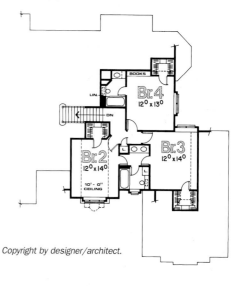

Upper Level Floor Plan

Copyright by designer/architect.

Plan #121089

Dimensions: 54' W x 51'8" D
Levels: 2
Square Footage: 1,976
Main Level Sq. Ft.: 1,413
Upper Level Sq. Ft.: 563
Bedrooms: 4
Bathrooms: 2½
Foundation: Basement
Materials List Available: Yes
Price Category: D

Enjoy the natural light that streams into every room through a variety of window types.

Features:

- **Entry:** This two-story entryway is distinguished by its many windows, which flood the area with light.

- **Great Room:** Tall windows frame the large fireplace in this room. A high, sloped ceiling accentuates its spacious dimensions, and its convenient position makes it a natural gathering place for friends and family.

- **Kitchen:** An island provides an extra measure of convenience in this well-designed kitchen. The sunny breakfast area with its many windows is defined by the snack bar that it shares with the kitchen area.

- **Master Suite:** Placed in the opposite side of the home for privacy, this master suite features unusual detailing on the ceiling. The bath includes a corner whirlpool tub and double vanity.

Main Level Floor Plan

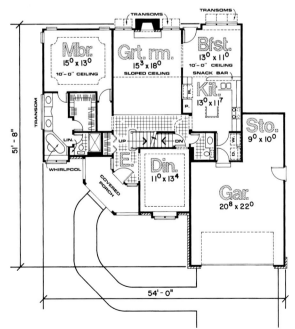

Upper Level Floor Plan

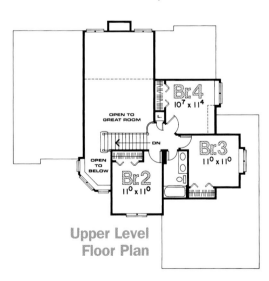

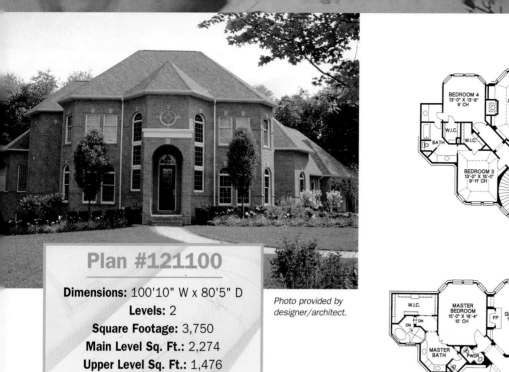

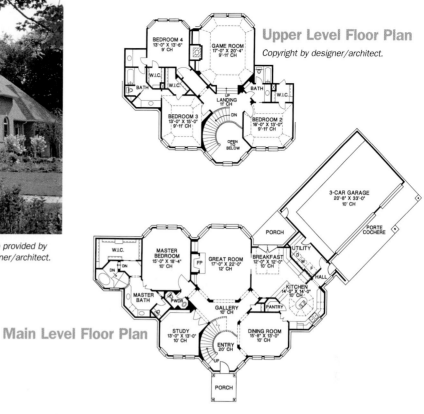

Upper Level Floor Plan
Copyright by designer/architect.

BEDROOM 4
13'-0" X 13'-6"
9' CH

GAME ROOM
17'-0" X 20'-4"
9'-11 CH

BATH

W.I.C.

W.I.C.

BATH

W.I.C.

UP
LANDING
11' CH
DN

BEDROOM 3
13'-0" X 15'-0"
9'-11" CH

BEDROOM 2
16'-0" X 13'-0"
9'-11" CH

OPEN
TO
BELOW

3-CAR GARAGE
20'-8" X 33'-0"
10' CH

PORTE
COCHERE

Plan #121100

Dimensions: 100'10" W x 80'5" D
Levels: 2
Square Footage: 3,750
Main Level Sq. Ft.: 2,274
Upper Level Sq. Ft.: 1,476
Bedrooms: 4
Bathrooms: 3½
Foundation: Slab
Materials List Available: No
Price Category: G

Photo provided by designer/architect.

W.I.C.

MASTER
BEDROOM
15'-0" X 18'-4"
10' CH

FP

GREAT ROOM
17'-0" X 22'-0"
12' CH

BREAKFAST
12'-0" X 12'-0"
10' CH

PORCH

UTILITY

KITCHEN
14'-0" X 14'-0"
10' CH

HALL

DN

MASTER
BATH

PWDR

GALLERY
10' CH

PANTRY

STUDY
13'-0" X 15'-0"
10' CH

ENTRY
20' CH

DINING ROOM
15'-8" X 13'-0"
10' CH

UP

PORCH

PORCH

Main Level Floor Plan

Plan #111033

Dimensions: 67' W x 65' D
Levels: 2
Square Footage: 2,824
Main Level Sq. Ft.: 2,120
Upper Level Sq. Ft.: 704
Bedrooms: 4
Bathrooms: 3
Foundation: Slab
Materials List Available: No
Price Category: G

Main Level Floor Plan

Two Car
Garage
21'4"x 21'4"

Patio

Porch

Master
Bedroom
14'x 17'

Family
19'4"x 17'

Breakfast

Bedroom
12'x 12'

Dining
15'x 11'3"

Living
11'4"x 11'4"

Porch

Upper Level Floor Plan

Copyright by designer/architect.

Bedroom
13'x 16'

Bedroom
11'6"x 12'

Photos provided by designer/architect.

Rear View

Plan #161016

Dimensions: 59'4" W x 58'8" D
Levels: 2
Square Footage: 2,101
Main Level Sq. Ft.: 1,626
Upper Level Sq. Ft.: 475
Bedrooms: 3
Bathrooms: 2½
Foundation: Basement
Optional crawl space
available for extra fee
Materials List Available: Yes
Price Category: D

Note: Home in photo reflects a modified garage entrance. This home, as shown in the photograph, may differ from the actual blueprints. For more detailed information, please check the floor plans carefully.

Images provided by designer/architect.

Features:

- Great Room: Made for relaxing and entertaining, the great room is sunken to set it off from the rest of the house. A balcony from the second floor looks down into this spacious area, making it easy to keep track of the kids while they are playing.

- Kitchen: Convenience marks this well laid-out kitchen where you'll love to cook for guests and for family.

- Master Bedroom: A vaulted ceiling complements the unusual octagonal shape

of the master bedroom. Located on the first floor, this room allows some privacy from the second floor bedrooms. It is also ideal for anyone who no longer wishes to climb stairs to reach a bedroom.

Rear Elevation

You'll love the exciting roofline that sets this elegant home apart from its neighbors as well as the embellished, solid look that declares how well-designed it is—from the inside to the exterior.

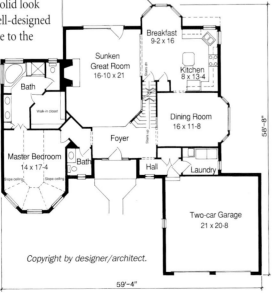

Main Level Floor Plan

Upper Level Floor Plan

Copyright by designer/architect.

Plan #121022

Dimensions: 76' W x 58'8" D
Levels: 2
Square Footage: 3,556
Main Level Sq. Ft.: 2,555
Upper Level Sq. Ft.: 1,001
Bedrooms: 4
Bathrooms: 4
Foundation: Basement
Materials List Available: Yes
Price Category: H

Dramatic soaring ceilings are the hallmark of the large and luxurious home.

Features:

• Ceiling Height: 8 ft. except as noted.

• Gathering Room: Guests and family will be drawn to this room with its cathedral ceiling and its fireplace flanked by built-ins.

• Den: To the right of the entry, French doors lead to a handsome den with a tall, spider-beamed ceiling.

• Great Room: This room will be flooded with sunlight thanks to stacked windows that take advantage of its 18-ft. ceiling.

• Formal Dining Room: Upon entering the 13-ft. entry, your guests will see this elegant room with its arched windows and decorative ceiling.

• Master Suite: Unwind at day's end in this luxurious suite featuring two walk-in closets, a sky-lit whirlpool and his and her vanities.

Main Level Floor Plan

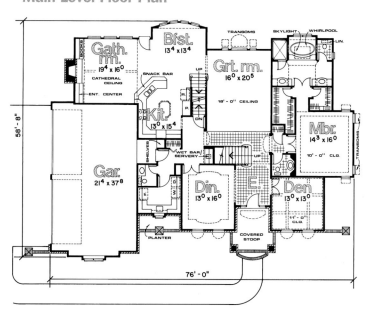

Upper Level Floor Plan

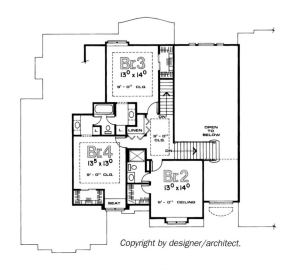

Plan #121019

Dimensions: 70' W x 60' D
Levels: 2
Square Footage: 3,775
Main Level Sq. Ft.: 1,923
Upper Level Sq. Ft.: 1,852
Bedrooms: 4
Bathrooms: 3
Foundation: Basement
Materials List Available: Yes
Price Category: H

The grand exterior presence is carried inside, beginning with the dramatic curved staircase.

Features:

• Ceiling Height: 8 ft.

• Den: French doors lead to the sophisticated den, with its bayed windows and wall of bookcases.

• Living Room: A curved wall and a series of arched windows highlight this large space.

• Formal Dining Room: The living room shares the curved wall and arched windows found in the living room.

• Screened Porch: This huge space features skylights and is accessible by another French door from the dining room.

• Family Room: Family and guests alike will be drawn to this room, with its trio of arched windows and fireplace flanked by bookcases.

• Kitchen: An island adds convenience and distinction to this large, functional kitchen.

• Garage: This spacious three-bay garage provides plenty of space for cars and storage.

Main Level Floor Plan

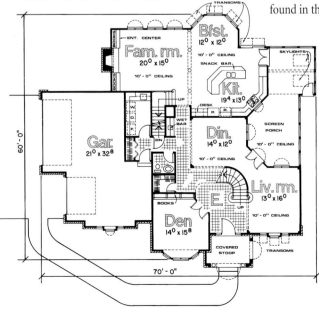

Upper Level Floor Plan

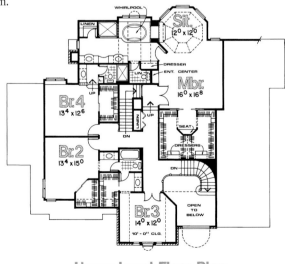

Plan #121046

Dimensions: 65'3" W x 57'2" D
Levels: 2
Square Footage: 2,655
Main Level Sq. Ft.: 1,906
Upper Level Sq. Ft.: 749
Bedrooms: 4
Bathrooms: 2
Foundation: Slab
Materials List Available: Yes
Price Category: F

CAD FILE AVAILABLE

This home beautifully blends traditional architectural detail with modern amenities.

Features:

• Ceiling Height: 8 ft. unless otherwise noted.

• Foyer: This two-story entry enjoys views of the uniquely shaped study, a second-floor balcony, and the formal dining room.

• Formal Dining Room: With its elegant corner column, this dining room sets the stage for formal entertaining as well as family gatherings.

• Kitchen: This well-appointed kitchen features a center island for efficient food preparation. It has a butler's pantry near the dining room and another pantry in the service entry.

• Breakfast Area: Here's the spot for informal family meals or lingering over coffee.

• Rear Porch: Step out through French doors in the master bedroom and the breakfast area.

Main Level Floor Plan

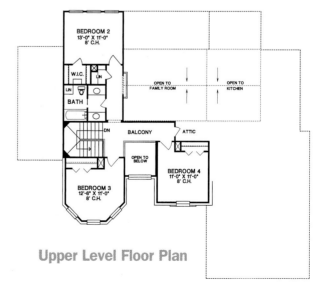

Upper Level Floor Plan

**Main Level
Floor Plan**

Copyright by designer/architect.

**Upper Level
Floor Plan**

Plan #361012

Dimensions: 54'8" W x 63'8" D

Levels: 2

Square Footage: 2,602

Main Level Sq. Ft.: 1,867

Upper Level Sq. Ft.: 735

Bedrooms: 4

Bathrooms: 3

Foundation: Crawl space

Materials List Available: No

Price Category: F

Images provided by designer/architect.

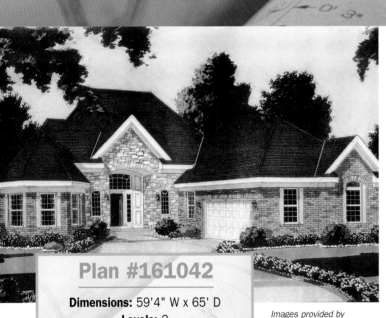

**Main Level
Floor Plan**

Copyright by designer/architect

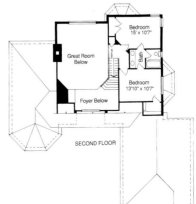

**Upper Level
Floor Plan**

Plan #161042

Dimensions: 59'4" W x 65' D

Levels: 2

Square Footage: 2,198

Main Level Sq. Ft.: 1,706

Upper Level Sq. Ft.: 492

Bedrooms: 3

Bathrooms: 2½

Foundation: Basement

Materials List Available: Yes

Price Category: D

Images provided by designer/architect.

Upper Level Floor Plan

Copyright by designer/architect.

Main Level Floor Plan

Plan #151032

Dimensions: 84'4" W x 48'4" D
Levels: 2
Square Footage: 2,824
Main Level Sq. Ft.: 2,279
Upper Level Sq. Ft.: 545
Bedrooms: 4
Bathrooms: 3
Foundation: Crawl space, slab (basement option for fee)
CompleteCost List Available: Yes
Price Category: F

Illustration provided by designer/architect.

Upper Level Floor Plan

Main Level Floor Plan

Copyright by designer/architect

Plan #171018

Dimensions: 48' W x 72' D
Levels: 2
Square Footage: 2,599
Main Level Sq. Ft.: 1,967
Upper Level Sq. Ft.: 632
Bedrooms: 4
Bathrooms: 4
Foundation: Slab, crawl space
Materials List Available: Yes
Price Category: E

Illustration provided by designer/architect.

Plan #661010

Dimensions: 61' W x 64' D
Levels: 2
Square Footage: 2,887
Main Level Sq. Ft.: 2,212
Upper Level Sq. Ft.: 675
Bedrooms: 4
Bathrooms: 3
Foundation: Slab
Materials List Available: No
Price Category: F

Images provided by designer/architect.

The special details in this home were specifically designed for a lakefront property.

Features:

• Pool: The proximity of the pool to the home will pull the beautiful water views inside.

• Kitchen: This open kitchen is easily accessible from the family room but sufficiently detached from the dining area to preserve the atmosphere of formal occasions.

• Study: If work requires after-hours peace and quiet, this combination den and study near the master suite is away from the main flow of traffic but close to the foyer for business visitors.

• Family Room: This family room can be incorperated into entertainment plans for feeding large groups or opening the interior to the rear paio and pool with the sliding glass door wall.

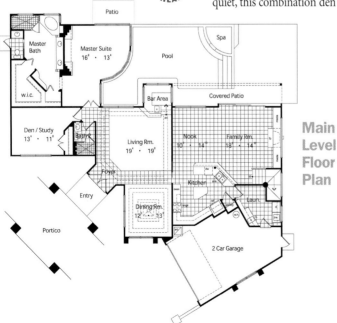

Main Level Floor Plan

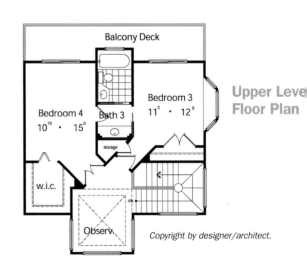

Upper Level Floor Plan

Copyright by designer/architect.

Master Bathroom

Kitchen

Living Room

Plan #121023

Dimensions: 85'5" W x 74'8" D

Levels: 2

Square Footage: 3,904

Main Level Sq. Ft.: 2,813

Upper Level Sq. Ft.: 1,091

Bedrooms: 4

Bathrooms: 2½

Foundation: Basement

Materials List Available: Yes

Price Category: H

CAD FILE AVAILABLE

Spacious and gracious, here are all the amenities you expect in a fine home.

Features:

- Ceiling Height: 8 ft. except as noted.

- Foyer: This magnificent entry features a graceful curved staircase with balcony above.

- Sunken Living Room: This sunken room is filled with light from a row of bowed windows. It's the perfect place for social gatherings both large and small.

- Den: French doors open into this truly distinctive den with its 11-ft. ceiling and built-in bookcases.

- Formal Dining Room: Entertain guests with style and grace in this dining room with corner column.

- Master Suite: Another set of French doors leads to this suite that features two walk-in closets, a whirlpool flanked by vanities, and a private sitting room with built-in bookcases.

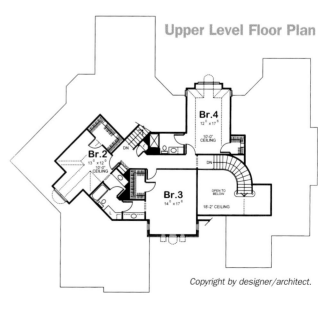

Plan #151024

Dimensions: 60' W x 73'8" D
Levels: 2
Square Footage: 3,623
Main Level Sq. Ft.: 2,391
Upper Level Sq. Ft.: 1,232
Bedrooms: 3
Bathrooms: 3
Foundation: Crawl space, slab;
optional full basement plan available
for extra fee
CompleteCost List Available: Yes
Price Category: F

Photo provided by designer/architect.

The 2-story foyer gives elegance to this traditional home with four fireplaces, 10-ft. ceilings, and multiple pairs of French doors.

Features:

• Great Room: With French doors leading to the covered porch, the study, and the master suite, this room is a natural hub for guests and family.

• Study: Off the great room, this impressive study features an 11-ft. ceiling and gas fireplace.

• Master Suite: Enter from the great room, and enjoy the fireplace, two walk-in closets, the whirlpool tub, and a private patio.

• Kitchen/Hearth Room: Always the traditional center of activity, this area includes a computer area, an island, ample storage, a butler's pantry, and a separate laundry/hobby room with a sink.

• Game Room: Upstairs, the game room is just the place for hosting large groups.

CAD FILE AVAILABLE

Main Level Floor Plan

Copyright by designer/architect.

Upper Level Floor Plan

Plan #151019

Dimensions: 63'4" W x 53'10" D
Levels: 2
Square Footage: 2,653
Main Level Sq. Ft.: 1,407
Upper Level Sq. Ft.: 1,246
Bedrooms: 3
Bathrooms: 2
Foundation: Crawl space, slab; optional full basement plan available for extra fee
CompleteCost List Available: Yes
Price Category: F

Photo provided by designer/architect.

Majestic French doors at the entry and a balcony overlooking the open foyer set the gracious tone that marks every aspect of this fabulous design.

Features:

- Great Room: Step down into this large room with its gas fireplace and atrium door to the patio.
- Study: Sliding doors and a 9-ft. ceiling give presence to this room.
- Dining Room: Entertaining is easy in this conveniently-placed room with sliding glass doors leading to a rear screened porch as well as the patio.
- Upper Level: Bedrooms 2 and 3 share access to a bath and the balcony that overlooks the foyer.
- Master Suite: A 10-ft. pan ceiling and French doors give elegance to the spacious suite, and you'll enjoy practicality and luxury in the bath, with its two walk-in closets, a corner whirlpool tub, and split vanities.

CAD FILE CAD AVAILABLE

Main Level Floor Plan

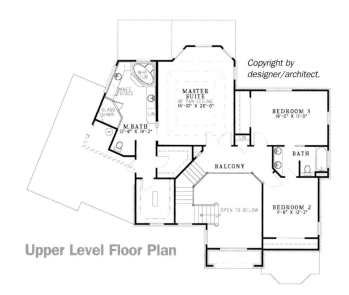

Copyright by designer/architect.

Upper Level Floor Plan

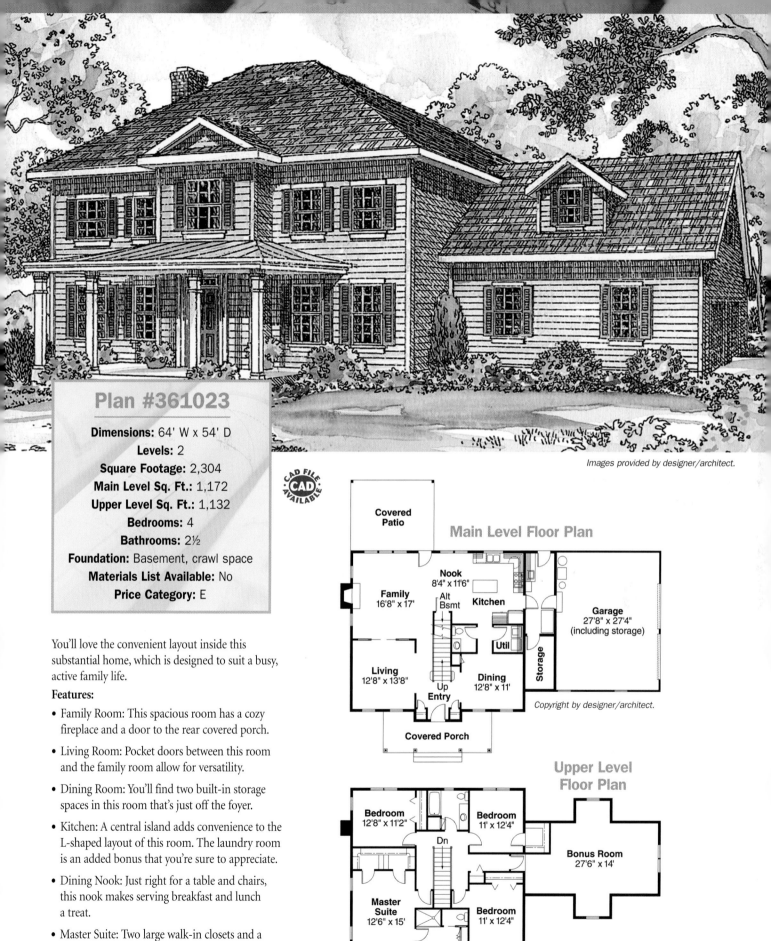

Plan #361023

Dimensions: 64' W x 54' D
Levels: 2
Square Footage: 2,304
Main Level Sq. Ft.: 1,172
Upper Level Sq. Ft.: 1,132
Bedrooms: 4
Bathrooms: 2½
Foundation: Basement, crawl space
Materials List Available: No
Price Category: E

Main Level Floor Plan

Covered Patio

Family 16'8" x 17'

Nook 8'4" x 11'6"

Alt Bsmt

Kitchen

Garage 27'8" x 27'4" (including storage)

Util

Storage

Living 12'8" x 13'8"

Dining 12'8" x 11'

Up

Entry

Covered Porch

Upper Level Floor Plan

Bedroom 12'8" x 11'2"

Bedroom 11' x 12'4"

Dn

Bonus Room 27'6" x 14'

Master Suite 12'6" x 15'

Bedroom 11' x 12'4"

You'll love the convenient layout inside this substantial home, which is designed to suit a busy, active family life.

Features:

- Family Room: This spacious room has a cozy fireplace and a door to the rear covered porch.

- Living Room: Pocket doors between this room and the family room allow for versatility.

- Dining Room: You'll find two built-in storage spaces in this room that's just off the foyer.

- Kitchen: A central island adds convenience to the L-shaped layout of this room. The laundry room is an added bonus that you're sure to appreciate.

- Dining Nook: Just right for a table and chairs, this nook makes serving breakfast and lunch a treat.

- Master Suite: Two large walk-in closets and a bath with split vanities and a built-in cabinet add luxury to the generous bedroom.

Plan #161040

Dimensions: 63'4" W x 48' D

Levels: 2

Square Footage: 2,403

Main Level Sq. Ft.: 1,710

Upper Level Sq. Ft.: 695

Bedrooms: 4

Bathrooms: 3½

Foundation: Basement

Optional slab available for extra fee

Price Category: E

Designed with attention to detail, this elegant home will please the most discriminating taste.

Images provided by designer/architect.

Features:

- Great Room: The high ceiling in this room accentuates the fireplace and the rear wall of windows. A fashionable balcony overlooks the great room.

- Dining Room: This lovely formal dining room is introduced by columns and accented by a boxed window.

- Kitchen: This wonderful kitchen includes a snack bar, island, and large pantry positioned to serve the breakfast and dining rooms with equal ease.

- Master Suite: This master suite features a dressing room, private sitting area with 11-ft.

ceiling, whirlpool tub, double-bowl vanity, and large walk-in closet.

- Additional Bedrooms: Three additional bedrooms complete this spectacular home.

Rear Elevation

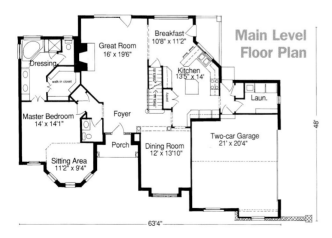

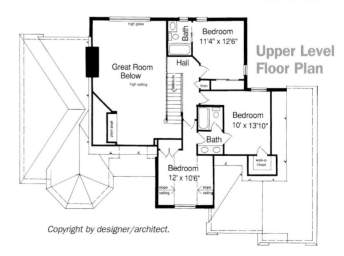

Copyright by designer/architect.

Plan #101019

Dimensions: 58'4" W x 55'2" D
Levels: 2
Square Footage: 2,954
Main Level Sq. Ft. 2,093
Upper Level Sq. Ft. 861
Bedrooms: 4
Bathrooms: 3½
Foundation: Crawl space or basement
Materials List Available: No
Price Category: F

Illustration provided by designer/architect.

CAD FILE AVAILABLE

This luxurious home features a spectacular open floor plan and a brick exterior.

Features:

- Ceiling Height: 9 ft. unless otherwise noted.
- Foyer: This inviting two-story foyer, which vaults to 18 ft., will greet guests with an impressive "welcome."
- Dining Room: To the right of the foyer is this spacious dining room surrounded by decorative columns.
- Family Room: There's plenty of room for all kinds of family activities in this enormous room, with its soaring two-story ceiling.
- Master Suite: This sumptuous retreat boasts a tray ceiling. Optional pocket doors provide direct access to the study. The master bath features his and her vanities and a large walk-in closet.
- Breakfast Area: Perfect for informal family meals, this bayed breakfast area has real flair.
- Secondary Bedrooms: Upstairs are three large bedrooms with 8-ft. ceilings. One has a private bath.

Main Level Floor Plan

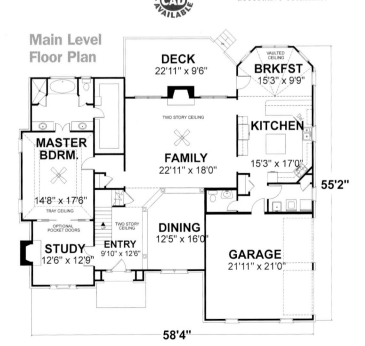

Upper Level Floor Plan

Copyright by designer/architect.

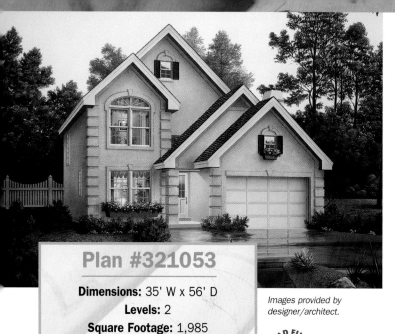

Main Level Floor Plan

Images provided by designer/architect.

CAD FILE AVAILABLE

Upper Level Floor Plan

Copyright by designer/architect.

Plan #321053

Dimensions: 35' W x 56' D

Levels: 2

Square Footage: 1,985

Main Level Sq. Ft.: 1,114

Upper Level Sq. Ft.: 871

Bedrooms: 4

Bathrooms: 3½

Foundation: Basement

Materials List Available: Yes

Price Category: D

Main Level Floor Plan

Images provided by designer/architect.

CAD FILE AVAILABLE

Upper Level Floor Plan

Copyright by designer/architect.

Plan #151030

Dimensions: 59' W x 73' D

Levels: 2

Square Footage: 2,802

Main Level Sq. Ft.: 2,058

Upper Level Sq. Ft.: 744

Bonus Room Sq. Ft.: 493

Bedrooms: 3

Bathrooms: 3½

Foundation: Crawl space, slab; optional basement plan available for extra fee

CompleteCost List Available: Yes

Price Category: F

Plan #611046

Dimensions: 60' W x 76' D
Levels: 2
Square Footage: 3,956
Main Level Sq. Ft.: 2,521
Upper Level Sq. Ft.: 1,435
Bedrooms: 5
Bathrooms: 3½
Foundation: Slab
Materials List Available: No
Price Category: H

Photo provided by designer/architect.

CAD FILE AVAILABLE

Main Level Floor Plan

Upper Level Floor Plan
Copyright by designer/architect.

Plan #151615

Dimensions: 82'6" W x 53'8" D
Levels: 2
Square Footage: 3,558
Main Level Sq. Ft.: 2,066
Upper Level Sq. Ft.: 1,492
Bedrooms: 4
Bathrooms: 4½
Foundation: Crawl space or slab
CompleteCost List Available: Yes
Price Category: G

Photo provided by designer/architect.

CAD FILE AVAILABLE

Main Level Floor Plan

Main Floor

Upper Level Floor Plan

Copyright by designer/architect.

Upper Floor

Plan #151011

Dimensions: 59'6" W x 74'4" D
Levels: 2
Square Footage: 3,437
Main Level Sq. Ft.: 2,184
Upper Level Sq. Ft.: 1,253
Bedrooms: 5
Bathrooms: 4
Foundation: Crawl space, slab; optional fee for basement or daylight basement
CompleteCost List Available: Yes
Price Category: F

CAD FILE AVAILABLE

Images provided by designer/architect.

Beauty, comfort, and convenience are yours in this luxurious, split-level home.

Main Level Features:

- Ceiling Height: 10 ft. unless otherwise noted.

- Master Suite: The 11-ft. pan ceiling sets the tone for this secluded area, with a lovely bay window that opens onto a rear porch, a pass-through fireplace to the great room, and a sitting room.

- Great Room: The pass-through fireplace makes this spacious room a cozy spot,

while the French doors leading to a rear porch make it a perfect spot for entertaining.

- Dining Room: Gracious 8-in. columns set off the entrance to this room.

- Kitchen: An island bar provides an efficient work area that's fitted with a sink.

- Breakfast Room: Open to the kitchen, this room is defined by a bay window and a spiral staircase to the second floor.

- Laundry Room: Large enough to accommodate a folding table, this room can also be fitted with a swinging pet door.

Upper Level Features:

- Play Room: French doors in the children's playroom open onto a balcony where they can continue their games.

- Bedrooms: The 9-ft. ceilings on the second story make the rooms feel bright and airy.

Optional basement foundation or optional daylight basement foundation available for an additional $250.

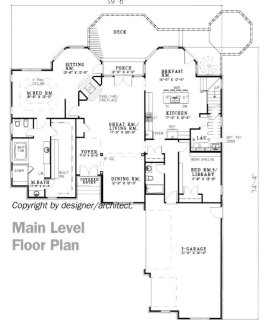

Copyright by designer/architect.

**Main Level
Floor Plan**

**Upper Level
Floor Plan**

Plan #151033

Dimensions: 81' W x 93' D
Levels: 2
Square Footage: 5,548
Main Level Sq. Ft.: 3,276
Upper Level Sq. Ft.: 2,272
Bedrooms: 4
Bathrooms: 4
Foundation: Crawl space, slab
CompleteCost List Available: Yes
Price Category: I

Photo provided by designer/architect.

From the exercise room to the home theatre, you'll love the spaciousness and comfort in this beautifully-designed home.

Features:

- Family Room: Everyone can gather around the stone fireplace and built-in media center.

- Hearth Room: Open to the breakfast/kitchen area, this room also has a lovely gas fireplace.

- Computer Areas: Set up work areas in the computer room, as well as the kid's nook.

- Dining Room: Sit by the bay window or go through the swinging door to the adjoining hearth room.

- Master Suite: Somewhat secluded, the bedroom has a vaulted 10-ft. boxed ceiling while the bath features a TV, whirlpool tub, a separate shower, and corner vanities.

- Porch: The rear screened-in porch lets in extra light through skylights on its roof.

Main Level Floor Plan

Upper Level Floor Plan

Copyright by designer/architect.

Plan #111031

Dimensions: 56' W x 53' D
Levels: 1.5
Square Footage: 2,869
Main Level Sq. Ft.: 2,152
Upper Level Sq. Ft.: 717
Bedrooms: 4
Bathrooms: 3
Foundation: Slab, basement
Materials List Available: No
Price Category: G

Images provided by designer/architect.

This home is ideal for any family, thanks to its spaciousness, beauty, and versatility.

Features:

• Ceiling Height: 9 ft.

• Front Porch: The middle of the three French doors with circle tops here opens to the foyer.

• Living Room: Archways from the foyer open to both this room and the equally large dining room.

• Family Room: Also open to the foyer, this room features a two-story sloped ceiling and a balcony from the upper level. You'll love the fireplace, with its raised brick hearth and the

two French doors with circle tops, which open to the rear porch.

• Kitchen: A center island, range with microwave, built-in desk, and dining bar that's open to the breakfast room add up to comfort and efficiency.

• Master Suite: A Palladian window and linen closet grace this suite's bedroom, and the bath has an oversized garden tub, standing shower, two walk-in closets, and double vanity.

Copyright by designer/architect.

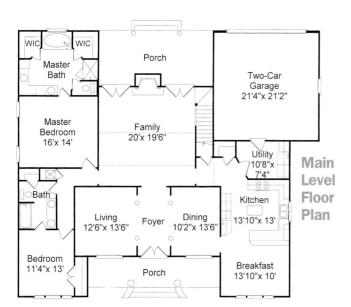

Main Level Floor Plan

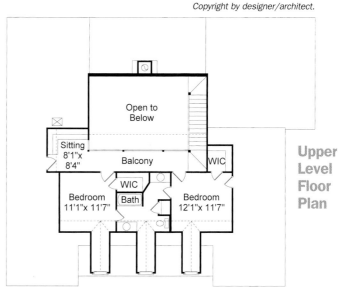

Upper Level Floor Plan

Entry

Kitchen

Living Room

Living Room

Preparing to Use a Clay Chiminea

Before getting started, there are a couple of general rules about using a clay chiminea. Make sure the chiminea is completely dry before lighting a fire, or else it will crack. Also, line the bottom of the pot with about 4 inches of sand. Finally, always build the fire slowly, and never use kerosene or charcoal lighter fluid.

To cure a new clay chiminea, follow these simple steps:

- Build a small paper fire inside the pot. For kindling, use strips of newspaper rolled into a few balls. Place one newspaper ball on the sand inside the chiminea. Ignite it with a match. Then add another ball, and another, one at a time, until the outside walls of the chiminea are slightly warm. Allow the fire to burn out; then let the pot cool completely before the next step.

- Once the chiminea feels cool, light another small fire, this time using wood. Again, let the fire burn out naturally, and then allow the unit to completely cool.

- Repeat the process of lighting a wood fire three more times, adding more kindling and building a larger fire with each consecutive attempt. Remember to let the chiminea cool completely between fires.

After the fifth fire, the chiminea should be cured and ready to use anytime you want a cozy fire.

Plan #121018

Dimensions: 95'9" W x 70'2" D
Levels: 2
Square Footage: 3,950
Main Level Sq. Ft.: 2,839
Upper Level Square Footage: 1,111
Bedrooms: 4
Bathrooms: 2 full, 2 half
Foundation: Basement
Materials List Available: Yes
Price Category: H

A spectacular two-story entry with a floating curved staircase welcomes you home.

Features:

- Ceiling Height: 8 ft. except as noted.
- Den: To the left of the entry, French doors lead to a spacious and stylish den featuring a spider-beamed ceiling.
- Living Room: The volume ceiling, transom windows, and large fireplace evoke a gracious traditional style.
- Gathering Rooms: There is plenty of space for large-group entertaining in the gathering rooms that also feature fireplaces and transom windows.
- Master Suite: Here is the height of luxurious living. The suite features an oversized walk-in closet, tiered ceilings, and a sitting room with fireplace. The pampering bath has a corner whirlpool and shower.
- Garage: An angle minimizes the appearance of the four-car garage.

Main Level Floor Plan

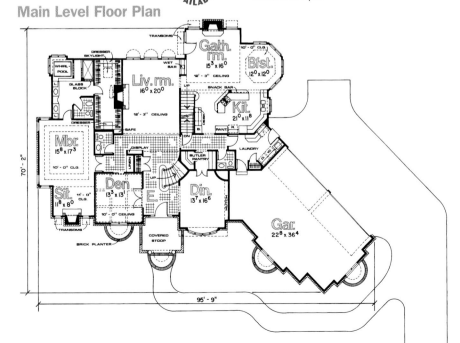

Upper Level Floor Plan

Copyright by designer/architect.

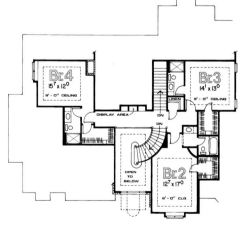

Plan #321065

Dimensions: 80' W x 62' D
Levels: 2
Square Footage: 3,420
Main Level Sq. Ft.: 1,894
Upper Level Sq. Ft.: 1,526
Bedrooms: 4
Bathrooms: 3½
Foundation: Daylight basement
Materials List Available: Yes
Price Category: G

You'll love the hip roofs, elliptical windows, and quoins that grace the exterior of this home, which is as comfortable for family living as it is stylish.

Features:

- Ceiling Height: The 9-ft. ceilings throughout this this home complement its airy, spacious feeling.

- Family Room: Positioned to be a natural gathering spot, this room is large enough to entertain a crowd, but you can decorate it to create cozy nooks for quiet evenings.

- Hearth Room: A vaulted ceiling distinguishes this room, which connects to the wet bar and family room through a gallery.

- Kitchen: Family cooks will relish the cooktop island, walk-in pantry, angled breakfast bar, and computer desk in this large room.

- Master Suite: A coffered ceiling, two walk-in closets, and a lavish bath make this private suite both practical and luxurious.

Images provided by designer/architect.

Main Level Floor Plan

Upper Level Floor Plan

Copyright by designer/architect.

As Your Landscape Grows

At Planting

Fringe tree

Spreading English yew

Spirea

Landscapes change over the years. As plants grow, the overall look evolves from sparse to lush. Trees cast cool shade where the sun used to shine. Shrubs and hedges grow tall and dense enough to provide privacy. Perennials and ground covers spread to form colorful patches of foliage and flowers. Meanwhile, paths, arbors, fences, and other structures gain the patina of age.

Constant change over the years—sometimes rapid and dramatic, sometimes slow and subtle—is one of the joys of landscaping. It is also one of the challenges. Anticipating how fast plants will grow and how big they will eventually get is difficult, even for professional designers.

To illustrate the kinds of changes to expect in a planting, these pages show a landscape design at three different "ages." Even though a new planting may look sparse at first, it will soon fill in. And because of careful spacing, the planting will look as good in 10 to 15 years as it does after 3 to 5. It will, of course, look different, but that's part of the fun.

At Planting. Here's how the corner might appear in spring immediately after planting. The fence and mulch look conspicuously fresh, new, and unweathered. The fringe tree is only 4 to 5 feet tall, with trunks no thicker than broomsticks. (With this or other trees, you can buy bigger specimens to start with, but they're a lot more expensive and sometimes don't perform as well in the long run.) The spireas and spreading English yews, transplanted from 2-gallon nursery containers, spread 12 to 18 inches wide. The perennials, transplanted from quart- or gallon-size containers, are just low tufts of foliage now, but they

grow fast enough to produce a few flowers the first summer.

Three to Five Years. The fringe tree has grown about 6 inches taller every year but is still quite slender. Some trees would grow faster, as much as 1 to 2 feet a year. The spireas, like many fast-growing shrubs, have reached almost full size. From now on, they'll get thicker but not much taller. The slower-growing English yews make a series of low mounds; you still see them as individuals, not a continuous patch. Most perennials, such as the coneflowers, Shasta daisies, daylilies, and dianthus shown here, grow so crowded after a few years that they need to be divided and replanted.

Ten to Fifteen Years. The fringe tree is becoming a fine specimen, 10 to 12 feet wide and tall. Unless you prune away enough of its lower limbs to let some sunlight in, the spireas will gradually stop blooming, get weaker, and need to be replaced with shade-tolerant shrubs such as more English yews or with shade-loving perennials and ferns. The original English yews will have formed a continuous ground cover by now and may have spread enough to limit the space available for perennials. Because the perennials get divided every few years anyway, it's no trouble to rearrange or regroup them, as shown here.

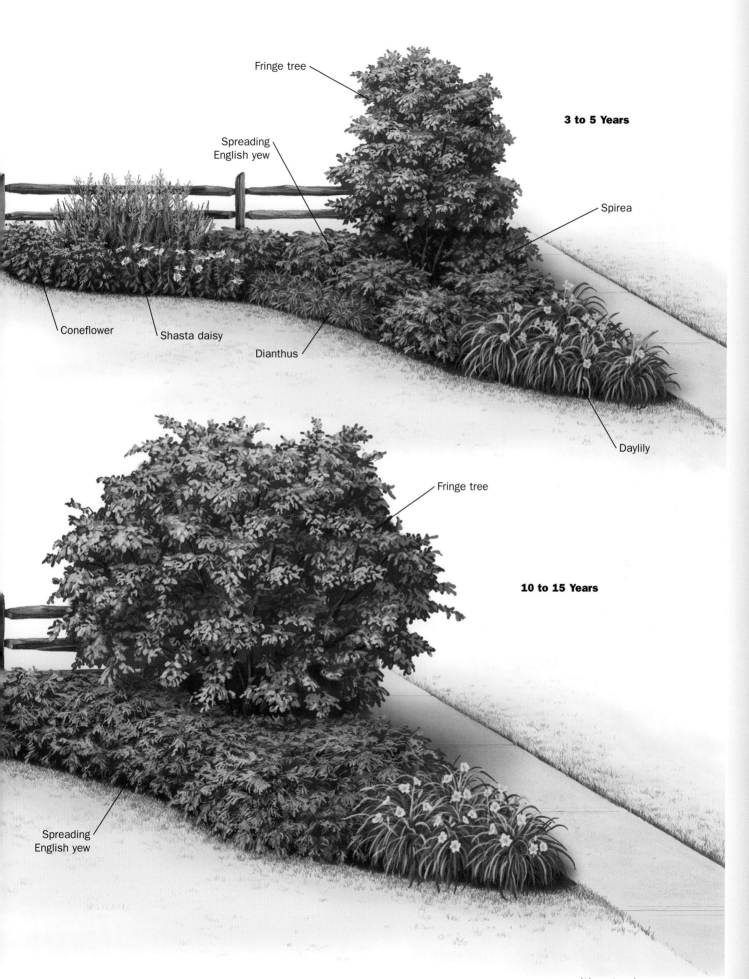

Fringe tree

3 to 5 Years

Spreading
English yew

Spirea

Coneflower

Shasta daisy

Dianthus

Daylily

Fringe tree

10 to 15 Years

Spreading
English yew

Down to Earth

Harmonize your deck with its surroundings

A second-story deck is a perfect spot for viewing your garden and yard. Too often, however, the view of the deck from the yard is less pleasing. Perched atop skinny posts, towering over a patch of lawn, an elevated deck looks out of place, an ungainly visitor that is uncomfortable in its surroundings.

In the design shown here, attractive landscaping brings the deck, house, and yard into balance. Plants, combined with lattice panels attached to the posts, form a broad pedestal of visual support for the deck. Decreasing in height from the deck to the yard, the planting makes it easier for our eyes to move between the levels.

The planting is as pretty as it is functional. At one corner, a fringe tree provides delightful scented spring flowers that can be enjoyed from the deck above or lawn below. Clematis climbs lattice panels on the sides of the deck, while an espaliered flowering dogwood fans in front.

Wrapping around the deck at ground level, a selection of shrubs, grasses, and perennials offers colorful flowers and foliage throughout the growing season. Grass paths lead to the enclosed area beneath the deck. Cover the ground there with wood chips and use the space to store garden tools or bicycles.

See site plan for **B**.

Fringe tree **A**

Gold-variegated hakonechloa **G**

Hollyhock mallow **H**

Dwarf Hinoki **D** cypress

Plants & Projects

In this design, flowers in shades of blue, pink, and white bloom in sequence from spring to fall, complemented by green, gold, and purple foliage. The lattice provides instant screening, and the clematis vine, perennials, and grasses will flower and fill their space in just a year or two; the trees will take several years to grow as large as we've shown here. Annual maintenance includes cutting back the perennials and grasses in fall or spring and training the espaliered dogwood, a process that takes patience but is fun to do.

A Fringe tree (use 1 plant)
A small multitrunked deciduous tree, it is festooned with spectacular fleecy clusters of fragrant flowers in late spring. Leaves turn gold in the autumn.

B Kousa dogwood (use 1)
Espaliered below the deck, this deciduous tree displays large white flowers in early summer, followed by red fruits and red-purple fall color. Flaking multicolored bark looks interesting all year.

C Sweet autumn clematis (use 2)
A vigorous deciduous vine covered with fragrant white flowers in late summer and puffy silvery seed heads in fall.

D Dwarf Hinoki cypress (use 2)
A small pyramidal conifer with curly sprays of dark green foliage.

E False indigo (use 5)
Candlelike spikes of sky blue flowers stand out in early summer above dense clumps of blue-green foliage. Big gray seedpods follow on this native perennial.

F Gaura (use 4)
Delicate white and pink flowers on arching stems sparkle from early summer to frost on this tough perennial wildflower.

G Gold-variegated hakonechloa (use 12)
Arching gracefully from thin stems, the long tapering leaves of this perennial grass have a creamy background overlaid with green and traces of bronze.

H Hollyhock mallow (use 7)
For weeks in midsummer, a thicket of tall stems carry fresh pink flowers. The bright green foliage looks good in spring and fall.

I 'Karl Foerster' feather reed grass (use 10)
This clumping perennial grass pushes stalks of slender silvery seed heads well above its leaves in midsummer. Handsome in winter.

J 'Longwood Blue' bluebeard (use 4)
Fluffy blue flowers on this deciduous shrub attract lots of butterflies in late summer. Gray-green foliage is attractive, too.

K 'Palace Purple' heuchera (use 8)
A broad patch of this perennial ground cover fills the front of the bed. Dark purple-bronze foliage contrasts with the other plants and the lawn.

L Peony (use 3)
A bushy perennial with lovely foliage all season and beautiful flowers in late May. Try a single pink form here; it won't flop like the heavier double-flowered kinds.

M Lattice panels
Wooden lattice panels enclose the base of the deck and support the espalier and vines.

c Sweet autumn clematis

M Lattice panels

K 'Palace Purple' heuchera

J 'Longwood Blue' bluebeard

I 'Karl Foerster' feather reed grass

B Kousa dogwood

I 'Karl Foerster' feather reed grass

F Gaura

D Dwarf Hinoki cypress

L Peony

Deck

Lawn

1 square = 1 ft.

Site: Sunny

Season: Spring

Concept: A pleasing mix of woody plants, perennials, and grasses leads the eye from ground to deck.

Note: All plants are appropriate for USDA Hardiness Zones 5, 6, and 7.

Plan #111049

Dimensions: 60' W x 50' D

Levels: 2

Square Footage: 2,205

Main Level Sq. Ft.: 1,552

Upper Level Sq. Ft.: 653

Bedrooms: 3

Bathrooms: 2

Foundation: Pier

Materials list available: No

Price Code: E

Images provided by designer/architect.

This stately beach home offers many waterfront views.

Features:

- Ceiling Height: 8 ft.
- Entrance: This home features raised stairs, with two wings that lead to the central staircase.
- Front Porch: This area is 110 square feet.
- Living Room: This huge room features a wood-burning fireplace and large windows, and it leads to the rear covered porch and a spacious deck. It is also open to the kitchen and dining area.
- Kitchen: This room has ample counter space

and an island that is open to the dining area.

- Master Suite: This upper level room has a large balcony. This balcony is a perfect place to watch the sun set over the beach. This room also a walk-in closet.
- Master Bath: This room has all the modern amenities, with separate vanities, large corner tub and walk-in shower.
- Lower Level Bedrooms: These rooms each have a walk in closet and share a bathroom.

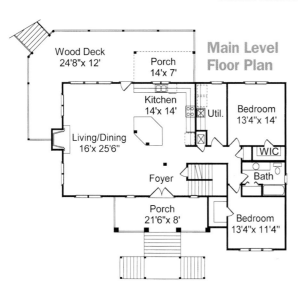

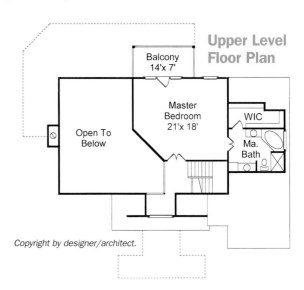

Copyright by designer/architect.

Rear View

Removing Carpet Stains in Kid's Rooms

Kids will be kids, and so accidents will happen. The cardinal rule for removing a stain from carpeting is to always clean up a spot or spill immediately, using white cloths or paper towels. Blot, never rub or scrub, a stain. Work from the outer edge in toward the center of the spot, and then follow up with clean water to remove any residue of the stain. Blot up any moisture remaining from the cleanup by layering white paper towels over the spot and weighing them down with a heavy object.

To remove a water-soluble stain, blot as much of it as possible with white paper towels that have been dampened with cold water. If necessary, mix a solution of 1¼ teaspoon of clear, mild, nonbleach laundry detergent with 32 ounces of water, and then spray it lightly onto the spot. Blot it repeatedly with white paper towels. Rinse it with a spray of clean water; then blot it dry.

To treat soils made by urine or vomit, mix equal parts of white vinegar and water, and blot it onto the spot with white paper towels; then clean with detergent solution.

To remove an oil-based stain, blot as much of it as you can; then apply a nonflammable spot remover made specifically for grease, oil, or tar to a clean, white paper towel. Don't apply the remover directly to the carpet, or you may damage the backing. Blot the stain with the treated towel. Wear rubber gloves to protect your hands. Use this method for stains caused by crayons, cosmetics, ink, paint, and shoe polish.

For spots made by cola, chocolate, or blood, apply a solution of 1 tablespoon of ammonia and 1 cup of water to the stain; then go over it with the detergent solution. Do not use ammonia on a wool carpet. Try an acid stain remover—lemon juice or white vinegar diluted with water.

To remove chewing gum or candle wax, try freezing the spot with ice cubes, and then gently scrape off the gum or wax with a blunt object. Follow this with a vacuuming. If this doesn't work, apply a commercial gum remover to the area, following the manufacturer's directions.

Upper Level Floor Plan

Copyright by designer/architect.

Plan #181041

Dimensions: 37' W x 30'8" D

Levels: 2

Square Footage: 1,556

Main Level Sq. Ft.: 952

Upper Level Sq. Ft.: 604

Bedrooms: 3

Bathrooms: 2

Foundation: Full basement

Materials List Available: Yes

Price Category: C

Illustration provided by designer/architect.

Main Level Floor Plan

Main Level Floor Plan

Copyright by designer/architect.

Plan #481005

Dimensions: 67'4" W x 53' D

Levels: 2

Square Footage: 2,825

Main Level Sq. Ft.: 1,412

Upper Level Sq. Ft.: 1,413

Bedrooms: 4

Bathrooms: 2½

Foundation: Walk-out basement

Materials List Available: No

Price Category: F

Illustration provided by designer/architect.

Upper Level Floor Plan

Plan #181063

Dimensions: 55' W x 41' D
Levels: 2
Square Footage: 2,037
Main Level Sq. Ft.: 1,347
Upper Level Sq. Ft.: 690
Bedrooms: 4
Bathrooms: 2
Foundation: Full basement
Materials List Available: Yes
Price Category: D

Images provided by designer/architect.

CAD FILE AVAILABLE

Main Level Floor Plan

Upper Level Floor Plan

Copyright by designer/architect.

Plan #361022

Dimensions: 34' W x 54' D
Levels: 2
Square Footage: 1,844
Main Level Sq. Ft.: 1,159
Upper Level Sq. Ft.: 685
Bedrooms: 3
Bathrooms: 2
Foundation: Crawl space
Materials List Available: No
Price Category: D

Images provided by designer/architect.

CAD FILE AVAILABLE

Main Level Floor Plan

Upper Level Floor Plan

Copyright by designer/architect.

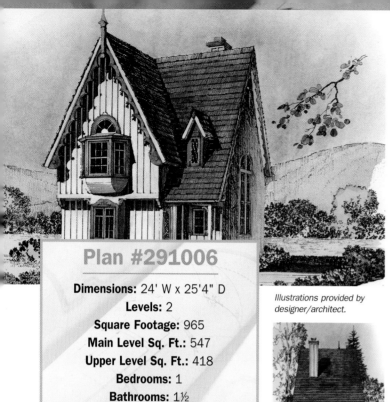

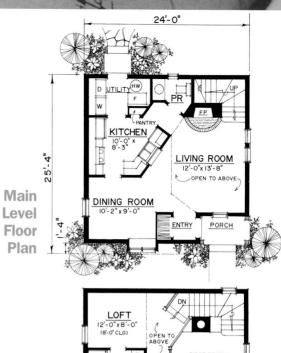

Main Level Floor Plan

24'-0"

25'-4"

1'-4"

D | UTILITY | HW
F
W
PANTRY
PR
UP
KITCHEN
10'-0" x 8'-3"
FP
LIVING ROOM
12'-0" x 13'-8"
OPEN TO ABOVE
DINING ROOM
10'-2" x 9'-0"
ENTRY
PORCH

Illustrations provided by designer/architect.

Plan #291006

Dimensions: 24' W x 25'4" D

Levels: 2

Square Footage: 965

Main Level Sq. Ft.: 547

Upper Level Sq. Ft.: 418

Bedrooms: 1

Bathrooms: 1½

Foundation: Crawl space

Materials List Available: No

Price Category: A

Upper Level Floor Plan

LOFT
12'-0" x 8'-0"
(8'-0" CLG)
DN
OPEN TO ABOVE
RIDGE BEAM
OPEN TO BELOW
TUB/SHWR
BATH
MASTER BEDROOM
12'-0" x 11'-0"
(12'-0" CEILING)
PLANT SHELF
WIC

Copyright by designer/architect.

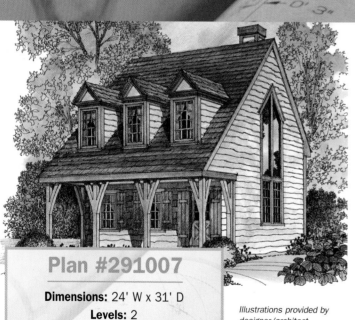

Plan #291007

Dimensions: 24' W x 31' D

Levels: 2

Square Footage: 1,065

Main Level Sq. Ft.: 576

Upper Level Sq. Ft.: 489

Bedrooms: 1

Bathrooms: 1½

Foundation: Crawl space

Materials List Available: No

Price Category: B

Illustrations provided by designer/architect.

Upper Level Floor Plan

5'-0" KNEEWALL
CEILING CLIP
DN
LOFT
12'-4" x 8'-0"
BATH
WOOD RAIL
EXPOSED BEAM
VAULTED CEILING
MASTER BED
13'-2" x 11'-0"
CEILING CLIP
W.I.C.
5'-0" KNEEWALL

Main Level Floor Plan

24'-0"

31'-0"

D | UTIL. | WH
F
W
PR
UP
FP
KITCHEN
11'-0" x 8'-4"
LIVING ROOM
13'-0" x 13'-8"
OPEN TO ABOVE
DINING
15'-0" x 9'-0"
ENTRY
PORCH
24'-0" x 7'-0"

Copyright by designer/architect.

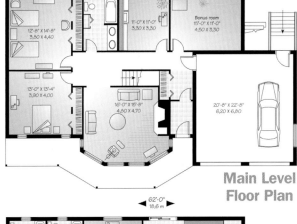

**Main Level
Floor Plan**

Illustration provided by designer/architect.

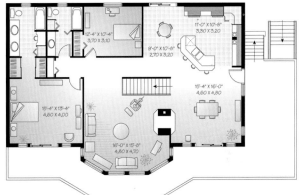

**Upper Level
Floor Plan**

Copyright by designer/architect.

Plan #181122

Dimensions: 62' W x 36'4" D

Levels: 2

Square Footage: 3,105

Main Level Sq. Ft.: 1,470

Upper Level Sq. Ft.: 1,635

Bedrooms: 4

Bathrooms: 3

Foundation: Finished basement

Materials List Available: Yes

Price Category: G

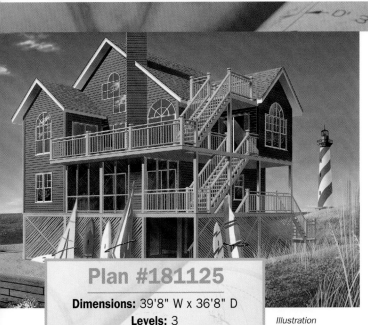

**Main
Level
Floor
Plan**

Plan #181125

Dimensions: 39'8" W x 36'8" D

Levels: 3

Square Footage: 2,392

Main Level Sq. Ft.: 967

Upper Level Sq. Ft.: 1,076

Third Level Sq. Ft.: 349

Bedrooms: 4

Bathrooms: 3½

Foundation: Pillars

Materials List Available: Yes

Price Category: E

Illustration provided by designer/architect.

**Top Level
Floor Plan**

Copyright by designer/architect.

**Upper
Level Floor Plan**

Plan #181081

Dimensions: 58' W x 33' D
Levels: 2
Square Footage: 2,350
Main Level Sq. Ft.: 1,107
Second Level Sq. Ft.: 1,243
Bedrooms: 3
Bathrooms: 2½
Foundation: Basement
Materials List Available: Yes
Price Category: F

Illustration provided by designer/architect.

This traditional country home features a wrap-around porch and a second-floor balcony.

Features:

- Ceiling Height: 8 ft. unless otherwise noted.

- Family Room: Double French doors and a fireplace in this inviting front room enhance the beauty and warmth of the home's open floor plan.

- Kitchen: You'll love working in this bright and convenient kitchen. The breakfast bar is the perfect place to gather for informal meals.

- Master Suite: You'll look forward to retiring to this elegant upstairs suite at the end of a busy day. The suite features a private bath with separate shower and tub, as well as dual vanities.

- Secondary Bedrooms: Two family bedrooms share a full bath with a third room that opens onto the balcony.

- Basement: An unfinished full basement provides plenty of storage and the potential to add additional finished living space.

Main Level Floor Plan

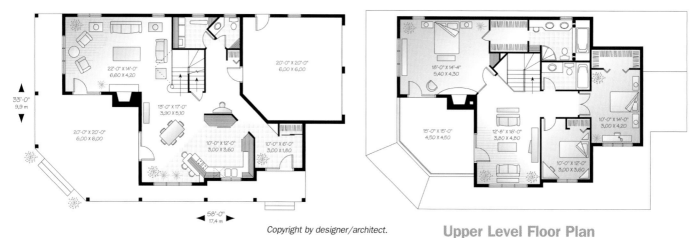

Copyright by designer/architect.

Upper Level Floor Plan

Plan #361007

Dimensions: 42' W x 40' D
Levels: 2
Square Footage: 1,306
Main Level Sq. Ft.: 1,047
Upper Level Sq. Ft.: 259
Bedrooms: 3
Bathrooms: 2
Foundation: Crawl space
Materials List Available: No
Price Category: B

Images provided by designer/architect.

This lovely, compact home is perfect for empty-nesters or a small family.

Features:

- **Great Room:** This spacious room has double doors to the deck, a vaulted ceiling, and a cozy area around the woodstove.

- **Porch/Deck:** The wraparound deck provides lots of space for sitting out to enjoy fine weather, but you'll want to sit under the roof when it's raining.

- **Nook:** Great windows and a vaulted ceiling make this room an ideal place for a dining area.

- **Kitchen:** The vaulted ceiling adds an unexpected touch to this step-saving kitchen design.

- **Studio/Bedroom:** Double doors from the deck provide a private entrance; you may want to use this room as a home office or studio space.

- **Loft:** The loft has an adjoining bath, spacious storage areas, and view to the rooms below.

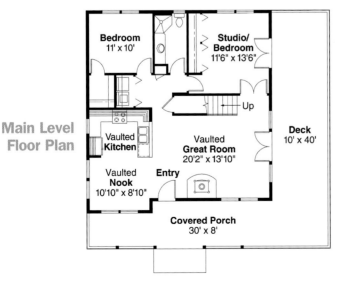

Main Level Floor Plan

Bedroom 11' x 10'
Studio/Bedroom 11'6" x 13'6"
Vaulted Kitchen
Vaulted Great Room 20'2" x 13'10"
Deck 10' x 40'
Vaulted Nook 10'10" x 8'10"
Entry
Up
Covered Porch 30' x 8'

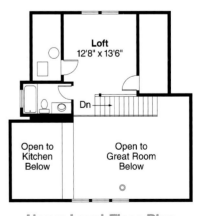

Upper Level Floor Plan

Loft 12'8" x 13'6"
Dn
Open to Kitchen Below
Open to Great Room Below

Copyright by designer/architect.

Plan #281004

Dimensions: 36' W x 50' D

Levels: 2

Square Footage: 1,426

Main Level Sq. Ft.: 1,086

Upper Level Sq. Ft.: 340

Bedrooms: 3

Bathrooms: 2½

Foundation: Walk-out basement

Materials List Available: Yes

Price Category: B

Illustration provided by designer/architect.

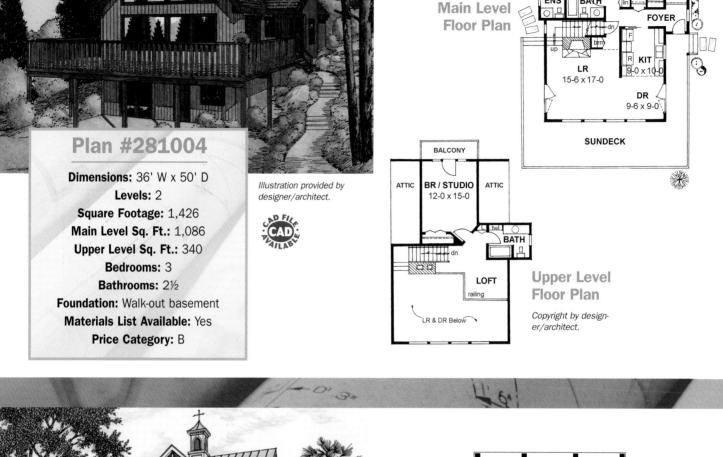

Main Level Floor Plan

MBR 12-0 x 12-0 | BR 2 10-0 x 13-0
ENS | BATH | lin | FOYER
up | brm | dn | F | R | KIT 9-0 x 10-0
LR 15-6 x 17-0
DR 9-6 x 9-0
SUNDECK

Upper Level Floor Plan

BALCONY
ATTIC | BR / STUDIO 12-0 x 15-0 | ATTIC
twl | BATH
dn | LOFT railing
LR & DR Below

Copyright by designer/architect.

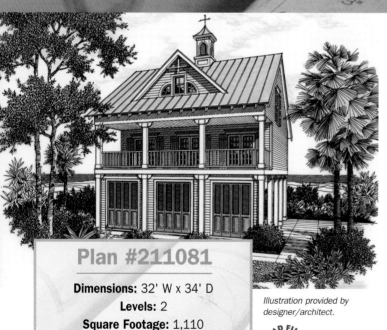

Plan #211081

Dimensions: 32' W x 34' D

Levels: 2

Square Footage: 1,110

Main Level Sq. Ft.: 832

Upper Level Sq. Ft.: 278

Bedrooms: 2

Bathrooms: 2

Foundation: Crawl space

Materials List Available: No

Price Category: B

Illustration provided by designer/architect.

Ground Level Floor Plan

covered porch
entry & utility 18 X 11 | sto 18 X 8 | carport 34 X 10
WASH | DRY
equipment area

Copyright by designer/architect.

bath | wic | kit | pan | dining 11 X 8
sink | ref | rng
mbr 18 X 12 | living 18 X 16 | 2 story clg
foy
porch 32 X 8

Main Level Floor Plan

attic space
bath | wic
br 2 12 X 12 | open to living below
attic space | observation rm | attic space

Upper Level Floor Plan

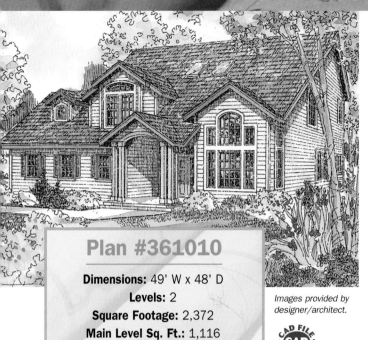

Plan #361010

Dimensions: 49' W x 48' D
Levels: 2
Square Footage: 2,372
Main Level Sq. Ft.: 1,116
Upper Level Sq. Ft.: 1,256
Bedrooms: 3
Bathrooms: 2½
Foundation: Crawl space
Materials List Available: No
Price Category: E

Images provided by designer/architect.

Main Level Floor Plan
Copyright by designer/architect.

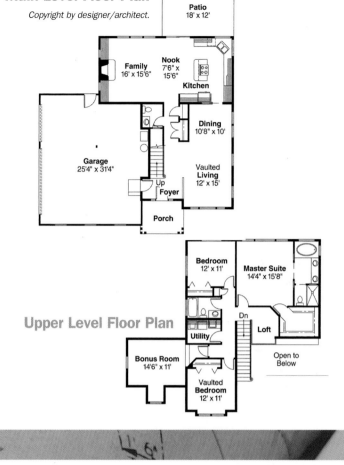

Patio 18' x 12'

Family 16' x 15'6"

Nook 7'6" x 15'6"

Kitchen

Dining 10'8" x 10'

Garage 25'4" x 31'4"

Vaulted Living 12' x 15'

Up
Foyer

Porch

Upper Level Floor Plan

Bedroom 12' x 11'

Master Suite 14'4" x 15'8"

Utility

Dn
Loft

Open to Below

Bonus Room 14'6" x 11'

Vaulted Bedroom 12' x 11'

Plan #181053

Dimensions: 56' W x 53'2" D
Levels: 2
Square Footage: 2,353
Main Level Sq. Ft.: 1,606
Upper Level Sq. Ft.: 747
Bedrooms: 3
Bathrooms: 2½
Foundation: Basement, crawl space
Materials List Available: Yes
Price Category: E

Images provided by designer/architect.

Main Level Floor Plan

53'-2"
15.95 m

56'-0"
16.8 m

Upper Level Floor Plan

Copyright by designer/architect.

OPEN TO BELOW

BONUS ROOM 20'-4" x 14'-0"
6.10 x 4.20

Main Level Floor Plan

PORCH

FAMILY 21 x 16

BRKFST. 10 x 7

SEWING 11 x 16

KIT. 12 x 12

GARAGE 21 x 21

LIVING 18 x 18

PORCH

Upper Level Floor Plan

BEDROOM 14 x 16

OPEN

OPEN

OPEN

BEDROOM 10 x 13

BEDROOM 10 x 13

Copyright by designer/architect.

Plan #381006

Dimensions: 59'10" W x 52' D

Levels: 2

Square Footage: 2,230

Main Level Sq. Ft.: 1,370

Upper Level Sq. Ft.: 860

Bedrooms: 3

Bathrooms: 2½

Foundation: Basement, crawl space

Materials List Available: Yes

Price Category: E

Images provided by designer/architect.

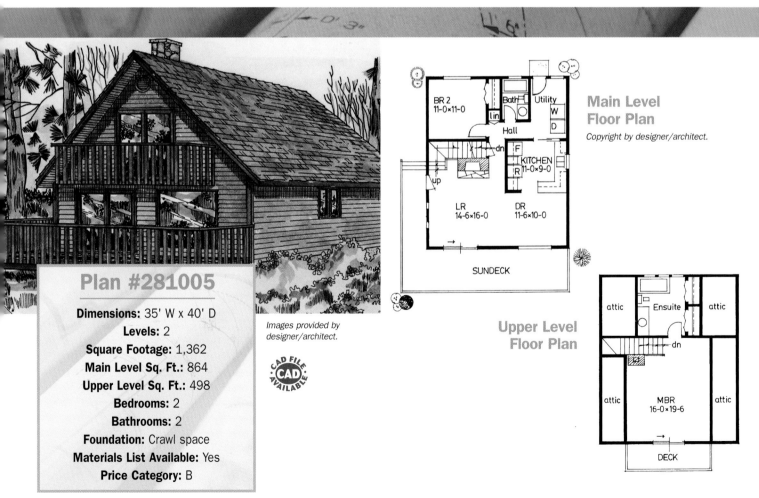

BR 2 11-0×11-0

Bath

Lin

Utility

W D

Hall

dn

up

F R

KITCHEN 11-0×9-0

LR 14-6×16-0

DR 11-6×10-0

SUNDECK

Main Level Floor Plan

Copyright by designer/architect.

Upper Level Floor Plan

attic

Ensuite

attic

dn

attic

MBR 16-0×19-6

attic

DECK

Plan #281005

Dimensions: 35' W x 40' D

Levels: 2

Square Footage: 1,362

Main Level Sq. Ft.: 864

Upper Level Sq. Ft.: 498

Bedrooms: 2

Bathrooms: 2

Foundation: Crawl space

Materials List Available: Yes

Price Category: B

Images provided by designer/architect.

CAD FILE AVAILABLE

Main Level Floor Plan

12'-0" X 12'-0"
3,60 X 3,60

12'-4" X 8'-0"
3,70 X 2,40

13'-8" X 24'-0"
4,10 X 7,20

37'-0"
11,1 m

26'-4"
7,9 m

Illustration provided by designer/architect.

CAD FILE AVAILABLE

13'-8" X 13'-8"
4,10 X 4,10

10'-0" X 10'-0"
3,00 X 3,00

Upper Level Floor Plan

Copyright by designer/architect.

Plan #181131

Dimensions: 26'4" W x 39' D

Levels: 2

Square Footage: 1,590

Main Level Sq. Ft.: 966

Upper Level Sq. Ft.: 594

Bedrooms: 3

Bathrooms: 2

Foundation: Full basement

Materials List Available: Yes

Price Category: B

Main Level Floor Plan

11'-0" X 9'-0"
3,30 X 2,70

12'-0" X 12'-8"
3,80 X 3,80

11'-8" X 7'-0"
3,50 X 2,10

18'-8" X 11'-8"
5,60 X 3,50

24'-0" X 12'-0"
7,20 X 3,60

26'-0"
7,8 m

44'-0"
13,2 m

Illustration provided by designer/architect.

CAD FILE AVAILABLE

11'-4" X 9'-4"
3,40 X 2,80

16'-0" X 12'-8"
4,80 X 3,80

Upper Level Floor Plan

Copyright by designer/architect.

Plan #181132

Dimensions: 44' W x 26' D

Levels: 2

Square Footage: 1,437

Main Level Sq. Ft.: 856

Upper Level Sq. Ft.: 581

Bedrooms: 3

Bathrooms: 1½

Foundation: Walk-out basement

Materials List Available: Yes

Price Category: C

Plan #391001

Dimensions: 32' W x 40' D
Levels: 2
Square Footage: 2,015
Main Level Sq. Ft.: 1,280
Upper Level Sq. Ft.: 735
Bedrooms: 3
Bathrooms: 2½
Foundation: Basement
Materials List Available: Yes
Price Category: D

Images provided by designer/architect.

Follow your dream to this home surrounded with decking. The A-frame front showcases bold windowing (on two levels), and natural lighting fills the house.

Features:

• **Dining Room:** This dining room and the family room are completely open to each other, perfect for hanging out in the warmth of the hearth.

• **Kitchen:** This L-shaped kitchen features an expansive cooktop/lunch counter.

• **Utility Areas:** A utility room handles the laundry and storage, and a half bath with linen closet takes care of other necessities.

• **Master Suite:** This main-floor master suite is just that—sweet! The spa-style bath features a corner tub nestled against a greenhouse window. Plus, there are double sinks and a separate shower.

• **Upstairs:** The sun-washed loft keeps overlooks the activity below while embracing two dreamy bedrooms and a sizable bath with double sinks.

Main Level Floor Plan

Upper Level Floor Plan

Copyright by designer/architect.

Plan #111047

Dimensions: 36' W x 54' D
Levels: 2
Square Footage: 1,863
Main Level Sq. Ft.: 1,056
Upper Level Sq. Ft.: 807
Bedrooms: 4
Bathrooms: 3
Foundation: Pier
Materials List Available: No
Price Category: E

Designed for a coastline, this home is equally appropriate as a year-round residence or a vacation retreat.

Features:

- Orientation: The rear-facing design gives you an ocean view and places the most attractive side of the house where beach-goers can see it.

- Entryway: On the waterside, a large deck with a covered portion leads to the main entrance.

- Carport: This house is raised on piers that let you park underneath it and that protect it from water damage during storms.

- Living Room: A fireplace, French doors, and large windows grace this room, which is open to both the kitchen and the dining area.

- Master Suite: Two sets of French doors open to a balcony on the ocean side, and the suite includes two walk-in closets and a fully equipped bath.

Main Level Floor Plan

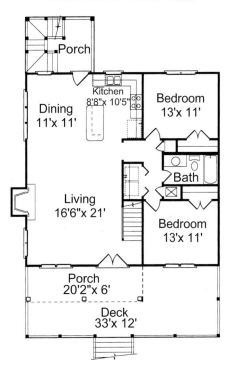

Upper Level Floor Plan

Copyright by designer/architect.

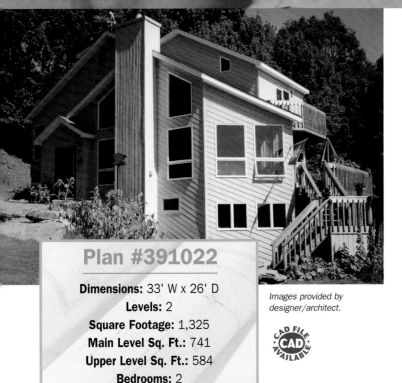

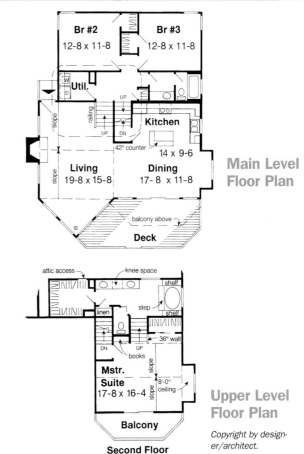

Plan #391022

Dimensions: 33' W x 26' D
Levels: 2
Square Footage: 1,325
Main Level Sq. Ft.: 741
Upper Level Sq. Ft.: 584
Bedrooms: 2
Bathrooms: 1½
Foundation: Walk-out basement
Materials List Available: Yes
Price Category: B

Images provided by designer/architect.

CAD FILE AVAILABLE

Main Level Floor Plan

Br #2
12-8 x 11-8

Br #3
12-8 x 11-8

Util.

UP

Kitchen
14 x 9-6

42" counter

UP
DN

Living
19-8 x 15-8

Dining
17-8 x 11-8

balcony above

Deck

Upper Level Floor Plan

attic access

knee space

shelf

linen

step

shelf

36" wall

DN

UP
books

Mstr. Suite
17-8 x 16-4

8'-0" ceiling

Balcony

Second Floor

Copyright by designer/architect.

Plan #181683

Dimensions: 34' W x 434'6" D
Levels: 2
Square Footage: 1,737
Main Level Sq. Ft.: 1,010
Upper Level Sq. Ft.: 727
Bedrooms: 3
Bathrooms: 2
Foundation: Basement
Materials List Available: Yes
Price Category: B

Images provided by designer/architect.

CAD FILE AVAILABLE

34'-6"
10.55 m

13'-0" X 12'-4"
3.90 X 3.70

18'-0" X 13'-8"
4.50 X 4.10

12'-10" X 18'-2"
3.85 X 5.45

34'-0"
10.2 m

9'-0" X 12'-4"
2.70 X 3.70

13'-0" X 15'-0"
3.90 X 4.50

12'-0" X 12'-0"
3.60 X 3.60

Main Level Floor Plan

Upper Level Floor Plan

Copyright by designer/architect.

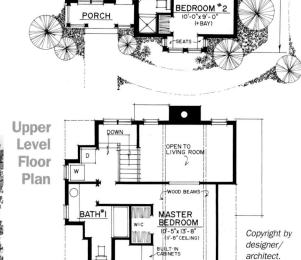

Main Level Floor Plan

32'-0"

KIT.
8'-0" x 9'-8"

STOR

F WH FP

LIVING ROOM
15'-7" x 14'-0"

PORCH

28'-7"

WALL ABOVE

UP

DINE
11'-0" x 8'-3"

ENTRY

B 2

BEDROOM #2
10'-0" x 9'-0"
(+BAY)

PORCH

SEATS

Plan #291008

Dimensions: 32' W x 28'7" D

Levels: 2

Square Footage: 1,183

Main Level Sq. Ft.: 772

Upper Level Sq. Ft.: 411

Bedrooms: 2

Bathrooms: 2

Foundation: Crawl space

Materials List Available: No

Price Category: B

Illustrations provided by designer/architect.

Upper Level Floor Plan

DOWN

D

W

OPEN TO LIVING ROOM

WOOD BEAMS

BATH #1

WIC

MASTER BEDROOM
10'-5" x 13'-8"
(11'-8" CEILING)

BUILT-IN CABINETS

Copyright by designer/architect.

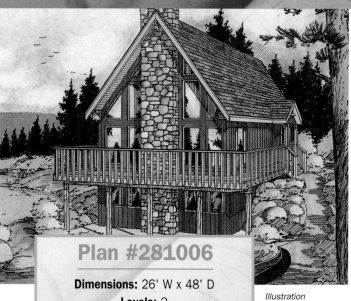

Plan #281006

Dimensions: 26' W x 48' D

Levels: 2

Square Footage: 1,702

Main Level Sq. Ft.: 1,238

Upper Level Sq. Ft.: 464

Bedrooms: 3

Bathrooms: 2

Foundation: Walk-out basement

Materials List Available: Yes

Price Category: C

Illustration provided by designer/architect.

CAD FILE AVAILABLE

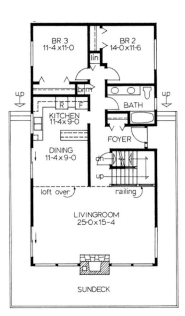

BR 3
11-4 x 11-0

BR 2
14-0 x 11-6

lin

up

R F

KITCHEN
11-4 x 9-0

DINING
11-4 x 9-0

BATH

FOYER

dn

up

loft over

railing

LIVINGROOM
25-0 x 15-4

SUNDECK

Main Level Floor Plan

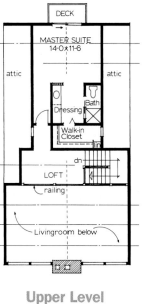

DECK

MASTER SUITE
14-0 x 11-6

attic

attic

Dressing

Bath

Walk-in Closet

dn

LOFT

railing

Livingroom below

Upper Level Floor Plan

Copyright by designer/architect.

**Main Level
Floor Plan**

*Photo provided by
designer/architect.*

**Upper Level
Floor Plan**

*Copyright by design-
er/architect.*

Plan #111040

Dimensions: 37' W x 52' D
Levels: 2
Square Footage: 1,650
Main Level Sq. Ft.: 1,122
Upper Level Sq. Ft.: 528
Bedrooms: 4
Bathrooms: 2
Foundation: Pier
Materials List Available: No
Price Category: D

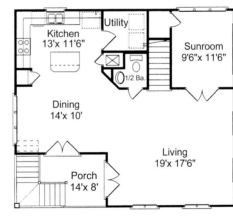

**Main
Level
Floor
Plan**

*Photo provided by
designer/architect.*

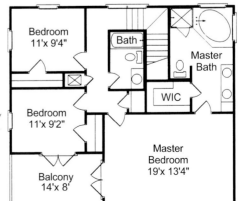

*Copyright by
designer/architect.*

**Upper
Level
Floor
Plan**

Plan #111042

Dimensions: 34' W x 30' D
Levels: 2
Square Footage: 1,779
Main Level Sq. Ft.: 907
Upper Level Sq. Ft.: 872
Bedrooms: 3
Bathrooms: 2½
Foundation: Pier
Materials List Available: No
Price Category: D

Main Level Floor Plan

Sun Room

Bedroom 10'4" x 12'6"

Bedroom 10'6" x 11'

Up

Kitchen

Dining 9' x 9'4"

Living 16'6" x 17'8"

Deck

Deck

Master Suite 21' x 12'6"

Dn

Open to Below

Upper Level Floor Plan

Copyright by designer/architect.

Plan #361026

Dimensions: 34' W x 38' D

Levels: 2

Square Footage: 1,401

Main Level Sq. Ft.: 948

Upper Level Sq. Ft.: 453

Bedrooms: 3

Bathrooms: 2

Foundation: Crawl space

Materials List Available: No

Price Category: B

Images provided by designer/architect.

CAD FILE AVAILABLE

Plan #111021

Dimensions: 34' W x 44'0" D

Levels: 2

Square Footage: 2,221

Main Level Sq. Ft.: 1,307

Upper Level Sq. Ft.: 914

Bedrooms: 4

Bathrooms: 3

Foundation: Pier

Materials List Available: No

Price Category: F

Images provided by designer/architect.

Bedroom 12'x 11'

Bedroom 12'x 11'

Kitchen 12'x 13'

Living 21'x 19'2"

Dining 12'4"x 13'6"

Porch 21'x 8'

Main Level Floor Plan

Study 10'x 10'

Sitting Area 10'9"x 10'

Master Bedroom 12'x 16'

Bedroom 12'4"x 13'

Balcony 21'x 8'

Upper Level Floor Plan

Copyright by designer/architect.

Main Level Floor Plan

Dining 12'8"x 12'

Bedroom 13'x 12'

Living 18'6"x 22'

Bedroom 13'x 11'9"

Porch

Deck

Plan #111027

Dimensions: 48' W x 57' D
Levels: 2
Square Footage: 2,601
Main Level Sq. Ft.: 1,623
Upper Level Sq. Ft.: 978
Bedrooms: 3
Bathrooms: 2
Foundation: Pier
Materials List Available: No
Price Category: G

Upper Level Floor Plan

Master Bedroom 18'6"x 20'

Study 13'x 15'6"

Balcony

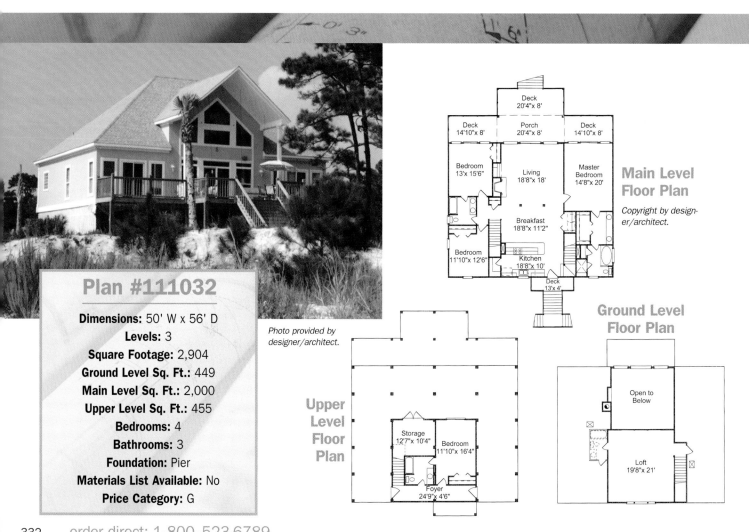

Main Level Floor Plan

Deck 20'4"x 8'

Deck 14'10"x 8'

Porch 20'4"x 8'

Deck 14'10"x 8'

Bedroom 13'x 15'6"

Living 18'8"x 18'

Master Bedroom 14'8"x 20'

Breakfast 18'8"x 11'2"

Bedroom 11'10"x 12'6"

Kitchen 18'8"x 10'

Deck 13'x 4'

Plan #111032

Dimensions: 50' W x 56' D
Levels: 3
Square Footage: 2,904
Ground Level Sq. Ft.: 449
Main Level Sq. Ft.: 2,000
Upper Level Sq. Ft.: 455
Bedrooms: 4
Bathrooms: 3
Foundation: Pier
Materials List Available: No
Price Category: G

Upper Level Floor Plan

Storage 12'7"x 10'4"

Bedroom 11'10"x 16'4"

Foyer 24'9"x 4'6"

Ground Level Floor Plan

Open to Below

Loft 19'8"x 21'

Illustration provided by designer/architect.

Plan #181133

Dimensions: 38' W x 40' D
Levels: 2
Square Footage: 1,832
Main Level Sq. Ft.: 1,212
Second Level Sq. Ft. 620
Bedrooms: 3
Bathrooms: 2
Foundation: Walkout, crawl space.
Slab or basement for fee.
Materials List Available: Yes
Price Category: D

You'll enjoy sunshine indoors and out with a wraparound deck and windows all around.

Features:

• Ceiling Height: 8 ft.

• Family Room: Family and friends will be drawn to this large sunny room. Curl up with a good book before the beautiful see-through fireplace.

• Screened Porch: This porch shares the see-through fireplace with the family room so you can enjoy an outside fire on cool summer nights.

• Master Suite: This romantic first-floor master suite offers a large walk-in closet and a luxurious private bathroom enhanced by dual vanities.

• Secondary Bedrooms: Upstairs you'll find two generous bedrooms with ample closet space. These bedrooms share a full bathroom.

• Basement: This large walkout basement with large glass door is perfectly suited for future expansion.

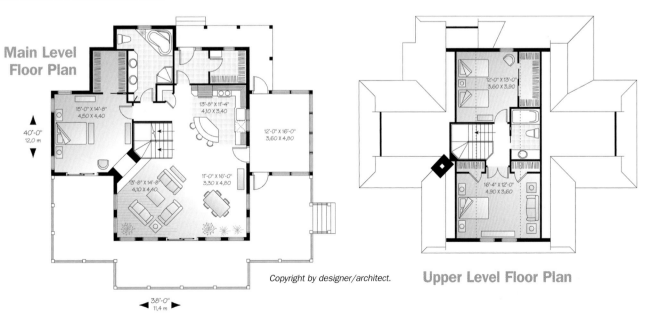

Main Level Floor Plan

Upper Level Floor Plan

Copyright by designer/architect.

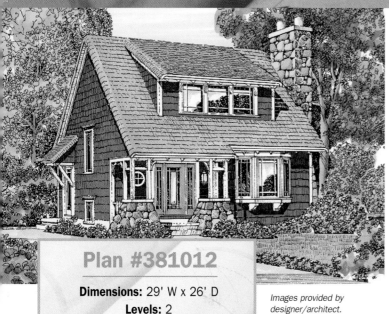

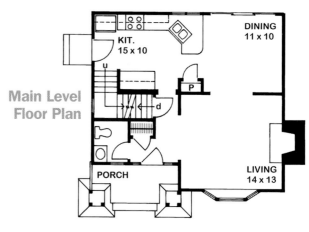

Main Level Floor Plan

KIT. 15 x 10

DINING 11 x 10

PORCH

LIVING 14 x 13

Images provided by designer/architect.

BEDROOM 10 x 9

st.

st.

Upper Level Floor Plan

Copyright by designer/architect.

st.

BEDROOM 15 x 11

st.

Plan #381012

Dimensions: 29' W x 26' D

Levels: 2

Square Footage: 1,035

Main Level Sq. Ft.: 605

Upper Level Sq. Ft.: 430

Bedrooms: 2

Bathrooms: 1½

Foundation: Basement

Materials List Available: Yes

Price Category: B

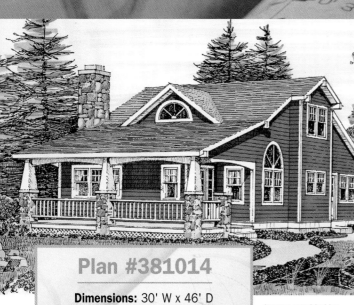

BEDROOM 12 x 15

BEDROOM 13 x 9

Main Level Floor Plan

KIT. 10 x 8

shelves   loft over

fp

DINING 12 x 9

LIVING 14 x 14

PORCH

Images provided by designer/architect.

storage

Upper Level Floor Plan

Copyright by designer/architect.

LOFT 15 x 10

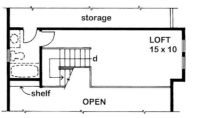

shelf

OPEN

Plan #381014

Dimensions: 30' W x 46' D

Levels: 2

Square Footage: 1,315

Main Level Sq. Ft.: 1,100

Upper Level Sq. Ft.: 215

Bedrooms: 2

Bathrooms: 2

Foundation: Basement

Materials List Available: Yes

Price Category: B

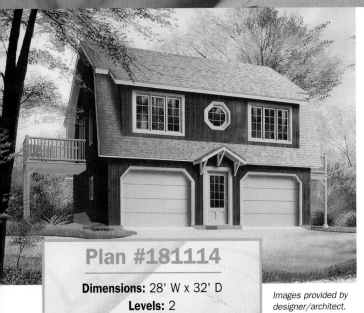

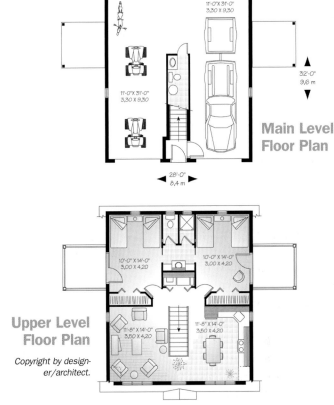

Main Level Floor Plan

11'-0"X 31'-0"
3,30 X 9,30

11'-0"X 31'-0"
3,30 X 9,30

32'-0"
9,6 m

28'-0"
8,4 m

Upper Level Floor Plan

Copyright by designer/architect.

10'-0" X 14'-0"
3,00 X 4,20

10'-0" X 14'-0"
3,00 X 4,20

11'-8" X 14'-0"
3,50 X 4,20

11'-8" X 14'-0"
3,50 X 4,20

Plan #181114

Dimensions: 28' W x 32' D

Levels: 2

Square Footage: 992

Garage Level Sq. Ft.: 96

Second Level Sq. Ft.: 896

Bedrooms: 2

Bathrooms: 1½

Foundation: Slab

Materials List Available: Yes

Price Category: A

Images provided by designer/architect.

CAD FILE AVAILABLE **CAD**

Main Level Floor Plan

Deck

Deck

Deck

Vaulted Master Suite
15'8" x 12'

Great Room
24'4" x 32'2"

Vaulted Country Kitchen
13'2" x 14'6"

Up

Entry

Utility

Covered Porch
24' x 8'

Upper Level Floor Plan

Copyright by designer/architect.

Open to Great Room Below

Vaulted Loft

Vaulted Bedroom
10'8" x 11'

Vaulted Bedroom
10' x 11'6"

Dn

Plan #361293

Dimensions: 56' W x 42' D

Levels: 2

Square Footage: 1,987

Main Level Sq. Ft.: 1,466

Upper Level Sq. Ft.: 521

Bedrooms: 3

Bathrooms: 2½

Foundation: Basement, crawl space

Materials List Available: No

Price Category: D

Images provided by designer/architect.

CAD FILE AVAILABLE **CAD**

Illustration provided by designer/architect.

Plan #181128

Dimensions: 36' W x 36' D
Levels: 2
Square Footage: 1,634
Main Level Sq. Ft.: 1,087
Second Level Sq. Ft.: 547
Bedrooms: 3
Bathrooms: 2
Foundation: Basement
Materials List Available: Yes
Price Category: D

This stone-accented rustic vacation home offers the perfect antidote to busy daily life.

CAD FILE AVAILABLE

Features:

- Ceiling Height: 8 ft. unless otherwise noted.
- Family Room: Family and friends will be unable to resist relaxing in this airy two-story family room, with its own handsome fireplace. French doors lead to the front deck.
- Kitchen: This eat-in kitchen features double sinks, ample counter space, and a pantry. It offers plenty of space for the family to gather for informal vacation meals.

- Master Suite: This first-floor master retreat occupies almost the entire length of the home. It includes a walk-in closet and a lavish bath.
- Secondary Bedrooms: On the second floor, two family bedrooms share a full bath.
- Mezzanine: This lovely balcony overlooks the family room.
- Basement: This full unfinished basement offers plenty of space for expansion.

Main Level Floor Plan

36'-0"
10,8 m

Upper Level Floor Plan

Copyright by designer/architect.

Plan #181062

Dimensions: 58' W x 55' D
Levels: 2
Square Footage: 1,953
Main Level Sq. Ft.: 1,301
Second Level Sq. Ft.: 652
Bedrooms: 3
Bathrooms: 2½
Foundation: Half basement,
half crawl space
Materials List Available: Yes
Price Category: D

Images provided by designer/architect.

Features:

- Ceiling Height: 8 ft.

- Wall of Doors: The entire back of the house is filled by five sets of multi-pane glass doors.

- Formal Dining Room: This dining room is located adjacent to the kitchen for convenient entertaining.

- Kitchen: This efficient kitchen is a pleasure in which to work, thanks to plenty of counter

space, a pantry, double sinks, and access to the laundry room.

- Great Room: This great room is open to the atrium. As a result it is filled with warmth and natural light. You'll love gathering around the handsome fireplace.

- Master Suite: This private first-floor retreat features a walk-in closet and a luxurious full bath with dual vanities.

A magnificent glass enclosed vertical atrium is the focal point of this beautiful country home.

CAD FILE CAD AVAILABLE

Main Level Floor Plan

Copyright by designer/architect.

Upper Level Floor Plan

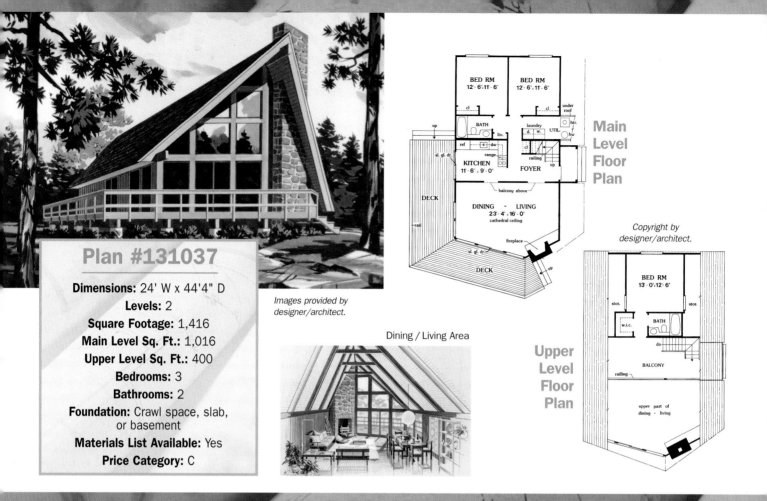

Plan #131037

Dimensions: 24' W x 44'4" D

Levels: 2

Square Footage: 1,416

Main Level Sq. Ft.: 1,016

Upper Level Sq. Ft.: 400

Bedrooms: 3

Bathrooms: 2

Foundation: Crawl space, slab, or basement

Materials List Available: Yes

Price Category: C

Images provided by designer/architect.

Dining / Living Area

Main Level Floor Plan

Upper Level Floor Plan

Copyright by designer/architect.

Plan #151790

Dimensions: 73'8" W x 55'8" D

Levels: 2

Square Footage: 3,378

Main Level Sq. Ft.: 2,216

Upper Level Sq. Ft.: 1,162

Bedrooms: 3

Bathrooms: 2½

Foundation: Crawl space

Materials List Available: No

Price Category: G

Images provided by designer/architect.

Main Level Floor Plan

Main Floor

Upper Level Floor Plan

Upper Floor

Copyright by designer/architect.

Illustration provided by designer/architect.

Plan #291005

Dimensions: 16' W x 36'10" D
Levels: 2
Square Footage: 896
Main Level Sq. Ft.: 448
Upper Level Sq. Ft.: 448
Bedrooms: 2
Bathrooms: 1½
Foundation: Crawl space
Materials List Available: No
Price Category: A

You'll be as charmed by the interior of this small home as you are by the wood-shingled roof, scroll-saw rake detailing, and board-and-batten siding on the exterior.

Features:

- **Porch:** Relax on this porch, which is the ideal spot for a couple of rockers or a swing.

- **Entryway:** Double doors reveal an open floor plan that makes everyone feel welcome.

- **Living Room:** Create a cozy nook by the windows here.

- **Kitchen:** Designed for convenience, this kitchen has ample counter space as well as enough storage to suit your needs. The stairway to the upper floor and the half-bath divide the kitchen from the living and dining areas.

- **Upper Level:** 9-ft. ceilings give a spacious feeling to the two bedrooms and full bathroom that you'll find on this floor.

Main Level Floor Plan

Upper Level Floor Plan

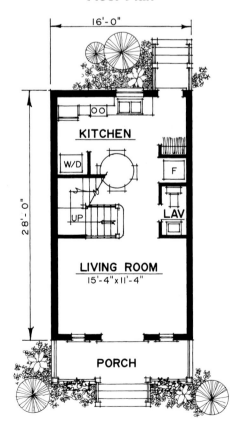

Copyright by designer/architect.

Images provided by designer/architect.

Plan #361008

Dimensions: 42' W x 48' D
Levels: 2
Square Footage: 1,749
Main Level Sq. Ft.: 1,280
Upper Level Sq. Ft.: 469
Bedrooms: 3
Bathrooms: 3
Foundation: Crawl space, basement, or slab
Materials List Available: No
Price Category: C

This charming home is ideal for a small family whose members value spending time both together and apart.

Features:

• Great Room: This room opens to the deck for entertaining ease and has a vaulted ceiling and chimney for an airtight woodstove.

• Nook: You'll love the vaulted ceiling here and in the kitchen, and the many windows in this nook.

• Kitchen: The U-shaped counter area creates a step-saving design.

• Studio/Bedroom: The bath, walk-in closet, and door to the deck make this ideal as a master suite, at-home office, or studio space.

• Bedroom: Also with an adjoining bath, this room has a large closet and wide window area.

• Loft: This area can also be a master suite with a huge closet, great window area, and luxury bath.

Main Level Floor Plan

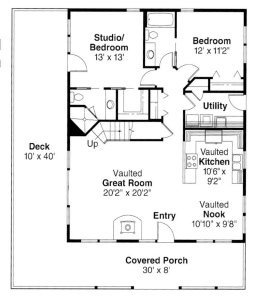

Upper Level Floor Plan

Copyright by designer/architect.

Let Us Help You
Plan Your
Dream Home

Whether you've always dreamed of building your own home or you can't find the right house from among the dozens you've toured, our collection of two-story plans can help you achieve the home of your dreams. You could have an architect create a one-of-a-kind home for you, but the design services alone could end up costing up to 15 percent of the cost of construction—a hefty premium for any building project. Isn't it a better idea to select from among the hundreds of unique designs shown in our collection for a fraction of the cost?

What does Creative Homeowner Offer?

In this book, Creative Homeowner provides hundreds of home plans from the country's best architects and designers. Our designs are among the most popular available. Whether your taste runs from traditional to contemporary, Victorian to early American, you are sure to find the best house design for you and your family. Our plans packages include detailed drawings to help you or your builder construct your dream house. **(See page 342.)**

Can I Make Changes to the Plans?

Creative Homeowner offers three ways to help you achieve a truly unique home design. Our customizing service allows for extensive changes to our designs. **(See page 343.)** We also provide reverse images of our plans, or we can give you and your builder the tools for making minor changes on your own. **(See page 346.)**

Can You Help Me Manage My Costs?

To help you stay within your budget, Creative Homeowner has teamed up with the leading estimating company to provide one of the most accurate, complete, and reliable building material take-offs in the industry. **(See page 344.)** If that is too much detail for you, we can provide you with general construction costs based on your zip code. **(See page 346.)** Also, many of our plans come with the option of buying detailed materials lists to help you price out construction costs.

How Can I Begin the Building Process?

To get started building your dream home, fill out the order form on page 347, call our order department at 1-800-523-6789, or visit ultimateplans.com. If you plan on doing all or part of the work yourself, or want to keep tabs on your builder, we offer best-selling building and design books available at www.creativehomeowner.com.

Our Plans Packages Offer:

"Square footage" refers to the total "heated square feet" of this plan. This number does not include the garage, porches, or unfinished areas. All of our home plans are the result of many hours of work by leading architects and professional designers. Most of our home plans include each of the following:

Frontal Sheet
This artist's rendering of the front of the house gives you an idea of how the house will look once it is completed and the property landscaped.

Detailed Floor Plans
These plans show the size and layout of the rooms. They also provide the locations of doors, windows, fireplaces, closets, stairs, and electrical outlets and switches.

Foundation Plan
A foundation plan gives the dimensions of basements, walk-out basements, crawl spaces, pier foundations, and slab construction. Each house design lists the type of foundation included. If the plan you choose does not have the foundation type you require, our customer service department can help you customize the plan to meet your needs.

Roof Plan
In addition to providing the pitch of the roof, these plans also show the locations of dormers, skylights, and other elements.

Exterior Elevations
These drawings show the front, rear, and sides of the house as if you were looking at it head on. Elevations also provide information about architectural features and finish materials.

Interior Elevations and Details
Interior elevations show specific details of such elements as fireplaces, kitchen and bathroom cabinets, built-ins, and other unique features of the design.

Cross Sections
These show the structure as if it were sliced to reveal construction requirements, such as insulation, flooring, and roofing details.- requirements, such as insulation, flooring, and roofing details.

Frontal Sheet

Floor Plan

Foundation Plan

Roof Plan

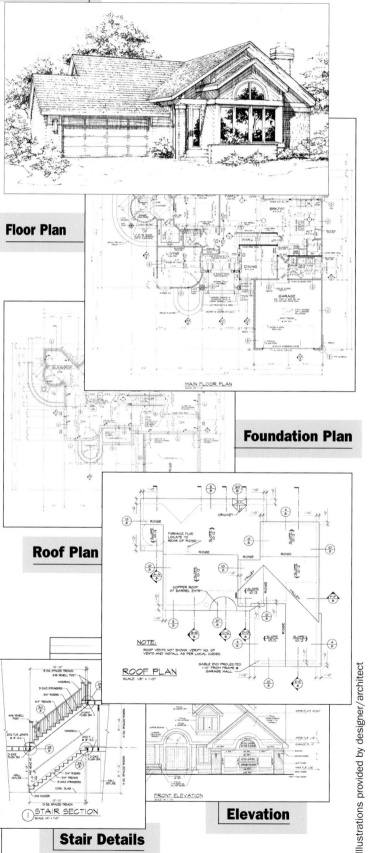

Cross Sections

Stair Details

Elevation

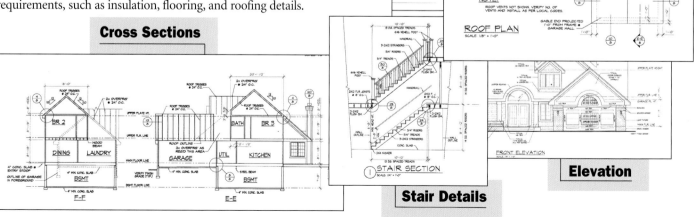

Illustrations provided by designer/architect

Customize Your Plans in 4 Easy Steps

1 **Select the home plan** that most closely meets your needs. Purchase of a reproducible master is necessary in order to make changes to a plan.

2 **Call 1-800-523-6789 to place your order.** Tell our sales representative you are interested in customizing your plan. To receive your customization cost estimate, our modification company will contact you (via fax or email) requesting a list or sketch of the changes requested to one of our plans. There is a $50 nonrefundable consultation fee for this service. If you decide to continue with the custom changes, the $50 fee is credited to the total amount charged.

3 **Fax or email your request** to our modification company. Within three business days of receipt of your request, a detailed cost estimate will be provided to you.

4 **Once you approve the estimate,** a 75% retainer fee is collected and customization work begins. Preliminary drawings typically take 10 to 15 business days. After approval of the design, the balance of your customization fee is due before modified plans can be shipped. You will receive five sets of blueprints, a reproducible master, or CAD files, depending on which package was purchase.

Modification Pricing Guide

Categories	Average Cost For Modification
Add or remove living space	Quote required
Bathroom layout redesign	Starting at $150
Kitchen layout redesign	Starting at $120
Garage: add or remove	Starting at $600
Garage: front entry to side load or vice versa	Starting at $300
Foundation changes	Starting at $220
Exterior building materials change	Starting at $200
Exterior openings: add, move, or remove	$75 per opening
Roof line changes	Starting at $600
Ceiling height adjustments	Starting at $280
Fireplace: add or remove	Starting at $90
Screened porch: add	Starting at $300
Wall framing change from 2x4 to 2x6	Starting at $250
Bearing and/or exterior walls changes	Quote required
Non-bearing wall or room changes	$65 per room
Metric conversion of home plan	Starting at $495
Adjust plan for handicapped accessibility	Quote required
Adapt plans for local building code requirements	Quote required
Engineering stamping only	Quote required
Any other engineering services	Quote required
Interactive illustrations (choices of exterior materials)	Quote required

Note: *Any home plan can be customized to accommodate your desired changes. The average prices above are provided only as examples of the most commonly requested changes, and are subject to change without notice. Prices for changes will vary according to the number of modifications requested, plan size, style, and method of design used by the original designer. To obtain a detailed cost estimate, please contact us.*

Terms & Copyright

These home plans are protected under the terms of United States Copyright Law and may not be copied or reproduced in any way, by any means, unless you have purchased reproducible masters, which clearly indicate your right to copy or reproduce. We authorize the use of your chosen home plan as an aid in the construction of one single-family home only. You may not use this home plan to build a second or multiple dwellings without purchasing another blueprint or blueprints, or paying additional home plan fees.

Architectural Seals

Because of differences in building codes, some cities and states now require an architect or engineer licensed in that state to review and "seal" a blueprint, or officially approve it, prior to construction. Delaware, Nevada, New Jersey, and New York require that all plans for houses built in those states be redrawn by an architect licensed in the state in which the home will be built. We strongly advise you to consult with your local building official for information regarding architectural seals.

Before Customization

After

Turn your dream home into reality with

a **Material Take-off** and

When purchasing a home plan with Creative Homeowner, we recommend you order one of the most complete materials lists in the industry.

What comes with a Material Take-off?

Quote

- Basis of the entire estimate.

- Detailed list of all the framing materials needed to build your project, listed from the bottom up, in the order that each one will actually be used.

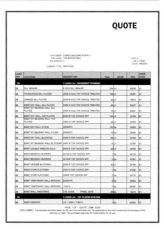

Comments

- Details pertinent information beyond the cost of materials.

- Includes any notes from our estimates.

Express List

- A combined version of the Quote with SKUs listed for purchasing the items at your local Lowe's.

- Your Lowe's Commercial Sales Specialist can then price out the materials list.

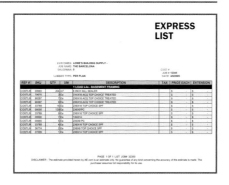

Construction-Ready Framing Diagrams

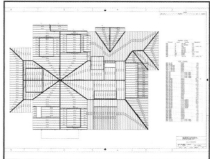

- Your "map" to exact roof and floor framing.

Millwork Report

- A complete count of the windows, doors, molding, and trim.

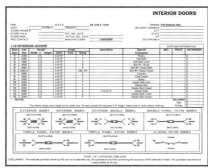

Man-Hour Report

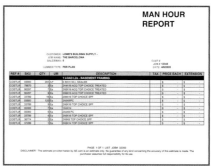

- Calculates labor on a line-by-line basis for all items quoted and presented in man-hours.

Why a Material Take-off?

Accurate. Professional estimators break down each individual item from the blueprints using advanced software, techniques, and equipment.

Timely. You will be able to start your home-building project quickly — knowing the exact framing materials you need and how to get them with Lowe's.

Detailed. Work with your Lowe's associate to complete your quote with the remaining products needed for your new home.

So how much does it cost?

Pricing is determined by the total square feet of the home plan — including living area, garages, decks, porches, finished basements, and finished attics.

Square Feet Range	MT Tier*	Price
Up to 5,000 total square feet	XB	$345.00
5,001 to 10,000 total square feet	XC	$545.00

* Please see the Plan Index to determine your plan's Material Take-off Tier (MT Tier).
 Note: All prices are subject to change

Call our toll-free number (800-523-6789), or visit ultimateplans.com to order your Material Take-off.

What else do I need to know?

When you purchase your products from Lowe's you may receive a gift card for the amount of your Material Take-off. Please go to LowesforPros.com for complete details of the program.

Turn your dream home into reality.

Decide What Type of Plan Package You Need

How many Plans Should You Order?

Standard 8-Set Package. We've found that our 8-set package is the best value for someone who is ready to start building. The 8-set package provides plans for you, your builder, the subcontractors, mortgage lender, and the building department.

Minimum 5-Set Package. If you are in the bidding process, you may want to order only five sets for the bidding round and reorder additional sets as needed.

1-Set Study Package. The 1-set package allows you to review your home plan in detail. The plan will be marked as a study print, and it is illegal to build a house from a study print alone. It is a violation of copyright law to reproduce a blueprint without permission.

Buying Additional Sets

If you require additional copies of blueprints for your home construction, you can order additional sets within 60 days of the original order date at a reduced price. The cost is $45.00 for each additional set. For more information, contact customer service.

Reproducible Masters

If you plan to make minor changes to one of our home plans, you can purchase reproducible masters. These plans are printed on bond or vellum paper that is easy to alter. They clearly indicate your right to modify, copy, or reproduce the plans. Reproducible masters allow an architect, designer, or builder to alter our plans to give you a customized home design. This package also allows you to print as many copies of the modified plans as you need for the construction of one home.

CAD (Computer Aided Design) Files

CAD files are the complete set of home plans in an electronic file format. Choose this option if there are multiple changes you wish made to the home plans and you have a local design professional able to make the changes. Not available for all plans. Please contact our order department or visit our Web site to check the availability of CAD files for your plan.

Mirror-Reverse Sets/Right-Reading Reverse

Plans can be printed in mirror-reverse—we can "flip" plans to create a mirror image of the design. This is useful when the house would fit your site or personal preferences if all the rooms were on the opposite side than shown. As the image is reversed, the lettering and dimensions will also be reversed, meaning they will read backwards. Therefore, when ordering mirror-reverse drawings, you must order at least one set of right-reading plans. A $50.00 fee per plan order will be charged for mirror-reverse (regardless of the number of mirror-reverse sets ordered). Some plans are available in right-reading reverse, this feature will show the plan in reverse, but the writing on the plan will be readable. A $150.00 fee per plan order will be charged for right-reading reverse (regardless of the number of right-reading reverse sets ordered). Please contact our order department or visit our website to check the availibility of this feature for your chosen plan.

EZ Quote: Home Cost Estimator

EZ Quote is our response to one of the most frequently asked questions we hear from customers: "How much will the house cost me to build?" EZ Quote: Home Cost Estimator will enable you to obtain a calculated building cost to construct your home, based on labor rates and building material costs within your zip code area. This summary is useful for those who want to get an idea of the total construction costs before purchasing sets of home plans. It will also provide a level of comfort when you begin soliciting bids. The cost is $29.95 for the first EZ Quote and $14.95 for each additional one. Available only in the U.S. and Canada.

Materials List

Available for most of our plans, the Materials List provides you an invaluable resource in planning and estimating the cost of your home. Each Materials List outlines the quantity, dimensions, and type of materials needed to build your home (with the exception of mechanical systems). You will get faster, more-accurate bids from your contractors and building suppliers. A Materials List may only be ordered with the purchase of at least five sets of home plans.

CompleteCost Estimator

CompleteCost Estimator is a valuable tool for use in planning and constructing your new home. It provides more detail than a materials list and will act as a checklist for all items you will need to select or coordinate during your building process. CompleteCost Estimator is only available for certain plans (please see Plan Index) and may only be ordered with the purchase of at least five sets of home plans. The cost is $125.00 for CompleteCost Estimator.

Lowe's Material Take-off (See page 344.)

Order Toll Free by Phone
1-800-523-6789
By Fax: 201-760-2431

Orders received 3PM ET, will be processed and shipped within two business days.

Order Online
www.ultimateplans.com

Mail Your Order
Creative Homeowner
Attn: Home Plans
24 Park Way
Upper Saddle River, NJ 07458

Canadian Customers
Order Toll Free 1-800-393-1883

Mail Your Order (Canada)
Creative Homeowner Canada
Attn: Home Plans
113-437 Martin St., Ste. 215
Penticton, BC V2A 5L1

Before You Order

Our Exchange Policy

Blueprints are nonrefundable. However, should you find that the plan you have purchased does not fit your needs, you may exchange that plan for another plan in our collection within 60 days from the date of your original order. The entire content of your original order must be returned before an exchange will be processed. You will be charged a processing fee of 20% of the amount of the original order, the cost difference between the new plan set and the original plan set (if applicable), and all related shipping costs for the new plans. Contact our order department for more information. Please note: reproducible masters may only be exchanged if the package is unopened and CAD files cannot be exchanged and are nonrefundable.

Building Codes and Requirements

All plans offered for sale in this book and on our website (www.ultimateplans.com) are continually updated to meet the latest International Residential Code (IRC). Because building codes vary from area to area, some drawing modifications and/or the assistance of a professional designer or architect may be necessary to comply with your local codes or to accommodate specific building site conditions. We strongly advise you to consult with your local building official for information regarding codes governing your area.

Multiple Plan Discount

Purchase **3** different home plans in the **same order** and receive **5% off** the plan price.

Purchase **5** or more different home plans in the **same order** and receive **10% off** the plan price.
(Please Note: Study sets do not apply.)

Blueprint Price Schedule

Price Code	1 Set	5 Sets	8 Sets	Reproducible Masters	CAD	Materials List
A	$400	$440	$475	$575	$1,025	$85
B	$440	$525	$555	$685	$1,195	$85
C	$510	$575	$635	$740	$1,265	$85
D	$560	$605	$665	$800	$1,300	$95
E	$600	$675	$705	$845	$1,400	$95
F	$650	$725	$775	$890	$1,500	$95
G	$720	$790	$840	$950	$1,600	$95
H	$820	$860	$945	$1,095	$1,700	$95
I	$945	$975	$1,075	$1,195	$1,890	$105
J	$1,010	$1,080	$1,125	$1,250	$1,900	$105
K	$1,125	$1,210	$1,250	$1,380	$2,030	$105
L	$1,240	$1,335	$1,375	$1,535	$2,270	$105

Note: All prices subject to change

Lowe's Material Take-off Tier (MT Tier)

MT Tier*	Price
XB	$345
XC	$545

* Please see the Plan Index to determine your plan's Material Take-off Tier (MT Tier).

Shipping & Handling

	1-4 Sets	5-7 Sets	8+ Sets or Reproducibles	CAD
US Regular (7–10 business days)	$18	$20	$25	$25
US Priority (3–5 business days)	$25	$30	$35	$35
US Express (1–2 business days)	$40	$45	$50	$50
Canada Express (3-5 business days)	$100	$100	$100	$100
Worldwide Express (3–5 business days)		** Call for price quote **		

Note: All delivery times are from date the blueprint package is shipped (typically within 1-2 days of placing order).

Order Form
Please send me the following:

Plan Number: _____ **Price Code:** _____ (See Plan Index.)

Indicate Foundation Type: (Select ONE. See plan page for availability.)

❏ Slab ❏ Crawl space ❏ Basement ❏ Walk-out basement

❏ Optional Foundation for Fee _____ $_____
(Please enter foundation here)

**Please call all our order department or visit our website for optional foundation fee*

Basic Blueprint Package

	Cost
❏ Cad Files	$_____
❏ Reproducible Masters	$_____
❏ 8-Set Plan Package	$_____
❏ 5-Set Plan Package	$_____
❏ 1-Set Study Package	$_____
❏ Additional plan sets: __ sets at $45.00 per set	$_____
❏ Print in mirror-reverse: $50.00 per order	$_____

**Please call all our order department or visit our website for availibility*

❏ Print in right-reading reverse: $150.00 per order $_____

**Please call all our order department or visit our website for availibility*

Important Extras

❏ Lowe's Material Takeoff (See Price Tier above.)	$_____
❏ Materials List	$_____
❏ CompleteCost Materials Report at $125.00 Zip Code of Home/Building Site _____	$_____
❏ EZ Quote for Plan #_____ at $29.95	$_____
❏ Additional EZ Quotes for Plan #s_____ at $19.95 each	$_____
Shipping (see chart above)	$_____
SUBTOTAL	$_____
Sales Tax (NJ residents only, add 7%)	$_____
TOTAL	$_____

Order Toll Free: 1-800-523-6789   By Fax: 201-760-2431
Creative Homeowner
24 Park Way
Upper Saddle River, NJ 07458

Name _____
(Please print or type)

Street _____
(Please do not use a P.O. Box)

City _____ State _____

Country _____ Zip _____

Daytime telephone (   )_____

Fax (   )_____
(Required for reproducible orders)

E-Mail _____

Payment ❏ Bank check/money order. No personal checks.
Make checks payable to Creative Homeowner

❏ VISA   ❏ MasterCard   ❏ American Express Cards   ❏ DISCOVER

Credit card number _____

Expiration date (mm/yy) _____

Signature _____

Please check the appropriate box:
❏ Building home for myself   ❏ Building home for someone else

SOURCE CODE **LD200**

Copyright Notice

Index

For pricing, see page 347.

Index

For pricing, see page 347.

Plan #	Price Code	Page	Total Finished Area Square Feet	Materials List Available	Complete Cost	MT Tier
141031	E	77	2367	No	No	XB
141032	E	77	2476	Yes	No	XB
141034	H	277	3656	Yes	No	XC
151011	F	304	3437	Yes	Yes	XB
151014	F	125	2698	Yes	Yes	XB
151015	F	128	2789	Yes	Yes	XB
151016	C	229	1783	Yes	Yes	XB
151019	F	298	2642	Yes	Yes	XB
151020	I	163	4532	Yes	Yes	XB
151021	F	187	3385	Yes	Yes	XB
151024	H	297	3623	Yes	Yes	XB
151025	H	128	3914	Yes	Yes	XB
151026	C	196	1574	Yes	Yes	XB
151027	E	248	2323	Yes	Yes	XB
151028	E	223	2252	Yes	Yes	XB
151029	F	249	2777	Yes	Yes	XB
151030	F	302	2949	Yes	Yes	XB
151031	F	162	3130	Yes	Yes	XB
151032	F	293	2824	Yes	Yes	XB
151033	I	305	5548	Yes	Yes	XC
151087	F	48	4228	Yes	Yes	XB
151100	E	14	2268	Yes	Yes	XB
151118	F	14	2784	Yes	Yes	XB
151121	G	141	3108	Yes	Yes	XB
151615	G	303	3558	No	Yes	XB
151790	G	338	4176	No	Yes	XB
161015	C	107	1768	No	No	XB
161016	D	288	2101	Yes	No	XB
161017	F	84	2653	No	No	XB
161018	F	112	2816	No	No	XB
161019	E	53	2428	No	No	XB
161020	D	129	2082	Yes	No	XB
161021	D	88	1897	No	No	XB
161022	D	113	1898	No	No	XB
161023	G	186	3445	No	No	XB
161024	C	116	1698	No	No	XB
161025	F	117	2738	No	No	XC
161027	E	201	2388	No	No	XB
161029	I	158	4589	Yes	No	XB
161030	I	284	4562	Yes	No	XB
161031	F	198	5381	Yes	No	XC
161032	I	138	4517	Yes	No	XB
161033	I	184	5125	Yes	No	XC
161034	D	124	2156	No	No	XB
161035	H	170	3688	No	No	XC
161036	H	164	3664	No	No	XB
161038	E	75	2209	No	No	XB
161039	E	89	2320	Yes	No	XB
161040	E	300	2403	Yes	No	XB
161041	F	81	2738	Yes	No	XB
161042	D	292	2198	Yes	No	XB
161043	D	87	1856	Yes	No	XB
161044	I	118	4652	Yes	No	XC
161045	D	160	2077	Yes	No	XB
161051	E	126	2484	Yes	No	XB
161052	E	118	1727	Yes	No	XB
171005	E	105	2276	Yes	No	XB
171007	C	250	1650	Yes	No	XB
171014	D	105	1815	Yes	No	XB
171017	E	232	2558	Yes	No	XB
171018	E	293	2599	Yes	No	XB
181034	F	233	2687	Yes	No	XB
181039	C	200	1661	Yes	No	XB
181041	C	316	1556	Yes	No	XB
181047	B	234	1458	Yes	No	XB
181053	F	323	2682	Yes	No	XB
181056	F	209	2889	Yes	No	XB
181061	D	214	2111	Yes	No	XB
181062	D	337	1953	Yes	No	XB
181063	D	317	2037	Yes	No	XB
181064	F	24	2802	Yes	No	XB
181074	C	234	1760	Yes	No	XB
181079	G	146	3016	Yes	No	XB
181080	D	64	2042	Yes	No	XB
181081	E	320	2350	Yes	No	XB
181085	D	238	2183	Yes	No	XB
181094	D	240	2099	Yes	No	XB
181102	E	65	2265	Yes	No	XB
181114	A	335	992	Yes	No	XB
181117	B	328	1325	Yes	No	XB
181122	G	319	3105	Yes	No	XB
181125	E	319	2392	Yes	No	XB
181128	C	336	1634	Yes	No	XB
181131	B	325	1442	Yes	No	XB
181132	B	325	1437	Yes	No	XB
181133	D	333	3734	Yes	No	XB
181137	E	25	2353	Yes	No	XB
181151	E	226	2283	Yes	No	XB
181683	B	328	2722	Yes	No	XB
201103	E	64	2490	Yes	No	XB
211069	C	264	1600	Yes	No	XB
211070	C	32	1700	Yes	No	XB
211072	G	245	3012	Yes	No	XB
211073	G	245	3119	Yes	No	XB
211074	G	168	3486	Yes	No	XB
211075	H	183	3568	Yes	No	XB
211076	I	180	4242	Yes	No	XC
211077	I	182	5560	No	No	XC
211081	B	322	1110	NA	No	XB
211108	F	130	2888	Yes	No	XB
211111	G	156	3035	Yes	No	XB
211125	I	147	4440	Yes	No	XC
221022	G	278	3382	No	No	XB
221024	C	88	1732	No	No	XB
221025	G	157	3009	No	No	XB
231020	D	200	2166	No	No	XB
231023	G	209	3215	No	No	XB
231026	H	209	3784	No	No	XB
231030	I	141	4200	No	No	XB
241009	D	42	1974	No	No	XB
241010	D	89	2044	No	No	XB
241012	E	241	2743	No	No	XB
241013	F	42	3072	No	No	XB
241014	G	241	3046	No	No	XB
251008	D	239	1808	Yes	No	XB
251010	D	49	1854	Yes	No	XB
251011	D	49	2008	Yes	No	XB
251012	D	58	2009	Yes	No	XB
251013	D	58	2073	Yes	No	XB
251014	E	25	2210	Yes	No	XB
261001	H	161	3746	No	No	XC
261002	F	179	2976	No	No	XC
261003	F	167	2974	No	No	XC
261004	F	43	2707	No	No	XC
261005	E	47	2419	No	No	XB
261007	F	46	2635	No	No	XB
261008	E	167	4897	No	No	XB
271010	C	85	1724	Yes	No	XB
271012	B	90	1359	Yes	No	XB
271022	B	100	1317	Yes	No	XB
271025	E	197	2223	Yes	No	XB
271027	E	91	2463	Yes	No	XB
271030	D	102	1926	Yes	No	XB

Index

For pricing, see page 347.

Plan #	Price Code	Page	Total Finished Area Square Feet	Materials List Available	Complete Cost	MT Tier
271032	G	153	3195	No	No	XB
271056	F	31	2820	No	No	XB
271062	E	101	2356	No	No	XB
271064	F	127	2864	No	No	XB
271066	E	101	2249	No	No	XB
271067	G	40	3015	No	No	XC
271068	E	100	2214	No	No	XB
271069	E	106	2376	No	No	XB
271071	G	40	3194	No	No	XC
271083	C	99	1690	Yes	No	XB
271089	E	109	2476	No	No	XB
271090	F	109	2708	No	No	XB
271091	F	108	2854	No	No	XB
271092	F	129	2636	No	No	XB
271093	F	31	2813	No	No	XC
271094	G	108	3242	No	No	XC
271095	G	111	3220	No	No	XB
281001	E	131	2423	Yes	No	XB
281003	E	232	2370	Yes	No	XB
281004	B	322	1426	Yes	No	XB
281005	B	324	1362	Yes	No	XB
281006	C	329	1702	Yes	No	XB
281007	B	15	1206	Yes	No	XB
291005	A	339	896	No	No	XB
291006	A	318	965	No	No	XB
291007	B	318	1065	No	No	XB
291008	B	329	1183	No	No	XB
291009	C	50	1655	No	No	XB
291010	C	59	1776	No	No	XB
291011	D	15	1898	No	No	XB
291012	E	59	2415	No	No	XB
291013	H	152	3553	No	No	XC
291014	I	152	4372	No	No	XC
301006	D	48	2162	Yes	No	XB
311003	E	103	2428	Yes	No	XB
311014	E	126	2344	Yes	No	XB
321041	E	257	2286	Yes	No	XB
321042	G	8	3368	Yes	No	XB
321043	E	95	2401	Yes	No	XB
321044	F	18	2618	Yes	No	XB
321045	D	122	2058	Yes	No	XB
321046	E	19	2411	Yes	No	XB
321047	E	122	2461	Yes	No	XB
321048	G	9	3216	Yes	No	XB
321049	G	19	3144	Yes	No	XB
321050	E	119	2336	Yes	No	XB
321051	F	208	2624	Yes	No	XB
321052	D	251	2182	Yes	No	XB
321053	D	302	1985	Yes	No	XB
321054	F	18	2828	Yes	No	XB
321055	E	257	2505	Yes	No	XB
321056	D	95	2050	Yes	No	XB
321057	C	214	1524	Yes	No	XB
321058	C	213	1700	Yes	No	XB
321059	E	119	2521	Yes	No	XB
321060	C	213	1575	Yes	No	XB
321061	G	271	3169	Yes	No	XB
321062	G	11	3138	Yes	No	XB
321065	G	309	3420	Yes	No	XB
331001	D	10	1846	No	No	XB
331002	E	10	2299	No	No	XB
331003	F	41	2661	No	No	XB
331004	G	41	3125	No	No	XB
331005	H	142	3585	No	No	XB
341001	F	110	2867	Yes	No	XB
341002	E	27	2528	Yes	No	XB
341006	E	110	2588	Yes	No	XB

Plan #	Price Code	Page	Total Finished Area Square Feet	Materials List Available	Complete Cost	MT Tier
341007	I	111	4068	Yes	No	XB
341008	E	26	2508	Yes	No	XB
341011	E	98	2560	Yes	No	XB
341014	E	21	2128	Yes	No	XB
341015	E	20	2418	Yes	No	XB
341016	F	99	2630	Yes	No	XB
341020	F	98	2614	Yes	No	XB
361006	E	324	2230	Yes	No	XB
361007	B	321	1306	No	No	XB
361008	C	340	1749	No	No	XB
361009	C	80	1775	No	No	XB
361010	E	323	2372	Yes	No	XB
361012	F	292	2602	No	No	XB
361017	D	81	2116	No	No	XB
361021	D	260	1887	No	No	XB
361022	D	317	1844	No	No	XB
361023	E	299	2304	No	No	XB
361024	E	115	2296	No	No	XB
361025	D	87	1904	No	No	XB
361026	B	331	1401	No	No	XB
361027	E	250	2140	No	No	XB
361293	D	335	1987	No	No	XB
371003	E	146	2297	No	No	XB
371004	D	36	1815	No	No	XB
371008	F	123	2656	No	No	XB
381002	E	233	2225	Yes	No	XB
381003	D	244	1925	Yes	No	XB
381004	D	244	1860	Yes	No	XB
381005	D	80	2030	Yes	No	XB
381006	C	324	1749	No	No	XB
381007	F	37	2600	Yes	No	XB
381011	B	37	1175	Yes	No	XB
381012	B	334	1035	Yes	No	XB
381013	B	114	1375	Yes	No	XB
381014	B	334	1315	Yes	No	XB
381015	B	114	1280	Yes	No	XB
381017	C	115	1540	Yes	No	XB
381019	E	24	2535	Yes	No	XB
381021	B	83	1425	Yes	No	XB
391002	E	143	2281	Yes	No	XB
391009	G	74	3440	Yes	No	XC
391018	H	44	3747	Yes	No	XC
391022	B	328	1325	Yes	No	XB
391023	E	104	2244	Yes	No	XB
391024	F	246	2647	No	No	XB
391026	B	240	1470	Yes	No	XB
391027	B	86	1434	Yes	No	XB
391032	D	93	2129	Yes	No	XB
391033	D	36	2007	Yes	No	XB
391036	D	93	1954	Yes	No	XB
391041	D	246	1880	No	No	XB
391043	D	127	2143	Yes	No	XB
391048	D	86	3447	Yes	No	XB
481035	G	150	6277	No	No	XC
491005	B	316	1997	Yes	No	XB
611044	H	173	4369	No	No	XB
611045	H	178	4512	No	No	XB
611046	H	303	4697	No	No	XB
611048	I	153	4870	No	No	XB
611126	E	172	3186	No	No	XB
641001	G	224	5298	No	No	XC
661010	F	294	3664	No	No	XB
661056	D	147	2486	No	No	XB
661066	D	140	2685	No	No	XB
661205	G	166	3856	No	No	XB
661229	J	283	7224	No	No	XC

The fastest way to get started building your dream home from Creative Homeowner is with a Material Take-off

One of the most complete materials lists in the industry

Work with your Lowe's associate to get all the products you need

To learn more go to page 344 or visit

online at LowesforPros.com